Samuel Bedijo, OSB

The Moral Problem Posed by Individualism in the Church in Africa

A Case Study in Nebbi Catholic Diocese in North-Western Uganda

THEOLOGISCHE REIHE, BAND 100

Samuel Bedijo, OSB

The Moral Problem Posed by Individualism in the Church in Africa

A Case Study in Nebbi Catholic Diocese in North-Western Uganda

eos

First impression 2015

Dissertation Submitted to the Faculty of Theology of the Catholic University of Eastern Africa for the Doctoral Degree in Theology with Specialisation in Moral Theology in August 2013

The printing was supported
by the Congregation of the Missionary Benedictines

Nihil obstat
Feast of St. Adrian, 9th January 2015
Fr. Calisto Nyagilo, Censor
Archdiocese of Nairobi

Imprimatur
Feast of St. Adrian, 9th January 2015
S.E. John Cardinal Njue
Archbishop of Nairobi

mail@eos-verlag.de – www.eos-verlag.de
ISBN 978-3-8306-7729-1

A catalogue record for this book is available from the German Library
http://dnb.ddb.de

EOS – Editions of Sankt Ottilien
www.eos-books.com | mail@eos-verlag.de
Printed in Germany

DEDICATION

To the God who is Communion: Father, Son, Holy Spirit.
And to my parents, Enriko Uvonji (RIP) and Irene Panyir,
Who taught us to believe in God and to learn from God's love.

Acknowledgement

We owe utmost thanks to God who has given us the grace and health in the process of this exercise. This has not been a merely academic work but it has helped us to reflect more deeply into what the Church stands to be for: representing and making Christ known.

We are deeply thankful to our parents and home community for their unforgettable upbringing and education in faith; equal gratitude to all our catechists and school teachers for their priceless instructions which opened us to, and widened our horizon on, relationship.

We register our gratitude to the Abbot President of the Congregation of St. Ottilien in Germany, Fr. Jeremias Schroeder, OSB, who not only granted us the opportunity for this study but also recommended the financial support to this end. In the same context we are immensely thankful to Fr. Pius Mühlbacher, OSB, who funded our fieldwork from his own means, which made it possible for the three months of field study. To the International Benedictine Study House Community in Nairobi, we are grateful for an atmosphere of community life and study.

We are thankful to the Administration of the Catholic University of Eastern Africa, in their different capacities, for the assistance that contributed to the success of this study. We must give special acknowledgement to the gatekeepers, receptionist and secretaries of the University for their friendly and kind gestures in showing us where to go.

We are particularly and immensely indebted to Rev. Professor Constance Bansikiza, First Supervisor; and Rev. Dr. Richard N. Rwiza, Second Supervisor: our heartfelt gratitude to them both for their cooperation among themselves, availability and student-attention despite their other duties and schedules, for their wise counsels and attendant guidance, critical reading and indicative suggestions of pertinent sources. Rev. Dr. Fabién Lonema was helpful with some rare literary materials which helped to unlock some riddles.

Many people have been helpful to us during our field study as acknowledged in Appendix 3 of this work. To them all, our sincere gratitude: parents, youth, Catechists, priests, the religious, pupils and students, school teachers, civil servants, Non-Governmental charity personnel and field assistants for the firsthand information they provided. Their contributions did not only offer responses to our questionnaire and oral interviews but also helped us to get an image of the Church both from within and without.

We are grateful to Frau Thekla Röther of Uznach, Frau Ida Wipf of Rorschacherberg and Frau Dr. Elisabeth Sulser Ebnöther of Wessen (RIP), in Switzerland, for their motherly love, prayer and financial contributions which helped us in specific ways in the course of this study; and Br. Victor of the Benedictine community at St. Otmarsberg abbey in Switzerland for his fraternal and quiet help.

Finally, our affectionate thanks to the Youth and the St. Kizito Companions group of Parombo Parish in Nebbi Catholic Diocese for their witness and love for the Church.

Nairobi, April 2015
Samuel Bedijo, OSB

Table of Content

CHAPTER TWO
Alur Traditional Communitarian Values

CHAPTER THREE
Christian Communitarian Values

CHAPTER FOUR
An Ethical Analysis of Individualism

CHAPTER FIVE
The Individual in the Light of Christian Anthropology

CHAPTER SIX
Towards the Building of Ecclesial Communion

CHAPTER SEVEN
Moral Theological Recommendations

APPENDICES

Abbreviations and Signs

AA	*Apostolicam Actuositatem*
AAS	*Acta Apostolicae Sedis*
ABC	*Africa Bible Commentary*
AFARD	Agency for Accelerated Regional Development (Nebbi)
AFER	*African Ecclesial Review*
AFJN	Africa Faith and Justice Network
AGD	*Ad Gentes Divinitus*
AM	*Africae Munus*
AMECEA	Association of Member Episcopal Conferences in Eastern Africa
AT	*Africae Terrarum*
ATR	African Traditional Religion
ca.	*circa* (Latin), about such a year
CA	*Centesimus Annus*
CCC	*Catechism of the Catholic Church*
Ch.	*Chapter*
CfL	*Christifideles Laici*
CISA	Catholic Information Service for Africa
Cor.	*Letter to the Corinthians*
CT	*Catechesi Tradendae*
DCE	*Deus Caritas Est*
DBT	*Dictionary of Biblical Theology*
DV	*Dei Verbum*
EA	*Ecclesia in Africa*
EBT	*Encyclopedia of Biblical Theology*
ed./eds.	editor/editors
EE	*Ecclesia de Eucharistia*
ECE	*Ex Corde Ecclesiae*
EN	*Evangelii Nuntiandi*
ES	*Ecclesiam Suam*
ETCSM	*Encyclopedia of Theology: The Concise Sacramentum Mundi*
EV	*Evangelium Vitae*
FC	*Familiaris Consortio*
FR	*Fides et Ratio*
Fr.	Father, Church title referring to a Priest
GDC	*General Directory for Catechesis*

GE	*Gravissimum Educationis*
Gen.	Genesis (Bible reference to the Old Testament Book of Genesis)
Gen. ed.	General editor
GS	*Gaudium et Spes*
HBD	*Harper's Bible Dictionary*
HCT	*Handbook of Catholic Theology*
Ibid.	the same author and title from the immediately preceding citation (Latin, *ibidem*, in the same place)
Idem	the same author just cited but another title (Latin, *idem*, the same)
IDB	*The Interpreter's Dictionary of the Bible*
ISBE	*The International Standard Bible Encyclopedia*
JBC	*The Jerome Biblical Commentary*
Jn.	John (the Gospel according to Saint John)
LG	*Lumen Gentium*
Lk.	Luke (the Gospel according to Saint Luke)
Mk.	Mark (the Gospel according to Saint Mark)
MC	*Mystici Corporis*
MM	*Mater et Magistra*
Msgr.	Monsignor, Church title for an ecclesiastical dignitary
Mt.	Mathew (the Gospel according to Saint Mathew)
§	after an article number, shows the specific paragraph under that number
ND	*The Christian Faith in the Doctrinal Documents of the Catholic Church*
NDCE	*New Dictionary of Christian Ethics*
NDCS	*The New Dictionary of Catholic Spirituality*
NDT	*The New Dictionary of Theology*
NGO	Non-Governmental Organisation
NIV	*The NIV Theological Dictionary of New Testament Words*
NJBC	*The New Jerome Biblical Commentary*
NT	New Testament
op. cit.	in the work already cited, same author, same title (Latin, *opere citato*)
Op. Tot.	*Optatam Totius*
OT	Old Testament
PaG	*Pastores Gregis*
PdV	*Pastores Dabo Vobis*
PO	*Presbyterorum Ordinis*
QA	*Quadragesimo Anno*

rev. ed.	revised edition (of a book cited)
RH	*Redemptor Hominis*
RM	*Redemptoris Missio*
Sac. Car.	*Sacramentum Caritatis*
SCCE	Sacred Congregation for Catholic Education
Sr.	Sister, a consecrated member of a Religious Order
SRS	*Sollicitudo Rei Socialis*
St.	Saint
TMA	*Tertio Millennio Adveniente*
UUS	*Ut Unum Sint*
VD	*Verbum Domini*
Vol.	Volume
VS	*Veritatis Splendor*
Zenit	Vatican News Agency

General Introduction

0.1. Background of the Study

Individualism, that spirit in which one is locked in on oneself, is a rather subtle, almost unnoticed problem, which seems to lie at the root of countless social evils. This is what our study intends to investigate, from within the Church. The title of this study is: *The Moral Problem Posed by Individualism in the Church in Africa: A Case Study in Nebbi Catholic Diocese in North-Western Uganda*. The purpose of situating the study in the Uganda context, with a narrower look at Nebbi Catholic diocese, makes for a case study. Individualism is treated in this present study as a moral problem. The concept of *problem* as used here refers to a situation which impedes progress and to which solution must be sought. It is *moral* in the understanding that it weakens or impedes right relationship not only among persons but also in the ecclesial community.

The study is undertaken in the Church context and looks at life within the Church. It is important to clarify, in some detail, what is meant by the term *church*. Cessario writes that the Church is a communion of persons where individuals are shaped and guided by the truth of the divine and evangelical law;[1] that is, a communion in which persons are held together by love of God and of neighbour. According to the *Catechism*, the word *church* designates People of God: an assembly called together by God and belongs to God.[2] In the *Handbook of Catholic Theology*, Löser writes that: "The church is the communion of those who believe in the gospel, have been incorporated into the "body of Christ" by baptism, come together at the table of the Eucharist, and give expression to their faith in witness and service."[3] *The International Standard*

---

1 Romanus Cessario, *Forward*, in Servais Pinckaers, *The Sources of Christian Ethics*, 3rd ed., English translation by Sr. Mary Thomas Noble, Edinburgh, T&T Clark, 1995, p. xiii.

2 *The Catechism of the Catholic Church*, Nairobi, Paulines Publications Africa, 1994, n. 751. The Anglo-Saxon group of words: English, *church*, Scottish, *kirk*, German, *Kirche*, Dutch, *kerk*; and Latin, *ecclesia*; from Greek, *ekklesia*, deriving from *ek-kalein* (*ek*, out of, out from; *kalein*, to call), 'call out of or from.' The Greek, *Kyriake*, from *Kyrios*, Lord; *iokos*, house, thus, *kyriake*, 'house of the Lord,' that is, 'belonging to the Lord,' or 'The Lord's house; The Lord's household.'

3 Werner Löser, "Church," in Wolfgang Beinert and Francis Schüssler Fiorenza (eds.), *Handbook of Catholic Theology*, New York, The Crossroad Publishing Company, 2000, p. 99. Citation henceforth: *HCT*.

Bible Encyclopedia defines *church* as 'belonging to the Lord.'[4] In *Key Ideas in Human Thought*, the term *church* is described as "Lord's house," meaning: a universal social membership in contrast to sects. In this understanding, the Church acknowledges the legitimacy of the State and other secular institutions for maintaining social order.[5] The usage, *church*, does not refer to a sect. Stackhouse writes that: "In theology and much ordinary usage, "sect" refers to a body of believers who follow a particular practice, doctrine, or leader distinct from that of the majority or "orthodox" norm, but within the same religion."[6] From this we may discern that sectarianism seems to portray group individualism.

Three biblical words, *ekklēsia, synagōgē, ḳāhāl*, serve to clarify the communal character of the Church.[7] These terms refer to assembly, gathering or community, although there are different shades of meaning. In classical Greek, *ekklesia* denoted the popular assembly of the competent citizens of a city-state, *polis*, on matters of organising it and solving its problems, which sometimes involved religious acts of prayers and sacrifice to deities. Another Greek term, *synagōgē*, meant assembly, gathering. Its original usage had a wide coverage in the sense of collection or gathering of things or people. What is common to both *ekklēsia* and *synagōgē* is the reference to an assembly of people, social institutions, their associated beliefs and practices which make a distinct religious grouping.[8]

In the New Testament the word *ekklēsia* has been used with reference to the assembly, meeting, or congregation of Christians. It translates the Old Testament Hebrew word, *qāhāl*, an assembly gathered before the Lord, rendering *ekklēsia* a comprehensive usage (*synagōgē*, gathering, assembly; *ochlos*, crowd; *plēthos*, plenitude, multitude). Synagogue, in popular Hebrew translation, took the term *ēdâ*, 'congregation,' denoting a summons to an assembly and the act itself of assembling. These linguistic variations and their gradual developments came to indicate the religious assembly of Christians.[9]

4 G. W. Bromiley, "Church," in Geoffrey W. Bromiley (Gen. ed.), *The International Standard Bible Encyclopedia*, Vol. 1, reprint, Michigan, William B. Eerdmans Publishing Company, 1989, p. 693, the word *church* from the Greek word *kyriakós*.

5 Davina Allan, "Church," in *Key Ideas in Human Thought*, edited by Kenneth McLeish, p. 123, uses the Greek phrase *kuriakon* [*doma*] to mean 'Lord's house.'

6 Max A. Stackhouse, "Sect," in John Macquarrie and James Childress (eds.), *A New Dictionary of Christian Ethics*, London, SCM Press Ltd., 1997, p. 566b.

7 John L. McKenzie, *Dictionary of the Bible*, New York, Macmillan Publishing Company, 1965, pp. 133b-136a.

8 Verlyn D. Verbrugge (ed.), *The NIV Theological Dictionary of New Testament Words*, Grand Rapids, Zondervan Publishing House, 2000, p. 388-396.

9 Ibid., the word *synagōgē*, deriving from *syn*, with; *agō*, gather, bring together.

However, as Joseph Cardinal Ratzinger (later Pope Benedict XVI) observes in his book, *Called to Communion*, it is to be noted that:

> ...there is a twofold distinction between the Old Testament *qahal* and the Greek plenary assembly of enfranchised citizens. Even women and children, who in Greece could not be active agents of political events, belonged to the *qahal*. A closely connected fact is that in Greece it is the males who determine by their decisions what is to be done, while the assembly of Israel gathers to "listen to what God proclaims and to assent to it"... It is thus clear what it means for the nascent Church to call herself *ecclesia*."[10]

It is in this picture that the Church is understood as "people of God" or "family of God."

Ernest Best argues that, "In the NT, the term *church* never signifies a building or a denomination. Rather, it always denotes a group of people, either all the Christians in a city, or those gathered for worship in a particular house, or all Christians in all the churches, the whole church."[11] From this understanding, we can conclude that the Church is, by its character, communitarian, not individualistic or sectarian (a faction or divisive group). In our study we are referring to the word *church* in the strict sense of the community of Christians gathered together by their common faith in Christ. Although it is made up of individuals it remains a community which is guided by the precepts of the Gospel as we have already noted above.

In our understanding, individualism stands contrary to what we have said about the Church. It is neither to be likened to, nor equated with, individuality by which is recognised the inherent and legitimate self-defining personhood and personality which is proper to every individual human being. Individualism is here understood as that spirit in which, and by which, someone is bent in on oneself with marginal or no regard for a true human relationship and the values that sustain this relationship. The English language dictionaries we have consulted define it in the following manner. The *Macmillan English Dictionary* defines it as the behavior of someone who does things in their own way without worrying about what other people think or do.[12] *The Concise One Volume Reference Book of the English Language* defines it as the conduct or feeling centered in self, egoism, self-interest, selfishness; idiosyncrasy, personal pe-

10 Joseph Cardinal Ratzinger (Pope Benedict XVI), *Called to Communion: Understanding the Church Today*, translated by Adrian Walker, San Francisco, Ignatius Press, 1996, pp. 31-32.

11 Ernest Best, "Church" in Paul J. Achtemeier (Gen. ed.), *Harper's Bible Dictionary*, Bangalore, Theological Publications in India, 2002, p. 168.

12 *MacMillan English Dictionary for Advanced Learners: International Student Edition*, Oxford, Oxford University Press, 2002.

culiarity; an attitude, tendency or system in which each individual works for his own ends; independent action as opposed to co-operation.[13] The *Concise Oxford English Dictionary* defines it as self-centered feeling or conduct, egoism.[14] The *Webster's New World Dictionary* defines it as the leading of one's life in one's own way.[15] Could we say that such a manner of life is to be found in the Church as such, and in Nebbi Catholic Diocese in particular? And, if this would be true, in what manner would the diocese be truly Christian and truly human, a Church of the place, if it harbours individualism?

The participants at Vatican Council II dedicated a paragraph on the need to transcend individualistic ethic.[16] The same point has been expressed in the *Instrumentum Laboris* (Working Paper) in preparation for the 1994 Special Assembly of the Synod of Bishops for Africa, under the topic of human promotion.[17] Reference is here made in a general outlook of the wider society and not in the Church context. This leaves us with an unavoidable question: Is the Church in Africa without a tinge of individualism within itself?

In their Pastoral Letter, *Let Your Light Shine*, the Catholic Bishops of Uganda spell out that: "Justice should be studied in all sectors of life, including the church herself. All Christians must be involved in this mission of detecting injustices in order to find common means of eliminating them from our church and society."[18] If our understanding of it is correct, we would say that individualism seems to be a major, if not the most, root cause to injustice.

Apparently, Nebbi Catholic Diocese is becoming more a local Church, that is, a Church of the place, particularly with regard to: (i) personnel, as reflected in the dwindling number of missionaries and an increasing number of indigenous priests, religious and catechists;[19] (ii) a growing awareness of church support through contributions of fund and material support to priests from the laity; (iii) the presence of different groups and associations by which the faith-

13 *The Concise One Volume Reference Book of the English Language: English Dictionary*, München, Orbis Verlag, 1990.

14 *Concise Oxford English Dictionary*, 11th edition, revised, Oxford, Oxford University Press, 2008.

15 *Webster's New World Dictionary and Thesaurus*, Cleveland, Wiley Publishing Inc., 2002.

16 Vatican Council II, Pastoral Constitution on the Church in the Modern World *Gaudium et Spes*, n. 30: *AAS* 58 (1966), p. 1049-1050.

17 Synod of Bishops – Special Assembly for Africa, *The Church in Africa and Her Evangelising Mission Towards the Year 2000: Instrumentum Laboris*, Vatican City, General Secretariat of the Synod of Bishops and Libreria Editrice Vaticana, 1993, n. 113.

18 Catholic Bishops of Uganda, Pastoral Letter *Let Your Light Shine*, Kisubi, Marianum Press, 1992, n. 34.

19 Cf., Nebbi Catholic Diocese, *Acts of the First Diocesan Synod of Nebbi Catholic Diocese: Angal, 13th-24th January 2003*, Nebbi, Catholic Press, 2003, p. 27f.

ful are enabled to realise and define themselves as members of the local church communion; (iv) the use of local language and gestures in the liturgy; (v) readable Bible translation in the local language of the people.

The reality of being a local Church seems to suggest that Nebbi Catholic Diocese will, strenuously, learn to become more conscious of its identity and diligently work to become truly itself in its own environment and situation, without obscuring its: (a) sincerely unique African human root in which Christianity finds a home; (b) authentic Christian faith which defines and shapes it; (c) truly African-Christian identity which characterises it.

0.2. Purpose of the Study

This study seeks to find out whether Alur, together with Christian, communitarian values, could help to reverse or curb down the problem of individualism in Nebbi Catholic Diocese, with a focus on strengthening ecclesial communion. To arrive at this it is helpful first to investigate whether there is any strain of individualism in the diocese, our case study. This leads to weighing its impact on the internal life of the Church, its pastoral work, and the image it might portray of the Church in the society in which the Church exists, a society that the Church works to shape after its image of God's family.

0.3. Rationale

The English Dictionaries we have consulted define the word *rationale* as a set of reasons or a logical basis for a course of action or belief; a reasoned exposition or a statement of reasons. Our enquiry is chiefly motivated by pastoral experience through youth seminars, retreats, recollections; encounters with Christian communities, Catholics who have crossed over to the evangelicals, encounters with both male and female Religious communities in Nebbi Catholic Diocese.

0.4. Central Question

Is individualism to be found in Nebbi Catholic Diocese?

0.5. Working Hypothesis

The assumption that helped to guide our fieldwork and the reading of the works cited in this study is that: there seems to be individualism in Nebbi Catholic Diocese.

0.6. Relevance of the Study

Our study looks for a moral response to the problem of individualism in the Church. Such a response involves working from different perspectives and disciplines, both theoretical and practical: including church administration and resource management (both human and material), spirituality, pastoral activities, liturgical practices as well as approaches to catechesis and formation. Although this present work is a case study, the subject under enquiry might have resonance in the Church elsewhere in Uganda or Africa. We hope that the questions raised in our study might contribute to further academic research on the same subject or its connection in other disciplines of church life. Besides, we hope that suggestions from this study might express moral sensitivity to how the Church mobilises its resources and organises itself as a community held together and guided by Christian faith, love with hope.

0.7. Scope and Delimitation

Our study has a couple of limitations. First, it is undertaken within the discipline of moral theology and thus approaches the problem of individualism in this context. Second, it looks at individualism within the context of the Catholic Church in an African situation. Third, it is not the whole of Africa, but in Uganda. Fourth, the field research has been largely carried out in Nebbi Catholic Diocese. Fifth, we have not come across a published work specifically on the subject of individualism in the Church in Africa: either in Nebbi Catholic Diocese itself, or the Catholic Church in Uganda, nor the wider Catholic Church in Africa. Sixth, the scope of our fieldwork does not allow us to give an exhaustive account of the problem of individualism in the Church, even in Nebbi Diocese itself, chiefly due to different contexts and intensities in which the same reality might find expression. Seventh, the subject of individualism is rather broad and can be studied under different perspectives, whether in the political, economic, cultural, social or religious contexts. Nevertheless, we would assume that these contingent human factors can find expression in the Church and can influence its life as well.

0.8. Literature Review

We have not identified a published work specifically on the subject of individualism as a moral problem in the Church in Africa, Uganda or Nebbi Catholic Diocese itself. Nonetheless, our study can benefit from relevant church documents, theological and non-theological reflections of individual authors that can open up the possibility of a study on the subject or serve to answer some of the questions pertaining to it within the scope of this study.

The first, and perhaps the only, comprehensive ethnographical study of the people in Nebbi is the work of Crazzolara, one of the first Comboni missionaries. His book, *The Lwoo*, provides a detailed descriptive material about the Alur and their neighbouring peoples: Lendu, Kebu, Madi and Lugbara.[20] The Alur are the dominant ethnic group in Nebbi; its social system has incorporated these other groups. Although there are implicit indications, Craszzolara's work is focused on ethnographical information and does not treat the subject of individualism in these communities.

Apart from Crazzolara's work, the earliest study of the Alur political system was carried out by Southall, a British political theorist, under the title: *Alur Society*. He alludes to an individualistic attitude only once in this work with reference to how the Alur are unsparing towards a leader who would neglect communal values and in that way sacrificing the social-cultural institution to his own benefits. He makes the critique: "...a people so assertive and, within limits, individualistic as the Alur, who...behave towards chiefship with something of the ambivalence of Americans, who detest government but would die for the constitution."[21] Both Crazzolara and Southall provide helpful materials on the tradition and customs of the Alur by highlighting central communitarian values, which provide good possibilities of dialogue with Christian values. However, our study remains with this question of enquiry: Does it mean that there is, or has been, no trace of individualism in the ordinary life of the Alur people with regard to the chain of relationships that affect their day-to-day life?

The works we have consulted on the subject of individualism are studies that have been largely carried in Euro-American cultural contexts. A seminal work on individualism appeared in the work of the French political analyst, Alexis Charles Henri Maurice Clérel de Tocqueville (1805-1859), *Democracy in America* (the fruit of a study travel in America in 1831-1832), where he studied the problem in the context of democracy. His study illustrates how individualism works generally in democracies.[22] This study is of interest as it closely looks at the mores in family life, religious traditions, participation in

20 Joseph Pasquale Crazzolara, *The Lwoo – Part I: Lwoo Migrations*, Verona, Istituto Missioni Africane, 1950; idem., *The Lwoo – Part II: Lwoo Traditions*, Verona, Editrice Nigrizia, 1951; idem., *The Lwoo – Part III: Clans*, Verona, Editrice Nigrizia, 1954. Citations from this same title, *The Lwoo*, will henceforth show page numbers.

21 Aidan William Southall, *Alur Society: A Study in Process and Types of Domination*, reprinted, Nairobi, Oxford University Press, 1970, p. 190.

22 Robert Nisbet, *Prejudices: A Philosophical Dictionary*, Cambridge, Harvard University Press, 1982, p. 184.

local politics, and free associations, as factors which shape people's attitude towards, and thus their response to, the wider community or society. About mores he writes: "I mean the term "mores" (*moeurs*) to have its original Latin meaning; I mean it to apply not only to "*moeurs*" in the strict sense, which might be called the habits of the heart, but also to the different notions possessed by men, the various opinions current among them, and the sum of ideas that shape mental habits."[23] The study shows how individualism can jeopardise communal or societal progress when individuals are bent in on their own interests; how they can neglect or take advantage of the social institution for their own interests, a situation which sets tension between the individual or group and the larger social reality. Although the study of Clérel provides a social-political analysis, it depicts individualism as a form of *habit of the heart*, which can be comparatively applied to life within the Church in its human reality.

Another work on individualism, which is of interest to our study, is that carried out by Paul Zweig, entitled, *The Heresy of Self-Love*.[24] This work is written in the discipline of comparative literature. In it, Zweig attempts to clarify the versions of narcissistic (a self-absorption) attitude that have strongly shaped the Euro-American industrial lifestyle. He demonstrates how this self-absorption (narcissism) can weaken not only the individual's own self-authenticity but community life itself. The study shows that individualism: (a) is that spirit by which one sinks into self-cultivation; (b) hardening into self-exaltation; and (c) eventually gravitating towards the heart of accepted values. The real problem is that it can become socialised, that is, the arrogance of the *self* which individualism imposes on the social system, running through the social institutions and working itself into a structural expression. The dilemma that arises from the exposition made by Zweig is: how communal or societal life could be imagined when its individual members are each sunk into pursuing personal interests. While this study is informative and vividly illustrates the social evil stemming from a misdirected self-love, it leaves room for a moral theological reflection, which our study seeks to bring out.

Another study on individualism is the collaborative work of Bellah and his colleagues – three American sociologists, a philosopher, and a theologian – a work entitled, *Habits of the Heart*. The findings of this study illustrate: (a) the way individualism distorts the sense of selfhood; (b) how it obscures or downplays objectivity; (c) how it influences choice, based on feeling; (d) how

23 Adler Mortimer J. (ed.), *Great Books of the Western World*, Vol. 44: *Tocqueville*, translated by George Lawrence, Chicago, Encyclopedia Britannica, Inc., 2nd edition, Ninth Printing, 2007, p. 150a.

24 Paul Zweig, *The Heresy of Self-Love: A Study of Subversive Individualism*, Princeton, University of Princeton Press, 1980.

it defects commitment to socially accepted values; and thus (e) shapes moral behaviour to the extent of dissociating from other people whose value systems or points of view are not congruent with our own. They write:

> Now if selves are defined by their preferences, but those preferences are arbitrary, then each self constitutes its own moral universe, and there is finally no way to reconcile conflicting claims about what is good in itself... All can appeal to in relationships with others is their self-interest...or their intuitive sympathies... Where sympathy or already-congruent values are not enough to resolve moral disagreements between ourselves and others, we have no recourse except to withdraw from them... In the absence of any objectifiable criteria of right and wrong, good or evil, the self and its feelings become our own moral guide.[25]

This work shows the fierceness of individualism, especially as it takes on a structural expression, where community or society exists at the mercy of self-serving individuals. The authors observe that individualism stands starkly against equality in communion and threatens the survival of freedom itself. They argue that cultural traditions and practices can still serve as a corrective to the problem: "...those cultural traditions and practices that, without destroying individuality, serve to limit and restrain the destructive side of individualism and provide alternative models..."[26] This study reveals how individuals can live their faith in their own way or bring it to weigh on family life and the social arena without questioning themselves about the common good. This leaves us with a graphic face of society: either the individual or like-minded individuals. The field findings of this study draw some striking parallels with our own. However, their study leaves some room for us to investigate how individualism might affect the internal life of the Church itself.

Another work of interest to us is that of Thomas Schindler, *The Social Dimension*, in which he links individualism, in part, with the Roman Catholic Church tradition, where he argues:

> My thesis is that U.S. individualism, by emphasizing the separateness of the individual and by loosening the individual's ties to society, subordinates the social to the personal. I will further argue that, while the Roman Catholic tradition is an important and powerful resource for overcoming the problems caused by individualism, it can serve as this resource only as the relation of the Roman Catholic church to U.S. culture is critically assessed. This assessment is necessary, in my judgment, because the Roman Catholic stance on morality, even

25 Robert Neelly Bellah, Richard Madsen, William M. Sullivan, Ann Swiddler and Steven M. Tipton, *Habits of the Heart: Individualism and Commitment in American Life*, Berkeley, University of California Press, 1985, p. 76.

26 Ibid., p. viii.

> though not itself individualistic, has at times been presented in ways that can easily be read as agreeing with U.S. individualism.[27]

Schindler discusses individualism in an attempt to bridge the gap between personal morality and the social dimension of morality. This work points out that individualism corrupts the moral life and moral decision-making of individuals. However, he places his discussion of the problem in the context of social justice that affects the wider society; he does not situate the problem to measure what happens within the Church itself. This gap is the interest of our enquiry.

In the four studies we have just cited, what is common is that individualism portrays an attitude or expressive behaviour which is much inclined toward self-cultivation. This isolates the individual or like-minded individuals into a world of self-interest or group-interest, a withdrawal from or withholding of relational interest and sympathy.

Writing in the African situation, Elochukwu E. Uzukwu, in his work, *A Listening Church*, has hinted on individualism only in passing, where he contrasts the individualistic notion of the person as enshrined in the Greco-Roman philosophy with the African communitarian consciousness.[28] He does not question whether individualism would find expression in the African society; and much so in the Church in Africa. Nevertheless, his argument against "Monoepiscopal Autocracy and Clericalism" in the Church in Africa seems to suggest that there is a mechanism of individualism taking on an institutional or structural expression within the Church itself. He writes that: "Problems encountered by the SCCs in entrenching the localization of the church in its primary structure and in beginning the development of a new kind of ministry are fundamentally rooted in male clerical power."[29] It could be argued that 'male clerical power' is a structural mechanism of male egoism. This seems to show that individualism becomes an ecclesial problem. From this illustration, could we not say, at least in general, that there is individualism in the Church in Africa? This is what our case study tries to investigate.

A study that depicts individualism as a moral problem in the African society is that of Richard N. Rwiza, entitled, *Formation of Christian Conscience in Modern Africa*. In this study he brings out an important factor provoking individualism in the African society. Comparing between rural and urban lifestyle, he observes that the long cherished African communitarian morality is being

27 Thomas F. Schindler, *Ethics: The Social Dimension – Individualism and the Catholic Tradition*, Wilmington, Michael Glazier, Inc., 1989, pp. 9-10.

28 Elochukwu E. Uzukwu, *A Listening Church: Autonomy and Community in African Churches*, Maryknoll, New York, Orbis Books, 1996, pp. 41-46, 106-107.

29 Ibid., p. 119.

eroded by influences of modern society. He particularly notes that the formation of conscience which was once based upon community values is now giving way to models that detach and push the individual into a polarised world of struggle for personal survival. In the urban life is emerging an anonymous "I" which is weakening the traditional African communitarian "we" personality. Rwiza remarks that: "With urbanization the traditional concept of solidarity is giving way to individualism, values of secularism and personal privacy."[30] This evidence lays open the possibility of enquiring into what factors there might be, which are causing or provoking individualism. However, while the study looks at the problem in the wider societal context it does not ask directly whether the same problem might find expression in the Church. This leaves room for investigating whether individualism might find expression within the Church itself; which is the focus of our present research.

0.9. Methodology

A problem is a situation that invites a deeper reflection on the matter in question, sincere explanation and constructive suggestions. To do this we would need an approach which involves: (a) considering pertinent historical events; (b) assessing situations that really exist; (c) finding rationally constructive alternatives; (d) searching out for concrete stimuli towards realising those alternatives; (e) leaving room for an open and continuous study of the subject in question.

Our study methodology is bifocal: social-anthropological and moral-theological. The social-anthropological approach has been employed to check out for embedded cultural values. It was helpful during fieldwork, carried out by means of questionnaire and oral interviews. This made it possible to gather firsthand information. It was done in the following manner: (a) the researcher distributed 300 questionnaire leaflets, 287 were filled in and returned, 13 were not returned; (b) the researcher travelled and stayed with interviewees in their homes, communities and work places; (c) the researcher carried night study in fifteen selected Trading Centers in the month of July, 2008. This intended to compare what changes or differences there might be between the typically traditional lifestyle in the villages and the pattern found in the trading centers; (d) the researcher worked with the help of field assistants in the distribution of questionnaire; as guides in visiting specified places and persons; and in conducting night study. Gathering information targeted the different groups as listed in the *Acts of the First Diocesan Synod of Nebbi Catholic Diocese*:

30 Richard N. Rwiza, *Formation of Christian Conscience in Modern Africa*, Nairobi, Paulines Publications Africa, 2001, pp. 28-31.

individuals and groups including priests, members of religious communities, the Christian family, catechists, diocesan pastoral coordinator, youth, Catholic Action, Catholic Charismatic Renewal, seminarians, ex-seminarians and ex-religious. Out of the fifteen parishes in the diocese, the researcher was unable to visit one. Besides, we interviewed cultural elders in order to get familiar with cultural values. Parents were interviewed in order to get their views on the behaviour of the youth. Some personnel in the non-governmental organisation (NGO) offices were also interviewed in order to get their views on the question of individualism in the Church. These are NGOs sponsoring Catholic projects directly or working with the Church in order to reach out to people. Furthermore, we interviewed civil servants, including primary and secondary school teachers as well as pupils and students. Names of individual informants mentioned in the text or footnotes represent similar points of view on the specified question; a full list of informants is provided in Appendix 3.

The moral-theological approach makes use of Sacred Scripture, Christian Tradition, and the teachings from official church documents. The study also makes use of pertinent theological reflections of individual authors. This approach is interdisciplinary, taking into account the different disciplines that can possibly enlighten our enquiry, such as we have acknowledged above under literature review and those that will be cited in the main work.

0.10. Structure of the Work

This work is divided into seven chapters, each with its introduction and conclusion. The first chapter presents a general outline of Nebbi Catholic Diocese. First it makes a general description of the diocese; then takes on a historical approach, which looks back at the mission method employed in implanting the present diocese as a Church of the place in its unique environment. It concludes with an assessment of the achievements that have been made, which suggests what else might be built upon this foundation.

Chapter Two examines Alur traditional communitarian values with the intention of presenting the human reality into which Nebbi Catholic Church is born. The Alur have been chosen for three reasons: (a) they were the first recipients of the Gospel message from the first missionaries; (b) from among them the earliest converts took part in spreading the gospel; (c) they are the more dominant ethnic group in Nebbi and their tradition has influenced other neighbouring ethnic groups of the place as the study of Crazzolara and Southall indicate (both acknowledged above under literature review).

Chapter Three discusses Christian communitarian values. It begins by presenting the Trinity as the foundation to Christian communion. Under the same point it continues to present Christ as the model of Christian moral life in the sense that He is God's gift and call to humans and in him is the human response to God; it proceeds to present the Holy Spirit as Giver of life and who renews life in Christ; and finally it presents the Church as a 'new covenant' and 'new creation' community. The second point discusses the Christian Creed as a proclamation of commitment to ecclesial communion. It identifies five marks of the Church and argues that these marks can serve to build unity in the Church. It further refers to faith and witnessing, and the corporate personality that ensues from this faith. It finally turns attention to Christian conversion as an on-going process which turns believers to God and to one another.

Chapter Four is central in this work; it approaches individualism as a moral problem in the Church. It begins by clarifying the concept of individualism and continues to look at it as a problem with a moral significance. The third point makes a critique of individualism as a misleading ethic which is harmful not only to the individual but also to the community. It further argues that the subtlety of individualism lies in its subversive diffusion: what begins with a single individual diffuses to affect others.

Chapter Five is an attempt to respond to the problem of the individual. It intends to bring the individual believer to understand herself or himself as someone who exists within the wider ecclesial reality, without which s/he diminishes. The question of the individual is approached in light of Christian anthropology, which views the human person in relation to Christ. The discussion begins by clarifying what Christian personhood means. It continues to present the individual as someone with a legitimate autonomy, an embodied moral subject, who is capable of self-realisation, but living in an historical context, responsible, relational, and finally, a participant in the social reality of the Church as family of God.

Chapter Six complements the fifth chapter: it explores what possibilities there might be which can provide for the building of ecclesial communion, wherein the individual believer can attain self-realisation. After clarifying the notion of ecclesial communion, it searches for images of ecclesial communion from practices in early Christianity and how this continued through the times of the Church Fathers as recorded in their writings – we select a few of them to illustrate this. This brings us to a discussion on the social nature of the Church, highlighting the models or images of the Church in the attempt to deepen our understanding of ecclesial communion. The chapter further presents the Church as a moral community; and ends with an exposition on the models of morality as ways that might help in translating the images of the Church into the lived experience of believers.

Chapter Seven attempts to make some moral theological recommendations that may help to respond to the problem of individualism from within the ecclesial community. The approach is open to both theological and non-theological possibilities. From what has been presented in the preceding chapters, attention is paid to the different aspects and contexts of ecclesial life including the structural set-up, pastoral, administration, resource management, and church law. The chapter makes three recommendations: the use of the word of God, integral formation, and collaboration in ecclesial activities. A short, General Conclusion is given to summarise what has been discussed in the seven chapters.

CHAPTER ONE
A Profile of Nebbi Catholic Diocese

INTRODUCTION

This chapter presents a general profile of Nebbi Catholic Diocese on these three premises: What was the missionary zeal? How has Christianity been imparted? How does the present Church build on that foundation? The approach is both descriptive, looking at realities into which the diocese is incarnated; and historical, looking at the mission method employed in implanting the Church.[1] This is discussed under seven points: the first five provide a general description of physical realities that exist; the last two look at how the diocese sets itself to work in this reality.

1.1. Location

Nebbi Catholic Diocese is situated in North-Western Uganda. It covers the civil administrative district of Nebbi, stretching between latitudes 2^0 30′ and 2^0 45′ north of the Equator; longitudes 30^0 45′ and 31^0 10′ east of the Prime Meridian.[2] It is bordered by Arua Catholic Diocese to the North; Gulu Catholic Archdiocese to the East, across the River Nile; Hoima Catholic Diocese to the South-East, across the tip of Lake Albert and the Albert Nile; Mahagi Catholic Diocese in the Democratic Republic of Congo, stretching from South to West.[3]

The terrain naturally divides the area into three geo-social belts: the highland is home to the *Okoro,* its inhabitants commonly known as *Jumalu* (highland dwellers); the midland inhabited by the *Padyere* (midland dwellers); the Lowland, stretching along a third of the western banks of Lake Albert, for about eighty kilometers along the Albert Nile, is inhabited by the *Junam* (riv-

---

1 A useful reference on evangelisation in West Nile (presently Nebbi and Arua Catholic dioceses) is the work of Toni La Salandra, "The History of the Catholic Church in West Nile" (unpublished), electronic text downloaded from website: http://www.aruadiocese.org/toni_la_salandra.pdf, from the main webpage of Arua Catholic Diocese: http://www.aruadiocese.org/history.htm (accessed on 11 June 2006).

2 Nebbi District Administration Office, "State of the Environment Report 2004," p.1; can also be accessed on Website: http://www.nemaug.org (accessed, 13 September 2008). We obtained a copy of this document from the District Census Officer, Richard Uryem, interviewed by the researcher, at Nebbi, 29 May 2008.

3 Mahagi Catholic Diocese participated in the first Nebbi diocesan synod. Its Ordinary, Bishop Marcel Uthembi, addressed the issue of inculturation. See *Acts of the First Synod*, p. 58-59.

erine or lake people). The physical land area of Nebbi district covers a total of 3,288 km^2 with a perimeter of 353 km (1.2% of total national area).

1.2. Demography

The ethnic groups in Nebbi are predominantly Nilotic (98%), comprising the Alur, Madi, Kebu, Lendu, Lugbara and Acooli (Acholi). The Alur are the majority in number (91%). The predominant local language is Alur, with slight variations in accent between the Jumalu, Padyere and Junam; others are Kebu, Lendu, Madi and Lugbara. Alurland runs astride the Uganda-Democratic Republic of Congo border. A larger section of the Alur is on the Congo side with more chieftains than those in Uganda. The Alur belong to the Lwo-speaking family.[4] In his book, *East African Societies*, Shorter writes that: "The Uganda or central Lwoo are represented by the Alur, the Chope and the Acholi; the eastern Lwoo, on the Kenya-Uganda border, and on the western shores of Lake Victoria in Kenya and Tanzania, by the Padhola and the Luo."[5]

Nebbi Diocese covers the entire Alurland on the Uganda side, part of which is in The Democratic Republic of Congo (since the territorial demarcation between the British and Belgian colonial administrations. West Nile region became a British protectorate in 1914). The distribution of other ethnic groups in Nebbi Catholic Diocese is as follows: Lendu and Kebu are mainly in Kango, Zeu and Atyak (in the highland); Madi in Akanyu, Nebbi (midland); Lugbara in Atyak (highland), Nebbi, Kucwiny (midland) and Wadelai (lowland); Acholi-Labwor in Wadelai; Hema pastoralists are sparsely distributed. The diocese has two parishes outside the civil district of Nebbi: Uleppi and Rhino-Camp, both in Arua civil district, with a predominantly Madi population.[6] This presents a mosaic of customs which must be taken into consideration. Nevertheless, despite this wide blend of ethnic groups, their social-cultural roots rest on the three principles of kinship, chiefship and religion which define their general lifestyle. This is recorded in the studies of Crazzolara and Southall.[7]

---

4 Crazzolara, *The Lwoo – Part I – Lwoo Traditions*, Verona, Editrice Nigrizia, 1951, p. 179ff; idem., *The Lwoo – Part III – Clans*, Verona, Editrice Nigrizia, 1954, p. 401; Southall, *Alur Society,* p. 3.

5 Aylward Shorter, *East African Societies*, reprint, London, Routledge, 2004, p. 23.

6 Fr. Lino Opio, Nebbi Diocesan Pastoral Coordinator, interviewed by the researcher, at Nebbi, 23 June 2008.

7 Crazzolara, *The Lwoo*, p. 409, "The Aluur, both aboriginals and later associates, include Okebo, Lendu, Madi, and Lango strains…"; Southall, *Alur Society*, p. 200-204, 212-214, 345.

1.3. Diocesan Statistics

Nebbi Catholic Diocese was erected in 1996, cut from Arua Diocese: both of them are under Gulu Archdiocese in northern Uganda. Nebbi Diocese comprises five deaneries with fifteen parishes. Its first ordinary, Bishop John Baptist Odama (23 February 1996 – 2 January 1999) later became the first Archbishop of Gulu Archdiocese. Its second ordinary Bishop was Martin Luluga (2 January 1999 – 2011) transferred from Gulu.[8] Its third Ordinary is Bishop Sanctus Lino Wanok (2011…).

The diocese covers an area of 5,098 km^2. The report of the Comboni Missionaries recorded in the diocesan synod document places the number of Catholics in Nebbi at 70% of the total population.[9] The latest population census in the diocese was conducted in 2002, which places the figure at 477,169 persons. Out of these 353,346 are Catholics, served by 713 local catechists, 1 lay missionary, 39 African Sisters, 9 African Brothers, 1 permanent deacon, 60 diocesan priests (including the bishop), 12 missionary priests. There are five different religious congregations in the diocese.[10]

Background information shows that until December 2000 there were 144 priests ordained in Arua Catholic Diocese. Out of them 30 were incardinated in Nebbi Catholic Diocese at its beginning in 1996.[11] The current number of priests by ethnic community is: 1 Kebu, 2 Madi, and 56 Alur. This generally represents the ethnic groups in the diocese; however, there is still the challenge of raising more numbers to the priesthood from other ethnic groups in the diocese. The number of Catholics per priest is relative: some parishes have more number of the laity than others. On average every parish has two ordained priests. The distribution of parishes by regions is relatively equal: of the fifteen parishes, 5 are in Okoro, 5 in Padyere, 5 in Junam.

1.4. Economic Activity

The topography has influenced population distribution and economic activities: the highlands register higher population and agricultural produce than the midland and riverine. According to the information from the office of the

8 *Acts of the First Diocesan Synod of Nebbi Catholic Diocese*, p. 6, dates the erection on 22.02.1996.

9 *Ibid.*, p. 28.

10 Fr. Lino Opio, interviewed by the researcher, at Nebbi, 23 June 2008.

11 Fr. Aquilino Acidri, Arua Diocese Pastoral Coordinator, interviewed by the researcher, at Ediofe, 19 May 2008; see also La Salandra, "The History of the Catholic Church in West Nile," p. 129.

District Census Officer, the record on Nebbi District Poverty Assessment-Livelihood Survey, 2006, indicates that over 80% of the population depends on agriculture for livelihood.[12] Until 2008 Nebbi district comprises three civil administrative counties with 16 sub-counties, 87 parishes, and 1329 villages in 31 local stations. The predominant economic activity in Nebbi is agriculture, which employs 85% of the population; 79% practice subsistence farming. Only 40% of the produce is sold for cash. The cash crops are predominantly cotton and coffee. Cotton is grown in Padyere and Junam counties; coffee is grown in Ukuro highlands. The Junam practice fishing both for subsistence and cash. Nebbi has poor infrastructures with regard to social-economic developments. The roads are poor, except one tarmac road running from Pakwach on the River Nile to Arua town. There are two banks: Stanbic Bank Limited and Centenary Bank, the latter run by the Catholic Church in Uganda, to which Nebbi Catholic Diocese is a shareholder.

There are three townships: Paidha in Ukuro, Nebbi in Padyere, Pakwach in Junam, operating both as administrative and business centers. Other locations are smaller trading centres operating simple business where people access household needs. However, these centres are going through social-cultural transformation, the confluence of rural and urban-like lifestyle. The trading centers attract mainly the youth, seeking casual jobs or personal business. Much of Nebbi is still rural and remote. This means that the majority of people are still closer to traditional lifestyle and practices. The family community is still viable, with its members close to one another. The homestead and family neighbours are either close of kin or together with those who have integrated with them. In the villages, close families still share the same compound, meals, practicing co-activities like house-building, joint-hoeing, harvesting, marriage, burial functions, inter-family and inter-homestead visits.

1.5. Social Institutions

The Church's traditional social institutions in Nebbi are in the health and education sectors. The history of evangelisation in West Nile written by La Salandra shows that these two institutions have been the most effective ways of communicating Gospel values. These contributions have been the foundations upon which the civil society has as well built.[13]

12 Nebbi District Administration Office, "State of the Environment Report 2004," Website: http://www.nemaug.org (accessed, 13 September 2008).

13 La Salandra, "The History of the Catholic Church in West Nile," p. 131-136.

1.5.1. Health Sector

Medical service is one way by which Nebbi Catholic Diocese carries out its mission of evangelisation. According to Fr. Opio, there are two main hospitals, two maternity centers, and one dispensary which were founded by the Catholic Church.[14] According to Mr. Ringe, the district LC5 chairperson, there are three general hospitals, fifty-seven health units and five Non-Governmental Organisation (NGO) or private dispensaries. The district has health centres in forty-five parishes while forty-two parishes are without. The table below shows the distribution of health services in Nebbi. Those which are church-founded fall under the NGO category.[15]

Figure 1: Distribution of Health Facilities in Nebbi

Health Sub-District		*Ownership*	*Total*	*Hospital*	*HC4*	*HC3*	*HC2*
Okoro County	18	Government	12	0	0	6	7
		NGO	6	1	0	3	2
Padyere County	20	Government	16	1	0	6	10
		NGO	4	1	0	3	0
Jonam County	17	Government	13	0	1	5	7
		NGO	4	0	0	2	2
Total			**57**	**3**	**1**	**25**	**28**

Source: Nebbi District State of the Environment Report, 2004

The diocese has three chaplaincies at the main hospitals of Angal, Nyapea and Nebbi. The researcher interviewed Sr. Susu (administration staff) and Fr. Centis (chaplain) at Angal hospital. Both commented that the Church needs to train and supply qualified medical doctors and administration personnel from among the religious, priests and deserving laity, even if they noted that it is expensive to do so. They added that health service is an avenue to inculcate Church teaching and charity by witness and service.[16]

14 Fr. Lino Opio, interviewed by the researcher, at Nebbi, 23 June 2008.

15 David Ringe, LC5 Chairperson, interviewed by the researcher, at Nebbi, 29 May 2008.

16 Sr. Merciana Susu, interviewed by the researcher, 25th and 26th May 2008; Fr. Felice Centis, 25 May 2008.

The Pontifical Council for Pastoral Assistance understands the Church's health care as a service to life, and health care workers as ministers of life. In its *Charter for Health Care Workers*, it states that: "The work of health care persons is a very valuable service to life. It expresses a profoundly human and Christian commitment, undertaken and carried out not only as a technical activity but also as one of dedication to and love for neighbor."[17] The document continues to explain that health care is a ministerial collaboration with the love of God, which brings to real life situations the continuation of the healing love of Christ.[18] Moreover, it is a participation in the pastoral and evangelising action of the Church, and thus, it is a ministry of salvation.[19]

1.5.2. School Education

The Alur word for education is *ponji*, "teaching, instruction;" from the verb, *ponjo*, "instruct, teach, communicate knowledge;" the subjective noun *ponjiri*, "learning; maturity in knowledge, to advance in wisdom, good judgment and ability to decide" refers to the person advancing in knowledge through learning. Mr. Ukok explained that for the Alur, education has to do with knowing values and appropriating them; which is tested through relationships.[20] This is in the context of traditional or informal education as they did not develop a formal school education.

Ogula, an educationist, explains that:

> In the first instance, education may refer to the process of developing desirable knowledge, values and skills. It is a process by which society transmits its cultural heritage from one generation to the next. Education also refers to a terminal state of the knowledge, values and skills that a person has acquired to enable him/her live comfortably and happily in his/her environment.[21]

The *Concise English Dictionary* and *Webster's New World Dictionary* define education in terms of imparting knowledge, instruction in skills and shaping moral character. From this understanding, the basic idea of education is

---

17 Pontifical Council for Pastoral Assistance, *Charter for Health Care Workers*, Vatican translation, Boston, Pauline Books & Media, 1999, n. 1.

18 Ibid., n. 4.

19 Ibid., n. 5.

20 Andrea Ukok, interviewed by the researcher, at Rero, 26 June 2008.

21 Paul A. Ogula, "The Impact of the Church on Education in Africa: Paper Presented at the 13th Interdisciplinary Theological Session, Faculty of Theology," Nairobi, The Catholic University of Eastern Africa, 2nd - 4th March, 2011 (unpublished), p. 3.

value-centered and has to do with imparting knowledge through guidance and experience.

Knowledge is person-centred; it aims at the integral growth of the person. Thus, the focus of education is the shaping of moral character. In his book, *The Ethical Animal*, Waddington argues that: "The moulding of the newborn infant into an ethicizing being is not due wholly to intrinsic forces, but requires an interaction between him and his external circumstances."[22] Agreeing with Waddington, Häring observes that education must lead to the maturation of the person; and: "Maturation includes, above all, discernment, a sense of dignity, awareness of freedom, and motivation. There is no truly human education where there is not a constant growth in moral insights."[23]

Growth in moral insight involves both informal and formal education. The *Policy Book* of Arua Catholic Diocese distinguishes between informal and formal education as a guide for its working strategy.[24] *Informal education* refers to the imparting of traditional, life-centred values. It is received from parents, peer groups and the community. It is a life-application education although not acquired in a systematic and scientific manner. In this way: (a) learners are taught good manners and social values such as kindness, respect, friendliness and solidarity; (b) life skills such as cultivation and handicraft are taught; (c) kinship values of relationships or ancestral lineage are instilled. This is still common in Nebbi Catholic Diocese, especially in the villages.

Formal education is scientific, systematic and progressive, carried out in organised institutions with specialised teachers instructing learners. In Nebbi Catholic Diocese this category includes pre-primary or nursery, primary and secondary schools; post-secondary or tertiary institutions, mainly vocational or specialised technical and training institutions. In the diocese there are 9 secondary schools, 4 technical and vocational schools which are church-founded. Primary schools (except pre-primary or nursery schools) are directly under the Government, even if they were church-founded.

However, it is to be noted that the school already takes on the identity of a plural community, which may not necessarily instill moral and traditional values as in the first kind of education. In order to make an assessment of school education, we may need to consider how this has developed in the country. This will help us to assess how the Diocese takes part in it. Here we shall pay

22 C. H. Waddington, *The Ethical Animal*, The University of Chicago Press, Phoenix Book, 1967, p. 27.

23 Bernard Häring, *Manipulation: Ethical Boundaries of Medical, Behavioural and Genetic Manipulation*, Slough, St. Paul Publications, 1975, p. 14.

24 Arua Catholic Diocese, *Policy Book: A Pastoral Guide for Christian Communities*, 3rd printing, Arua, Diocese Publications, 2000, p. 52.

attention to the Government policy on school education and how it has affected the Church's ministry in this field.

1.5.2.1. The Uganda Government Education Policy

Late 1960s the Government liberalised school education and introduced the Grant-Aided system. The State undertook material provisions to meet capital expenses, recurrent costs and financial payment of teachers' salaries. This meant staff-sharing: the Government posted qualified teachers to church schools regardless of religious affiliation. Due to changes in Government, the 1970s to the first half of the 1980s saw a decline in the school sector. In 1992 the Government introduced a new long-term education policy to reverse a decaying situation in the education sector. In 1997 the Government introduced free primary school education under the Universal Primary Education programme. Afterwards, in 2007 the Government introduced Universal Secondary School. This aimed at equipping citizens with suitable capacity to participate in the educational programmes, designed to promote national development.

Article 30 of the 1995 Constitution stipulates that all persons have a right to education.[25] Article 34 entitles children to access basic education from parents and the State. This article defines the Government's education objectives in the following manner: (i) The State shall promote free and compulsory basic education; (ii) The State shall take appropriate measures to afford every citizen equal opportunity to attain the highest education standard possible; (iii) Individuals, religious bodies and other non-governmental organisations shall be free to found and operate educational institutions if they comply with the general educational policy of the country and maintain national standards. However, it is to be noted that even though this development recognises the Church's role in school education, it has as well modified the extent to which the Church can play a part. Does this national programme promote the moral formation of learners?

1.5.2.2. The Diocese's Contribution

According to Bansikiza, the school is a vital institution for the restoration of moral formation in Africa.[26] This concern has been expressed by the Catholic Bishops of Uganda, where they recall that: "The Catholic Church has had as

25 Constitution of the Republic of Uganda, Article 30: "Right to education." Electronic text retrieved from website: http://en.wikisource.org/wiki/Constitution_of_the_Republic_of_Uganda (accessed, 4 November 2009).

26 Constance Bansikiza, *Restoring Moral Formation in Africa*, Eldoret, AMECEA Gaba Publications, Spearhead Nr. 155, 2001, pp. 78-80.

its aim, since its first arrival in Uganda, the education of the sons and daughters of Uganda that they may assume responsibility for their own country."[27]

Nebbi Catholic Diocese participates in the national school programmes at all levels. All the diocesan schools and specialised institutions are registered with the Ministry of Education and Sports, thereby following the same national examinations under the Uganda National Examinations Board for all qualifications. However, the Church can still offer its unique contribution to the society through the Church-founded schools; but that is not enough, the Church must also have a part in the public schools and specialised institutions by providing teaching staff in them. It cannot only provide chaplains; it must also train some of its priests and, where possible, support its deserving catechists and lay people in the teaching profession with specific qualifications in the secular subjects. The Directory of the Episcopal Conference of Uganda recommends the ministry of presence in schools and institutions of learning. It lays that the Church must: "Identify committed and exemplary persons – priests, religious Sisters and Brothers, and lay people for the ministry of presence and actual teaching."[28]

Nebbi Diocese *Education Policy* book states that: "Indeed education has been the concern of the Catholic Church and she believes that a human person has a right to a harmonious education at all levels, that is, academic, moral, religious and physical in order to acquire new attitudes, better knowledge, greater skills and improved habits linked to values."[29] It continues to explain that: "Our responsibility, therefore, is to let our schools become educational communities, communities where pupils/students, staff and parents converge… It is imperative and urgent that we, the Church, take appropriate steps to make our role more effective in schools so as to realize the evangelizing Mission of the Church."[30] In the *Forward* of the same document, the Bishop calls for a concerted effort in order to improve school education in the diocese. He makes the appeal: "We have to admit that the Church has not made full use of the opportunities at her disposal to promote her values in her schools, and this has

27 Catholic Bishops of Uganda, Pastoral Letter *Shaping Our National Destiny*, Kisubi, Marianum Press, 1962, p. 30.

28 Uganda Episcopal Conference, *Directory and Some Practical Suggestions of Promoting Catholic Education in Schools and Institutions of Learning*, Kampala, Catholic Secretariat, 2003, p. i.

29 Nebbi Catholic Diocese, *The Education Policy for Nebbi Catholic Founded Schools: Policy Implementation Handbook*, 1st edition, Nebbi, Catholic Press, 2003, p. 4.

30 Ibid., p. 5.

led to a decline in our academic ladder. With this policy book… let us all work for quality education."[31]

The question of "quality education" has received scholarly interest in the field of education with a focus on instilling a sense of good moral life and communitarian habits. Under the editorship of Teklemarian and Akala, various contributors at the Catholic University of Eastern Africa have written on what ways can be taken to ensure effective school education in Africa in the 21st century. In the *Forward*, the editors observe that: "Effective schools are not measured merely in terms of their academic/intellectual performance as demonstrated in written examinations. Effectiveness should involve the satisfaction obtained as a result of schooling, the social concerns developed and expressed to one's neighbor, the ethical principles one embraces and the whole rounded physical, emotional, and moral growth obtained."[32] The central point is that education must furnish learners with the awareness of, and the link with, the community or society in which they are being prepared to serve, the society whose burdens they must learn to shoulder.

1.5.2.3. Evaluation

What we have said above gives a clue about the state of school education in the diocese. The researcher interviewed the LC5 Chairperson of Nebbi District. The record of the District Education Department, obtained from his office, gives the district literacy level as shown below:[33]

Figure 2: Nebbi District Literacy Level: male-female comparison

General		***Urban***		***Rural***	
Male	*Female*	*Male*	*Female*	*Male*	*Female*
70%	30%	78.2%	46.1%	65.7%	27.6%

Source: Nebbi District State of the Environment, 2004

The overall literacy level in Nebbi is rated at 53% of which women make 30% and men 70%. The gap is visibly pronounced both in the urban and rural con-

31 Ibid., p. 2.

32 Amanuel A. Teklemariam and Winston Jumba Akala (eds.), *Effective Schools for 21st Century in Africa*, Faculty of Education 4th Interdisciplinary Sessions, March 17 – 18, 2010, Nairobi, CUEA Press, 2011, p. vii.

33 David Ringe, interviewed by the researcher, at Nebbi, 29 May 2008. The figures referred to are the records of the District Education Department.

texts. This reality reflects both an institutional and structural problem, which demonstrates that women do not stand an equal chance to go to school as men do. They are more tied to domestic chores. This sets a gender imbalance with regard to female participation in the society much as in the Church. As noted, the disparity is deeper between the village and township populace.

Since 2003/4, there has been a shift of development in the education sector in Uganda, especially with regard to implementing the Government programme of Universal Primary Education. The Government education reform policy is to provide basic education for all as part of the Millennium Development Goals.[34] This programme has revolutionised education in the country, with a massive enrolment, especially in the primary schools. This can be illustrated from the 2003 general comparison ratio of schools in Northern Uganda, as shown in the table below:

Figure 3: General School Comparison of Ratios in Northern Uganda

Teacher : Pupil Ratio		***Pupil : Textbook Ratio***
National	1 : 15	Not applicable
Kotido	1 : 200	1 : 15
Masindi	1 : 120	1 : 15
Nebbi	1 : 100	1 : 10
Pader	1 : 100	Not applicable
Gulu	1 : 150	Not applicable

Source: ActionAid Uganda 2003; Ministry of Education and Sports, 2003

This figure shows that in Nebbi the school generally registers low results. On average, one teacher must attend to one hundred pupils, as compared to the national ratio of attending to fifteen pupils. The same figure shows that ten pupils are to share one textbook. From this information, there are three points to note, with regard to the spiritual and moral growth of the school-going youth:

First, the massive access to the school does not obviously imply quality. The large teacher-pupil ratio suggests that there is a heavy workload. This

34 Ministry of Education and Sports, *The National Report on the Development of Education in Uganda at the Beginning of the 21st Century: Report to the 47th Session of the International Conference on Education*, Geneva, 8th-11th September 2004. Article by Doris Kakuru Muhwezi, "Paper Commissioned for the EFA Global Monitoring Report 2003/4: The Leap to Equality."

means that the teacher has to focus more on academic pursuit than paying attention to the spiritual and moral needs of the pupils.

Secondly, the Church in Nebbi Catholic Diocese no longer enjoys the full influence over the schools as in the past. On the government syllabus, Christian Religious Education (CRE) is now an optional subject; more emphasis is placed on science subjects. In our questionnaire report, twenty-three respondents identified themselves as teachers (Catholic by affiliation) from twelve primary schools; sixteen of them reported that they did not take CRE during their college training. The reason was that this subject is not marketable. Out of forty-seven student respondents, from ten secondary schools, thirty-one wrote that they did not like CRE because it promises no job, even if one passed it highly; and there are no competent teachers for it. Only the schools run by the Church have CRE as a core subject. But even in this case more attention is paid to passing examination rather than taking a life-application approach. It can be deduced from this that moral formation is largely left with parents, elders, catechists, the religious and priests.

Thirdly, there is the problem of school drop-outs, more especially at the primary level. The record of the District Education Sector rates the school drop-outs at 5.1% of the total number enrolled. The majority of these are girls (65.2%) than boys (43.8%). Nearly 80% of girls enrolled in Class One do not complete their primary education.[35] The reasons include lack of parental motivation and support, domestic violence, peer pressure, negative cultural practices, the reality of poverty which forces them to resort to petty business, caring for siblings, early marriage, and early pregnancy. According to Bishop Luluga the situation has kept women away from leadership roles, particularly in the education and administrative sectors, in civil society and in the Church. This is attributed to the negative attitude towards the education of women, embedded in the tradition of the people.[36] From this information, we can deduce that the Church still has a role to play in the moral formation of the society through school education.

Findings from questionnaire and oral interviews revealed that the youth are faced with an influx of confusing life models. From his long pastoral experience, Fr. Onegwa observed that there is a growing situation of cultural and moral downturn among the youth.[37] The catechists we interviewed reported that the youth, especially those in school life, demand pragmatic answers for immediate needs including sexual expression, freedom, money, job, person-

35 "Nebbi District State of the Environment Report 2004," p. 53.

36 Bishop Martin Luluga, interviewed by the researcher, at Nebbi, 27 May and 23 June 2008.

37 Fr. Emilio Onegwa, interviewed by the researcher, at Nyapea, 7 June 2008. Fr. Emilio is one of the oldest priests of the diocese, ordained on 24. 06. 1956.

al property and leisure.[38] The comment of Akelo, a mother, summarised the general experience of parents interviewed by this researcher: "Fluid social changes are luring and confusing the youth."[39] Mr. Candia, a secondary school teacher, in charge of discipline, remarked that there is a decline in the behaviour of school youth.[40] An element of negative cultural practice goes under the pretext of "social entertainment" which effectively attracts the youth. In our night studies at seventeen trading centers we discovered that the youth spend long hours into the night at video shows or entertaining themselves by playing cards, chewing leaves of intoxicating plants, doing petty business, and errant sexual behaviours.[41]

According to Mr. Unencan, a police officer, the Church has an important role in the moral education of the youth; it cannot be replaced by the civil institution.[42] We can deduce that the challenges of moral education call for the joint efforts of parents, pastoral agents, school teachers and civil servants together, in shaping a society with cherished human values. In what follows we shall discuss the unique role which the Church plays in the society as a moral authority.

1.6. The Church as a Moral Authority in the Society in Nebbi

What is the consciousness of Nebbi Catholic Diocese, as Church, about the human society in which it exists? And, vice-versa, what is the consciousness of the society about this Church? From our field finding, the society in Nebbi can fall under four categories. At the lowest levels are the *villagers*, forming the majority, who are closest to their traditional ways. Next, is the *elite* class, more literate, including civil servants, school teachers and medical servants; these are more critical and liberal compared to those in the villages. Another group is the *business* class, comprising those in personal or group business who may support the Church but may not frequent it. In the fourth category we can identify the *non-governmental organisations*, comprising the more free and independent associations but church-friendly. According to Lakwonyero,

38 Vincent Aguda and Anthony Urombi, interviewed by the researcher, at Angal Catechist Training Centre, 26 June 2008; Charles Udaga, interviewed by the researcher, at Rero Chapel and Angelo Upoki, interviewed by the researcher, at Makwera Chapel, both on 3 July 2008.

39 Carolina Akelo, interviewed by the researcher, at Boro Community, Rero, 4 July 2008.

40 Stephen Candia, interviewed by the researcher, at Parombo Secondary School, 1 June 2008.

41 Names of Field Assistants, selected Trading Centres, and dates of night study are provided in appendix 3.

42 George Unencan, Police Officer, interviewed by the researcher, at Parombo Police Post, 27 June 2008.

non-governmental or charity organisations find the Church a good interface for them to reach down to the people at the grassroots level.[43] In its work of evangelisation, the Church addresses itself to all these categories.

In our field interviews with respondents representing each of these categories, we found out that the Church is seen as a "moral authority."[44] This means that the Church commands respect for its message, especially with regard to its inclusive social teaching. According to Häring the Church's moral authority is within the Gospel message and the convincing appeal to various people's consciences. He writes that: "Its effectiveness will correspond with the purity and depth of the salvation-knowledge of those who speak and act for her, their good reasoning… The teaching authority of the church has direct competence only for those who, by faith and baptism, are her members. But… her social teaching, prophecy and critique intend to reach the upright conscience of all people."[45]

In his book, *Authority in Morals*, Gerald Hughes gives four criteria for a rationally convincing appeal to the Church's moral authority. First, the question must be one which we have not settled satisfactorily ourselves. Secondly, there must be some external grounds for believing that the authority appealed to is likely to be correct in the point in question. Thirdly, the grounds for believing in the authority must be sufficiently strong that they outweigh any tendency we may have to disagree with its conclusions on internal ground. Fourthly, it is undesirable to rely on authority in circumstances where it is practicable to settle the point in question without making any appeal to authority.[46]

Appeal to the Church's moral authority therefore requires from the part of the Church: competence, credibility, reliability, and relevance to reality. To bring the Church's moral authority to life needs an organised working arrangement. This specifically refers to its structural set-up and pastoral approach.

---

43 Alfred Lakwonyero, AFARD Director, interviewed by the researcher, at Nebbi, 25 May 2008.

44 Anthony Uyungi, retired school teacher (17 May 2008); Peter Unyutha, retired civil servant (16 May 2008); John Urunge, retired Catechist (28 June 2008); Kwonga, ATR believer (20th July 2008); Charles Umbidi, Paramount Chief of Panyimur Chieftaincy (20 July 2008) – all interviews conducted by the researcher.

45 Bernard Häring, *Free and Faithful in Christ: Moral Theology for Priests and Laity,* Vol. 3: *Light to the World Salt for the Earth*, Slough, St. Paul Publications, 1981, p. 257.

46 Gerald Hughes, *Authority in Morals: An Essay in Christian Ethics*, London, Heythrop Monographs, pp. 92ff.

1.7. The Diocesan Structural Set-up

This section describes how Nebbi Catholic Diocese is structured, which depicts the way it is set to work, namely, its pastoral and administrative framework.[47] By the term *structure* we are referring to the intelligible and feasible framework, an arrangement of a work strategy, a make-up pointing to and streamlining a specified path of action. However, a structure awaits implementation and continuous evaluation to realise it.

1.7.1. Pastoral and Administrative Functioning

The notion of *diocese* was clarified at Vatican Council II, recorded in its document, *Christus Dominus*, on the pastoral office of the bishop as a service to Christ the Lord:

> A diocese is a portion of the people of God which is entrusted to a bishop to be shepherded by him with the cooperation of the presbytery. Thus by adhering to its pastor and gathered together by him through the Gospel and the Eucharist in the Holy Spirit, it constitutes a particular church in which the one, holy, catholic, and apostolic Church of Christ is truly present and operative.[48]

Renken clarifies that this notion reveals the constitutive elements of the diocese: bishop, priests, people of God, making up a particular Church. Commenting on canon 369 of the Code of Canon Law, he writes that, "The diocese is not a mere administrative division of the universal Church... The canon focuses upon the people of God who form the particular church."[49] This depicts the diocese as the conscious and active communion of all believers contributing to the wholeness of not only what the Church is but more so who the Church is by its intelligible and operative designation. It is plausible that the diocese needs a structure to organise its physical reality, direct its life and coordinate its activities.

Nebbi Diocese is divided into five deaneries, each with a priest chosen as its dean whose work is to coordinate pastoral and administrative activities, and general discipline among fellow priests. Each deanery comprises three parishes on average. Each parish is divided into sub-parish units called zones,

---

47 This structure is taken directly from Arua Catholic Diocese from which Nebbi Catholic Diocese is created. See *Acts of the First Synod of Arua Diocese*, Kisubi, Marianum Press, 1987, chart inside back cover.

48 Vatican Council II, Decree Concerning the Pastoral Office of Bishops in the Church, *Christus Dominus*, n. 11 § 1: *AAS* 58 (1966), pp. 677.

49 John A. Renken, "Notion of Diocese," in John Beal, et al., *New Commentary on the Code of Canon Law*, Bangalore, Theological Publications in India, 2003, p. 507.

each with a zonal head-catechist. The zone is further divided into smaller unit stations (a minimum of two) commonly known as chapels, each served by the chapel head-catechist, jointly with assistant catechists and other pastoral agents. The use *chapel*, in the local understanding, primarily refers to the church building where the assembly of believers commonly prays on Sunday and performs other regular functions. By extension, the use *chapel* vaguely refers to the constitutive community itself. Each chapel is dedicated to a patron saint. Meanwhile, in the local consciousness and parlance, the word *eklezia* (church) is used with reference to the physical church building itself, although the sense of a communion of communities and communion of believers is implied. The chapel, in turn, comprises Small Christian Communities (SCC), a homestead of believers made up of individual families with their corporate members. Fr. Odokodit explained that ideally the diocesan structure facilitates the dissemination of information and coordination of pastoral activities, the flow of communication and policy implementation.[50]

1.7.2. Assessment

The pastoral-administrative structure can be best assessed by the moral cohesion it brings about in the life of the Church, how it helps the Church to pull its strength together for wholeness. In his Encyclical Letter on the Church as Mystical Body of Christ, *Mystici Corporis*, Pope Pius XII has indicated that the Church's organic structure involves both charism and hierarchy in an inseparable whole. He clarifies that, "One must not think, however, that this ordered or 'organic' structure of the body of the Church contains only hierarchical elements and with them is complete..."[51] His point here is that the life of the Church cannot rest on the ordained priests alone without the laity. Church historians recall that this papacy was faced with the problem of totalitarian regimes marked by the Second World War (1939 – 1945), Nazi regime, and Communism.[52] But what is rewarding for the Church is the theological development which opened more space for the laity both in the internal life of the Church and outward activity in the society. Bokenkotter writes that this document summed up recent theological developments which clarified the unity of the Church in the mystical Body of Christ.[53] The Pope encouraged the forming

50 Fr. John Hercules Odokodit, interviewed by the researcher, at Nebbi, 23 May 2008.

51 Pius XII, Ecyclical Letter *Mystici Corporis* (29 June 1943), par. 17; *AAS* 35 (1943), p. 200.

52 See Hubert Jedin (ed.), *History of the Church*, vol. X: *The Church in the Modern Age*, translated by Anselm Biggs, London, Burns & Oates, 1981, pp. 143-248.

53 Thomas Bokenkotter, *A Concise History of the Catholic Church*, revised and expanded edition, New York, Doubleday, 1990, p. 353.

of Catholic associations by which believers, especially the laity, could take active part in the society and fill it with Christian values. He noticed that a greater availability of the Church in the civil society can be realised by involving the laity who are more directly immersed in the daily encounter with the world. In his study within the context of the Church in Uganda, Bitole argues that this document of Pope Pius XII can help to challenge the laity to appreciate their vital role in the Church.[54] The fullness of the Church in its human reality is not complete with the clergy alone.

Our study seeks to find ways of overcoming the problem of individualism in the Church. The question of *structure* provides an important premise for finding ways of resolving this problem with a focus on building ecclesial communion. Improving church structure will strengthen ecclesial life both in the internal acts of worship, as well as the work of evangelisation and social activities. In his Apostolic Exhortation on the role of the Christian family in the modern world, *Familiaris Consortio*, Pope John Paul II states that the pastorship of the Church needs a working structure at all levels down from the SCC.[55] This will enable it to set root more firmly at the most elementary level. But, he clarifies that this structure is only necessary to ensure an effective life-application through competence, sensitivity, fidelity to the Gospel and the living Tradition of the Church.[56]

Structure is to facilitate participation. A study done by Fabien Lonema, although in a juridical approach, gives clarification on this. The central point is ecclesial unity, where all the faithful work together for common growth. He writes that: "The common priesthood of all the believers in Christ, with its ministerial character and restituting to the ordained ministry its authentic and evangelical vocation to the service of the community of the faithful, has placed the premises for an organic restructuring of the pastoral work in the cooperative and missionary sense."[57] The channel for these structures of participation is the parish council. But, *structures of participation* does not imply that there should arise in the Church clerical authoritarianism or anti-clerical democracy. We may understand that both of these two negative terminologies are forms of individualism; and are incompatible with the spirit of ecclesial communion.

---

54 Joseph Bitole Kato, *Awakiening the Laity: Ugandan Pastoral Approach*, Eldoret, AMECEA Gaba Publications Spearhead Nos. 161-163 (2003), pp. 34-35.

55 John Paul II, Apostolic Exhortation *Familiaris Consortio* (The Role of the Christian Family in the Modern World, 22 November 1981), Boston, St. Paul Books & Media, 1999, n. 70-72: *AAS* 74 (1982), p. 167-170.

56 Ibid., n. 68.

57 Fabien Lonema, "Structures of Participation in the Parish," in *African Christian Studies*, vol. 26, Nr. 1 (March 2010), p. 114.

Nebbi Catholic Diocese has Church councils at every level, drawn from the unit of the Christian family, up through the SCC, chapel, zone, parish, deanery, diocesan council, to the curia. This provides for the involvement of all church members, including children. It presents a communion and conciliar structure, a framework within which all activities can be coordinated, including pastoral ministries, finance, development projects and education. It channels all activities under the two sectors of administration and pastoral. This picture of a Church, with its roots deep in the family, gives an impression that it is a people-oriented Church. But it also presents a challenge on the practical side, namely, the strength that moves such a structure lies in the spirit needed to sustain it.

According to the report of the diocesan pastoral coordinator, the policy of Nebbi Catholic Diocese is that, every parish is to be developed into an operative spiritual center.[58] This means that there is need for suitable facilitators for the task, not necessarily priests. Different reports recorded in the first diocesan synod document show that there are capable religious, catechists and other laity whom the parish or diocese can involve in steering the different pastoral activities.[59] To understand the present reality better we have to read into the historical passage of evangelisation through which the present Church came to be; and from it, to discern what possible ways can give strength for continuity.

1.8. Missiological Perspective: A Historical Analysis

Primary evangelisation in Nebbi Catholic Diocese was carried out by the Comboni missionaries (named after their founder, Daniel Comboni, 1831-1881).[60] The itinerary diary of Bishop Geyer shows that the first group of missionaries entered Alurland on 17 February 1910, at Pa-Koba across the River Nile, opposite present day Pakwach.[61] He reports that they met a welcoming

58 Fr. Lino Opio, interviewed by the researcher, at Nebbi, 23 June 2008.

59 *Acts of the First Diocesan Synod of Nebbi Catholic Diocese*, pp. 22-40.

60 The Comboni missionaries evangelised the entire Northern Uganda, the present Catholic dioceses of Nebbi, Gulu, Arua, Lira, Moroto and Kotido – all under Gulu Archdiocese. Cf., La Salandra, *op. cit.*, pp. 137-138.

61 Francis Xaver Geyer, *Durch Sand, Sumpf und Wald: Missionsreisen in Zentral-Afrika*, Freiburg i. Br., Herdersche Verlagshandlung, 1914, p. 403. The place Pa-Koba is named after Koba, the chieflet of the place.

people, the "Alur"[62] and "Acooli."[63] They were a religious people; even if they did not know God fully as Christians do, they called God "*Juok.*"[64]

The mission method inseminated by Comboni was *collaboration* (working together) to *implant* (establishing) the Church, a Church which must become self-propagating. His motto was: "Save Africa with Africa."[65] By this he meant that Africans themselves are to be made the evangelisers of Africans. Agostoni, a Comboni missionary priest, comments that in their vision of *implanting* the local Church (*plantatio ecclesiae*) the missionaries specifically meant establishing the leaders of the Church at all levels. He observes that their contribution as missionaries is now through qualitative commitments for the basic and on-going formation of priests, religious and laity. The local Church must now be financially self-supporting, deepen a missionary spirit to make it self-propagating, and must become self-ministering in terms of personnel.[66]

This same message of a self-propagating Church was recommended by Pope Paul VI on his visit to Africa (in Uganda). It was during this visit that the Pope inaugurated the Symposium of Episcopal Conferences of Africa and Madagascar (SECAM) in 1969. He encouraged the Church in Africa to grow in self-confidence, self-reliance and maturity; it must go forward courageously and build a full-fledged Christianity: "By now you Africans are missionaries to yourselves."[67]

In its document, *General Directory for Catechesis*, the Sacred Congregation for the Clergy defines a self-propagating Church in terms of Gospel proclamation, making disciples, teaching, bearing witness, baptising, doing this in memory of Christ, and holding together in love.[68] It is on this rationale of establishing a truly local Church that primary and ongoing evangelisation can take place.

---

62 Ibid., p. 404.

63 Ibid., p. 415.

64 Ibid., p. 532.

65 Aldo Gilli, *Daniel Comboni: The Man and His Message*, Bologna, EMI, 1980, p. 135; Pietro Chiocchetta, *Daniel Comboni: Papers for the Evangelization of Africa*, Bolonga, EMI, 1982, p. 46.

66 Tarcisio Agostoni, *The Comboni Missionaries: An Outline History 1867 – 1997*, Rome, Comboni Missionaries, 2003, p. 572.

67 Paul VI, Address to the Symposium of Episcopal Conference of Africa and Madagascar and the People of Africa, Kampala, 31 July 1969, *Allocution 9*: *AAS* 61 (1969), p. 575; Catholic Bishops of Uganda, Pastoral Letter *Let Your Light Shine*, Kisubi, Marianum Press, 1992, nn. 9-10.

68 Sacred Congregation for the Clergy, *General Directory fot Catechesis*, Nairobi, Paulines Publications Africa, 1997, n. 46.

1.8.1. Mission Method: Past and Present

In his Encyclical Letter on the Church founded by Christ, *Ecclesiam Suam*, Pope Paul VI writes that catechesis is the practical instrument of evangelisation, the content of which is dialogue of salvation, by which the Church communicates Christ to the human world which it approaches.[69] The same expression continues in his Apostolic Exhortation on the proclamation of the Gospel, *Evangelii Nuntiandi*, where he states that the Church exists in order to evangelise.[70] This consists in bringing the message of God's salvation to every sector of the human race so that by its strength it may enter into the hearts of men and women and thus renew the human race.[71]

As pointed out by Pope John Paul II, in his Post-Synodal Apostolic Exhortation, *Ecclesia in Africa*, the efficacy of this dialogue-mission depends to a great extent on the method employed in conveying the Gospel message. Basing on the propositions from the first Special Assembly of the Synod of Bishops for the Church in Africa, he explains that it is the process by which catechesis takes flesh in the various cultures, a path towards full evangelisation, until the Gospel proclaimed takes root in the life-situation of the hearers.[72]

In their work of evangelisation in Nebbi (West Nile in general) the Comboni missionaries tried to apply their founder's mission leitmotif: (i) saving Africa with Africans themselves; (ii) the missionary work in Africa must be Catholic; (iii) Africa must be its own regenerator.[73] Their main mission method can be explained under three aspects: the catechumenate, mission school, and Christian homestead communities.

1.8.1.1. The Mission Station Catechumenate

In *A Dictionary of Canon Law*, the term *Catechumenate* is defined as "catechesis identified with the preparation of the adult candidate for baptism and the Eucharist and post Baptismal instruction of the neophyte in the mysteries

69 Paul VI, Encyclical Letter *Ecclesiam Suam* (Paths of the Church, 6 August 1964), NCWC translation, Boston, Pauline Books and Media, 1999, n. 70: *AAS* 56 (1964), p. 641.

70 Paul VI, Apostolic Exhortation *Evangelii Nuntiandi* (On Evangelization in the Modern World, 8 December 1975), Nairobi, Paulines Publications Africa, 2000, n. 14: *AAS* 68 (1976), p. 13.

71 Ibid., n. 18: *AAS* 68 (1976), pp. 17-18.

72 John Paul II, Post-Synodal Apostolic Exhortation *Ecclesia in Africa* (The Church in Africa, 14 September 1995), Nairobi, Paulines Publications Africa, 1995, n. 59: *AAS* 88 (1996), p. 37.

73 Gilli, *Daniel Comboni: The Man and His Message*, pp. 135-160.

of faith, known as the period of mystagogia."[74] In Nebbi Catholic Diocese, the Catechumenate, at its early beginning, provided basic literacy with the aim of raising catechists and the general laity who could facilitate the propagation of the faith in the homesteads. It was perceived as a community of charity, an intensive training lasting twelve months. The good fruit of this strenuous work can be seen today in the strong commitment of the elderly who went through those programmes.

The first formal catechumenate was opened at Omach in 1910 with the help of a catechist, Daudi Bikumi, from Hoima.[75] The first converts to be baptised at Omach became instrumental in laying the foundation of evangelisation in Alurland some two years ahead of the missionaries. La Salandra reports that they became catechists.[76] It is to be borne in mind that missionaries were not permitted by the British colonial administration to cross to the western part of the River Nile until November 1916. Meanwhile, as Southall recalls, the Alur on the eastern bank of the Nile were ordered by the British administration to cross to the western side in 1914 to avoid sleeping sickness spreading from Bunyoroland.[77]

Fr. Centis remembers these lay men and women as exemplary ancestors of evangelisation in Nebbi Catholic Diocese, who were active in spreading the Gospel among the people.[78] The diocese could keep an annual memorial of them specifically in their honour, to the edification of the faithful. Here we see an indelible mark of collaboration in the founding and evangelisation of the diocese. La Salandra recalls that: "The first protagonists of the expansion of the Christian faith in West Nile have been Ugandan lay people... When the Verona Fathers reached Omach, there was an Alur catechist teaching in Panyimur."[79] It was a lay person, Areni, who gave the first baptism to a cultural leader, chief Okello, of the Panyimur clan. It was him who encouraged the first missionary priest to set foot across the River Nile.[80]

However, the Church has to modify its approach today, specifically for two reasons. First, the government has abolished the catechumenate. The only possibility the Church has is a short and quick catechetical instruction to pupils in

74 John Burke (Compiler), *A Dictionary of Canon Law*, revised edition, Akure, Don Bosco Publications – Nigeria, 2006, p. 126.

75 Felice Centis, *The Cross at Omach*, Comboni Missionaries Diamond Jubilee Pamplet, Angal, 1985, p. 6.

76 La Salandra, "The History of the Catholic Church in West Nile," pp. 13-14.

77 Southall, *Alur Society,* p. 282; La Salandra, *op. cit.*, pp. 15-16.

78 Centis, *The Cross at Omach*, p. 11.

79 La Salandra, "The History of the Catholic Church in West Nile," p. 5.

80 Ibid., pp. 11-12.

primary schools for the renewal of their baptismal promise (made for them by parents and the ecclesial community), leading to first Holy Communion; and to students in secondary schools for the sacrament of Confirmation (and those who did not renew baptismal promise during primary school). Secondly, the society is going through fast and overwhelming social-cultural changes, which are shaking the very foundations of embedded traditional moral values. This has an impact on the life of the people, especially those exposed to the wider social context through school education, business or mass media. The school is a more informed, but at the same time diffusive, community by its articulate programmes of imparting knowledge and information. The problem faced here is the critical and liberal mind these school youth have. They ask pragmatic questions and expect clear answers; they question Church pictures and statues. This calls the diocese to find appropriate catechesis methods, cogent to contemporary social models and expressions.

Today, in communicating the basic truths of faith the Church needs to modify its approach in catechesis by emphasising more the social teachings, based on the theological and social virtues. According to MacIntyre, reference to a virtue approach has three points in focus: (a) virtues are considered as qualities necessary to achieve the goods internal to practices; (b) virtues are qualities contributing to the good of a whole life; (c) virtues relate to the pursuit of a good for human beings, the conception of which can only be elaborated and possessed within an ongoing social tradition.[81]

In view of the teaching of the Sacred Congregation for Catholic Education, the catechumenate, in this paradigm of the school context, takes the form of mission, which is a critical, systematic transmission of culture in the light of faith and bringing forth the power of Christian virtue by the integration of culture with faith and faith with living.[82] While short phrases are good for memorising, there is also the need for a life-application method in catechesis. Fr. Amandu, a qualified secondary school teacher, stated that many school youth, in their objection, do not like attending catechism instruction because of its formulation in a style they call "boring repertoire."[83] This reality brings up the question of designing a life-application teaching methodology that can appeal to the youth.

Pope John Paul II understands the universal Catechism as a help to formulating local catechism texts that fit with the cultural situation in every locality

81 Alasdair MacIntyre, *After Virtue*, 3rd edition, reprint, Notre Dame, University of Notre Dame Press, 2008, p. 273.

82 Sacred Congregation for Catholic Education, *The Catholic School*, Rome, Libreria Editrice Vaticana, 1997, n. 49.

83 Fr. Amandu John, interviewed by the researcher, at Urusi, 2 June 2008.

and region. He expresses this in the Apostolic Constitution on the publication of the Catechism, *Fidei Depositum*, where he writes: "This catechism... is meant to encourage and assist in the writing of new local catechisms, which must take into account various situations and cultures, while carefully preserving the unity of faith and fidelity to Catholic doctrine."[84]

1.8.1.2. The School Approach

Chiocchetta, a Comboni missionary priest, writes that the school approach was aimed at providing personnel and structures through which Africa could establish a self-governing and self-propagating Church with capable clergy, the religious and laity.[85] In Nebbi, Bishop Geyer's diary records that with the cooperation and support of the local chiefs, the missionaries learnt the local language, built the first mission station, a residential house and a school at Omach.[86] Alur and Acholi chiefs in the area responded by sending their children to this first mission school.[87] However, this first stage slowly phased out as missionaries moved to other missions opened in Acholiland (Gulu, 1911; Palaro, 1912; Kitgum 1915); in Madiland (Moyo, 1917); in Lugbaraland (Arua, 1917) and in Alurland (Orussi, 1916; Angal, 1917; Nyapea, 1932; Warr and Pakwach, 1952).[88]

In Alurland, the school catechumenate was a child-to-parent approach: missionaries evangelised the youth in order to evangelise adults. Thus, the youth who came from schools also played a role in winning people to the Gospel message. This time registered massive conversion to the Christian faith. In this context, school teachers became more important than catechists. With a hand of control over these teachers the Church could as well control the school; and in this manner, maintain discipline among the teachers and pupils. To some extent, as Mugo observes, being a baptised Catholic Christian or coming from a family of baptised parents became an advantage of acceptance into Catholic mission schools.[89] However, the subtlety of this approach was that religious

84 John Paul II, Apostolic Constitution *Fidei Depositum* on the Publication of the Catechism of the Catholic Church Prepared Following the Second Vatican Ecumenical Council (11 October 1992), Rome, Libreria Editrice Vaticana, 1992, Part IV § 4, "The Doctrinal Value of the Text" in *The Catechism of the Catholic Church*, Nairobi, Paulines Publications Africa, 1994, pp. 26-27: *AAS* 86 (1994), pp. 113-121.

85 Chiocchetta, *Daniel Comboni: Paper for the Evangelization of Africa*, p. 77.

86 Geyer, pp. 425-440; Agostoni, *The Comboni Missionaries*, p. 166-7.

87 Centis, *The Cross at Omach*, p. 3.

88 La Salandra, "The History of the Catholic Church in West Nile," pp. 15-30, 57.

89 E. Mugo, *African Response to Western Christian Religion*, Nairobi, East African Literature Bureau, 1975, p. 53.

affiliation took the form of social convenience rather than an internalised and transforming faith.

Besides, the presence of Protestant mission schools was a factor which propelled the Catholic missionaries to intensify their efforts of impressing Catholic identity through the school. This meant more teaching staff, both European and African; as well as material resources. The situation leaves us with the impression that religion had another human side of competition among Christian evangelisers. During his study sojourn in Alurland that time, Southall made the following remark:

> Education and Christianity are aspects of the same thing. The term used for converts is "readers." The whole younger generation are nominal Christians. As far as a nominal allegiance is concerned, Roman Catholicism is becoming the majority faith and a form of Protestantism a minority one… baptism into the Catholic Church has become a social necessity for the majority. Everyone wishes to have a Christian name, and unless living near the Protestant mission or one of its most energetic teachers, or unless closely related to an influential Protestant adherent, every child aims at baptism as a Catholic.[90]

However, the school scenario changed when Uganda achieved independence in 1962.[91] The government policy was to have a direct control over all schools: a move to nationalise, coordinate all activities, to have free determination and interaction between the government and schools. This situation weakened Church influence in the schools, with the result that teachers disentangled themselves from the yoke of Church moral obligations and discipline. For them this change meant that the domination of colonisation was overcome and removed. They were free; the government paid them higher salary than the Church; they were now transferable and mobile. Bigala describes such a situation thus:

> With the 1964 education Act, all government-aided schools in Uganda were declared open to pupils from all denominations… The catechumenates were seen as the only church schools left. During the 1960s and 1970s, official church attitude toward school education was confused and uncertain. Other church development activities multiplied but those for promoting school education remained minimal.[92]

90 Southall, *Alur Society*, pp. 175-176. What Southall refers to as "a form of Protestantism" is what La Salandra in his "The History of the Catholic Church in West Nile" (pp. 36-37) identifies as "Quakers."

91 Cf. La Salandra, p. 133-135.

92 J. C. B. Bigala, "The Church's Contribution to Education," in Joseph Therese Agbasire and Boniface K. Zabajungu (eds.), *Church Contribution to Integral Development: A New Vision*,

Christian religious education suffered. Lay Catholic school teachers, who once served more as school catechists, now took a lax attitude towards morality. Many of them abandoned their role as agents of religion. They became unwilling to teach religion. Unfortunately, the more dedicated catechists were not prepared for this task. Catholic missionaries had overlooked or underestimated the strength of catechists. Besides, their formation trend did not prepare free thinkers who could link faith to the social arena, unlike their Protestant counterparts whose approach to education and formation produced elites who influenced people even in high political profiles. Even harder, was that the priests and religious alone could not manage the number of Church schools. This drawback meant that the Church's influence over the youth dwindled significantly; and the parents who listened to their children's faith story were cut off. The government placed more emphasis on academic pursuit. As Kasozi observes of the general situation in Uganda, this change considerably marginalised religious and moral education, with the result that the standard of school education declined.[93]

If the 1960s saw the nationalisation of schools by the Government, the 1990s saw the universal primary and secondary school policy. This has brought to an end the mission catechumenate that provided for basic literacy, to read and write. Children now go to school. The youth have become one of the greatest pastoral problems in the diocese; and many priests do not know what to do that will attract them to the Church. The Church has to find another way of approaching faith instruction and moral education of the youth. Today, in Nebbi Catholic Diocese, religious instruction is given to school youth only for a short duration of time as we have noted above. The problem here is that this program is more academic in style. Like the school approach, these youth are drilled through a hurried intellectual cramming of Church teaching (the programme must agree with the government syllabus and within the specified time). 'Dogma' becomes theory, which does not sink into the heart. Many of the youth, after completing school catechism, do not know what to say at times of individual confession with a priest.[94] Ukwong calls the completion of

---

Fourth Uganda Theological Week: African Theology in Progress, Vol. 2, Eldoret, AMECEA Gaba Publications Spearhead, Nr. 108-109 (1989), p. 176.

93 A. B. K. Kasozi, *The Crisis of Secondary School Education in Uganda 1960-1970*, Kampala, Longman, 1979, p. 31.

94 The same is true of many boys and girls who join religious congregations. Most of them coming from secondary schools admitted to this researcher that they do not know how to make personal confession with a priest.

this catechesis a "baptismal graduation."[95] What is more, the problem of religious education is deepened due to lack of teachers to take it as we have noted above, except in those schools where priests, religious Brothers or Sisters are available to teach it. This is another clear factor why many young Catholics in schools are cheaply attracted to the evangelicals whose approach is a lively, drama performance.

Assessment

How effective was the school approach to raising personnel for a self-ministering and self-propagating Church? Missionaries had good intention for the school approach as a path to evangelisation but they were unaware of or neglected some fundamental factors that would have set a firm ground upon which the Church would stand. First, the child-to-parent methodology overlooked the human value of parent-to-child or elder-to-youth pedagogy which was an effective tool in upbringing and education. By keeping elders at a distance, evangelisation had little impact on elders and leaders in the society.

Secondly, the school method did not pay attention to dialogue, an instrumental tool in discerning positive cultural values and practices of the people of the place. Dialogue, through respectful and attentive listening, is an important possibility to inculturating Gospel values into the lived experience of the people. Without this approach, conversion seems to remain superficial; it does not go to the heart.

Thirdly, the school approach created some suspicion towards the Christian message as the school children would not sufficiently explain Gospel stories or interpret them to the lived experience of their parents and elders. This has created a conscience of looking at the Church as a closed system or institution of 'the just' (*jumaleng*, the holy ones) against a sinful people; building a holy community of the children while leaving their parents outside signaled rejection, exclusion, and separation.

Fourth, entrusting the work of catechesis to school teachers was a miscalculation. This approach did not foresee the vital role that specially trained catechists would play in the spiritual and moral formation of youth. As we have stated above, the crisis was felt when all schools were nationalised. School teachers pay more attention to the academic life of their pupils. On the contrary, the catechist focuses on the spiritual and moral good of the human person.

95 Gabriel Ukwong Mayele, "The Catholic Church among the Alur of North Western Uganda: A Pastoral Analysis of the Church's Work in the Light of Vatican II" (unpublished work). A Masters/Licentiate thesis submitted to the Catholic Higher Institute of Eastern Africa (CHIEA), Nairobi 1986, p. 39.

Besides, the school teacher does not pay pastoral visits to families and homesteads of Christians as the catechist or other pastoral agent does.

Nevertheless, the school approach has not been sterile; it can still provide an avenue for evangelisation. First, through the school the Church has produced persons working in different public and private offices in their different capacities. The Church can work with them in those areas to impart Christian values for the good of the society, whether in Nebbi itself or at national levels. Secondly, the diocese has chaplaincies in the schools through which Gospel values can be communicated. Thirdly, it is on this foundation that there is today in the diocese the Catholic Teachers' Association. This is an organ through which the diocese still stands the chance of imparting Christian values for the good of the society. It is one way of involving Catholic teachers in public life; and upholding Catholic presence in the school as a witness of its mission and service to society. This needs to be strengthened.

1.8.1.3. Establishing Christian Homestead Communities

In his evaluation, La Salandra comments that missionary approach to evangelisation had some expansionist inkling. This inclination would not fully help to achieve the primary aim of establishing firm ecclesial communities. He observes that, "Missionary concern was chiefly extension, meanwhile the Christian community needed some inner consolidation. This came in a way through a better education and through establishing small Christian Communities."[96] The Christian homestead approach was a vibrant factor of evangelisation in the nascent Church in Nebbi Catholic Diocese. Missionaries visited the homes of chiefs and through them had access to the people who zealously received the word of God. In retrospect, this gave birth to what is now called Small Christian Communities. Domenico Mananu and Regina Ugwetha, who lived the experience, recalled those early days of evangelisation, when the common practice was that these homestead communities would meet to share the word of the Gospel, and pray the rosary, awaiting the priest's next visit.[97]

With time the number of these Christian homesteads increased and the few priests could not manage to visit them regularly. Attention shifted to centralising the Church. Most activities now shifted from the village to the parish center. This development had a moral significance, in that believers began to feel isolated from the priest. The priest's personal influence, the power of presence, began to wane. Positively, this move created coordination with a centralised

96 La Salandra, "The History of the Catholic Church in West Nile," p. 127.

97 Domenico J. O. Mananu, at Angal, 27 May 2009; Regina Ugwetha, at Rero, 30 June 2008 both interviewed by the researcher.

system. Negatively, it created the impression of a parochial bureaucracy with more elaborate procedures. In the background, this has left the image of an arm-chair priest, more concerned with administration than pastorship.

1.8.2. Achievements

The development of mission method has left Nebbi Catholic Diocese as a Church of the place with three marks, which carry the mission statement of the first missionaries: to establish a Church which is self-directing, self-evangelising and self-supporting. This saw the involving of the laity in the work of evangelisation, particularly in their homesteads. It also saw the establishment of parishes with regard to consolidation and centralisation of pastoral and administrative activities; this inculcated the sense of communion, solidarity and the spirit of working together for a more universal goal within the diocese.

Of much impact has been the establishment of Christian homestead communities, the SCC. This was introduced in the diocese since early 1980s, as a pastoral programme of the AMECEA Bishops. It has brought to the faithful a growing awareness of 'being church' in their own environment and situation. This has had the advantage of developing self-confidence in the faithful as members of the Church, especially in their homestead ecclesial communities. The book, *Small Christian Communities Today*, co-edited by Healey and Hinton, shows that the SCC practice has not only gained universal importance but has also attracted scholarly interest.[98] Healey continues to demonstrate, in his book, *Building the Church as Family of God*, the impact of SCCs within and outside the AMECEA region. He observes that what is unique of the AMECEA approach is its "pastoral, parish-based" orientation which enriches ecclesial growth. This is different from the Latin American Basic Ecclesial Communities model whose empasis is "liberation, social-action."[99]

The SCC method has been formally adopted as a pastoral priority by the Bishops in the AMECEA region since 1973, where they expressly state:

> We believe that in these countries of Eastern Africa it is time for the church to become really 'local,' that is: self-ministering, self-propagating and self-supporting… Church life must be based on the communities in which everyday life and work takes place: those basic and manageable social groupings whose

98 Joseph G. Healey and Jeanne Hinton (eds.), *Small Christian Communities Today: Capturing the New Movement*, Nairobi, Paulines Publications Africa, 2006. Experiences shared in this book enlist contributors from Latin America, North America, Europe, Asia, and Oceania.

99 Joseph G. Healey, *Building the Church as Family of God: Evaluation of Small Christian Communities in Eastern Africa*, Nairobi, AMECEA Gaba Publications – CUEA Press, 2012, p. 102.

> members can experience real interpersonal relationships and feel a sense of communal belonging, both in living and working. We believe that Christian communities at this level will be best suited to develop real intense vitality and to become effective witnesses in their natural environment.[100]

Another important development in Nebbi Catholic Diocese has been the opening of the Catechist Training Centre at Angal since 1988. It serves as an inter-diocesan Catechist Center, offering a two-year training programme. This has deepened the awareness of a self-evangelising Church, with a particular focus on the role of the catechist in the diocese. This raises an important question: Who is a catechist?

In *A Dictionary of Canon Law*, the *catechist* is broadly rendered as: "a clergyman, religious or layperson who instructs a person in the Catholic faith. By word and example, the catechist shares his or her personal faith with other members of the community and/or with those who seek to join the Church."[101] However, this definition seems to leave some room for further investigation. The word *catechist* is derived from biblical Greek, *katēchōn*, teacher of the Gospel; the verb *katēcheō,* to inform, instruct, teach. The one who receives this instruction is called *katēchoumenos*, catechumen.[102] For example, in Acts 18:26, Priscilla and Aquila instructed Apollos in the Way of the Lord. In 1 Cor. 14:17-19, St. Paul reproaches those who 'praise' God in tongues but forget building up others through sound instruction. In Gal. 6:6, *katēchēsis* means "instruction in sound doctrine." In Rom. 2:18, it leads to knowing God's will, with a moral maturity in distinguishing between right and wrong. The anonymous sermon attributed to Clement of Rome, about mid-second century (2 Clem. 17:1, 2) gives testimony that catechesis (religious instruction) became a stable practice in the early Church:

> Let us, then, repent with our whole heart, so that none of us will be lost. For if we have been commanded to do this too – to draw men away from idols and *instruct* them – how much more is it wrong for the soul which already knows God to perish? Consequently we must help one another and bring back those weak in goodness, so that we may all be saved; and convert and admonish one another.[103]

100 Catholic Bishops of Eastern Africa, "Planning for the Church in Eastern Africa in the 1980's: Record of the AMECEA Study Conference held at St. Thomas Aquinas Seminary, Nairobi, 14-21 December 1973," in *AFER*, Vol. 16, Nos. 1 and 2, 1974, pp. 9-10.

101 Burke (Compiler), *A Dictionary of Canon Law*, p. 126.

102 *NIV*, p. 667.

103 Clement of Rome, *Second Letter to the Corinthians,* in Cyril C. Richardson (ed.), *Early Christian Fathers*, New York, Touchstone, 1996, p. 200, italic emphasis – *instruct* – ours.

Thus, the English words *catechism* (handbook of Christian instruction) and *catechesis* (religious instruction) derive directly from the Greek word, *katēchēsis*.

In this present study we are referring to the *catechist* as a non-ordained pastoral agent in the parish, who has been trained and serves the Church in the following manner: (a) proclaiming the word of God in the community, leading Sunday liturgy where there is no priest to celebrate the Eucharist with the community; (b) pastoral visit to families and the sick; (c) administering Holy Communion on Sunday in the absence of the ordained priest; (d) taking Holy Communion to the sick; (e) preparing people for receiving the sacraments; (f) accompanying the local community in its various activities as a team role; (g) some of them taking care of Eucharistic centers and leading the community for adoration.[104] In Nebbi Catholic Diocese, the catechist is commonly called *japonji dini*, "teacher of religion," with reference to her/his teaching role; and *jatela mi yic*, "leader in the faith," regarding her/his leading role in the community. An ordained priest is commonly referred to as *wego mi tipu*, "spiritual father," for his fatherly function (but this has a bend towards paternalism). The consecrated Religious are commonly called *jurudini*, "religious persons," in view of their distinctive dedication, exemplary life and caring service.

The question regarding the role of catechists in the Church in Africa has attracted academic interest. In their editorial remark in the book, *Missionaries to Yourselves*, Shorter and Kataza note that: "The future of the Church in Africa is to a large extent bound up with how the role of the catechist develops."[105] They explain that this will depend on how theological reflection about the role of the catechist will be developed in the African reality of the Church. Commenting on this study, Bühlmann observes, in his book, *The Coming of the Third Church*, that one of the promising indicators of growth in the Church in Africa is the vital role of the catechist. He argues that the theology of the catechist fits in well with the communitarian character of the Church. This means that the catechist serves not merely as an animator or a paid worker but as a team player in the community.[106]

At Angal Catechist Training Center, the researcher interviewed trainees from three dioceses: Nebbi, Arua, and Hoima. Their responses specified the need for practical skills in the art of community-building that would enable

104 Fr. Lino Opio, interviewed by the researcher, at Nebbi, 23 May 2008.

105 Aylward Shorter and Eugene Kataza (eds.), *Missionaries to Yourselves: African Catechists Today*, London, Geoffrey Chapman, 1972, p. iii.

106 Walbert Bühlmann, *The Coming of the Third Church: An Analysis of the Present and Future of the Church*, Maryknoll, Orbis Books, 1978, p. 265.

them to work effectively with those they are being prepared to serve.[107] This regards the application of the Gospel to actual life.

Conclusion

In this chapter, we have tried to give a sketch of Nebbi Catholic Diocese. The points discussed intend to illustrate areas and possibilities where the diocese can strive to build itself up as a communion and how it can make its contribution to shaping life in the society. Location intends uniqueness and growth in a place. Demography gives an awareness of the Church's service towards the people of the place. The discussion of Statistics attempts to illustrate two things: (a) what realities the Church exists in, what it assumes to itself and to which it offers the Gospel message and its values; (b) the human, material, and financial resources which the Church has at its disposal for communicating the Gospel message.

Institutions in the fields of education and health illustrate practical ways by which the Church becomes the bearer of Gospel values through witness and service. The pastoral-administrative structure illustrates how the Church mobilises its resources, organises itself, and the spirit needed to implement it. The mission method is the manner in which Gospel message and values are imparted.

One point is central in this chapter: we have noted that Nebbi Catholic Diocese, right from its nascent stage, is a people-Church, which has enlisted the joint efforts of its members, both laity and clergy. This serves as an historical consciousness which can guide it to move forward. Next chapter will discuss the traditional communitarian values of the Alur in Nebbi Catholic Diocese, as a human environment in which the Church sets a home.

107 The researcher conducted this interview on 26 June 2008. Their names appear in Appendix 3.

CHAPTER TWO
Alur Traditional Communitarian Values

Introduction

This chapter pays attention to the human reality in Nebbi, into which the Church is born and grows. It examines Alur traditional communitarian values, focusing on the moral content of culture, tradition, kinship, chiefship and religious practices as the foundamental elements of moral cohesion, binding individuals together into community. The reflection ends with a brief assessment of those traditional values, and a conclusion.

2.1. The Meaning of Traditional Communitarian Values

The content of the chapter heading revolves around the following basic terms which will guide our discussion: *traditional values*, *community* and *meaning*. In his book, *African Christian Theology*, Shorter writes that traditional values are "...those insights which are precious and original – even if they can only be identified in certain places and at certain times."[108] The word *community* is defined in *A New Dictionary of Christian Ethics* in terms of commitment to shared values by which a group of persons are bound together.[109] This is more elucidated by Lonergan, where he writes that: "A community is not just a number of men within a geographical frontier. It is an achievement of common meaning... Common meaning is potential when there is common field of experience, and to withdraw from that common field is to get out of touch."[110] Therefore, traditional communitarian values, as used in this study, refer to those insights, perceived meanings, aspirations and practices that serve as touchstones in shaping and sustaining togetherness or life in common. What

108 Cf. Aylward Shorter, *African Christian Theology: Adaptation or Incarnation?* Marknoll, Orbis Books, 1977, p. 27.

109 Henry Clark, "Community," in John Mcquarrie and James Childress (eds.), *A New Dictionary of Christian Ethics*, London, SCM Press Ltd., 1997, pp. 105-106.

110 Bernard Lonergan, *Method in Theology*, New York, The Seabury Press, 1979, p. 79.

is central is the content and *meaning*[111] attached to those embedded values and aspirations.[112]

According to Splett, the notion of *meaning* points out to that which is appropriate, relevant, and justifiable. There is distinction between subjective and objective notions of meaning. Subjectively, *meaning* refers to that which is in the mind or thoughts of an individual (his/her feeling, opinion, discernment). Objectively, it refers to that which has significance, purpose, value and a rational goal which primarily includes and affects the subjective.[113] Traditional communitarian values are therefore those which serve common purposes; they are objective, relevant and justifiable. Before we discuss the traditional Alur communitarian values we shall give some space to clarify what is meant by the term *value*; and its moral significance.

2.1.1. Value Unites Community

The general usage of the term *value* is multifaceted. Davina writes that the concept of value refers to "...generalized, abstract ideas held by human individuals or groups about what is desirable, proper, good or bad... what individuals value is strongly influenced by the culture of the society in which they happen to live... it is this value consensus which provides the framework of social order."[114] Underlying the concept of value is therefore *consensus*, which makes a moral demand on every member of the community because it expresses the aspiration, aptitude and objective focus of that community. Sofield, Hammet and Juliano make the following definition: "Consensus is a process of decision-making in which the whole community agrees to a common course of action that preserves the values of all and is eventually owned by all."[115]

111 Ibid., pp. 57-85, gives a detailed treatment on "meaning" as an important element for theological methodology in evangelisation. He notes that meanings are intrinsic components of culture (p. 78).

112 We acknowledge here the work of Michael C. Kirwen (ed.), *African Cultural Knowledge: Themes of Embedded Beliefs*, Nairobi, Mias Books, 2005. His approach to rediscovering those embedded values of African peoples is helpful for the Church in Africa to knowing and understanding its people's beliefs, aptitudes and worldview.

113 Jörg Splett, "Meaning" in Karl Rahner (ed.), *Encyclopedia of Theology: The Concise Sacramentum Mundi*, English edition, New York, Crossroad Publishing Company, 1982, pp. 945-946.

114 Davina Allan, "Values," in Kenneth McLeish (ed.), *Key Ideas in Human Thought*, New York, Facts on File, Inc., 1993, pp. 769-770.

115 Loughlan Sofield, Rosine Hammett and Carroll Juliano, *Building Community: Christian, Caring, Vital*, Notre Dame, Ave Maria Press, 1998, p. 112. These authors write in the context of Church community. We are concerned here with clarifying the concept of *consensus* as such.

Shorter's definition of *value* gives moral relevance to it where he writes that: "Put very simply, value is the worth we ascribe to a choice – choice of an object, an opinion, a course of action, a relationship, a role, an experience."[116] From this, it is doubtless that *value* is central to the shaping of a communitarian spirit. Mbiti writes that:

> Values safeguard and uphold the life of the people in their relationship with one another and the world around them. Values and morals cover topics like truth, justice, love, right and wrong, good and evil, beauty, decency, respect for people and property, the keeping of promises and agreements, praise and blame, crime and punishment, the rights and responsibilities of both the individual and his community, character, integrity…[117]

Value has a moral significance in the sense that it regulates relationship through the choices and decisions that we make and the actions that follow from them. We can say that value is what we recognise to be good and helpful for our life; what brings fulfillment in our life; it is what promotes our spiritual, material and moral welfare. Values bind us together in these three basic aspects. They are our common ground for true human relationship and growth.

2.1.2. The Moral Content

Values form an integral part of culture. According to Chukwu: "Most of what we are preserving and perpetuating as culture, is due to the values associated with it by a people or a group... Wherever there is culture there are values."[118] Thus, values are hinges about which revolve common beliefs and customs: "The communal beliefs and customs that are important to a society are parts of its culture. These would include religious beliefs, moral norms, and occupations."[119] In order to understand the moral content of values it is important to see how they affect our life itself; and our relational attitudes, those mental or neutral predispositions by which we respond in particular and distinctive ways.

116 Shorter, *African Christian Theology*, p. 111.

117 John S. Mbiti, *Introduction to African Religion*, 2nd ed., reprint, Nairobi, East African Educational Publishers, 2003, p. 12.

118 Cletus N. Chukwu, *Introduction to Philosophy in an African Perspective*, Eldoret, Zapf Chancery, 2002, p. 155.

119 Ibid., p. 156.

Donceel distinguishes five major groups or hierarchies of values.[120] These values significantly shape our moral aptitude; they affect our choices and decisions, our mind and our motivations. We are indebted to him in the following presentation which summarises his reflection. In the first group are the *sensory values*, which satisfy any of our bodily drives in general, like food, drink, rest, comfort, and sex. The second hierarchy comprises the *vital values*, deriving from the harmonious development of the body, including health, strength, forceful and harmonious activity, physical beauty and playing. These have their greatest appeal during later childhood and adolescence. The third group comprises the *social values*, or *values of peace and association*, which satisfy the individual as a member of a group, like love of parents, heterosexual attraction, friendship, human society, reputation and power. Its dedication is to the common good: the cult of altruism. The fourth are *spiritual values*, which appeal to the spiritual faculties of a person, the intellect and will. These are further subdivided into: (a) *intellectual* or *theoretical values*, devoted to knowledge, discovery, truthfulness and objectivity which, especially through education, help to remove ignorance, superstition and unhealthy taboos; (b) *aesthetic values*, concerned with artistic beauty in its many forms, by which we come to appreciate the goodness of our environment and strive to make it homely; (c) *moral values*, more devoted to goodness, honesty, justice and generosity, enabling people to enhance good relationship among themselves. In the fifth hierarchy are the *religious values*, which refer to God and to our life after death. In theological reflection, some of these values presuppose the supernatural virtues of faith, hope, and charity; others are accessible to unaided human reason. What is central in these values is the growth of every individual to human maturity; they enable the individual to become a social person. What, then, is the moral siginifance of values?

Values are basic human goods: according to Grisez and Shaw values are basic human goods which form the purposes for being truly human;[121] that is, values specify the reason for common dedication and fidelity to one's community: "The human good is at once individual and social. Individuals do not just operate to meet their needs but operate to meet one another's needs. As the community develops, its institutions facilitate cooperation, so individuals

120 J. F. Donceel, *Philosophical Anthropology*, New York, Sheed and Ward, 1967, pp. 207-208; see also Chukwu, *Introduction to Philosophy*, p. 157-166; Häring, *Free and Faithful in Christ,* Vol. 1, pp. 177-180.

121 Germain Grisez and Russell Shaw, *Beyond the New Morality: The Responsibilities of Freedom*, Notre Dame, Indiana, University of Notre Dame Press, 1988, p. 78.

develop skills to fulfill the roles and perform the tasks set by the institutional framework."[122]

Values are aspects of our personhood: this means, as Lonergan explains, "One has to grow in sincerity and responsiveness to values if one's humanity is to be authentic."[123]

Values are communitarian pointers: they enable us to discover and develop a sense of togetherness, leading to the realisation of integral fulfillment. Häring emphasises that all values look to the basic freedom and knowledge which must open every individual to personal commitment and responsibility: "All particulars of morally relevant values and of all types of value rest in the basic value, in the *good*: ultimately in God who is the fullness of all love."[124] The appreciation and internalisation of values will enable people to embody those values in their own lives and become "value-persons."[125] Understood this way, values are internal to communitarian life and reasons for choice, decision and acting to that effect.

Values specify common meaning, by which every individual is enabled to grow in personal experience, understanding, judgment, choice and decision. It is important to note, as Maguire observes, that morality is not an abstract principle but rooted in the experience of persons and their environment.[126] It is upon values that there are taboos (abstention) and norms (regular ways of conduct) prohibiting certain kinds of behavior and recommending others. Norms of conduct serve to express, to protect, regulate and promote values; they are not just any random or indiscriminate supposition.

The human person is the center of all earthly values: moral theological reflection places people at the centre of all earthly values. As Häring explains, "The person himself is the basic value, the centre of values. He is also the bearer of value. The attitudes and dispositions which realise in the person the openness and unity that constitute his personality may be called moral virtues. They are, as it were, refractions of the basic value."[127] The moral significance of *value* is therefore the worth of persons and what befits their well-being. It is upon values that people develop the art of good living in various ways. Gula maintains that morality pertains to value. All morality is organically linked to

122 Lonergan, p. 52.

123 Ibid., p. 51.

124 Häring, *Free and Faithful in Christ*, Vol. 1, p. 183.

125 Ibid., p. 90.

126 Daniel C. Maguire, *The Moral Choice*, Garden City, Doubleday and Company, Inc., 1978, p. 72.

127 George V. Lobo, *Moral Theology Today: Christian Living According to Vatican II*, Bangalore, Theological Publications in India, 1999, p. 224.

the foundational moral experience of the sacredness, or worth, of persons as persons.[128]

Values give a moral meaning to attitudes of relationship: Häring notes that values play a significant role in shaping individuals to become heart-persons: *heart* in the biblical sense of the wholeness of the person, with a relational depth, sensitivity and experience, open to "...building bridges to others, grasping the unique value of each one as a person and the manifold values embodied by persons, and thus calling for an ever new embodiment of these values in one's own life."[129] Values do not only shape the attitudes of the person but also enrich them as persons in relationship. Human values are transmitted through the media of culture and tradition.

2.1.3. The Role of Culture

The anthropological concept of the term *culture* refers to the way of communicating inherited relational human values from generation to generation. A classical definition was given by Burnet Tylor, a British anthropologist, as "...that complex whole which includes knowledge, belief, art, morals, law, custom, and any other capabilities and habits acquired by man as a member of society."[130] A modernist definition is given by Geertz, depicting culture as: "A system of inherited conceptions expressed in symbolic forms by means of which human beings communicate, perpetuate and develop their knowledge about, and their attitudes towards, life."[131] Agreeing with Geertz, Shorter argues that the classicist definition given by Tylor attends to *acquired* learning but misses the important link of *inheritance*. Shorter clarifies that: "Culture is therefore essentially a transmitted pattern of meanings embodied in symbols, a pattern capable of development and change, and it belongs to the concept of humanness itself."[132]

A good synthesis of the concept of culture is made by Amarlopavadas where he clarifies that: "...what remains objectively central is the value-sys-

128 Richard M. Gula, *Reason Informed by Faith: Foundations of Catholic Morality*, Mahwah, Paulist Press, 1989, p. 13.

129 Häring, *Free and Faithful in Christ*, Vol. 1, p. 90.

130 Edward Burnett Tylor, *Primitive Culture: Researches into the Development of Mythology, Philosophy, Religion, Art, and Custom,* Vol.1, London, John Murray, 1871, p. 1. Electronic text digitalised by Google, original from The University of Michigan, 2nd edition, 30 May 2006, downloaded from website: http://books.google.co.uk/books/about/Primitive_culture.html?id=AucLAAAAIAAJ&redir_esc=y (accessed 3 September 2011).

131 Clifford Geertz, *The Interpretation of Cultures*, New York, Basic Books, 1973, p. 89.

132 Aylward Shorter, *Towards a Theology of Inculturation*, Eugene, Wipf and Stock Publishers, 1999, p. 5.

tem in commonness: worldview or vision of life, meanings, goals, categories and thought patterns, experience, tradition, behavior patterns, organization of relationship and roles. Contexts in expression vary from one place to another but the inner dynamic points to the same values."[133]

The Alur word for culture is *kúrá*, referring to character, behaviour to reckon with; and its cognate *kúrá-jo*, human conduct; the people's path of life embodying qualities such as friendship, fraternity, solidarity, kindness, respect, good judgment, generosity and care. Writing about the Alur, Ongom defines *kúrá* (culture) as the means by which a person gets involved in life, the means through which one's unique self is developed and expressed.[134] A person of *kúrá* embodies community character, s/he is a reliable person. *Kúrá* does not only embody moral principles and ways of conduct; it also defines the people's entire way of life. It is about how people are to behave because they are human beings.

From what we have observed above, culture has two basic functional connotations: (a) it is a self-defining inner quality someone must have, upon which their life depends; (b) it binds the individual to the community. According to Jonsen, culture is a unified way of life, intending responsibility, which unfolds two shades of meaning: (a) *accountability*, which consists in personal integrity and the respect someone's life commands in others; (b) *commitment*, a creative, dedicated effort and faithfulness in upholding common purposes and goals.[135] Closely linked to culture is tradition.

2.1.4. The Place of Tradition

According to Stout, the term *tradition* has two concepts: (a) what is handed down from generation to generation (from the Latin back-form, *traditum*); (b) the mode by which it is transmitted (Latin, *traditio*).[136] Tradition is relevant to morality because it embodies original insights and lived experience, which serve to evaluate the moral heritage of a given people. What is central is the reference to value and meaning. Constantino makes the point, where he argues

---

133 D. S. Amalorpavadass, "Church and Culture" in Joseph A. Komonchak, Mary Coillins and Dermot Lane (eds.), *New Dictionary of Theology*, Dublin, Gill and Macmilla, 1990, pp. 201-206; also Henry Clark, "Culture" in *NDCE*, pp. 140-142.

134 Quirine K. Ongom, "An Integrative Approach to Christian Spiritual Direction with Reference to the Alur of Uganda," (MA/Specialized Licentiate in Spirituality, unpublished) CUEA, Nairobi, July 1993, p. 8.

135 Cf. Albert R. Jonsen, "Responsibility," in John Macquarrie and James Childress (eds.), *A New Dictionary of Christian Ethics*, Dublin, Gill and Macmillan, 1990, p. 545-549.

136 Jeffrey Stout, "Tradition in Ethics," in *NDCE*, pp. 629-630.

that creativity, innovation and ongoing developments in the different fields can be mutually enriching with tradition:

> A people's history must rediscover the past in order to make it reusable… Such a history must deal with the past with the view to explaining the present. It must therefore be not only descriptive but also analytical; it must deal not only with objective developments but also bring the discussion to the realm of value judgments. The past should not be the object of mere contemplation if the present is to be meaningful.[137]

According to Matyasi Geru, the Alur word for tradition is *thé-Kwaru*, ancestral foundation; and its cognate, *lág-Kwaru*, ancestral root; both usage denoting continuity.[138] It is the way of life that has been perceived, practiced, lived by, tested by experience, proven over time and handed down through generations. An elder, Ukathi, remarked: "One who does not cherish one's roots excommunicates oneself from community. Where does s/he belong?"[139] Tradition is therefore a verified path of life along which one must identify with, and respond to, countless relational values.

2.2. The Principles of Alur Communitarian Values

Alur communitarian values revolve around the three principles or foundations of kinship, chiefship and religion.

2.2.1. Kinship

In our field study we learnt that among the Alur, kinship has an important role in shaping relational attitudes not only among individuals, families, clans and sub-clans; but it also affects relationship in a number of ways which influence how the society works. We shall illustrate this by first analysing the concept and then show how it has worked to shape the lifestyle of the Alur people. We shall here begin with a conceptual analysis and proceed to present how kinship was expressed in everyday living in Alur society.

137 Renato Constantino, quoted in R. Armes, *Third World Film Making and the West*, Berkeley, University of California Press, 1978, p. vii.

138 Matyasi Geru, an elder of Padolo clan, interviewed by the researcher, at Rero, Padolo Community, 30 June 2008. The Alur word, *kwaru*, "grandparents; ancestors;" *thé-*, "underlying, at the base of, foundation;" *lág-*, "root, foundation," thus: *thé-kwaru*, and *lág-Kwaru*, denoting continuity and link with ancestral roots.

139 Ukathi, an elder of Parombo clan, interviewed by the researcher, at Parombo, 26 May 2008.

2.2.1.1. Conceptual Analysis

The perception given in the *New Catholic Encyclopedia* renders kinship as: "…a recognised relationship based upon a common ancestry which serves in every known society as the foundation for all other institutions."[140] In *A Dictionary of Canon Law* kinship is confined to consanguinity: "a blood relationship among two persons."[141] This juridical understanding seems to leave a wide gap in the comprehensive understanding of kinship as our research found out.

In their book, *Cultural Anthropology*, Grunlan and Mayers explain that kinship is the basis of social structure: a network of social relationships that goes beyond biological relationships and extends to cover large tribes. It serves as a road map by which social ties, patterns of behaviour, obligations and responsibilities are established. They observe that an effective approach to planting the Church firmly is to analyse and understand kinship systems and how they function.[142]

The Alur word for kinship is *waat*. In his study of the Alur, Southall bases this on lineage (blood descent) and marriage relationships.[143] However, for the Alur the concept covers more than lineage and marriage alone: (a) Lineage is the foundation of oneness and thus inseparability; (b) Marriage binds everyone to both parental domains. It is a factor which established the strongest bond between the Alur and neighbouring peoples: Madi, Lendu and Kebu;[144] (c) People become *waat* (kin) after living for a long time on the same compound or homestead even if they come from clans that normally intermarry. According to custom (ordinary practice), children from these different clans will not intermarry due to the immediacy that has developed; (d) Kinship sealed by the ritual of blood-letting (*theyo rimo*) or blood-swallowing (*mwonyo rimo*) involving two family heads of different clans which normally intermarry.[145] Once this is done, the two immediate families will not intermarry; they have become one blood. This in turn affects a wide range of relationships on both sides. Although this is no longer practiced (with the episode of HIV/AIDS) it

140 F. K. Lehman, "Kinship" in *New Catholic Encyclopedia*, Vol. 8, Washington, The Catholic University of America, 1967, p. 202.

141 Cf. Burke (Compiler), *A Dictionary of Canon Law*, p. 379.

142 Stephen A. Grunlan and Marvin K. Mayers, *Cultural Anthropology: A Christian Perspective*, 2nd edition, Michigan, Zondervan Publishing House, 1988, pp. 162-163.

143 Southall, *Alur Society*, p. 27, mentions "wat;" pp. 27-69 gives a detailed explanation on kinship.

144 Ibid., p. 83.

145 Ibid., p. 235.

remains a relic of communion and such families live to prolong their blood-sealed kinship.

2.2.1.2. Communitarian Function

Although writing in the North American context, the observation of Bellah and his comrades is resonant with our study finding of the Alur people in Nebbi. That is, how ever complex a society might become, the element of kinship cannot be erased. They note that: "In simple societies, however, kinship predominates over all other ways of relating… In such societies, it would not be rude for a young person to address an unrelated older person as "uncle," or "aunt," or "grandfather," or "grandmother." Even in a brief encounter such kinship terminology establishes a pattern of expected interaction."[146]

In this understanding kinship stands as a strong traditional communitarian factor which touches on the moral conduct of every community member. As Ayisi observes, "The terms which are used to express the values of kinship enjoin the individual members who are described in these social contexts to behave within the customarily prescribed meaning of the terms used."[147] This entails loyalty, meaning that someone belongs to the community of persons and concomitantly to the community of property. The terms of relationship intensify the content and depth of kinship, and expand solidarity. This means, as Mbiti writes: "…everyone is related to everyone."[148] That is, in the structure of kinship, one's relationship with another has a chain of connections to countless others.[149]

How does kinship intensify moral cohesion in Alur society? The study of Grunlan and Mayers on cultural anthropology can help us to respond to this question, although it is written in the American social-cultural context. They identify three main functions of kinship: socialisation, security and social aid, and social control.[150] We shall follow this arrangement to illustrate how kinship has helped to instill a communitarian spirit in Alur society. But we are to understand it more in terms of solidarity, unity, benevolence, charity and sharing, identity and belonging, autonomy, participation and neighbourhood.

146 Bellah, et al., pp. 113-114.

147 Eric O. Ayisi, *An Introduction to the Study of African Culture*, 2nd edition, reprint, London, Heinemann, 1980, p. 40.

148 John S. Mbiti, *African Religions and Philosophy*, 2nd ed. reprint, Oxford, Heinemann, 2006, p. 102.

149 Ibid., p. 200.

150 Stephen A. Grunlan and Marvin K. Mayers, *Cultural Anthropology: A Christian Perspective*, pp. 174-175; 204ff.

Socialisation: while sociologists use the term *socialisation;* anthropologists use the term *enculturation*, with reference to the process of learning and internalising embedded cultural values and models of behaviour from the entire kinship system.[151] Shorter clarifies that the term *enculturation* refers to the process by which one is inserted into one's own culture.[152] In other words, it is a cultural education or adaptive learning by which one gets immersed into one's own culture.[153] This involves inheriting norms, customs, values, traditions, social roles, symbols and language. In Alur society this is understood as *ngeyo kúrá* (knowing the way of life; learning through practice). According to Clausen, *socialisation* is the means by which social and cultural continuity is attained.[154] It helps individuals to become functioning members of their community or society, that is, they become social persons who participate in that system.[155]

In Alur society, socialisation is perceived as *mondo i kúrá* (entering or integration into the way of life). The study of Southall found that this comes about through integration. There is no initiation ritual among the Alur but a process of maturation with a gradual transition of youth from physiological immaturity into cultural terms when they begin to share in the social-cultural responsibilities.[156] Until this day, children and youth internalise community values as they grow up in the community. The family has its role of upbringing children; apart from it, the extended family plays the role of helping the young to learn the ways of life and good conduct. Girls are entrusted to aunts; boys to uncles. These elders act as mentors helping them to internalise general customs and specific conducts. Their role is comparable to that of spiritual directors or mentors in church practice.

In the Catholic Church, the term *socialisation* entered into official expression with Vatican Council II document on the Church in the Modern World, *Gaudium et Spes*.[157] But, before the Council, Pope John XXIII had already

151 Stephen A. Grunlan and Marvin K. Mayers, *Cultural Anthropology,* p. 71-72.

152 Shorter, *Toward a Theology of Inculturation*, p. 4.

153 Aylward Shorter, *African Culture: An Overview*, 1st reprint, Nairobi, Paulines, 2001, p. 57f.

154 John A. Clausen (ed.), *Socialization and Society*, Boston, Little Brown and Company, 1968, p. 5.

155 Cf. Joseph A. Scimecca, *Society and Freedom: An Introduction to Humanist Sociology*, 2nd edition, Chicago, Nelson-Hall Publishers, 1995, p. 55.

156 Southall, *Alur Society*, p. 28-29.

157 *GS*, n. 25 § 2: *AAS* 58 (1966), p. 1045; see Norman P. Tanner (ed.), *Decrees of the Ecumenical Councils*, Vol. II, p. 1084, the Latin text in front has "socializatio" translated into English as "socialisation." Also the commentary by Donald R. Campion, "The Church Today," in Walter M. Abbott and Joseph Gallagher (eds.), *The Documents of Vatican II*, p. 187.

used the expression "social relationships" or "social organisation" in his 1961 Encyclical Letter, *Mater et Magistra*, in the social context of the time, where he rejects the principles of socialism as incompatible with the Christian notion of being social.[158] He cites "...the multiplication of social relationships, that is, a daily more complex interdependence of citizens, introducing into their lives and activities many and varied forms of association..."[159] However, this understanding treats socialisation in the industrial mentality of production of material goods, which jeopardises the freedom of the individual and diminishes the bond of kinship as a human value. In Alur society socialisation can be best understood as a cultural value that expands relationship in a number of ways as explained below.

Solidarity: referring to the social security and aid that kinship provides among persons. The Alur understand social security in terms of solidarity, expressed in the words: *gwokiri*, supporting one another; and *konyiri*, aiding one another; leading to *gwoko pacu*, sustaining the home. For them solidarity is conceived as interdependence; it is that deep feeling, that we are fellow human beings sharing the same life principle. Solidarity is not just a family feeling or such as exists among close friends; it is rather that spirit of standing together in promoting one another. The Alur discouraged begging; it is degrading. An individual in need is supported to become self-reliant and fend for oneself. Selfishness is scorned and deplored; it is burren and futile. On the contrary, events like marriage, childbirth, death and burial are possibilities of expressing solidarity. Likewise, co-activities like house-building, joint-hoeing, planting and harvesting are possibilities of strengthening one another.[160]

Sharing and generosity: being charitable towards others by acts of love. This begins in the family. It is foundational to child education and runs through the entire process of upbringing. Mothers encourage their children in the simple act of sharing food with others, not only among siblings themselves, but also with those outside the family. By this act, those who receive learn to be thankful; those who give learn to be more generous. In a typically traditional Alur home, when someone arrives towards the end of a family meal, that

158 John XXIII, Encyclical Letter *Mater et Magistra*, n. 34: *AAS*, 53 (1961), p. 408. We have followed the text and numbering as in the translation by William J. Gibbons, et al. (eds.), *Encyclical of Pope John XXIII, Mater et Magistra: Christianity and Social Progress*, Study Club Edition, Glen Rock, Paulist Press, 1961, p. 17. The *AAS* Latin text speaks of "the order of social life" (...socialis vitae ordo...). The English translation: "social organization" downlodaded from: http://www.vatican.va/holy_father/john_xxiii/encyclicals/documents/hf_j-xxiii_enc_15051961_mater_en.html (accessed, 12 July 2010).

159 Ibid., n. 59, p. 25: *AAS* 53 (1961), p. 415.

160 Southall, *Alur Society*, p. 33. This is still common in Alur at the time of this research (May-August 2008).

person will accept to eat from the little that is there, even if a meal is to be prepared for them. Among the Alur, to be called *jakéc*, stingy, is a disgraceful name. This does not imply that someone must just give all that one has to others. It is rather great-mindedness in putting to the best use every possible resource at our disposal.

Sharing is practiced through socialisation and events by which one is exposed to the larger community context; through experiencing one another by which one comes to know the needs of others. Sharing is not only in material things but much deeper it consists in the readiness to avail our particular talents and gifts to the good of all, to promote them and bring them to realise their own personal gifts. Through generosity and sharing people learn that no one is self-sufficient.

Benevolence: is the heart of social security. It is the good heart and will that we have towards one another; keeping the good name of one another; having a place in our heart for one another. The Alur believe that the honour borne by someone is the good name that s/he has in the community. An especially intense event of social security and aid is shown when someone dies. Everyone is kin in the event of death. The Alur have the saying: *No one cleans their own wound; another must.* The funeral rite has a religious content. The name of the deceased is cleansed and set free from any known or unknown fault or debt to be paid back. An elder, Elia Ucama, recounted that, in tradition, everyone viewing the body of the deceased opens both hands and, raising them up, says silently: "Go in peace! I do not hold you. If you owe me anything, now it ends. If I owe you anything, forgive me for it. Forgive us for our wrongs to you. Remember us and speak well of us among all ancestors. We keep your name with us. Go in peace!"[161]

In the account given by Matyasi Geru, according to tradition, asking mourners over any debt and lifting up one's hands tells the people: (a) to let go; (b) not to remain with ill memory of the deceased; (c) peace with all the dead; (d) leaving a good name behind – a person of good memory has their name given to infants; (e) an admonition to community members that they must strive to live in harmony with one another. The Alur do not presume to speculate over judgment in the next world. The dead can no longer be accused; the living must solve their problems and build a good community. This is the true ancestor memorial.[162] It is this awareness of communion with ancestors that sustains social order.

Unity: provides for social control and order. Socialisation, solidarity, sharing, and benevolence are factors to unity. The Alur did not develop written

161 Elia Ucama, interviewed by the researcher, at Parombo, 26 May 2008.

162 Matyasi Geru, interviewed by the researcher, at Rero, 26 June 2008.

laws but they have customs and rules of conduct which have preserved respectful interpesronal relationships. Customs are important in regulating community cohesion. Leslie notes that, "The kinship organization specifies reciprocal and correlative rights, duties, and obligations... Custom is the name given to uniformities in socio-cultural systems. Uniformities are important because they make *anticipation and prediction* possible, custom, therefore, is a means of social regulation and control, of effecting compliance with itself in order to render effective conduct of social life possible."[163] The expression *anticipation and prediction* means that we are expected to act in certain prescribed modes of relationship which are compatible with operative customs. This has to do with correct attitudes and dispositions; not oddities of unrelated behaviours. It is helpful to note that *custom* has an important role to play in the day-to-day moral life of a people or community. According to Smalley, "Custom refers to the habitual behavior of a society. It represents the normal, typical response of any social group to the normal conditions of life, interpersonal relationships and environment. It is the daily, immediate working out of the effects of tradition, ethics, religion, values, and world view."[164] We may understand *custom* to mean a habitual, regular and disciplined gesture of relationship.

An illustration of custom in Alur society is the gesture of the chief or an elderly man towards women in general. Crazzolara writes: "If a *Rwoot* (chief/king) meets a woman on a narrow path, he has to withdraw into the grass and leave the road to her. He must show regard for women generally."[165] Custom preserves good relationship and order. Southall writes: "In Alur society… the basis lies in the system of groups organised on kinship principles. Consequently, it is not only with these groups that Alur children acquire respect for authority and discipline, but it is on them, too, that the Alur adult normally relies for securing the framework of orderly relations within which his daily life is lived."[166] In addition to what we have said, kinship provides for identity and belonging, which widens the community horizon through neighbourhood.

Identity and belonging: what about the individual? Where is one's place in the community? Our field respondents, acknowledged in this work, answered in the affirmative that there is no community without individuals and the individual cannot come to existence without the man and woman in marriage; the individual is the fruit of communion. The further question: Who is the in-

163 Leslie A. White, "The Concept and Components of Culture" in *Encyclopedia Britannica*, Vol. 16, p. 880-881. Italic highlights ours.

164 William A. Smalley, "Custom," in John Macquarrie and James Childress (eds.), *A New Dictionary of Christian Ethics*, p. 142.

165 Crazzolara, *The Lwoo*, p. 209.

166 Southall, *Alur Society*, p. 74-75.

dividual?" was answered: "One of us." In his study, Southall noted that in Alur society the individual is the centre of relationships, expressed in a wide range of kinship descriptions.[167] A good illustration is where neighbouring families gather together for a meal; or a homestead is gathered for common fields of action. At such events no parent corrects or rebukes their child in public; the child belongs to the whole community there, a daughter or son to all the parents; so the saying: *nyathin mwa*, our child. This understanding establishes the sense of being a son or daughter in a wider community framework. It is in the community that the individual finds integral personal wholeness. The community becomes the security of every individual member from childhood to adulthood.

Personal identity is again found in the name one has. The concept of *name* is given in the *New Catholic Encyclopedia* thus: "Among ancient peoples generally, a name was considered as the identification of the essence, nature, or function of an individual..."[168] As the study of Crazzolala illustrates, in Alur society the name somone takes is not a mere distinguishing appellation; one's personal name is both memorial and commitment.[169] In the African context, Osabuteu writes that: "In ancient as well as modern Africa, the name of a person marks a certain phenomenal characteristic which singularises him as long as he lives and even after death. It was this fact that led the ancients to give descriptive names to God according to the manner in which they felt his power manifested in the whole reality of nature."[170] In Nebbi Catholic Diocese it is common to find such theonomous names as *Mungumiyo* (God has given), *Mungudit* (God is great), *Munguleng* (God is holy), *Mungungeyo* (God knows), *Mungunyang* (God understands), *AniRwoth* (I am in the Lord), *AyomiRwoth* (I rest in the Lord), *Munguryek* (God is wise), *AyiyoRwoth* (I believe in the Lord, Christ), *AgenoRwoth* (I trust in the Lord), *Wanaciel* (We are one), *Mungujakisa* (God is merciful), *Uweki* (forgive). Such names not only point to the nature or characteristics of God but also appeal for peaceful living in the community. Identity and belonging therefore engender the legitimacy of autonomy, participation, neighbourhood, and togetherness.

Autonomy: the Alur understanding of autonomy has two meanings. First, it emphasises the spirit of fending for oneself, as in the saying: *atum pa Rwoth imaku ku peri*, "the bow of the chief, hold it together with your own," meaning that one cannot depend on others in every little detail of what one needs to do. Secondly, it encourages faithfulness to one's community; someone has to

167 Ibid., p. 34-36.

168 F. X. Murphy, "Names, Christian" in *New Catholic Encyclopedia*, Vol. 10, p. 201.

169 Cf. Crazzolara, *The Lwoo*, p. 24-25; 115-116.

170 Isaac D. Osabuteu, *The Principle Understanding: The African Religion and Philosophy*, Nairobi, Maillu Publishing House, 1990, p. 207.

do one's best part without having to be told what to do. Autonomy depicts the community as the cumulative strength of its individual members. It means that the individual is a living embodiment of the human values s/he has received and internalised within the community matrix.

Participation: refers to taking part in common purposes such as beliefs, ceremonies, rituals and festivals. It helps someone to internalise the values that hold people together. It deepens the sense of belonging to the community. The question of name comes up again here. In Alur society, as the works of Crazzolara and Southall show, every clan has its praise name (*pák*) which constitutes corporate personality.[171] In this way, the community has a decisive claim on the life of the individual. This means here is that the communitarian spirit operates on the principle of interdependence, as we have already said of co-activities.

Neighbourhood: referring to the relational attitude towards other peoples and persons. The Alur have the saying: *dhanu ceke waat*, all people are kin. In his study of Alur society, Southall noted that: "Another factor which assisted the Alur in maintaining and extending their system was the extent to which they and their subject peoples shared a basically similar metaphysical outlook. They both inhabited the same universe in this respect."[172] Kinship therefore widens the horizon of relationship beyond the confines of clan or ethnicity. It is based on the life principle shared by every human being, whether of the same ethnic group, a social group or race.[173] In this perspective kinship entails equality, reciprocity and courtesy.[174]

To the Alur, nobody is considered a stranger or inferior, once differences are clarified and that person or group has accepted to settle among them. For them the *stranger* represents the mysterious, a symbol of man's communication with the unknown spiritual world; their coming is a blessing. Crazzolara writes of the Lwo in general: "...another very human quality... had taken a strong hold on their minds: broadmindedness and liberality in looking upon and treating unrelated, strange or foreign peoples... any stranger, even from a hostile tribe... was sure of their hospitality..."[175] This trait seems to characterise all the societies of the Southern Lwo: Alur, Acholi, Palwo.[176] All the *Jii* language family: Naadh (Nuer), Jiaang (Dinka) and Lwo, share the same concept

171 Crazzolara, *The Lwoo*, pp. 408-447; Southall, *Alur Society*, 67-68.

172 Southall, *Alur Society*, p. 232.

173 Ibid., p. 40. The Alur word for "race" is *thék*; the Acholi have *kaká*, and the Madi, *súrú*.

174 Ibid., p. 234.

175 Crazzolara, *The Lwoo*, p. 75.

176 Southall, *Alur Society*, p. 236; Crazzolara, *The Lwoo*, pp. 75-77.

of *jii, joo, juu*, human beings, humankind, people, persons.[177] The specific Alur word is *dhanu*; the Madi have *madi,* a person, a human being, or humanity as a whole;[178] the Lendu[179] and Kebu[180] have the same concept; much as *ntu* in Bantu languages and *mtu* in Kiswahili. To the Alur, therefore, kinship harbours no individual or group egoism. It is inclusive and enlarges the horizon of relationship beyond the narrow confines of blood line or marriage alone.

We can summarise our reflection by referring to Mbiti's analysis of kinship, where he distinguishes six features which have a moral bearing: (i) it controls social relations as a means of knowing how people are related to one another; (ii) governs marital customs and regulations; (iii) determines the behavior of one individual towards another; (iv) it is the basis of strong communal solidarity; (v) extends to the animal, plant and metallurgical spheres through the totemic system; (vi) extends to the vertical plane, to the world of spirits and finally to God.[181]

2.2.2. Chiefship

The second traditional communitarian principle in Alur society is *chiefship*, based on the family structure and lineage system. In his assessment, Southall saw that: "Chiefship and kinship are the joint principles of Alur political organisation."[182] The idea refers to the embodiment of public well-being under the leadership of the chief. We are concerned with how this principle is a value that promotes community spirit.

Chiefship is a unifying institution. Scimecca defines *institution* as an established way of doing things.[183] It sets up predefined expectations of behaviour which constrain and control behavours of every member of the community or society. The function of chiefship is to cater for the harmonious coexistence among members of the society, based on the commonly perceived and inherited value system, meanings, purposes and goals. The Alur word for chiefship

177 Crazzolara, *The Lwoo*, p. 13-16; 17-25.

178 Dominic Dipio, "Bishop Caesar Asili: A Gift to the Universal Church – A Biography," preface by Msgr. Pierino Madrwa, Episcopal Vicar of Moyo Vicariate, Arua Diocese, 1996 (unpublished work), p. 19.

179 Southall, *Alur Society*, p. 152, footnote 1.

180 Crazzolara, *The Lwoo*, p. 361.

181 Mbiti, *African Religions and Philosophy*, p. 98-106.

182 Southall, *Alur Society*, p. 27.

183 Scimecca, *Society and Freedom*, p. 85.

is *kēr*; the chief is *Rwoth*; Alur chiefdom, *kēr Alur*. The *Ubimo* is the highest political office of the "over-all; supreme" chief or king.[184]

How did chiefship foster communitarian cohesion among the Alur? This can be illustrated in the context of structure as a framework for the proper functioning of the community. The concept of *structure* is depicted by Clayton in his study of the family institution as "...an organised system of social relationships (roles, positions, norms) that is pervasively implemented in society and that serves certain basic needs of society."[185] Taking its foundation from the family institution, chiefship functions through: (a) task sharing and team action; (b) symbols of leadership.

2.2.2.1. Task Sharing and Team Action

Chiefship in Alur society rests on the family structure. Southall writes that, "Authority and order within lineages and clans are built upon the values which are inculcated in the family, and extended outwards from the agnatic core of brothers, fathers and sons to embrace all kinsmen of the corporate lineage or clan section."[186] In his study, Clayton avers that kinship, based on the family model, provides for the framework of interaction among members of the community who share at least a set of symbols, meanings and language of communication.[187]

In Alur society, a group of families makes up the homestead, *ungú-pacu*[188] under the headship of the homestead elder, *jego pacu*, together with a team of elders, *judongo pacu*. This was already observed by Crazzolara: a number of homesteads together make a village or clan section under a chieflet assisted by the council of court elders, *judongo kaal*. The chief's court comprises his deputy or prime minister (*jago kaal*); court elders or ministers (*judongo kaal*) forming a court council (*dipo pa judongo kaal*) together with special consultants, informers, advisors and other functionaries in different capacities with defined

184 See "Ker Alur in the Peace Week" in Justice and Peace Commission of Archdiocese of Gulu, *Newsletter*, Vol. 9, Nr. 1, January 2009, p. 3 and 5. Electronic text from website: Gulu_JPC_Newsletter_Jan_2009.pdf (accessed, 3 May 2010).

185 Richard R. Clayton, *The Family, Marriage and Social Change*, Lexington, Massachusetts, D.C. Heath and Company, 1975, pp. 17-21.

186 Southall, p. 28.

187 Clayton, *The Family*, p. 18.

188 Alur word, *pacu*, "home;" *ungú*, "cluster, bunch;" thus: *ungú-pacu*, "homestead, village." This model of homestead proved helpful in establishing Small Christian Communities in Nebbi Catholic Diocese at its inception in the 1980s. This is the name that the SCC has taken in Nebbi Catholic Diocese: *Ungú Pacu pa Jukristo*, Christian Homestead (literally, Homestead of Christians).

roles.[189] The council of elders works through consultation and discourse. The chief/king is a symbol of unity; he relies on the council of elders.

Women had their own council with special roles reserved to them, especially in religious rituals (in alur society women have no king over them; they are mothers even if they are still young). A religious ritual would not start if the right woman was not present to perform her part. It is in this spiritual role that women had a clear competence equal to men. However, they did not have an explicit influential leadership role as men had. This is a gap that Alur culture created, which placed women and youth in an inferior positition in the community; they did not play any significant role in the process of decision making.

Autonomy and Delegation: chiefship promoted autonomy through the distribution and sharing of tasks at different levels. In *A Dictionary of Christian Ethics*, the word *autonomy* is defined in terms of internal rule and self-determination.[190] This concept underlines self-governance. Southall observed that in Alur society:

> Authority and order within lineages and clan are built upon the values which are inculcated in the family, and extended outwards... Contrariwise, political authority stems from chiefship and radiates or is delegated downwards to chieflets and the heads of corporate lineages or clan sections. These heads are therefore the meeting points of the two authority systems, familial and political.[191]

Closely linked with autonomy is *delegation.* The Alur did not develop a written set of laws to define the roles of persons with recognised social positions and their conducts. The content of delegation, as explained by Southall, lies in trust and it means placing a task in the hands of another. A person in a lower position can rightfully act on behalf of another in a higher position. However, this depends to a great deal on the respect he commands in those in his charge, that is, his good moral life. Conjoint to autonomy is subsidiarity.

Subsidiarity: is the practice by which a task can be more easily carried out at a lower level without having to refer to a higher authority. The English word, *subsidiarity*, derives from the Latin *subsidium*, help. In Alur society subsidiarity can be illustrated on the family custom (regular, respectful gesture of relationship). One respondent, Andrea Ukok, explained that: "When a young man marries, his father does not sit on a chair in his house; to do so would mean

189 Crazzolara, p. 201-209; Southall, pp. 121-125.

190 James F. Childress, "Autonomy," in *NDCE*, pp. 51-52. The term is derived from two Greek words, *autos*, self, and *nomos*, rule, norm, law (a clearly defined or stipulated way of conduct, to order relationships and activities).

191 Southall, p. 28.

that the father is rivaling his own son."[192] Subsidiarity increases roles and task sharing, and thus encourages personal moral responsibility in exercising one's gifts and talents to the good of community. Institutions of leadership operate at successive levels, from the family to the apex, at the chief's court (*kaal*). This set-up encourages team action which coordinates the various activities of communities at different levels and contexts. Writing in the field of management and administration, D'Souza notes that community structure specifies roles, which can facilitate good governance and administration.[193] This renders service to common goal and consensus.

Common goal and consensus: common goal refers to a community's shared vision and ideals. We have already clarified (above, in the discussion on *value*) that consensus has to do with the process of decision making based on the community's shared vision. The institution of chiefship is an organ of common goal and consensus, service, unity and moral cohesion. This sets some tension. Both Southall and Crazzolara have the same conclusions about the articulation of chiefship in Alur society. The chief's/leader's role is vital as a figure of unity but he is not an autocrat. Leadership is not absolutism over commoners.[194] Crazzolara writes: "A *Rwoot* (chief) must not pretend to rule alone; he must hear the elders. He must accept the assistance of the *Jegos* (court elders and advisors) of the country; in matters of moment he must ask and follow the advice of the sub-chiefs and elders of his people."[195] The chief does not presume to monopolise decisions; he relies on the advice of his council. The council had the legitimacy of deposing him if he abused his rights, and to make a new chief. This means that, as Southall has observed, the strength of leadership "...depends at all points on public faith..."[196] In cases where the chief/leader is selfish, harsh, scornful, or insensitive to the people's feelings he would be disowned.[197] The moral strength of the leader's authority is measured by the underlying values upon which the institution rests.

192 Andrea Ukok, a parent, interviewed by the researcher, at Rero, Panyimur Community, 26 June 2008.

193 Anthony D'Souza, *Leadership: Trilogy on Leadership and Effective Management*, 6th reprint, Nairobi, Paulines Publications Africa, 2003, p. 73.

194 Southall, p. 54.

195 Crazzolara, p. 209.

196 Southall, p. 86.

197 Crazzolara, p. 187-188.

2.2.2.2. Symbols of Leadership

In his study, Southall found out that in Alur society leadership is inseparable from religion and morality. This is symbolised in the regalia of leadership, including the chief's residence, tools and garments.[198] A symbol is a representation of the value and meaning, purpose and goal it depicts. The paramount chief of Panyimur clan, Rwoth Umbidi Charles, explained it in the following manner. The spear of the elder/chief signifies protection of the weak and defenseless, not for fighting. The stool is a seat of judgment, signifying neutrality and balance: the throne of the chief is made low and not elegantly, to mean stability, humility, equality and solidarity with the people. The costume of the chief designates royalty, meaning that he is vested with spiritual power. The ancestral shrine reminds him of his linking role between the spiritual and the worldly. His knife signifies impartiality, good judgment and justice. His staff is a symbol of unity and weakness: he needs and leans on the support of his people; besides, it is a symbol of peace: when two people are in bitter moods and an elder approaches them with his staff they stop that quarrel and submit to his counsel – by this, he is telling them that if they split, his authority is shattered. The royal drum and horn symbolise common concern and are sounded to call people together when someone dies or similar events occur. The residence of the chief (*kaal*) symbolises both convergence and reserve: the leader must be welcoming and a listener but, at the same time, must not over-expose himself due to his centrality and impartiality. The granary in the compound of the chief or elder is the symbol of a common treasury to meet dire needs of the people: the leader must be frugal and not wasteful. The chief does not handle money directly; people take care of him, he is a symbol of unity, center of cultural, social, economic and political life of the entire people whom he serves.[199]

By the symbols of authority the bearer is entrusted with the care of community values. The leader is the embodiment of public well-being.[200] In Alur society a leader is someone with a 'cool head' (sound judgment; capable of taking difficult decisions) acting as a bridge between the secular and the divine; a peace-judge among his people. He is a man from the people and of the people, with the people and available for them. The people are impatient with a leader whose life is not resonant with his office: he is betraying them. The Church may consider this cultural sensitivity, particularly from what people

198 Southall, p. 178; cf. p. 88.

199 Rwoth Charles Umbidi, interviewed by the researcher, at Panyimur, 20 July 2008.

200 Southall, p. 92.

perceive of the identity of the priest and religious, as symbolised in their residence, sacred vessels, formal garments and their state of life.[201]

2.2.3. Religious Values

The French sociologist, Durkheim, defined religion as "a unified system of beliefs and practices relative to sacred things, that is to say set apart and forbidden, beliefs and practices which unite into one single moral community, called a church, those who adhere to them."[202] We may detect that Durkheim knows religion in terms of "church" and perhaps close to Christianity alone. Our study is concerned with the moral community that religion creates, based on the sense of the sacred.

The Alur believe in the God whom they call *Jacwic* or *Nyakacwiya* (Creator) or *Rubanga* (Supreme Being), *Rubanga Nyakacwiya* (Omnipotent Creator). The nature of this God is communitarian, depicted in the appellative, *Alwāk*, a communion-God.[203] This belief acknowledges God as a transcendent being who is responsible for the existence of the world order and human beings alike. A study done by James Onyango among the Luo of Kenya illustrates this point: God who is transcendent and yet immanent (whose presence is with creation and sustains it).[204] The Alur, *Nyakacwiya*, which translates the Luo variant, *Nyasaye* (originator of life, with a feminine connotation) provides a point for theological reflection. Onyango writes that, "The semantics of the term, *Nya…* gives the Luo philosophy of the universe that all that exists: living or non-living, great or small, powerful or weak begins as *Nya* – from little or a tiny state."[205] Our point of reflection is concerned with the masculinity-femininity nature of God in the Alur belief in God. This provides us with a theological argumentation for gender balance. We find in the Alur traditional religion a fundamental human equality that exists between men and women

201 137 responses to our questionnaire had similar viewpoint: out of reverence, the people look at priests and the religious as people invested with spiritual powers and would not expect to see them live like any ordinary person.

202 Émile Durkheim, *The Elementary Forms of the Religious Life*, New York, Free Press, 1965 (1912), p. 62.

203 In the Alur language, *Jacwic*, Creator, depicts the masculine nature of God. The prefix, *Ja-*, is indicative masculine, but it can also be used neutrally in some cases, for example, *jakéc*, 'a stingy person,' can refer to both male and female; *janyáp*, 'a lazy person,' can be masculine or feminine. The appellative, *Nyakacwiya*, is feminine, the prefix, *Nya-*, 'daughter of,' is indicative feminine.

204 James Onyango Awino, "Towards an Analitical African Theology: The Luo Concept of God as a Case in Point," in *AFER*, Vol. 36, Nr.3 (June 1994), pp. 171-180.

205 Ibid., p. 174.

before God (*Jacwic*) which ideally provides reason for complementarity in their relationships.

Our enquiry intends to find out how this religious belief and practices ensuing from it have contributed to shaping relational attitude in Alur society. In our field study, out of forty persons randomnly interviewed by the researcher, twenty-seven said religion is the strongest binding factor. Out of 287 questionnaire responses, 173 (60%) said it has a strong appeal to community life. This suggests that, until now, religion has had a significant impact on the lifestyle of the Alur. We can highlight this under five points: identification of values, themes, memorial, co-creativity, and bond of community wholeness.

2.2.3.1. Identification of Human Values

Religious belief is a significant factor in identifying human values. In general this was observed, of the African people, by Pope Paul VI in his 1967 Motu Proprio, *Africae Terrarum*, where he writes:

> Many customs and rites, once considered bizarre and primitive, today, in the light of ethnological science, reveal themselves as integral parts of unique social systems, worthy of studies and respect. In this regard, We think it profitable to dwell on some general concepts characteristic of ancient African religious cultures because We think their moral and religious values deserve attentive consideration.[206]

He published this document, to express his opinion on Africa and its people, when a number of African countries had got political independence. His statement sought to overcome the theological and cultural bias which had until then relegated African religious practices to animism (belief in a supernatural spiritual power that organises and animates or ensouls the material universe: plants, animals, objects and nature). He acknowledges that a constant and general foundation of African tradition is a spiritual vision of life. Its religious expression is not animist but constitutes a spiritual view of life, which influences all living beings and visible nature itself as linked with the world of the invisible and spirit.[207] He understands that this spiritual *vision* is the most important and common element that portrays the idea of God as the source of reality: "This concept, perceived rather than analysed, lived rather than reflected on… The fact remains that the presence of God permeates African life as the presence of a higher being, personal and mysterious."[208] It must be noted, however,

206 *AT*, n. 7 § 2: *AAS* 59 (1967), p. 1077.

207 Ibid., n. 8 § 1: *AAS* 59 (1967), p. 1077.

208 Ibid., n. 8 § 2: *AAS* 59 (1967), pp. 1077-1078.

that the Pope's approach is dialogical, as he clarifies in his earlier Encyclical Letter, *Ecclesiam Suam*, where he writes:

> Obviously we cannot agree with these various forms of religion...honesty compels us to declare openly our conviction that the Christian religion is the one and only true religion...But we do not wish to turn a blind eye to the spiritual and moral values of the various non-Christian religions, for we desire to join them in promoting and defending common ideals in the spheres of religious liberty, human brotherhood, education, culture, social welfare, and civic order. Dialogue is possible in all these great projects...[209]

His insistence remains, that the Christian religion is the only and one true religion in contrast to the great Afro-Asiatic religions.

Mbiti gives the general picture of African religion where he writes that: "Africans are notoriously religious...Religion permeates all the departments of life so fully that it is not easy or possible to isolate it."[210] By this he means that the African is a living expression of their religion: "In traditional religion there are no creeds to be recited...each one is...a living creed."[211] Commenting on this statement, Gwinyai writes that it is "...the African religious feeling"[212] which influences their whole life. This is Magesa's thesis, too, in his study of African religion, where he talks of the ethical perspective of African religion[213] as that consciousness which gives the African a holistic definition.[214] However, Mbiti's statement, "notoriously religious," must be taken with some hesitation. It seems to push the African consciousness more into the invisible, abstract realities rather than the visible and rational: misfortune or luck, failure or success, opposition or disagreement tend to leave people with suspicion, mistrust and biased accusations; events are seen in terms of the spirit world influencing human life either with curses or blessings.

Bishop Geyer, the first Comboni missionary bishop to enter Alurland in 1910, reports in his itinerary diary: "From the more than thirty different, larger and smaller, Negro ethnic groups whom I met on my journey, all have in their

209 *ES*, n. 107-108: *AAS* 10 (1964), pp. 654-655.

210 Mbiti, *African Religions and Philosophy*, p. 1.

211 Ibid., p. 4.

212 Gwinyai H. Mozorewa, *The Origins and Development of African Theology*, Eugene, Wipf and Stock Publishers, 1987, p. 90.

213 Laurenti Magesa, *African Religion: The Moral Traditions of Abundant Life*, 1st reprint, Nairobi, Paulines Publications Africa, 2002, p. 38.

214 Ibid., p. 59ff.

language an expression for God."[215] The Alur believed in a God called *Jok*, perceived as totally free and above full human grasp; neither did they assign male or female characteristics to *Jok*. The image portrayed here is that, *Jok* (God) relates impartially to both sexes. People are subject to God and must direct their lives according to religious values. Would this understanding help to bridge the cultural gender imbalance that exists in Alur society?

2.2.3.2. Life Themes

An important aspect of religion is *theme,* resulting from attitudes towards values and their regular practice which influence decision and choice, and motivate specific actions. In this understanding, Aylward writes that: "Values are expressed as a repeated and consistent *leitmotif* in any number of contexts, through any number of images or symbols. They become a regularity or pattern in the thought of a people or culture."[216] These life themes include communitarian values such as benevolence, solidarity, shairng, and unity (as explained above under kinship). This can be illustrated with two practices among the Alur: harvest feast and assembly.

Harvest thanksgiving: offering and celebrating their first fruits, what they call *landu wi kác* (the first of harvest) or *mwooka*.[217] It is a commensal feast held in every homestead, signifying generosity and sharing. Jalobo, himself an Alur, writes:

> The sacrificial aspect of traditional African religious belief is very important because it shows and confirms the individual's self-awareness and wholeness of life and the center of sacrificial worship and offering is the family, within which the individual finds strong hold and point of reference. In the family, the elders offer libations (*onjo pii*, pouring water) to the ancestors. There are many types of sacrifices: those offered by specialists to the creator, but through the spirit of

215 Geyer, *op. cit*., p 532, translation ours. However, Geyer moves quickly to label the African religious practices as animism, ancestor cult and demonic belief (p. 533).

216 Shorter, *African Christian Theology*, p. 112. The term *leitmotif*, from German, *leitmotiv*, literally meaning, "a leading motive," refers to a recurrent theme (the main focus) throughout a musical or literary composition with a particular person, idea or situation. We are indebted to Shorter for the discussions on themes, memorial, co-creativity, and community wholeness (pp. 111-128); see also Aylward Shorter, "Concepts of Social Justice in Traditional Africa" in *ATR Special Topics*, published in *Pro Dialogo Bulletin* 12 (1977), 32-51. Electronic text from website: http://www.afrikaworld.netafrel/atr-socialjustice.htm (accessed, 14/8/2011).

217 Crazzolara, p. 205.

ancestors, and those offered by the elders in the form of libations to the dead members of that family.[218]

About the general practice of first fruits among African peoples, Pope Paul VI writes that: "...among the forms of sacrifice emerges, by clarity of meaning, the sacrifice of first fruits."[219] In Nebbi Catholic Diocese, the practice of *harvest offering* on the first day of the year has been developed on this background. What is collected on this day is dedicated for the support of pastoral agents.

Assembly: coming together for common purposes and concerns presupposes dialogue, communication, deliberation and decision making in common. The Alur have two types of assembly, *dipo* and *vura*. Similar traditional practices are found among the Madi, Lendu, Kebu and Lugbara.[220] *Dipo* is of a jural nature, a court, at which the council of elders sit to deliberate on matters addressed to them. *Vura* is a general assembly of the people, where general matters affecting the whole community or society are communicated to them by elders. Crazzolara observed of them (Lwo character): "The Lwoo are also remarkable for their calm, dignified, staid demeanor and way of transacting or discussing matters..."[221] They are "...frank, liberal, unpretending and reliable."[222] For the Alur, the question of theme signifies: (a) consultation, which checks against self-opinion; (b) open discussion in the process of decision making; (c) deliberating together; (d) acting on common purpose.

2.2.3.3. Memorial

The concept of *memorial* has two connotations. First, it refers to *ancestors,* those who lived before, regarded as mediators between the earthly human community and that in the spiritual world and ultimately with God. The study of Mbiti illustrates that in most of Africa there is a constellation of beliefs and practices with a focus on a mediator figure. The different examples which he cites show that there seems to be none without it.[223] In this context, Bujo depicts the concept of memorial as mystical communion with ancestors, where he writes that: "...the contact, communication and communion with

218 Jalobo Jacan Ngomlokojo, *Rituals of Religious Worship among the Traditional Alur*, Gulu, Catholic Press, 1985, pp. 127-128.

219 *AT*, n. 8 § 3: *AAS* 59 (1967), p. 1078.

220 Crazzolara, p. 237f; Dominic Dipio, "Bishop Caesar Asili, A Gift to the Universal Church: A Biography" (unpublished), p. 19.

221 Crazzolara, p. 75.

222 Ibid., p. 77.

223 Mbiti, *African Religions and Philosophy*, pp. 67-71; 74-89.

one's ancestors have their highly salvific and eschatological purpose."[224] He continues to explain that, "an ethically active subject always understands his action as making present the ethical experience of his ancestors and attempts to shape these actions accordingly."[225] This means that ancestors are an important source of the community's moral reflection.

In Alur society, as the study of Southall records, elders proper are the ancestors.[226] Communion and communication with them has a moral appeal to both the individual and community. On the personal level, memorial demands every individual to lead a truthful life, what the Alur call *gwoko ajá:* preserving truth, relating to others and their property as one would expect of them. On the communal level, it enjoins all members to uphold their community, what they call *gwoko pacu*, upholding the home. One informer, Upiyo Akile, emphasised that someone is a true community member when s/he works to keep it alive.[227]

Secondly, memorial is *historical consciousness.* By history is meant a transforming event that leaves an indelible impress in the life of a people. According to Katongole, "...memory is the embodied performance of the past into the present, the ethical task of remembering is nothing but living with a certain attentiveness to the stories, habits, and practices that shape our lives today and form us into the sort of characters or people we are."[228] In his study sojourn, Southall observed that in Alur society, memorial refers to the unbroken continuity with ancestors and historical events.[229] Historical consciousness draws attention to loyalties that operate in a comprehensive communion: the departed, the living, and those yet to be born. Memorial is linked with, and leads to, co-creativity.

224 Bénézet Bujo, *African Christian Morality at the Age of Inculturation*, Nairobi, St. Paul Publications, 1990, p. 78.

225 Idem., *Foundations of an African Ethic: Beyond the Universal Claims of Western Morality*, New York, The Crossroad Publishing Company, 2001, p. 34.

226 Southall, p. 102.

227 Upio Akile (Achilles), an elder of Panyona clan, interviewed by the researcher, at Rero, 29-32 July 2008. He hosted the researcher for three days, and was our main informer on "remembering the ancestors."

228 Katongole, *A Future for Africa: Critical Essays in Christian Social Imagination*, p. 19. Katongole is recalling the troubled political times in Uganda as reminder to living the present critically. In this context the task of memory is a conversation with the *present* (italics his). See also Peter Kanyandago, "Anthropological History and Interpreting African History and Culture," (unpublished paper, p. 5). Both of them are arguing from negative historical events.

229 Southall, pp. 98-103.

2.2.3.4. Co-creativity

Co-creativity refers to the transmission and enhancing of life in all espects. It has the religious meaning of participation in God's work, the divine blessing of giving life and sustaining it through the human agent. As Rwiza writes of Africa in general, "...the transmission of life is to a great extent still a deep-rooted aspiration, considered as a divine blessing and conceived with communal status and appreciation."[230] In Alur society, marriage is a communal event in the process of which many persons play vital roles: those who make preparatory contacts, parents, elders, peers and sponsors from both sides acting as mentors to the would-be spouses and in their married life.[231] Aunts are mentors to girls, uncles to boys. These mentors encourage family life and account to the council of elders for any serious abuse.[232] Co-creativity has three functions:

Memorial is a spiritual value, which acknowledges the presence of the sacred and divine intervention in human affairs. It underlines loyalty to the Creator whose love and care for human beings is personal and intimate. The Alur have appellatives denoting specific attitudes of relating with God (*Jok*). *Jacwic* or *Nyakacwiya*, Creator: Crazzolara records this belief, "*Jwok mucwiio dhano*" (*Jok* who created people).[233] *Jok-Anyodo*, God of birth, is linked with conception and childbirth. *Jok-ma-Taar*, God of brightness, God of light: who enlightens people and brings light for them to go about their work. Light is a motivation for activity. *Jok-Binga* (*binga*, darkness): God of night, invisible, whose ways are mysterious, human beings cannot manipulate God. Night symbolises silence and sleep, signifying rest from work, long pause between activities. The appellative for twins is *alwak* (group) from which God is named, *Jok-Alwák*, depicting God as communion, a God of the multitude, of together-

---

230 Rwiza, *Formation of Christian Conscience in Modern Africa*, p. 31.

231 We are not fully convinced with Bénézet Bujo's book title: *Plea for Change of Models for Marriage*, English translation by St. Paul Communications/Daughters of St. Paul, Nairobi, Paulines Publications Africa, 2009. The content of Bujo's arguments is correct, yet one has to note that the book title is somewhat vague, considering the emerging confusions surrounding marriage, which militate against the very African models of the marriage that Bujo advocates for. A second problem is the translation. The original German title reads: *Plädoyer für ein Neues Modell von Ehe und Sexualität* (Freiburg im Breisgau, Verlag Herder, 2007), which would read: "Plea for a New Model of Marriage and Sexuality," which poses another question: What "new" model? A third problem is that, while it is clear that Bujo advances the African model of marriage, the title does not precisely mention "Africa." See his discussion on p. 94-99.

232 Matilde Uronya, interviewed by the researcher, at Rero, 6 July 2008; and Donasiano Ucendi, interviewed by the researcher, at Ju-pa-Gilo, 6 July 2008. Both explained the roles of aunts and uncles as mentors to the youth and to young families.

233 Crazzolara, p. 204. In Alur language, *Jacwic* is masculine, while *Nyakacwiya* is feminine.

ness. Today scientific explanation clarifies the biological conception of twins but Alur traditional religion celebrated it as God's blessing, not as an accidental. Human existence therefore acknowledges the Creator as its source; the human community consciously belongs together in that same life principle.

Human activity has a religious and moral content, directed to enhancing life. Of the Alur, Jalobo writes that human life is at the centre of religion and morality: "Very closely related to rituals, symbols, marriages, having children and the whole belief system of traditional Africans, are also morals and values which are integral parts of individual self-awareness. Along this line, human life is very precious and highly valued, since each individual incorporates the three principles of spirit, life and immortality."[234] An action or attitude that blocks the progress of human value is sensitive to the community.

Persons with religious roles, arising from stabilised religious roles: minister to and take care of community life-values. Pope Paul VI reads into the African traditional religion a priestly function, with a root in the family: "There is the fact that in some African cultures, to the father of the family is attributed a function which is typically priestly, by which he acts as a mediator not only between the ancestors and his family, but also between the family and God, fulfilling cultic acts established by custom."[235] However, in Alur society, there are practices which break the taboos of sex division and exclusiveness. For example, in rituals after the birth of twins, men assume the role of women as 'spiritual mothers' (*min-jok*). Similarly, women assume male roles as custodians of sacred places, spirit possession, and priestly functions of making offerings to deities. Shorter has observed similar practices in most African societies. In his study of African Traditional Religion, he remarks that:

> Practically, the only areas in which men and women competed with some equality were those which could be termed "religious or cult". One could find both women and men as specialists in spirit possession societies, as 'custodians of holy places, priests/priestesses. Sexes were probably on an equal footing there because these situations were exceptional, religious or ritual situations.[236]

In Alur society, persons with religious roles are expected to live according to convincing spiritual discipline.[237] People avoid them if they abuse their rights. Southall writes that: "In Alur society the etiquette of rank imposes a strict code of behaviuor in certain specific situations, and otherwise permits

234 Jalobo Jacan Ngomlokojo, p. 126.

235 *AT*, n. 11: *AAS* 59 (1967), pp. 1078-1079.

236 Shorter, "Concepts of Social Justice in Traditional Africa," *op. cit.* p. 4.

237 Southall, pp. 117-120.

free association on a basis of apparent equality."[238] Holding spiritual office means that such a person embodies the supernatural and the natural, which must not be manipulated or used to manipulate.[239] It is important for pastoral agents working in such a setting to take note of their loyalties and the demands these loyalties place on the person of the priest or the religious whose status is defined by their religious function.

2.2.3.5. Moral Cohesion

Religion establishes the bond of community wholeness. Writing about the general religious consciousness of the African people, Pope Paul VI states that: "With regard to communitarian life, which in the African tradition was like an extension of family life itself, we notice that the participation in the life of the community, whether in the ambit of relatives or public life, is considered a precise duty and right of all."[240] In Alur society traditional religion cements the community as families and clan sections join at common rituals. This factor has helped to shape a common vision and relational disposition: taboos (prohibitions) arising from religious observance, such as respect for one another's property, has developed a respectful relationship. This orientation has given the notion of community life as the full fledge of the family where members know and support one other. It is this religious factor that has given the consciousness of understanding the community as home.

Among the Alur, religion has strengthened moral cohesion and made it possible for a clan to live in a locality for reasons of regular rituals. Clans or clan sections living geographically apart have recourse to centralised religious functions. Those living away from home visit home not only at critical moments but also for social-religious reasons. Those living in urban centres try to find their clan or ethnic community for socialisation (coming together for their common ethnic identity and ideals), consultation, or resolving conflicts according to custom.[241] This reflects what Rwiza calls "urban ethnicity."[242]

From the foregoing we can summarise by saying that Alur traditional religion is a strong social-cultural value: it regulates not only the spiritual aspect; but also the bodily, as well as the cosmic, which embody a sacred reality. In our

238 Ibid., p. xii.

239 Ibid., p. 197.

240 *AT*, n. 12: *AAS* 59 (1967), p. 1079.

241 Samuel Uketha and Moses Thokeronga, both interviewed by the researcher, at Entebbe, 1 July 2008.

242 Rwiza, *Formation of Christian Conscience in Modern Africa*, p. 30.

assessment, this perspective provides a theological premise or framework for dialogue with Christianity and the inculturation of Gospel values.

However, this leaves us with some space to ask how far this religious consciousness and practices have contributed to building the society in all dimensions as best possible. To what extent have kinship, chiefship and religion shaped communirian life among the Alur? Are there no loopholes to be filled in?

2.3. Assessment

From what we have seen above, there are significant communitarian values in Alur society which provide a variety of ways to eliminate individualism. We have noted that *kinship* promotes relationships that go beyond lineage and marriage alone. Its dynamics include benevolence, solidarity, generosity and sharing. *Chiefship* promotes consensus, and common goal, subsidiarity and delegation. *Religious* practices promote spiritual goods in the community. This presents a rich potential for evangelisation and communitarian life in Nebbi Catholic Diocese. The diocese can approach the society in Nebbi through these embedded values.

However, despite the positive picture of Alur traditional communitarian values that we have presented above, there are also significant loopholes which need close attention, including the situation of women, youth, inheriting positions, officialdom, and rivalry. From this we can make the following observations:

Women have not been fully proactively involved in the process of decision making. They have not had enough opportunity for significant roles in social-cultural prominence on the bias that their argument is immature like that of children. Besides, there is the male attitude which considers women and children as the property of their husbands. Matilde Uronya recounted that Alur tradition enshrined some practices in taboos such as prohibiting women from eating certain food stuffs; not sitting on a chair; not speaking in an assembly.[243] Such taboos of abstentions have in a way become a mechanism of silencing women. However, today educated women bearing civil roles (such as teachers, police, administrators, members of parliament) or professional roles (such as nurses, medical doctors, engineering, and building) challenge the rationality of this cultural practice.

The youth have been taken to be immature and incapable of sound reason, and thus, not included in the process of decision making. However, today the

243 Matilde Uronya, interviewed by the researcher, at Rero, 6 July 2008.

school has changed this logic; parents who did not attend school education now feel inferior and helpless to argue with their school-going children on topics like family planning, sexuality, human rights, truth, freedom or privacy and ownership of property.

The practice of inheriting the chiefly office on lineage, usually the first son of the chief, creates a form of institutionalised individualism in the mechanism of officialdom which discriminates against capable people who might do better.

Officialdom is sometimes marked with favour and not merit. It does not consider whether one deserves such a task. This does not augur well for community growth.

Rivalry for positions creates tension and division not only among contenders but also factions among supporters of one against the other. Mutual suspicion and accusation of witchcraft is sometimes linked with this rivalry. All these elements amount to a systematic display of the individual ego which, crystallising into group ego, eventually affects and weakens the entire community. In our assessment, these areas invite the Church in Nebbi to a deeper evangelisation to impart gospel values through catechesis and dialogue. This may enable the people to evaluate their traditional practices and improve them for a better appreciation of human values and community building.

Conclusion

This chapter has discussed the three principles of kinship, chiefship and religion, embodying the basic human values and practices that have significantly shaped the worldview and relational aptitude of the Alur people. We have said that value is a worth, a uniting point of reference, inasmuch as it shapes relational attitudes, opinions, choices, decisions and actions. It is relationship that filters and measures all values. We have noted that these principles may remain void of meaning when they do not point to some specific significant meaning, refering to that which is objectively relevant to reality. We have said that culture is a unified way of life that appreciates values and brings them to expression through relationship. We have further clarified that tradition, deriving from original insights tested by time, is a living awareness, communicated to continuing generations, binding them to common aspirations and purposes.

We have noted that kinship is a value based on the inherent principles of spirit, life and immortality. Although it rests on the foundations of lineage and marriage, kinship creates and expands relationships beyond these confines. In the full understanding, it means co-existence and interdependence.

We clarified that chiefship rests on the family structure. It is regulated by common goal and consensus, task sharing and team action, delegation and subsidiarity. However, it has not enlisted the active participation of women and youth in the process of decision making and roles of prominence in public life. This makes it difficult to implement common objectives effectively.

We explained that religion gives the society a spiritual character; it provides the possibility of deepening the spirit of belonging and community wholeness. In the following chapter we shall examine Christian communitarian values.

CHAPTER THREE
Christian Communitarian Values

Introduction

We have already clarified the concept of *value* in Chapter Two. We can recall here that values are touchstones which not only provide the framework for a common course of action but also regulate the life of the community. This chapter is concerned with the theological footholds upon which ecclesial community stands: the Trinity, the Creed, and conversion. That is, the Church is communitarian inasmuch as it is gathered together by the same faith; held together by a continual practice of conversion; and remains trinitarian in its lifestyle.

3.1. The Trinity: Origin of Christian Communion

Here we present the Trinity as the foundation of Christian communion. Our enquiry is whether the theology of the communion of God can serve to deepen the understanding of ecclesial relationship. The Trinity has been understood in Catholic Tradition as unity and wholeness. The Pseudo-Athanasian symbol (end of fifth century, A.D.) states: "Now this is Catholic faith: We worship one God in the Trinity and the Trinity in unity."[244]

In his book, *I Believe in the Holy Spirit*, Congar writes that faith in the Trinitarian God has no room for advancing personal claims that places an individual or group to centre stage while downplaying ecclesial good:

The 'Trinitarian symbolism' not only sets aside the image of narcissistic self-contemplation as an ideal of perfection – it also equally strongly rejects the ideal of a 'face to face' which is sufficient in itself, and points to a life of or a communion that is both differentiated and open. The Spirit...makes the divine communion open to what is not divine...He is therefore called 'love.' He is God's 'ecstasy' directed towards his 'other,' the creature.[245]

---

244 "The Pseudo-Athanasian Symbol Quicumque," in J. Neuner and J. Dupuis (eds.), *The Christian Faith in the Doctrinal Documents of the Catholic Church*, New York, Alba House, 1981, p. 11, n. 16; cf. Paul VI, The *Credo* of the People of God *Solemni hac Liturgia*, in Austin Flannery (ed.), *Vatican Council II*, Vol. 2: *More Post Conciliar Documents*, New York, Costello Publishing Company, 1982, p. 390: *AAS* 60 (1968), p. 437.

245 Yves Congar, *I Believe in the Holy Spirit, Vol. III*, p. 148, note 32.

In his book, *The Church in the Power of the Spirit*, Moltmann develops the theology of the Trinity as a Divine Community. Faith in the Trinity calls Christians "…to understand the Triune God as the God who is sociality, the God who calls sociality to life and invites men and women to fellowship with him. The community of Christ is permitted to see itself as an earthly reflection of the divine Trinity."[246] Faith in the Trinity provides a reflection on the self-consciousness and identity of the believer as a participant in the unity of the Church. But, the Church is: (a) *not a racial Church* that would permit racial separation and discrimination; (b) *not a class Church* that would bless separation or class conflict; (c) *not a male Church* that would tolerate patriarchal rule within itself, or society, but considers all as brothers and sisters in Christ; (d) *not a cultural or national Church* that would encourage or tolerate cultural or national arrogance; (e) *not a kind of 'holy autocracy'* but 'the sovereignty of all believers' that regards all as one in Christ, with equal dignity and rights according to the faith they profess.[247] Faith makes the Church a community of peace and joy;[248] in which divine law prevails, where privileges will not divide individuals or groups, but responsibility for one another will foster a culture of harmony, fraternity and loving service.[249]

The theology of the Trinity has a direct implication in the moral life of Christians. This point is explored in detail by LaCugna in her book, *God for Us*. Human communion comes from the communion of the Trinity. She writes: "Indeed, trinitarian theology is par excellence a theology of relationship: God to us, we to God, we to each other. The doctrine of the Trinity affirms that the 'essence' of God is relational, other-ward; that God exists as diverse persons united in a communion of freedom, love and knowledge."[250] Christian faith is a trinitarian faith which must be brought to life: "Living a trinitarian faith means living God's life with one another: living from and for God, from and for others…*in persona Christi...*"[251] She continues to illustrate that: "…living as persons in communion, in right relationship, is the meaning of salvation and the ideal of Christian faith. God is interactive, neither solitary nor isolated… The doctrine of the Trinity stresses the relational character of personhood over and against the reduction of personhood to individual self-consciousness, and also

246 Jürgen Moltmann, *The Church in the Power of the Spirit*, English translation by Margaret Kohl, London, SCM Press Ltd., 1998, p. xvii.

247 Ibid., p. 105ff.

248 Ibid., p. 78.

249 Ibid., p. 107.

250 Catherine Mowry LaCugna, *God for Us: The Trinity and Christian Life*, New York, HarperSanFrancisco, 1993, p. 243.

251 Ibid., p. 400.

emphasizes the uniqueness and integrity of personhood over and against the reduction of personhood to a product of social relations."[252] LaCugna argues that Christian moral life is the life application (*orthopraxis*) of a fitting human response to the glory of God (*orthodoxy*) definitively revealed in the person of Christ, a personal God. The believer must therefore strive to be fully a person as Christ reveals: "The uniqueness of Christian ethics stems from the uniqueness of the economy of Christ and the Spirit; an ethics that makes little reference to the specifics of the economy, even were its ethical norms to closely approximate the teaching of Jesus, would hardly qualify as Christian."[253]

In its document, *Gaudium et Spes*, the Second Vatican Council teaches that there is an intimate and *vital bond* between every human person and God in which lies their dignity and honor: "The dignity of man rests above all on the fact that he is called to communion with God."[254] In our understanding, the expression *vital bond* or *vital relationship* with God is more theologically satisfying, without prejudice to such a philosophical tenet of 'vital force' as postulated by Tempels, which he nevertheless convincingly advanced in favour of Africans who were in his time taken by Europeans for animists.

Tempels had a positive and solidaric philosophical approach as a missionary to explain that Africans (South of the Sahara) are humans with rational capacity. He sought to give a rational explanation that Africans have an objective philosophy of existence or ontology. In his attempt to make evangelisation successful he learned the people's language, aspiration and thought. His writing can better be understood in the context of his pastoral work among the people. He gives the central point of his writing: "This book is addressed to the colonials of goodwill."[255]

Nkafu, in his book, *African Vitalogy*, takes up this postulation of Tempels to develop his own philosophical discourse on the African concept of life's existence and its dynamic. He writes that African civilisation is "...a civilisation of relation: between man and nature, between man and the supernatural, that is, the vital force which is God, who communicates himself to man and everything... Relationship is a participation in the vital force... this confirms

252 Ibid., p. 292.

253 Ibid., p. 408.

254 *GS*, n.19: *AAS* 58 (1966), p. 1038. Italic emphases, *vital bond*, are ours. See also *CCC*, n. 27.

255 Placide Tempels, *Bantu Philosophy*, English edition from the French Version, *La Philosophie Bantoue* (1945), translated by Dr. A. Rubbens, Paris, Présence Africaine, 1959, p. 184. A Franciscan missionary from Belgium, Tempels lived among the Bantu peoples in the Congo during colonial time.

that vital force is the soul of the African, the principle of African identity."[256] For Nkafu, "the vital force" is God. However, what remains to question is why a people with such a 'vital force' stretching from the sky to earth, from sea to sea, would fail to account for the gender imbalance; wars fought for selfish ambitions; degradation of the natural habitat; irresponsible political regimes and similar moral problems on the African soil! This philosophical vision appears akin to pantheism, where the 'vital force' becomes immanent in plants, animals and humans alike. Allusion to 'vital force' would need some reserve in constructing an 'African-Christian' theological reflection. It is not enough to talk of a 'vital force' without pointing to the ultimate foundation and destiny of human beings. Our theological premise is based on the fullness of God's self-revelation and intervention in human history; the same cannot be said of 'vital force.' As Kabasélé argues, Christian faith acknowledges Jesus Christ above all spirits: spirits of ancestors or other kinds of spirits.[257] Christian theology refers to the Trinity as the source of life and existence. In the *Africa Bible Commentary*, Assohoto and Ngewa comment that the phrase "let us" (Gen. 1:26a) expressed in the plural, "...suggests the community of the Godhead, which involves three persons – the Father, Son and Holy Spirit."[258]

Christian trinitarian ethic underscores solidaric accountability: the believer is accountable both to God in the vertical relationship and to community on the horizontal dimension. Writing in the North American context Niebuhr developed the model of *character ethics* in view of God's self-gift to humans in Christ and the loving response by which Christians are to commit themselves to God in Christ.[259] The core of Niebuhr's reflection is about the transformation of heart by which the believer is to develop their character by practicing the pattern of Jesus' way of life and to communicate Christ. The human community or society is the place where the believer practices universal solidarity. Niebuhr argues that to be responsible is to respond in a framework of accountability to those whose actions call forth our response and with whom we are in solidarity because we together make a continuing society.[260] Faith creates a

256 Martin Nkafu Nkemnkia, *African Vitalogy: A Step Forward in African Thinking*, Nairobi, Paulines Publications Africa, 1999, p, 170-171.

257 See François Kabasélé, "Christ as Ancestor and Elder Brother," in Robert Schreiter (ed.), *Faces of Jesus in Africa*, 8th printing, Maryknoll, Orbis Books, 2002, p. 117.

258 Barnabe Assohoto and Samuel Ngewa, "Commentary on the Book of Genesis," in Tokunboh Adeyemo (Gen. ed.), *Africa Bible Commentary*, Nairobi, WordAlive Publishers, 2006, p. 11.

259 Cf. William C. Spohn, "Jesus and Moral Theology," in James Keating (ed.), *Moral Theology: New Directions and Fundamental Issues*, New York, Paulist Press, 2004, p. 35.

260 H. Richard Niebuhr, *The Responsible Self: An Essay in Christian Moral Philosophy,* New York, Harper & Row, 1963, pp. 61-65.

unity in which: "I place companions, human and subhuman and supernatural, in the one universal society which has its centre neither in me nor in any finite cause but in the transcendent One."[261] Through faith, human action participates in God's action: "Responsibility affirms: 'God is acting in all actions upon you. So respond to all actions upon you as to respond to this action.'"[262]

Christian solidarity engenders a co-naturality and interdependence which is to bring the deepest human longing for communion to expression. In the context of science and technology for the development of peoples, the topic of interdependence was the central mission statement of the World Council of Churches held at Bucharest in 1974. The formulation of this Council expresses the Christian Trinitarian reality: "...independence, in the sense of isolation from the human community is neither possible nor just. We, human persons, need each other within communities. We, human communities, need each other within the community of humanity. We, human communities, need nature within the community of creation. We, the creation, need God, our Creator and re-Creator..."[263]

The Trinitarian ethic is also covenantal and underlines moral character and conduct according to faith. St. Paul's Letter to the Ephesians (4:1-6) admonishes Christians to lead a life worthy of their vocation because of the binding principles: one Spirit, one Lord, one faith, one God. This means that the community to which we belong has a moral claim on our life; it widens the horizon of its every member and facilitates personal fulfillment. Gerkin writes that in this framework of response lies: "...the story of the transcendent God who creates, promises to be faithful, and calls God's people into covenant relationship with one another and with their Creator."[264]

In his Encyclical Letter, *Evangelium Vitae*, Pope John Paul II writes that true human communion is a living sign of the mutual self-giving that exists in the communion of the Trinity: "The God of the Covenant has entrusted the life of every individual to his or her fellow human beings, brothers and sisters, according to the law of reciprocity in giving and receiving, of self-giving and of the acceptance of others."[265] He continues with the same understanding in

261 Ibid., p, 124.

262 Ibid., p. 126.

263 The Bucharest Conference of the World Council of Churches on "Science and Technology for Human Development," June 1974, *Anticipation* 19, Geneva, November 1974; Jürgen Moltmann, *The Church in the Power of the Spirit*, p. 176 discusses this under the theme of 'interdependence.'

264 Charles V. Gerkin, *Widening the Horizons: Pastoral Responses to a Fragmented Society*, Philadelphia, The Westminster Press, 1986, p. 21.

265 John Paul II, Encyclical Letter *Evangelium Vitae* (*The Gospel of Life: A Message of Hope*), London, Fount Publishers, 1995, n. 76: *AAS* 87 (1995), p. 489.

his Post-Synodal Apostolic Exhortation, *Ecclesia in Africa*, where he discerns a providential trace of communion in the African religious consciousness. He invites the Church in Africa to develop this and bring it to the best expression for the enrichment of the universal Church and to humanity as a whole:

> Africa...is endowed with a wealth of cultural values and priceless human qualities which it can offer to the Churches and to humanity as a whole...cultural values, which are a providential preparation for the transmission of the Gospel...Africans have a profound religious sense of the sacred, of the existence of God the Creator and of a spiritual world. The reality of sin in its individual and social forms is very much present in the consciousness of these peoples, as is also the need for rites of purification and expiation.[266]

This does not only give the picture of a people who is responsive to the realities of life; it also presents an appeal for a constructive ordering of life within the Church. It is important to recall here that the Second Vatican Council, in its document on the Church in the world, *Gaudium et Spes*, admonishes Christians to show the true face of God. The Council discerns that one of the reasons why the world may remain in disbelief about the Christian religion is because Christians fail to present the face of God: "To the extent that they neglect their own training in faith, or teach erroneous doctrine, or are deficient in their religious, moral, or social life, they must be said to conceal rather than reveal the face of God and religion."[267] Commenting on this statement, Abbot observes that: "The Council here proposes an examination of conscience for believers. Have they contributed by their shortcomings to the disaffection of those who cannot or will not believe? The text specifically mentions defects of social conscience among Christians."[268]

According to Mwoleka, a trinitarian ecclesial lifestyle for the Christian community involves three things: (a) The Trinity is not an intellectual puzzle: the right approach is to imitate the Trinity; (b) A way of life together: the Trinity is shared and lived in our daily experiences. It is this spirit of togetherness that can bring forwardness in the Christian family and the different ecclesial aspects. It has to find expression in community meetings, discussions, deliberations, decisions and action plans, implementation of agreed course of action, continuous consultations and assessment of community actions; (c) To reveal the face of the Trinity by practicing charity, through which we can transform and go beyond the confines of self-absorption (cupidity) into other-centred

266 John Paul II, Post-Synodal Apostolic Exhortation *Ecclesia in Africa* (*The Church in Africa*), Nairobi, Paulines Publications Africa, 1995, n. 42: *AAS* 88 (1996), p. 28.

267 *GS*, n. 19: *AAS* 58 (1966), p. 1039.

268 Walter Abbott and Joseph Gallagher (eds.), *The Documents of Vatican II*, p. 217, note 45.

love (charity).[269] A trinitarian ecclesiology means that the Church (family, SCC, groups, clubs, associations, movements, parish, deanery, and diocese) must allow itself to be guided by the Spirit of God in the example of Christ.[270]

3.1.1. Christ: God's Call and Response

The Second Synod of Bishops for Africa (2009) refers to Christ 346 times, and Jesus 119 times.[271] This calls our attention to the place of Christ in the life of the Church in Africa and in the life of every believer. Vatican Council II Decree on Priestly Formation, *Optatam Totius*, recommends that the scientific exposition of teaching moral theology is to be founded on the mystery of Christ and sacred scripture. It is to show also the meaning of the vocation of the faithful and their part to play in bearing the fruits of charity for the life of the world.[272] This is because Christian moral life cannot be detached from Jesus Christ himself; it is a life of discipleship intrinsically linked to his life and person.

The challenge of discipleship involves a correct understanding of Jesus' portrait, striving to internalise and appropriate his attitude, to let our imagination and sensitivity be stirred by his own. On the one hand, in Jesus there is his divinity which calls the believer to honour him as "one" with the Father. It teaches us humility, to acknowledge the grace of Christ but to know our limitations due to sin. On the other hand, in Jesus there is humanity, which ponders his ministry, how God is becoming everything human in order to guide what is human to perfection according to how divine love works. However, Christian life is more than a call to discipleship; it is a call "to be" and "to live with" Jesus in the Father. St. Paul stresses the Christo-centric fellowship. In his First Letter to the Corinthians, he encourages us: "You can rely on God, who has called you to be partners with his Son Jesus Christ our Lord" (1 Cor. 1:9). St. John confirms this by saying: "What we have seen and heard we are telling you so that you too may be in union with us as we are in union with the Father and with the Son Jesus Christ" (1 Jn. 1:3).

---

269 Christopher Mwoleka, "Trinity and Community," in *AFER*, Vol. 17, No. 4, 1975, pp.203-206.

270 Idem., *Do This! The Church in the Third Millennium – What Face Shall It Have?* Peramiho, Benedictine Publications Ndanda, 1988. Mwoleka finds in the Trinity a model of Church that can contribute to the deepening not only of a trinitarian ecclesiology but also the application of the Gospel into daily living.

271 Zenit, *Keywords at the Africa Synod*, Permalink: http://www.zenit.org/article-27186?l=english Code: ZE09101309 – 2009-10-13 (downloaded, 14 October 2009).

272 Vatican Council II, Decree on Priestly Formation *Optatam Totius*, n. 16: *AAS* 58 (1966), p. 724.

In his Encyclical Letter, *Redemptor Hominis* (Redeemer of Man) Pope John Paul II teaches that every Christian believer – both clergy and laity – shares in the kingly function (*munus*) of Christ. It can only be practiced in the Church as a community of disciples. The Pope uses the expression *communion of disciples* technically to emphasise the spiritual meaning which distinguishes the Church from a merely social membership although being Church does not erase the human social reality. Being in the Church is not an empty social convenience but involves commitment and fidelity, by making our loyalty to God in Christ a relatively consistent way of life. The Church, in every believer, must become more conscious of its life and activity, even from the human point of view.[273]

The Pope continues to emphasise the place of Christ in the moral life of Christians in his Encyclical Letter, *Veritatis Splendor* (Splendor of Truth). He states that: "Jesus' way of acting and his words, his deeds and his precepts constitute the moral rule of Christian life."[274] He further clarifies that the moral question is a universal aspiration rooted in the heart of every human person, as illustrated in the encounter of the one who approached Jesus with the question, "What should I do?" (Mt. 19:16). He explains that: "In the young man, whom Mathew's Gospel does not name, we can recognize every person who, consciously or not, *approaches Christ the Redeemer of man and questions him about morality.* For the young man, the *question* is not so much about rules to be followed, but *about the full meaning of life.*"[275]

In his book, *Reason Informed by Faith*, Gula develops the place of Jesus in the Christian moral life within the context of discipleship.[276] First, Jesus is God's self-gift of a personal encounter with humans, the fullest revelation of the invitation of divine love; and in his own person the fullest human response to God. Thus, in the Judeo-Christian tradition, Christian morality can be understood as a 'revealed reality' as well as a 'revealed morality' in which God calls, and man and woman freely respond: Jesus is both *gift* and *call.* Second, morality is specifically Christian because it has Christ as the norm of the moral life. This is because of *who* Jesus is: God's personal revelation and encounter with humans. Thirdly, the biblical stories about the life of Jesus help to shape our character by informing our discernment. Internalising his portrait gives birth to

273 John Paul II, Encyclical Letter *Redemptor Hominis* (*Redeemer of Man*), English translation by Vatican Polyglot Press), Boston, Pauline Books and Media, 1979, n. 21: *AAS* 71 (1979), pp. 316-320.

274 Idem., Encyclical Letter *Veritatis Splendor*, (*Splendor of Truth*), English translation by Vatican Polyglot Press), Boston, Pauline Books & Media, 1993, n. 20: *AAS* 85 (1993), p. 1149.

275 Ibid., n. 7: *AAS* 85 (1993), p. 1138, italics as in the English translation text.

276 Gula, *Reason Informed by Faith*, pp. 185-197.

our commitment. This in turn shapes our perspective, dispositions, affections and intentions. *Perspective* refers to how we view and assess and interpret our experiences, that is, how our faith helps us to make choices, evaluate situations and to act. *Disposition* refers to a relatively stable way of our attitudes which affect our actions and manner of life. *Intention* refers to the purpose for which we act. *Affection* is the quicknes that makes us ready to carry out our action. These qualities shape our sensitivities and open us to relate with one another.

Discipleship entails fidelity to Christ. Orr and Bromiley write that *Christianity is Christ.* This is to say that Christ is the *Reason* and *Authority* of Christian life:

> Christianity takes its substance as well as its name from Jesus Christ. It is not a construct of human philosophy, though it points to true wisdom. It is not a system of theological dogmas, though dogmatic truths are involved. It is not just an inward and subjective experience, though it entails a personal relationship with God. It is no mere code of ethics, though it carries with it a way of life. In fact, it is not to be understood or explained in any anthropological terms except insofar as Jesus Himself is true man. It is supremely Christological: Christ is the beginning, center, and end.[277]

However, this cautions the believer against making Christ an ethical master without a critical assessment. Moltmann observes that: "In the Western Church a one-sided stress on the lordship of Christ has led to an ethicization of the freedom of faith in new obedience. This ethicization has often enough led to a new legality in which Christ was conceived of as a new lawgiver, and in which faith took its public form from this legality's demand."[278] What is at stake here is the oversimplification of faith in Christ without answering to the demands of God's incarnate love.

Fidelity goes together with commitment. As Rigali writes, Christian morality, at its core, is the commitment to Christ in his Church.[279] The Church is the place where the believer practices commitment to Christ through acts of love, in a creative and generative freedom. Christian fidelity is an integration of faith and reason to express the community's depth of commitment to God in Christ who is present in the world in and through the Church. This is subject to the guidance of the Holy Spirit.

---

277 James Orr and Geoffrey W. Bromiley, "Christianity," in *ISBE*, Vol. 1, p. 659.

278 Motlmann, p. 109.

279 Norbert Rigali, "On Theology of the Christian Life," in James Keating (ed.), *Moral Theology: New Directions and Fundamental Issues*, New York, Paulist Press, 2004, p. 19.

3.1.2. The Holy Spirit: Giver of Life

The place of the Holy Spirit in Christian communitarian life emphasises God's self-giving and abiding presence in the life of the Church. Jesus identifies himself with the 'spirit' of the Lord that rests upon him. By this he defines his mission of establishing the Kingdom of God's love in which people are to be at home with God and with one another (Lk. 4:18-19). He promises and gives the Spirit as Revealer and Teacher of truthfulness, to guide the Church in bearing witness to him in the world. The work of the Holy Spirit in the Church and in the lives of Christians is therefore to prolong Christ's presence and mission.

However, it is helpful to distinguish between the Holy Spirit and the 'human spirit.' There are two biblical words, *ruah* in the Old Testament, *pneuma*, in the New Testament, rendered in English by the general meaning of *spirit. The NIV Theological Dictionary of New Testament Words* makes the clear distinction that:

> At one end of pneuma's spectrum of meaning is the human spirit, or perhaps better, the human person insofar as he or she belongs to and interacts with the spiritual realm...the human spirit is that aspect of a person through which God encounters him or her...that dimension whereby human beings are most immediately open and responsive to God...that aspect of human awareness most sensitive to matters of the spiritual realm...[280]

The problem of the Spirit of God and the human spirit creates some moral difficulties that need attention. This is illustrated in the *Lineamenta* (Working Paper) to the 1994 Special Assembly of the Synod of Bishops for Africa. The document lists a score of problems in its report on the ATR. In the *religious sphere*, magic and divination are widespread; people are enclosed within a universe of fear; fear is the motive for religious cult. God is regarded as too remote and therefore absent from the daily lives of men; this leads to the cult of spirits as substitutions for God; the belief is widespread that certain natural things have supernatural powers. In the *ritual sphere*, some prayers invoke a curse; spirits and ancestors are sacrificed to. In the *religio-moral sphere*, the report mentions that some situations may call for human sacrifice; ritual murder is practiced. In the *religio-cultural sphere*, spirit possession is a usual phenomenon in some communities; secret cults are sometimes used to manipulate society. In the *religio-social sphere*, witchcraft and sorcery are persistent; the sense of neighbour is often restricted. Rites against witchcraft may play upon

280 *NIV*, p. 1053.

and deepen the hatred and divisions in the society.[281] Such examples place some reserve on claiming the role of the Holy Spirit in human dispositions and actions.

Congar clarifies that the Holy Spirit is not consubstantial with us; we cannot manipulate the Holy Spirit as a personal possession. We can appreciate and appropriate the presence of the Holy Spirit as grace, an abiding Presence of God with us and in us. The Holy Spirit is God's grace of unity, implying the effective and concrete social and familial communion.[282] Church unity is not just a structural uniformity but a living reality of the unity of God's Spirit, exercised in varied ways. It is the Holy Spirit who is the principle of wholeness, a power spreading faith and love according to the teaching of Christ. However, the Holy Spirit cannot be left hanging in the air between heaven and earth, in an abstract faith and liturgical performance without influencing the ordinary life of believers. "This communion consists in living and behaving as a conscious member of an organic whole."[283] It is the Holy Spirit who communicates the memory of Christ in every member and who binds them to the wholeness of the Church. The Holy Spirit defines and brings Christian discipleship to real life and directs it towards God in Christ.

Ronald A. Mercier writes that recourse to the action of the Holy Spirit for the moral lives of Christians can bring forth life from chaos, namely, moral chaos in a world that is losing the traditional sense of relationship among persons. The Holy Spirit is the giver of life, the ongoing source of relationship that invites one into relationship with others, with the world and with Christ. The Holy Spirit defines the individual as a *person in relationship*. This helps the believer to respond to the three moral gaps of *presence*, *power*, and *person*. Mercier writes that:

> In a world devoid of the experience of meaning or of God, the profoundly experiential identity of the Spirit as *presence* can reinvigorate that empty space. In a world that has lost a sense of moral purpose, a horizon that beckons us, the Spirit as *power* – a power oriented toward the creation of nature intended by God – provides a needed sense of common purpose and vision in which we participate. Most important, though, the Spirit as *person*, in whom we experience the gift of a relationship with God that creates and sustains us as persons rather

281 Special Assembly of the Synod of Bishops for Africa, *The Church in Africa and the Evangelizing Mission towards the Year 2000: Instrumentum Laboris*, Vatican City, Libreria Editrice Vaticana, 1993, n. 106.

282 Yves Congar, *I Believe in the Holy Spirit*, Vol. 2, pp. 21-22.

283 Ibid., p. 18.

than isolated individuals, beckons us out of isolation into community with God – and thus with others.[284]

The visible stage of the Spirit's presence, power and person is the Church for its internal life and for the life of the world. The presence and guidance of the Holy Spirit is to help the Church to discern if it is moving in God's ways. Ignatius of Laodicea gives a vivid image of the Holy Spirit in the life of the Church, where he writes:

> Without the Holy Spirit, God is distant; Christ remains in the past; the Gospel is a dead letter; the Church is a mere organisation; authority is domination; mission is propaganda; cult (liturgy) is a mere evocation; Christian action is an empty moral slavery. But in the Holy Spirit, the entire world order rises and groans in the birth pang of God's reign; the risen Christ is present; the Gospel is power of life; the Church is a Trinitarian communion; authority is a liberating service; mission is Pentecost; the liturgy is memorial and anticipation; human work is godly.[285]

We may conclude that, life in the Spirit defines the Church as a 'new covenant' community of love, joy, peace and harmony. Reflecting on the place given to the Holy Spirit in the *Instrumentum Laboris* (Working Paper) to the Second Synod of Bishops for Africa, Nwaigbo writes that, "When we examine our attitude towards the spread of the message of the gospel, it is clear that the degree to which we are willing to evangelize is linked to the degree to which we have understood the great work that the Spirit of Christ has done in our lives and in the life of the Church."[286]

3.1.2.1. The 'New Covenant' Motif

According to the *NIV Dictionary of New Testament Words*, the terminology "new" and its cognates are used both in the Old and New Testaments to denote "what has not been before." It carries a qualitative meaning referring to what is

---

284 Ronald A. Mercier, "The Holy Spirit and Ethics: A Personal Gift Making Persons," in James Keating (ed.), *Moral Theology: New Directions and Fundamental Issues*, New York, Paulist Press, 2004, p. 59.

285 Donagh O'Shea, "Pentecost" from website: http//www.goodnews.ie/jacobswelljoie.shtml (accessed, 16/4/2010), p.1. See also Raniero Cantalamessa, *La Parola di Vita: Riflessioni sulla Parola di Dio delle Domeniche e delle Feste dell'Anno: Anno C*, Roma, Cittá Nuova, 1979, Homily for Pentecost Sunday. I have not been able to find directly the corpus translation of the original text of Ignatius of Laodicea.

286 Ferdinand Nwaigbo, "*Instrumentum Laboris*: The Holy Spirit and the Sings of the Times for the Second Synod for Africa," in *AFER*, Vol. 51, Nr. 4 (December 2009) & Vol. 52, Nr. 1 (March 2010), p. 621.

more than that which has been until now. In Salvation history "new" refers to God's saving intervention in human history and his promise. In Jer. 31:31-34, God will put a new heart in his people as a "new covenant" which is God's faithful commitment to his people. In the New Testament, "new" refers to God's saving act in the person of Christ. The basic meaning of *covenant* centres on response and fidelity to God's self-giving love, with reference to Christ.[287]

Joseph Allen identifies six characteristics of God's covenantal love: (a) God binds us together as members of a covenant community; (b) God affirms the worth of each member; (c) God extends covenantal love inclusively; (d) God seeks to meet the needs of each member of the covenant community; (e) God is steadfast; (f) God is reconciling.[288] In synthesis, covenant signifies good relationship in a comprehensive conduct towards one another. As Schildenberger notes: "The line of conduct corresponding to such an ensuing unity goes by the name of *hesed*, namely, 'conduct towards others with regard to whom one stands in a relation of kinship, friendship, hospitality or service; the duty arising out of close bonds with one another; community; solidarity."[289]

The notion of biblical covenant is explained by Gula as an invitation to participate in God's love. He uses three terms – worth, solidarity and fidelity – which together provide the full context and content of covenant. This involves respecting one's own worth and that of others as constituted by God; living in solidarity with creation and with one another as covenantal partners; developing the virtue of fidelity as the proper characteristic of every covenantal relationship, sealed in Christ.[290]

The understanding of the new covenant morality is to help Christians to evaluate their cultural morality and bring it to a wider horizon of the ecclesial reality as family of God. Grisez writes that covenantal relationship deepens and transforms morality: "All human life is drawn into its context, and the primacy of the human good of religion is made clear. This relationship causes God's people to share in his qualities, including those which are more than human. Moral insights are deepened, and the richness of human goods is unfolded. A fresh perspective is provided for criticizing all conventional morality."[291] The notion of *new covenant* is closely linked with *new creation*.

287 *NIV*, pp. 630-632.

288 Joseph L. Allen, *Love and Conflict: A Covenantal Model for Christian Ethics*, Nashville, Abingdon Press, 1984, pp. 61ff.

289 Johannes Schildenberger, "Covenant," in Johannes B. Bauer (ed.) *Encyclopedia of Biblical Theology*, second impression, London, Sheed Ward, 1976, p. 142a.

290 Richard Gula, p. 92-99.

291 Germain Grisez, *The Way of the Lord*, Vol. 1: *Christian Moral Principles*, Quincy, Franciscan Press, 1997, p. 520.

3.1.2.2. The Church as 'New Creation'

The new creation morality consists in a relationship stirred by the spirit of Christ. By *new creation* is meant that Christians, in the conviction of faith, embody a new horizon both in the human-cultural and Christ-centred character of existing and living in a new identity, characterised by creative freedom. Using the paradigm of St. Paul, Robert Banks identifies three aspects of Christian freedom: involving independence, dependence, and interdependence. *Independence* means (a) freedom from certain things, like sin, the law, death and alien powers; (b) freedom for certain things like righteousness, conformity to Jesus, and suffering, which could be understood here as the painstaking endeavour to go beyond one's group's social-cultural horizons; (c) freedom, resulting into a personal life-giving experience of liberty. *Dependence* signifies (a) relying upon Christ, who terminated humanity's enslavement through his death and resurrection; (b) relying upon the Holy Spirit, who communicates Christ's life and purpose as a received divine gift rather than innate possibility. *Interdependence* (a) with others, since liberty leads to service and can only be practically defined in relation to their needs; (b) with the world, since the universe itself will experience the liberty of transformation along with those who are Christ's; (c) giving liberty a social and cosmic as well as personal and theo-centric dimension.[292] The Trinitarian morality is summarised in the Creed.

3.2. The Creed: Profession of Commitment to Communion

The New Dictionary of Theology defines *creed* as: "...a commitment, the giving of one's heart or self to someone or something. A creed is a statement that casts in verbal form the faith of an individual or a community."[293] The formulation of the Christian Creed dates back to the Council of Nicea (325 AD) and later Constantinople (381 AD) thus: "We believe in one God, the Father... one Lord Jesus Christ...one Holy Spirit... one, Holy, Catholic, and apostolic Church."[294] This definition shows that the Creed is a rule of faith and baptismal formula, which distinguishes it from any cultural, political or ideological

292 Banks, *Paul's idea of Community: The Early House Churches in Their Cultural Setting*, revised edition, sixth printing, Peabody, Hendrickson Publishers, 2007, p. 25.

293 Berard L. Mathaler, "Creeds," in Joseph A. Komonchak, Mary Collins, Dermot A. Lane (eds.), *The New Dictionary of Theology*, Dublin, Gill and Macmillan, 1990, p. 260. Etymology from the Latin, *credo*, deriving from two words: *cor*, "heart" and the verb, *do*, "I place, I put," literally meaning, "I place my heart," denoting an unreserved, wholehearted or wholesome commitment.

294 Norman P. Tanner (ed.), *Decrees of the Ecumenical Councils*, Vol. 1: *Nicea – Lateran V*, London, Sheed & Ward, 1990, p. 5; p. 24. Cf. J. Neuner and J. Dupuis (eds.), *The Christian Faith*

adherence. From this Creed emerge the four traditional marks of the Church: oneness, holiness, catholicity and apostolicity.

There are two other formulations that must be borne in mind. The *Symbol of the Roman Order of Baptism* (tenth century) mentions: "...the communion of saints."[295] The profession of faith of Pope Paul VI adds: "...the communion of all the faithful of Christ, those who are pilgrims on earth."[296] In the Creed therefore we have three communitarian principles for the life of the Church: (a) God who is communion – Father, Son, Holy Spirit – in whom we are united through Christ in the Holy Spirit; (b) the communion of saints; (c) the communion of all the faithful.

The question of faith is important and deserves some clarification. It is faith that will define and characterise the individual believer as much as the ecclesial community as specifically Christian. Faith evokes a sense of belonging and the spirit of commitment to that belonging. Basing his definition on the Old Testament covenantal relationship between Israel and Yahweh, O'Donnell explains that: "...faith has to do with that which is reliable, that which gives security, that which can be trusted. Faith presupposes a correspondence between that which is promised and that which is realized... The OT understanding of faith is thus far from intellectualistic; rather it involves an existential surrender of the whole person in obedience. It has to do with the totality of a person's life..."[297]

Christian faith is a loving response to the Gospel message and an appreciation of the values that it offers. A theological synthesis is made by Beinert where he writes that:

> Faith in theological understanding is the personal, fundamental option in which the human being, through grace and trusting in God's power effective in Jesus Christ, responds in consensus with the Church with his or her confession to the saving event of revelation. In contrast to its colloquial meanings (believe = think, suppose, be of the well-founded conviction, agree with an authority, trust in something on the basis of probability), faith in its theological meaning is an absolute assent based on inner certainty.[298]

From these expositions on the biblical and theological understanding of faith, it is clear to see that faith is a critical and decisive personal commitment,

---

in the Doctrinal Documents of the Catholic Church, New York, Alba House, 1981, 9 (p. 7); 12 (p. 9).

295 J. Neuner and J. Dupuis (eds.), 5 (p. 5).

296 Ibid., 39 (p. 29).

297 John O'Donnell, "Faith," in *NDT*, p. 376a-b.

298 Wolfgang Beinert, "Faith," in *HCT*, p. 249.

such as St. Peter makes: "Lord, to whom shall we go? You have the message of eternal life, and we believe; we have come to know that you are the holy one of God" (Jn. 6:68-69; cf. Mt. 16:16; Mk. 8:29; Lk. 9:20). Similarly, St. Augustine in his *Confessions*: "You awaken us to delight in praising you; for you made us for yourself, Lord, and our hearts find no peace until they rest in you."[299] The Christian faith is therefore not a supplement to philosophy, nor a mere intellectual loyalty to an institution; and neither is it a set of propositions about divine love, nor a mere cultic prescription about religious rituals – although these elements are still necessary for its expression. Christian faith is obediential and dialogical. It is *obediential*, that is, an inner listening (Latin, *obedire*, from *ob-*, towards, in the direction of; *audire*, listen to, heed, observe attentively) which places us at the crossroads between cultural values and the values that Christ offers. It is *dialogical* in that it calls for acknowledgement and assent to the values offered: values as possibilities through which persons are united to a common purpose (*dialogue*, from Greek, *dia*, through, across; *logos*, word, signifying communication). For Christians, it is Jesus himself who is the embodiment of obediential dialogue between God and human beings which he imparts on them through his grace of salvation. David Bohr writes that Christian faith is a decision to heed God's word revealed in Jesus and to put it into action: "At its deepest core faith is a total surrender to the ultimate graciousness of the Mystery in which we live, move and have our existence. It is an entering into a totally loving relationship with this Mystery whose love and mercy reconciles us, heals and energizes us."[300] Christian faith is not abstract but a commitment to the message that is proclaimed and translating it into life through witnessing.

3.2.1. Faith and Witnessing

Moltmann has paid especial attention to the Creed in view of the social nature of the Church. He explains that *church* means building a community of shared humanity, one of mutual recognition and of love with justice because Christ calls the Church to pass on to the world a new humanity.[301] In the Church the new order of humanity is thus: (a) men and women created in the image of God (Gen. 1:26) means equality where individual identity and distinction provide for mutuality, not tension; (b) all are called, justified and

299 St. Augustine, *Confessions*, 1.1.1, in Philip Schaff (ed.), *Nicene and Post-Nicene Fathers*, First Series, Vol. 1, Massachusetts, Hendrickson Publishers, 2004, p. 25.

300 Bohr, p. 123.

301 Moltmann, p. xix.

sanctified through the same Gospel message; (c) the same Holy Spirit is the sole Giver of life, who renews the face of the earth.

One central theme stands out clearly in the Creed: communion, which highlights the four marks of the Church: oneness, holiness, catholicity, apostolicity. Moltmann finds in the Creed useful insights for constructing a social ethic.[302] First, the *oneness* of the Church means unity in diversity, opening up to acceptance, loving, respecting and living in solidarity with its members near and far. Second, the Church's *holiness* consists in faith, hope, action and truthfulness. But truthfulness lies in humility in communicating the Gospel message, which is to contribute to shaping people's way of life. Humility points to the spirit of the Gospel; truthfulness rests in obedience to God in the example of Christ, with the help of the Holy Spirit. In this there is no room for advancing personal interests. Thirdly, the Church's *catholicity* implies free openness by which the Church addresses itself impartially to all parties in society in the quest for reconciliation and peace. A free but critical Christian involvement in the social-political, economic and cultural life supports the oppressed and the oppressor. God's word is directed to both. Fourth, the *apostolicity* of the Church means an expressive Christian witnessing to the building of a humane society which, however, involves suffering. It is by their profession of faith that believers form a corporate personality in the ecclesial communion. It is this strength which will enable them to live and act as one body with one spirit, namely, striving to build up the corporate personality that faith brings about.

3.2.2. Corporate Personality

The question of corporate personality in the Church is rather demanding and yet enriching for its life. McKenzie observes that "corporate personality" is a fluid term which may designate the individual or the group, yet neither without the other.[303] We use this expression with reference to ecclesial communion, by which is meant that the community does not exist without individual members and neither the individual without community. This does not confuse the individual against the community; it refers to the openness which acknowledges and gives room for self-realisation in the medium of community life. It means that Christians live from and participate in the fraternity and friendship of Christ, who identifies himself with all and seeks to gather them into the family of God.

302 Ibid., pp. 337-361.

303 John L. McKenzie, "Aspects of Old Testament Thought," in *JBC*, Vol. 2, article 77:69, p. 748.

Moltman argues that Christian communitarian ethic takes on a wide meaning which brings the Church to understand itself as: (a) *Christian*, that is, open to the world. The Church is in the world that gives it its human reality and from which it cannot shy away; (b) *Missionary*, by which is meant a critical existence, embracing all activities that serve to liberate man and woman from the various emblems of slavery masked under cultural, political, economic or religious models; (c) *Ecumenical*, pointing to a universal availability, responsive to Christ's mission amid the continuous historical tensions. Here, cultural or social sways that spark out tensions are no standards for the Church and cannot guide Christians in their life of faith; (d) *Political*, a participation in the political life without succumbing to fluctuating ideological tides but exercising an impartial disposition towards all groups, classes, tribes.[304]

The plausibility of corporate personality is such that, on the one hand, the Church stands for God to the world. On this plane, it is through its involvement in the realities of life that the Church will contribute to building a humane world. It is in confronting society with its critical freedom and giving authentic testimony of the revelation of a new life that the Church will convince society and enter into a fruitful and transforming dialogue with it. It is the appeal of its convincing image that will enrich and/or convert society to accept the Gospel message and its values. On the other hand, the Church stands for the world before God in solidarity with all men and women.[305] The Church embodies the world and strives to bring it to God as a pleasing sacrifice in Christ, at the working of the Holy Spirit. In other words, the Church is in the world and the world is in the Church. The Christian is as human as the politician, the economist, the socialist, the scientist; the difference lies in their vision as a Christian. This is what may help to explain Christian presence in the world in the symbolism of 'light for the world' and 'salt for the earth.' For its internal life, corporate Christian personality consists in ecclesial unity.

3.2.2.1. Unity

Unity is the possibility for Christians to practice love. It builds through the spirit of friendship and fraternity brought by Christ. Ecclesial unity is Trinitarian and knows no divissiveness. Pope John Paul II writes that in a human society or institution people are entrusted to one another in the uniting spirit of fraternity and solidarity.[306] And, the Church itself is not an abstract institution;

304 Moltman, p. 1-18.

305 Ibid., p. 45.

306 *EV*, n. 76: *AAS* 87 (1995), p. 489.

it lives in a human reality, for which unity among its members is its visible strength.

The Pope continues to demonstrate that ecclesial unity is built around two pillars of an ecclesiology of communion and likewise a spirituality of communion. In the Apostolic Exhortation *Christifideles Laici* (Vocation and Mission of the Lay Faithful), he defines ecclesial communion as "...the union with God brought about by Jesus Christ, in the Holy Spirit. The opportunity for such communion is present in the Word of God and in the Sacraments."[307] Unity does not ask to place people at an equal material level; it is an organic communion of diversity and complementarity.[308] Unity characterises the Church as mystery, communion and mission: "...called to relive the very communion of God and to manifest it and communicate it in history (mission)... Only from inside the Church's mystery of communion is the identity of the lay faithful made known, and their fundamental dignity revealed."[309] In the Apostolic Exhortation on the pastoral ministry of the ordained priest, *Pastores Dabo Vobis* (I Will Give You Shepherds) he continues to emphasise that: "It is within the Church's mystery, as a mystery of Trinitarian communion... that every Christian identity is revealed, and likewise the specific identity of the priest and his ministry."[310] By this he means that the identity of the priest is an identity of unity, fundamentally relational, uniting him with all other priests and the laity. He makes the same recommendation for the pastoral ministry of bishops, where he writes that: "As pastors...we have the task of gathering together the family of the faithful and in it fostering charity and brotherly communion."[311]

In his Apostolic Letter *Novo Millennio Inuente*, in preparation for the new Millennium of the year 2000, he proposes a spirituality of communion as the way of deepening ecclesial unity in every context and at every level. He writes that: "To make the Church the home of communion and school of communion... we need to promote a spirituality of communion, making it the guiding principle of education wherever individuals and Christians are formed,

307 John Paul II, Apostolic Exhortation *Christifideles Laici* (*Vocation and Mission of the Lay Faithful*), 1st reprint, Nairobi, Paulines Publications Africa, 1998, n. 19: *AAS* 81 (1989), p. 422.

308 Ibid., n. 20: *AAS* 81 (1989), pp. 425-427.

309 Ibid., n. 8: *AAS* 81 (1989), p. 405.

310 John Paul II, Post-Synodal Apostolic Exhortation *Pastores Dabo Vobis* (*I Will Give You Shepherds*), Nairobi, Paulones Publications Africa, 1998, n. 12 §2: *AAS* 84 (1992), p. 675.

311 Idem., Post-Synodal Apostolic Exhortation *Pastores Gregis* (*Bishops: Shepherds of the Lord's Flock*), Nairobi, Paulines Publications Africa, 2003, n. 5 § 2: *AAS* 96 (2004), pp. 829-830.

wherever ministers of the altar, consecrated persons, and pastoral workers are trained, wherever families and communities are being built up."[312]

Following Pope John Paul II, Pope Benedict XVI highlights, in his Post-Synodal Exhortation *Africae Munus* (Africa's Commitment), five conditions for a spirituality of communion: (a) the ability to perceive the light of the mystery of the Trinity shining on the faces of brothers and sisters around us; (b) to be attentive to our brothers and sisters as part of ourselves and to offer them deep and genuine friendship; (c) to acknowledge others as channels of divine graces; (d) to resist the selfish temptations which constantly beset us and provoke competition, careerism, distrust and jealousy; (e) to practice self-denial that opens us to the needs of others.[313] This will promote the virtue of solidarity.

3.2.2.2. Solidarity

Christian solidarity refers to the gratuity of love. In his Encyclical Letter, *Solicitudo Rei Socialis* (On Social Concern), Pope John Paul II defines solidarity in terms of interdependence, a system determining relationships among people; it is a moral and social virtue understood as charity. According to him, solidarity "…is not a feeling of vague compassion or shallow distress at the misfortunes of so many people, both near and far. On the contrary, it is a firm and persevering determination to commit oneself to the common good; that is to say to the good of all and of each individual, because we are all really responsible for all."[314] He continues to explain that: "Solidarity is undoubtedly a Christian virtue… In the light of faith, solidarity seeks to go beyond itself, to take on the specifically Christian dimension of total gratuity, forgiveness and reconciliation."[315] With reference to Africa, in his Post-Synodal Apostolic Exhortation, *Ecclesia in Africa,* he appreciates the spirit of solidarity but cautions against the temptation of individualism which might dilute this traditional value: "Africans have an acute sense of solidarity and community life… It is my ardent hope and prayer that Africa will always preserve this priceless cultural heritage and never succumb to the temptation of individualism, which is so alien to its best traditions."[316]

312 John Paul II, Apostolic Letter *Novo Millennio Ineunte*, Vatican City, Libreria Editrice Vaticana, 2001, n. 43: *AAS* 93 (2001), pp. 296-297.

313 Benedict XVI, Post-Synodal Apostolic Exhortation *Africae Munus* (Africa's Commitment), Nairobi, Paulines Publications Africa, 2011, n. 35: *AAS* 104 (6 April 2012), p. 257.

314 John Paul II, Encyclical Letter *Solicitudo Rei Socialis* (*On Social Concern*), Boston, St. Paul Books & Media, 1995, n. 38: *AAS* 80 (1988), pp. 565-566.

315 Ibid., n. 40: *AAS* 80 (1988), p. 568.

316 John Paul II, Post-Synodal Apostolic Exhortation *Ecclesial in Africa* (The Church in Africa), Nairobi, Paulines Publications Africa, 1995, n. 43 § 2: *AAS* 88 (1995), p. 28.

The Catechism calls solidarity a *communion in charity*: "In this solidarity with all men, living or dead, which is founded on the communion of saints, the least of our acts done in charity redounds to the profit of all. Every sin harms this communion."[317] The Catechism clarifies that the virtue of solidarity is not primarily about material goods although it leads to them: "Solidarity is an eminently Christian virtue. It practices the sharing of spiritual goods even more than material ones."[318] The basic theological notion is Christian communion, the belief that all men and women are sons and daughters of the same God: we are one people of God and belong to the one family of God. Solidarity finds expression through charity which gives it a living testimony.

3.2.2.3. Charity

Here we are using the term *charity* synonymously with *love*. Charity is a cementing factor to ecclesial life. Häring defines Christian loving as joining God in his fatherly love for all people.[319] Christian charity is primarily the loving spirit which will enable the believer to communicate God's love. It corrects and perfects such obscure philanthropic terms like 'fraternity,' 'class' or 'party solidarity,' 'equality' or 'citizenship' even if they may find religious expressions. Under these very same terms people have fallen prey to others through subjection and victimisation; under such mocking terms like 'relief *aids*' or 'liberation' clandestine hands have worked out more complex sufferings with daunting psychological agonies.

In his study on the principles of social ethics, Spiazzi illustrates that charity is a core relational principle.[320] He identifies five characteristics of Christian charity: *(a) Objectivity of love*, oriented toward the research and pursuit of the objective good over and above all the mechanisms of egoism; *(b) Gratuity of love*, which is detached and disinterested, by which giving is a self-giving in view of eternal life, not conditioned by harsh demands which imprison others; *(c) Love as oblation*, signifying self-dedication, devotion and service to others, beyond all limitations and divisions set by the antagonism between power and right; *(d) The interiority of love*, by which is established an intimate and profound communion with God and among believers. It gives rise to every form of external relationship; *(e) Generosity of love*, which is of itself creative and generative in giving, not because something is asked for but a willing readiness

317 *CCC*, n. 953.

318 Ibid., n. 1948, 1942.

319 Häring, *Free and Faithful in Christ*, Vol. 1, p. 210.

320 Raimondo Spiazzi, *Principi di Etica Sociale*, Bologna, Edizioni Stuio Domenicano, 1990, pp. 131.

like in almsgiving to rectify a real situation, cooperation in carrying out a task, forgiving, and good deeds. It is this love which can lead to conversion which turns hearts toward one another.

3.3. Christian Conversion

Häring defines Christian conversion as "...the ongoing activation of creative freedom and fidelity in Christ."[321] Christian conversion is however wide-ranging and engages the believer in countless ways all through life. Here we shall look at six aspects of conversion: cultural, intellectual, moral, religious, affective and social. In his book, *Method in Theology*, Lonergan identifies three aspects of conversion: intellectual, moral and religious.[322] Following Lonergan, Conn, in his book, *Christian Conversion*, adds two other aspects: affective and social.[323] In his book, *Catholic Moral Tradition*, David Bohr treats it in four perspectives: religious, intellectual, affective, and moral. Our field study has suggested to us another important aspect: cultural conversion, with which we shall begin.

Cultural conversion is the transformation of cultural models in the light of Christ. First, cultural conversion has a dialogical import where the Church is to present Christ and Gospel values with a liberating power. In his Post-Synodal Apostolic Exhortation, *Pastores Dabo Vobis*, on the formation of priests in the context of contemporary social-cultural realities, Pope John Paul II rejects reducing the Christian message to a mere alternative religion or social ethic. He writes that:

> There are spiritual and religious values in today's culture, and man, notwithstanding appearances to the contrary, cannot help but hunger and thirst for God. However, the Christian religion is often regarded as just one religion among many or reduced to nothing more than a social ethic at the service of man. As a result its amazing novelty in human history is often not apparent. It is a "mystery," the event of the coming of the Son of God who becomes man and gives to those who welcome him the "power to become the children of God" (Jn. 1:12). It is the proclamation, nay the gift of a personal covenant of love and life between God and man.[324]

---

321 Häring, *Free and Faithful in Christ*, Vol. 1, p. 378.

322 Lonergan, pp. 238-243.

323 Walter Conn, *Christian Conversion: A Developmental Interpretation of Autonomy and Surrender*, New York, Paulist Press, 1986.

324 *PdV*, n. 46 § 3: *AAS* 84 (1992), pp. 738-739.

Secondly, cultural conversion deserves attention in the process of inculturation, namely, the attempt to impart Gospel values in the unique cultural contexts in view of the problem of cultural incompatibility in the Church. According to Nkéramihigo:

> To achieve the inculturation of Christianity, it is necessary to develop a theology fundamentally Christological, and hence capable of arbitrating the conflict among cultures. It seems to me that Christianity is capable of providing the criterion which will facilitate the meeting of different cultures in the same field of appreciation... The revelation of God in Christ forbids any culture to set itself as a norm or model, and thus to verify in Christ the idea of God which it has developed on the basis of its cosmology, anthropology or history... The perfect *knowledge* of God proceeds therefore, for all peoples, from the unique Christological anthropology.[325]

Thirdly, cultural conversion discerns, purifies and elevates the man and woman of a culture and its values. According to Bohr, Christian conversion is the transformation of the whole person: "Conversion happens when we allow God's all-merciful, reconciling love to transform us into a whole new creation... We let him raise us up in Christ to new life... Conversion is a turnabout from the alienating effects of sin, from the self-satisfaction of mere existence subjected to the law of entropy and spiritual inertia."[326]

Religious conversion: creates the desire and thirst for ultimate meaning and love, the longing for true happiness; but this happiness grows in the present community. First, religious conversion means accepting to live from the fatherhood of God and practicing the Trinitarian life in the present community. Lonergan writes that: "Conversion is existential, intensely personal, utterly intimate. But it is not so private as to be solitary."[327] Secondly, religious conversion means embracing the values that energise and perfect the unity of life. In this context, McBrien points out that the "*final test* of religious conversion is whether or not it leads to and is continually manifested in *love for the neighbor.*"[328]

Intellectual conversion: according to the definition given by Walter Conn, it is the transforming of our worldview or imaginative perception that has shaped our life until now. Intellectual development affects our spiritual as well

325 Théoneste Nkéramihigo, "Inculturation and the Specificity of Christian Faith" in J. M. Waliggo, et al., *Inculturation: Its Meaning and Urgency*, Kampala, St. Paul Publications Africa, 1986, p. 72, italic his.

326 Bohr, p. 112.

327 Lonergan, pp. 130-131.

328 Richard P. McBrien, *Catholicism*, Study Edition, New York, HarperSanFrancsico, 1981, p. 963. Italic his.

as our moral life. This development moves through the stages of enthusiasm, to idealisation and reaches maturity at the stage of personal process where we bring to life those values which we have internalised.[329] This means that intellectual conversion is to bring faith and reason to work together in our choices and decisions, which must lead to good actions.

Affective conversion: helps us to get out of self-absorption and self-contemplation. A good explanation of the affect is given by Robeck where he writes about the human soul (Hebrew, *nephesh*), denoting the "self," filled with emotions, appetites and volition:

> By extrapolation *nephesh* can be used to refer to the seat of spiritual as well as physical needs and cravings… *Nephesh* can also be used in a more comprehensive sense to denote the seat of emotions and experiences. The *nephesh* may be sad… grieved… or in pain… and it may weep… It may be distressed… bitter… or troubled… it may tremble… The *nephesh* can also hate… On the other hand, it can rejoice… be cheered… bless the Lord… and love… Thus the term is associated with a full range of needs, desires, and feelings, as well as with thought and memory… The nephesh appears frequently not as the possession of *adam* but as what *adam* is.[330]

In other words, the affect as soul (*nephesh*) referring to the human person, can represent the totality of feeling. Porteous links the understanding of the human soul with expressions found in the New Testament: "… *nephesh* (soul) can represent the totality of feeling (Ex. 23:24). The *nephesh* hungers, and thirsts; is greedy; is satisfied; feels joy, sorrow, love, hatred, hope, despair, etc… It is used as the subject of emotions in Mk. 14:34; Lk. 1:46; Jn. 12:27."[331] It is here clear that the affect can lead to socialising egoistic feelings.

Affective conversion therefore calls for moving away from self-absorption to a self-giving love. It helps to direct one's positive feelings or intentional responses to an ongoing practice of charity. Bohr writes that: "The affective dimension of Christian love involves a movement away from narcissistic love to a self-giving love. Such conversion or movement requires of the disciple that he or she turn away from those attitudes, dispositions, and vices which make loving relationships and community unattainable."[332]

---

329 Conn, p. 116ff.

330 C. M. Robeck, Jr., "Soul," in *ISBE*, Vol. 4, pp. 587a-588a. Biblical references are omitted, shown by (…).

331 Porteous N. W., "Soul," in George Arthur Buttrick (ed.), *The Interpreter's Dictionary of the Bible: An Illustrated Encyclopedia, R - Z*, Vol. 4, 13th printing, Nashville, Abingdon Press, 1982, p. 429a.

332 Bohr, *Catholic Moral Tradition*, pp. 132-133.

Moral conversion: is defined by McBrien as the recognition of oneself as a free and responsible subject.[333] The value of the life of faith in the 'new creation' cannot be reduced just to Sunday observance alone. God's order of charity must be sought and applied in all spheres of the religious, cultural, social, economic and political life. Moral conversion is a shift from the level of thought and feeling to that of decision and action. It turns attention from personal satisfaction to values, especially inasmuch as we experience people as values and act to make them flourish.

Social conversion: can be attained through the will and decision to enhance our relationships. Häring writes that: "There is important interplay between the identity of the individual and the up-building of a healthy community and society. All the patterns of cooperation that foster love, and everything that provides grounds for fidelity and creative freedom, enrich our total milieu and strengthens our good disposition."[334] Understood thus, social conversion integrates and widens the cultural, intellectual, religious, affective and moral horizons.

An illustration of social conversion has been made by Pope John Paul II, where he calls the Church to make an examination of conscience and purify its memory of the past.[335] In his Apostolic Letter, *Tertio Millennio Adveniente* (On Preparation for the Jubilee of the Year 2000) he appeals to the universal Church to acknowledge and make reparation for the faults committed in the past by the sons and daughters of the Church.[336] He repeats the same appeal in the Bull of Indiction of the Great Jubilee Year 2000, *Incarnationis Mysterium* (Mystery of Salvation).[337] He brings social conversion to bear on the life within the Church itself with a focus on unity. This is spelt out in his Post-Synodal Apostolic Exhortation, *Ecclesia in America* (The Church in America) where he links it with fraternal charity, which must help to improve relationships between sectors, institutions and groups in the Church. Here he uses the New Testament word *metanoia*, with reference to a change of mentality: "It is not simply a matter of thinking in an intellectual sense, but of revising the rea-

---

333 McBrien, p. 962.

334 Häring, *Free and Faithful in Christ*, Vol. 1, p. 154.

335 Cf. Luigi Accattoli, *When a Pope Asks Forgiveness: The Mea Culpa's of John Paul II*, translated by Jordan Aumann, Boston, Pauline Books & Media, 1998, pp. xv-xxiv.

336 John Paul II, Apostolic Letter *Tertio Millennio Adveniente* (On Preparation for the Jubilee of the Year 2000), Boston, Pauline Books & Media, 1994, nn. 33-34: *AAS* 87 (1995), pp. 25-27.

337 John Paul II, Bull of Indiction of the great Jubilee year 2000 *Incarnationis Mysterium* (29 November 1998), Rome, Libreria Editrice Vaticana, n. 11: AAS (1999), p. 139.

sons behind one's actions in the light of the Gospel."[338] He continues to clarify that personal conversion is incomplete without the social dimension where we must strive to meet the demands of the Christian life in a variety of ways.[339]

Further reflection on the significance of social conversion has been made by the International Theological Commission in its document, *Memory and Reconciliation*. Here mention is made, that Christians have an objective responsibility by which all share in the wrongs of other Christians through solidarity.[340] They are encouraged to live in such a way as to show others the true face of the living God. This will come about through the practice of fidelity to Christ, unity in the Church, solidarity among believers and with the world, and bearing witness to the Gospel both in word and action.[341]

In summary, the point we have tried to make here is that conversion is an important Christian value which provides the possibility not only for building up but also to strength the ecclesial communion that has already been made. As Gula writes, Christian conversion is to bring the believer to live with a new spirit, the spirit of Christ.[342] It is this spirit that will make of the believer a truly human and truly Christian person. It is this spirit that will sustain the Church.

Conclusion

This chapter has highlighted three theological foundations upon which Christian communitarian values stand. It presented the Trinity as the source of Christian communion from which the Church takes its name. The second point illustrated that the Creed is not an empty recital but has a social appeal that can help for building ecclesial communion in practical ways. Thirdly, we have argued that conversion can help to open every believer to a deeper appreciation of the mysteries of Salvation to perfect God's providential gifts in them. It is conversion that leads to a true and creative freedom. The following chapter will discuss individidualism, the main subject of this dissertation.

338 John Paul II, *Ecclesia in America* (The Church in America), Vatican translation, Boston, Pauline Books & Media, 1999, n. 26: *AAS* 91 (1999), p. 761.

339 Ibid., n. 27: *AAS* 91 (1999), p. 761.

340 International Theological Commission, *Memory and Reconciliation: The Church and the Faults of the Past* (December 1999) published together with the *Homily of John Paul II: Mass for the Day of Pardon* (12 March 2000), Vatican translation, Boston, Pauline Books & Media, 2000, 5.1.

341 Ibid., n. 5.5 § 3

342 Gula, p. 100.

CHAPTER FOUR
An Ethical Analysis of Individualism

Introduction

This chapter makes an ethical analysis of individualism. The different sources cited will help to express our research finding in Nebbi Catholic Diocese. This is discussed under four main points. First, what individualism means. Second, the expressive forms it takes in the Church. Third, what might be causing, or provoking, or accentuating individualism. Fourth, there is an assessment of how it affects the moral life of both the individual and, through the individual, taking a community outlook.

4.1. The Meaning of Individualism

Out of 287 questionnaire responses, 173 (60%) described individualism commonly as a behaviour or way of life by which one distances oneself from others.[343] Out of 113 persons interviewed orally, 87 (77%) described it generally as a selfish manipulation of common meaning, aspiration, values, vision and consensus.[344] The general notion depicts the dissociating of oneself from others. It is cold and repulsive towards communal life. This has been explained as an antithesis or resistance to solidarity. Solidarity has been explained as: standing together, joining hands, supporting one another, common strength, sharing of resources. Intensely understood, individualism poses a radical moral problem which goes to the heart of community life. For the Alur this means *lalu waat*, undoing, disjoining, rifting apart, breaking the cord of kinship; and *nyotho waat*, corrupting, spoiling, destroying (the spirit of) kinship. It gives blind reasons for one to absent oneself from habitual participation in communal activities like eating together, sharing, burial, helping those in need, or coming together to solve community problems. We can link this with Schindler's definition, that individualism is a "loosening of the individual-community connection."[345]

---

343 See Appendix 1 and 2 of this work.

344 Appendix 3.

345 Schindler, *Ethics: The Social Dimension*, p. 45, and p. 57.

According to Clérel, individualism is that spirit in which one's feelings are turned in on oneself.[346] He clarifies this by distinguishing between individualism and egoism:

> Egoism is a passionate and exaggerated love of self which leads a man to think of all things in terms of himself and to prefer himself to all. Individualism is a calm and considered feeling which disposes each citizen to isolate himself from the mass of his fellows and withdraw into the circle of family and friends; with this little society formed to his taste, he gladly leaves the greater society to look after itself.[347]

For Clérel, egoism or selfishness comes from a blind instinct; individualism derives from a misguided judgment than from depraved feeling. While egoism sterilises the seeds of every virtue; individualism at first only sucks out the spring of public virtues, but in the long run it attacks and destroys all others too and finally merges in egoism. McClay comments that Alexis understood individualism as a conscious and calculated withdrawal from the responsibilities of citizenship and public life.[348] This clarification shows that individualism is an attitude, a mental predisposition, arising as much from deficiencies of mind as perversity of heart. It is therefore not an unconscious occurrence; but meditated because it involves one's decision and choice to act in such a manner.

In the 1910 *Catholic Encyclopedia*, individualism is described as: "…the tendency to magnify individual liberty, as against external authority, and individual activity, as against associated activity… through all forms of individualism runs the note of emphasis upon the importance of *self* in opposition to either restraint or assistance from without."[349] By "external authority" is meant all legitimate institutions that serve to regulate communal life. Thus, the problem revolves around personal freedom, by which someone chooses and acts with minimal or no regard for what those choices and actions might mean to

346 Adler Mortimer J. (ed.), *Great Books of the Western World*, Vol. 44: *Tocqueville*, translated by George Lawrence, Chicago, Encyclopedia Britannica, Inc., 2nd edition, Ninth Printing, 2007, p. 271a.

347 Ibid.

348 Wilfred M. McClay, "Individualism," in *First Principles*, ISI Web Journal, Intercollegiate Studies Institute, Wilmington, 03/13/08. Electronic text downloaded from Website: http://www.firstprinciplesjournal.aspx?article=144&loc=b&type=cbtp (accessed, 11th June 2010).

349 John Ryan Augustine, "Individualism," in *The Catholic Encyclopedia, Vol. 7*, New York, Robert Appleton Company, 1910; electronic text on: http://www.newadvent.org/cathen/07761a.htm (accessed, 13 June 2010).

others. This portrays individualism as a tendency inasmuch as it is a habitual behaviuor; and yet, it is more than a tendency by the way it presents itself as a conscious and willfull disposition.

4.1.1. Indications in the Bible

Is the Bible silent on individualism? Is there no pointer to it? In the *Encyclopedia of Catholicism*, Kenan argues that:

> The rise of modern individualism owes something to the historical Christian emphasis on the sanctity and dignity of the person (cf. Matt 10:30), though the often exaggerated distinction drawn by modern individualism between the individual and community – particularly in the moral, social, and economic spheres – is inconsistent with the traditional Christian belief in the inherently social nature of the person, the unity of humankind, and the ultimate dependence of the individual upon God.[350]

Biblical study seems to suggest that the problem found expression. Shinn tries to illustrate the images from both the Old and New Testaments that might contribute to individualistic impulses. Although he notes that earlier Old Testament sources emphasised the 'corporate personality' of the tribe or of Israel, he nevertheless makes the following observations: (a) the call for fidelity and personal decision came to distinguish the individual from the society; (b) the hope for the nation became the hope for a remnant; (c) the punishment of the family or tribe for the sins of some of its members gave way to law that fixed guilt and responsibility upon individuals (e.g., Deut. 24:16); (d) while the prophets felt solidarity with their people, they became lonely in their alienation from their kin, as with Jeremiah (Jer. 15:17, "I sat alone") and his writings, with a pitch of self-awareness never expressed before; (e) Ezekiel (18:1-4) stresses personal responsibility to the extent of an unreal denial of social solidarity; (f) the exilic and post-exilic psalmists frequently showed a penetrating quality of introspection and recognition of inner life of the individual; (g) late Jewish eschatology transferred the place of hope from the historical society, in which persons found gratification, and by anticipation, to a consummation in which each person would participate and be judged individually.

Shinn continues to argue that the same Hebrew concept of the person continues in the New Testament: Jesus taught that God numbers the hairs on the heads of persons; there is more joy in heaven over one repentant sinner than over ninety-nine who show no repentance; an act done to "one of the least of

350 Osborne B. Kenan, "Individualism," in Richard P. McBrien (ed.), *The HarperCollins Encyclopedia of Catholicism*, 1st edition, New York, HarperCollins Publishers Inc., 1995, p. 622b.

these my brethren" is done to God. However, Christ is not an individualist; there is a clear distinction in him:

> Jesus himself went to his lonely death on the cross. Yet the NT interprets this solitary man as representative person, suffering and conquering sin for all. He teaches and exemplifies love. He calls persons, not into solitary devotion, but into a community of faith. His followers understand themselves as the household of God, as the body of Christ, as a holy nation.[351]

There are certain technical words in Scripture whose usage seems to bring to a better focus the reality of individualism, as illustrated in what follows.

4.1.1.1. Old Testament

In biblical language individualism can be explained by the term *ambition*,[352] which links to a range of similar words like antinomism,[353] selfish, selfishness,[354] self-will, self-rivalry or wanton. The term *wanton* is understood in its intensive as "desire of a desire." It is an unchecked desire by which someone is bent in on oneself; it makes one insensitive to what one's action might bring upon others. McDonald writes that: "The terms that are translated "wanton" and its derivatives in the OT and the NT often refer to actions that are both selfish and contrary to the will of God, whether by direct opposition to Yahweh through idolatrous actions or in senseless and willful harm of human beings (2 Ch. 28:19) or animals (Gen. 49:6)."[355] These words and their derivatives portray an ungenerous self-seeking. From this we can highlight a few examples to exemplify how individuals can bend community values and concerns to their own selfish interests.

A *selfish ambition* is described in 1 Samuel 2:11-36, which sets a contrast between Samuel and the sons of the priest Eli at Shiloh. Samuel acts honestly in performing religious services to Yahweh; he thus wins divine and human approval. On the contrary, the sons of Eli and their attendants debase the priestly office through extortion of the best parts of meat brought as sacrifice to Yahweh. By doing this, they: (a) place their welfare or self-care above the demands

351 Roger Shinn L., "Individualism" in *NDCE*, pp. 295-297, quotation from p. 296.

352 Cf. A. J. Birkey, "Ambition," in *ISBE*, Vol. 1, p. 110.

353 Cf. A. S. Wood, "Antinomism," in *ibid*., pp. 141-142. The word *antinomy* derives from Greek *anti*, "against," and *nomos*, "law," basically meaning "against law" or "opposed to law."

354 R. A. Gwin, "Selfish; Selfishness," in *idem*, Vol. 4, p. 387. Here *selfishness* has three shades of meaning in the Bible: the Greek, *poneros*, "evil, wicked;" *eritheia*, "selfish ambition; (personal) rivalry;" *acharistos*, "ungrateful, not returning good deeds."

355 L. M. McDonagh, "Wanton," in *ISBE*, Vol. 4, p. 1013.

of the priestly office; (b) act contemptuously with the faithful; (c) despise Yahweh to whom such sacrifices are made by the faithful. De Vaux comments that: "The fault of Eli's sons lay, not in taking their portion of meat, but in demanding the meat raw... they were thus serving themselves before serving Yahweh."[356] Here we can understand individualism, in the religious sense, as impiety, acting unjustly towards God. The same book, 1 Sam. 8:3, reports that the sons of Samuel, whom he appoints to act as auxiliary judges close to himself, do not follow his examples but instead seek unlawful gains, accept bribery and pervert justice. It is this greedy self-seeking of Samuel's sons, coupled with Samuel's old age and ineffective leadership, which provoke the people to ask Samuel for a king. Turro comments that: "The people's request for a king was not only a wish to emulate the other nations but also a desire for effective leadership to meet the challenge of other nations."[357] These two examples both illustrate one thing is common, that such practices arise from self-seeking and, as Bohr observes, individualism creates moral corruption that goes to the heart of life, that is, a spirit of social irresponsibility and moral degeneration.[358] It is clear from this to see that the action of an individual, or a group of like-minded individuals, can affect others as well: individualism creates an institutional or structural social injustice.

4.1.1.2. New Testament

In the New Testament there are two antithetical Greek words, *philotimeomai*, "be fond of honour" and *eritheia*, "self-seeking ambition," distinguishing between that spirit by which one is disposed towards community building and the contrary self-bent spirit. The word *ambition* distinguishes between a generous will and a selfish will. It translates the Greek term *philotimeomai*, which denotes sacrifice through self-giving: a generous and pioneering ambition, with the aim of achieving a particular goal.[359] In Rom. 15:20, St. Paul uses the word to express his "eagerly striving" or "aspiring" to take the Gospel where Christ is not yet known.[360] The contrary word, *eritheia*, refers to that ambition which is motivated by selfishness. Jas. 3:14, 16, touches the core of individual-

356 Roland de Vaux, *Ancient Israel: Its Life and Institutions*, translated by John McHugh, Second edition, reprint, London, Darton, Longman and Todd Ltd., 1998, p. 379.

357 James C. Turro, "1-2 Samuel," in Raymond E. Brown, Joseph A. Fitzmyer, Roland E. Murhpy (eds.), *The Jerusalem Bible Commentary*, Vol. 1: *The Old Testament*, reprint, London, Geoffrey Chapman, 1972, p. 168a.

358 Bohr, p. 47.

359 A. J. Birkey, *op. cit.*

360 *The Interlinear NIV Parallel New Testament in Greek and English*, translated by Alfred Marshal, Michigan, Zondervan Publishing House, 1998, p. 650; *The New Greek-English Inter-*

ism, where ambition is motivated by "rivalry" and "selfishness" in the heart; it yields disharmony.[361] This shows that individualism arises from selfish ambition, which corrupts not only one's attitude and character but also affects one's decisions and choices, and one's relational aptitude as well.

St. James continues to show in his Epistle a practice of partiality in the community of believers, where influential or rich members are treated with honour while the poor and lowly are held in low esteem and despisal. He writes: "My brothers, do not let class distinction enter into your faith in Jesus Christ, our glorified Lord... In making this distinction among yourselves have you not used a corrupt standard?" (Jas. 2:1-4). The main problem he confronts is the attitude towards members of the community. For him, it is faith that defines their status before God. Class distinction seems to portray *categorical* (treating one another according to category) or group individualism, which can become a systematic mechanism of sidelining others, and eventually, working itself into a structural problem.

An illustration that depicts group egoism is reported in Acts 6:1-5 between Greek-speaking (Hellenists) and Hebrew- or Aramaic-speaking groups. The Hellenists complain that their widows are being sidelined in the distribution of charity collections.[362] The "Twelve" convene a community meeting at which the problem is resolved by appointing seven men as administrators. The Twelve occupy themselves with prayer and preaching while the Seven serve as deacons in the distribution of charity collections to the needy of the community. The problem is, however, not solved by a symbolic presence, by merely choosing men from both sides as group representatives; the assessment is based on the work of the Holy Spirit. All the Seven have Hebrew names, not Greek. They are approved by the whole group as men of good faith and reputation. What this account brings to light is a sectarian problem where one group wants to keep another or other groups at a distance. It illustrates the problem of group ego that works itself into a systematic marginalisation of one group by another.

In 1 Cor. 1: 10-13, St. Paul confronts another community situation where members are forming groups around personalities. He makes this appeal:

---

linear New Testament, translated by Robert K. Brown and Philip W. Comfort, edited by J. D. Douglas, Illinois, Tyndale House Publishers, Inc., 1990, p. 573.

361 *The Interlinear NIV Parallel New Testament in Greek and English*, p. 902-902; *The Greek-English Interlinear New Testament*, p. 802.

362 Justo L. González, *Acts: The Gospel of the Spirit*, Maryknoll, Orbis Books, 2001, pp. 88-94, elaborates on the problem in the context of justice. The central theme that runs throughout this book is that the Church today can learn from the early Church how to manage its material, human and pastoral resources to achieve greater fruits.

> I urge you, in the name of our Lord Jesus Christ, not to have factions among yourselves but all to be in agreement in what you profess; so that you are perfectly united in your beliefs and judgments... what I mean is this: everyone of you is declaring, 'I belong to Paul,' or 'I belong to Apollos,' or 'I belong to Christ.' Has Christ been split up? Was it Paul that was crucified for you, or was it in Paul's name that you were baptised?

This problem is sectarian in nature, namely, a split (schism) which threatens community progress. Robert Banks observes that: "Rather than referring to divisions between churches, schism for Paul designates division within a single community. It results, he says, either from a lack of agreement with one another or from a lack of care for one another (1 Cor. 1:12; 11:21) and is one of the works of the "flesh" (Gal. 5:20)."[363] So, we see in this that rejection or sidelining can cause division or split in ecclesial life. These examples show that both the Old and New Testaments, Pastoral Letters, and common practice in early Christian communities, do not give room for the self-seeking spirit because it can kill community spirit.

The Second Letter of St. Paul to Timothy shows how individualism is a distortion of self-love, a love misdirected in the heart. He cautions Timothy to take note of people who are "lovers of their own selves," whom he describes as: self-lovers, money-lovers, boasters, arrogant, blasphemers, disobedient to parents, unthankful, unholy, without natural affection, implacable, slanderers, incontinent, untamed, haters of good (things, people and common interest), betrayers, reckless, puffed up, pleasure-lovers rather than God-lovers. St. Paul observes that such people betray or mock piety and deny its power by the way they behave (cf. 2 Tim. 3:1-5).[364] Commenting on this text, St. Augustine writes that this "self-love" (an insatiable self-seeking) is the single fountain from which flows all forms of sinfulness; it is the root cause of all evils in the Church.[365] He argues this in contrast to what Chirstian love demands, drawing from the dialogue between Jesus and Peter (Jn. 21:12-19): "Do you love me?" a question repeated three times to which Peter answers: "I love you." John places this episode as an epilogue to his Gospel, an appendage after the actual

363 Robert J. Banks, *Paul's idea of Community: The Early House Churches in Their Cultural Setting*, revised edition, sixth printing, Peabody, Hendrickson Publishers, 2007, p. 65.

364 *The Interlinear Greek-English New Testament: The Nestle Greek Text with a Literal English Translation*, 3rd edition, London, Samuel Bagster and Sons Limited, 1974, p. 840.

365 St. Augustine, "Lectures or Tractate on the Gospel According to St. John: Tractate 123, John 21:10-15," translated by Rev. John Gibb and Rev. James Innes, in *A Select Library of the Christian, Nicene and Post-Nicene Fathers*, First Series, Vol. 7, *Augustin: Homilies on the Gospel of John, Homilies on the First Epistle of John, Soliloquies*, 4th printing, Peabody, Hendrickson Publishers, 2004, p. 445-446.

conclusion. Jesus wants to pass on to his disciples the most central thing – *love* – which will distinguish them as his disciples.

From what we have said here we may deduce that individualism is not lacking in the Old and New Testament as well as the Pastoral Letters. However, it is to be understood as an antithesis to God's love. Nevertheless, it remains a deeply anthropological problem which the Church cannot avoid to address. Scripture testifies that there are actions by which individuals, and through them like-minded groups, can work against commonly held values and aspirations and in this way can block community progress; it does this by taking away from the community what it direly needs for its life and continuity.

4.1.2. Anthropological Perspective

From what we have discussed above, it becomes clear that individualism is a human problem, but with a moral impact. It is a *problem* because it impedes progress. Giussani analyses this human problem under the categories of culture, love, work and identity.[366] The *cultural* horizon relates to the search for truth and meaning of reality. The question here lies in what one conceives of oneself as a human person and one's destiny; and how one seeks to mobilise and utilise the elements of one's own existence. In this context, bending to oneself alone can condense into a patterned system or structure that becomes a way of life. The question of *love* or affectivity or identity is the quest to arrive at a satisfying personal completeness, given one's experience in the world. In the dimension of *work*, through one's initiatives and creativity, one wants to express one's personality, and hopes to make an impress upon the reality of time and space, given the possibilities open to them, their potentialities and capabilities. The *political* aspect refers to human co-existence, in the attempt to organise, to shape and carry forward this co-existence on a more comprehensive and complex level. However, from all this arise tension and unease, conflict and compromise, ambiguity and uncertainty. The dilemma is whether one could arrive at cultural fulfillment, or grow in love, or advance in one's work, or make political progress in isolation. This is elaborated below.

4.1.3. Psycho-Moral Aspect

Individualism poses not only a moral problem but it also has a psychological impact inasmuch as it affects both the relational attitude and behavioural pattern of an individual. In his book, *The Heresy of Self-Love*, Zweig calls

366 Luigi Giussani, *Why the Church?* Montreal, McGill-Queen's University Press, 2001, pp. 154-155. Giussani is an Italian priest and educator, founder of the international Catholic movement, *Communion and Liberation* (*CCL*: Christ is Communion and Life).

individualism a "public privacy" because it is a subversive socialisation of one's ego.[367] This illustrates that individualism does not operate only at the individual level.

Nisbet argues that individualism is a "menacing current" against a communitarian conscience, throwing one back upon oneself and threatening in the end to confine someone entirely within the solitude of one's own heart.[368] He writes: "If there is any single root meaning of the word individualism, it lies in the notion of the discreet being, of I-am-myself-alone-free-of-all-bonds."[369] Although Nisbet writes in the North American context his reflection shows that individualism as such weakens community life.

In the general introduction of this study, we have stated that our enquiry is whether individualism could be found in the Church in Africa, with specific reference to Nebbi Catholic Diocese. The reflection of Pope John Paul II suggests that individualism can be found in the Church. In a General Audience to priests, he stated that the priestly life cannot achieve its purpose without renouncing individualism:

> Like the apostles, bishops and priests too are called together... This community of vocation doubtless implies an openness of one to the other and of each to all, so as to live and work in communion. This does not occur without renouncing an ever real, recurring individualism, without achieving self-denial in the victory of charity over selfishness.[370]

He refers to the ordained priest as belonging to a community of vocation, which cannot be fully realised in isolation. His ministry is a consecration to the service and growth of the Church.

Renouncing individualism is not restricted to the ordained ministers of the Church. A similar expression is found in the Pope's Letter to Families, *Nuntius*. This document is an explicit acknowledgment and response to the declaration of the year 1994 as the Year of the Family, made by the United Nations Organisation. Of individualism he writes:

> Individualism presupposes a use of freedom in which the subject does what he wants, in which he himself is the one to "establish the truth" of whatever he

367 Zweig, *The Heresy of Self-Love*, p. ix.

368 Nisbet, *Prejudices*, p. 184.

369 Ibid., p. 186.

370 John Paul II, General Audience of Wednesday, 4th August 1993, "Priests: Union with their Bishops and their Fellow Priests," in James P. Socias (compiler), *Priesthood in the Third Millennium: Addresses of Pope John Paul II 1993*, Princeton, Scepter Publishers, 1994, p. 104; also Giovanni Paolo II, *Udienza Generale*, Mercoledì, 4 agosto 1993, Cità del Vaticano, Libreria Editrice Vaticana, 1993, n. 2 § 2.

> finds pleasing or useful. He does not tolerate the fact that someone else "wants" or demands something from him in the name of an objective truth. He does not want to "give" to another on the basis of truth; he does not want to become a "sincere gift."[371]

In this Letter, individualism is understood as a falsification of freedom, and of the truth of being human. It is the denial of a sincere self-giving which weakens the family institution upon which both the Church and society stand.

Again, in the Post-Synodal Apostolic Exhortation, *Pastores Gregis*, addressed to Bishops as Pastors of the Church, he rejects individualism because it can weaken the apostolic communion enjoyed by all the Bishops of the Catholic Church. He writes: "The apostolic aspect of obedience is necessarily linked also to its communitarian aspect... As a result of this communal dimension, the bishop is called to live out his obedience by overcoming all temptations to individualism and by taking upon himself, within the wider context of the mission of the college of bishops, concern for the good of the whole Church."[372] This Exhortation follows the Tenth Ordinary General Assembly of the Synod of Bishops (held in Rome, 30th September – 27th October 2001) under the theme: "The Bishop: Servant of the Gospel of Jesus Christ for the Hope of the World." This Synod emphasised the specific ministry of the Bishop in view of the Church as communion. The Pope's rejection of individualism among bishops is in this context of communion by which their strength is increased and deepened. Even if he is writing in the wider ecclesial context, these examples show that individualism is incompatible with the life of the Church in all aspects and at all levels. The family context depicts the general composition of the Church; the ordained priesthood and episcopal offices refer to pastorship.

The Bishops in the SECAM region have conceived of and identified individualism with a cultural meltdown. They state that: "Africa is gradually losing its cultural identity... our sense of and respect for community life have melted into individualism, our spirit of kindness, hospitality and concern for others has taken flight at the approach of the disintegration of our traditional social and cultural life."[373] This situation calls attention to rediscovering those traditional communitarian values upon which the society is built and grows. However, this situation cannot be understood only outside the Church, consid-

371 John Paul II, *Nuntius*, n. 14: *AAS* 86 (1994), p. 894. Electronic text: *Letter to Families*, Irondale, Eternal Word Television Network, 1999, URL: http://www.etwn.com/library/papaldoc/jp2famlt.htm (downloaded on 29 October 2011).

372 *PaG*, n. 19: *AAS* 96 (2004), p. 851.

373 The 12th Plenary Assembly of the Symposium Episcopal Conferences of Africa and Madagascar (SECAM), *Christ Our Peace: Church as Family of God, Place and Sacrament of Reconciliation, Forgiveness and Peace in Africa*, 30th September - 9th October, Rome 2000, n. 12.

ering how many Christians there are in Africa, included in this statement. Is there such a situation in Nebbi Catholic Diocese? How does it find expression?

This enquiry brings us to look at the information obtained from our field study. Respondents to oral questions (113)[374] and questionnaire (287)[375] were drawn from a wide cross-section representing the cultural community, those practiticing traditional religion (traditionalists), Catholics, Church of Uganda, Moselms (five of them who preferred anonymity), the emerging Christian churches or organisations (commonly called *jang-Fruthandhi*, offshoots of Prostestant mainstream Church, namely, of Anglican root), civil servants and non-governmental organisations. Our finding can be analysed under four main points: expressive forms, factors causing individualism, responsibility, and relationship in the Church.[376]

4.2. Expressive Forms

Individualism finds expression in different ways as illustrated below:

Expression	Rating (how strong)				
	Very strong	Strong	Moderate	Minor	**Total**
No transparency in communicating	43	51	82	67	**243**
Not together in planning projects	66	92	61	48	**267**
Not together at implementing plans	61	96	42	26	**225**
Rivalry among individuals and groups	29	66	57	63	**215**
Favours in appointment and placement	48	76	92	60	**276**
Sidelining by pondered transfer or neglect	48	70	77	41	**236**
Mishandling (diverting, swindling) funds	36	88	72	60	**256**
Mishandling assets (diverting elsewhere)	55	73	95	30	**253**
Using (abuse of) office for personal gains	62	78	81	61	**282**
Telling cover-up lies	21	63	82	77	**243**
Threats, intimidation, silencing	62	64	92	46	**264**

374 See Appendix 3 of this work.

375 Appendix 1 and 2.

376 Appendix 1: Section Three: 1 – 4.

Poor or no accountability	53	85	77	66	**281**
Personal projects from common resources	27	81	42	67	**217**
One-man decision	71	92	76	18	**257**
Clericalism: the priest is everything	63	80	79	40	**262**
Syncretism: anonymous, double life	52	58	81	96	**287**
Power struggle: want to dominate	31	68	93	54	**246**
Stand-alone behaviour	36	61	81	101	**279**
Over-employment: one man in many offices	27	64	123	42	**256**
Opening busy or business-like outstations	21	40	61	162	**284**

Figure 4: Expressive Forms of Individualism in the Church

The figure above illustrates the complex subtlety of individualism, namely, how it can chill the heart of church life by weakening and disorganising its proper functioning. It obscures transparency; it makes it difficult to discuss common activities; it is one cause of tension and suspicion in the Church; it takes advantage of community resources and turns them to individuals. This shows how an individual or group of like-minded individuals can manipulate common ecclesial interests and goals to their own ends.

This information can help us to interpret the comment made by the Papal Nuncio as recorded in the document of the First Synod of Nebbi Catholic Diocese, by which he calls attention to collaboration in order to realise the synod goals. Referring to the Synod theme: "Who is the Church in Nebbi Catholic Diocese?" he makes the remark:

> Many times we look at the Church as a beautiful *what.* The Church is *not an association* to which one belongs. It is a gift from God, in which we are transformed. It is *not just an institution* we thank for the good it has done to make us what we are and we say farewell to it. We live in it day by day and continue to be in it and, with God's grace, we continue to belong. Let us not just stick to our vocation, e.g. I am a priest forever…without a mission.[377]

The Nuncio continues to emphasise the need for the spirit of cooperation for a greater strength: "You are the Church! We are, therefore, the instrument of God living among us. The priests should thus not sleep but must promote

377 *Acts of the First Diocesan Synod of Nebbi Catholic Diocese*, p. 12, italic emphases as in the text.

dialogue with the bishop… The presbyteral council is very important. If there is no dialogue between the bishop and priests the laity will suffer. If the religious do not cooperate with the priests, the laity will suffer. Promote this relationship."[378]

Collaboration and co-operation refer to joining efforts to work together. The question does not only refer to relationship between the Bishop and priests. The Lay Apostolate report in the same synod document mentions poor co-operation among leaders and poor relationship among the different groups.[379] About relationship in the Church, our field study got the information as illustrated below:

Description	***Rating: how strong***				
	Good	*Fair*	*Poor*	*Very poor*	***Total***
Men towards women	56	61	97	72	**286**
Women towards men	83	70	41	29	223
Men among themselves	69	88	73	57	287
Women among themselves	71	89	83	44	287
Adults towards youth	116	81	38	---	**235**
Youth towards adults	88	94	59	25	**266**
Inter-group relationships	70	83	82	22	**262**
Leader towards members	51	67	86	47	**251**
Members towards leader	60	81	68	44	**233**
Community, Groups towards catechists	61	76	82	39	**256**
Groups towards priests	91	97	54	22	264
Catechists towards community	111	84	59	27	**281**
Catechists towards priests	187	66	16	---	**269**
Priests among themselves	57	62	97	52	**268**
Priests towards parish council	57	62	72	40	**231**
Priests towards catechists	68	55	99	43	**265**

378 Ibid., p. 14.

379 Ibid., p. 31.

Priests towards laity, groups	89	97	83	18	**287**
Priests towards religious	41	76	99	51	**267**
Priests towards seminarians	48	91	80	44	**263**
Priests towards aspirants	62	85	81	38	**266**
Religious towards priests	71	83	43	28	**225**
Religious towards church community	126	90	---	---	216
Religious among themselves	67	87	71	41	**266**
Religious towards catechists	198	86	---	---	**274**

Figure 5: Regarding Relationship in the Church

The figure above presents aspects of relationship and how individualism cuts into them. It shows how these human relationships enter into the life of the Chuch as individuals interact with one another and how this will influence co-existence in the community. One factor which seems to come to the surface and to colour relationships in the Church is social-cultural. It is striking to observe the ratings of relationship among women themselves, among men themselves, male-female and adult-youth relationships; and those that feature between the leadership and community members. Out of 113 respondents to oral interview, 94 (83%) said that the social-cultural factor has a strong impact on relationship not only in the society but even in the Church itself. From this picture emerge two main problems that deserve mention, namely, clericalism and responsibility.

4.2.1. Clericalism

In our field finding (figure 4 above) 262 persons responded to this question; of them 222 (85%) admitted that there is clericalism in Nebbi Catholic Diocese although this is reported differently: sixty-three (24%) said it is very strong; eighty (30%) said it is strong; seventy-nine (30%) said it is moderate; and forty (15%) said it is a minor problem. How then can clericalism be understood as a form of individualism?

In the 1993 *Instrumentum Laboris* (Working Paper) to the First Special Assembly of the Synod of Bishops for Africa, clericalism is defined as "…a monopoly of mission by the clergy which would not integrate or promote the mission of the lay faithful."[380] This may be read in connection with what the document explains earlier, that: "In some places lack of trust still persists between the clergy and the lay faithful, in spite of the option of many Episcopal Conferences to promote the involvement of the laity."[381] Monopoly of mission and lack of trust affect decision making and the implementation of decisions that might be made. This can fail the Church especially on critical issues that might call for the participation of both the clergy and the laity. In his book, *Evangelization Today*, Häring illustrates that in the Church there is a new form of clericalism, where church authorities and groups claim for themselves decisions and judgments in matters where they widely lack true and informed competence.[382]

In his advocacy for involving all the faithful in church ministry, Magesa uses the synonym, *hierarchism*, by which he criticises clericalism for the overemphasis it places on the ordained priest as the protagonist of church life.[383] The argument is within the context of the Church entering the Third Millennium. He argues that church communion shall be stronger and more fruitful when the laity are involved in the different church ministries.

The term *hierarchism* projects another conscience of clericalism with an inclination towards the adulation of rank. In his book, *Social Psychology*, Myers links hierarchism to a social dominance orientation which tends to view people in terms of ranks or hierarchies to justify status difference.[384] Viewed in this context, clericalism does not only portray a hierarchical image of the Church; our field study has revealed that it also severs relationship among priests. Out of 287 questionnaire responses (figure 5 above), 149 (52%) mentioned poor relationship among priests, especially where the distinction is drawn between *Parish Priest* and *Curate*. The report of diocesan priests, as recorded in the *Acts of the First Nebbi Diocesan Synod*, mentions the tension arising out of competition among them: "We need to work in collaboration in running the Diocese. No need for unhealthy competition."[385] The report of catechists mentions poor relationship between them and the priests; cold relationship between catechists and the community.[386] This was reflected in our field finding where

380 Synod of Bishops – Special Assembly for Africa, *The Church in Africa and Her Evangelizing Mission Towards the Year 2000: Instrumentum Laboris*, n. 34 § 3.

381 Ibid., "Signs of the Times: Negative Signs," n. 23, point 4.

382 Bernard Häring, *Evangelization Today*, revised, Slough, St. Paul Publications, 1990, p. 124.

383 Laurenti Magesa, "Involving all in Ministry: A Challenge to the Church of the Third Millennium" in *AFER*, Vol. 42/1, February/April 2000, pp. 2-15.

384 David C. Myers, *Social Psychology*, Boston, McGraw-Hill, 2008, p. 312.

385 *Acts of the First Diocesan Synod of Nebbi Catholic Diocese*, p. 23.

386 Ibid., p. 36.

265 persons responded to the question regarding the relationship of priests towards catechists (Figure 5 above); of whom 142 (53%) reported that it is generally weak. By contrast, questionnaire responses – 253 (94%) out of 269 – show that catechists are more respectful in their relationship towards priests. Besides, 101 (35%) out of 287 mentioned poor clergy-laity relationship. By this they mean that the parish priest is paying marginal attention to the laity's role. Due to such a divide it creates, clericalism depicts an institutionalised individualism, which weakens not only clergy-to-laity or clergy-to-clergy relationship but the polity of the Church as an institution. Poor relationship suggests that there is poor communication and thus poor coordination of activities.

What Nwatu calls *priestcraft* carries another image and conscience of clericalism.[387] According to him, priestcraft is marked by self-indulgence, personal aggrandizement and accumulation of wealth. He argues that such a practice is gradually becoming the trend in the mainline Churches in Africa, with a growing number of the clergy not having sufficient regard for personal moral accountability to their congregation. This turns priests into 'landlords' enforcing aggressive and intimidating demands on the faithful of the parish. In his comment on Nwatu's article, Mutuka remarks that the problem of priestcraft in the Church deserves attention. He argues that this perverts the Church's pastroship.[388] We would understand priestcraft as an expressive form of individualism. Our informants questioned the personal business investments of priests and the religious. They referred to the diocesan Association of Priests as the proper channel for priests to set up a common income generating project.[389]

The preparatory document, *Instrumentum Laboris*, to the first Special Assembly of the Synod of Bishops for Africa decries the gap between the "haves" and "have-nots" in the civil society.[390] Our field study investigated whether such a practice may be found in the Church. The *Acts of the First Synod of Nebbi Catholic Diocese* registers the speech of the Apostolic Nuncio thus: "… sometimes we may send wrong signals as Church; Caritas, as a department, is

387 Felix Nwatu, "Africa and the Return to Priestcraft," in *AFER*, Vol. 35, Nr. 4, 1993, pp. 240-251.

388 Tarcisius Mutuka, "Africa and the Return of Priestcraft" in *AFER*, Vol. 35, Nr. 6, 1993, pp. 256-264.

389 Out of 287 responses, 36 commented that the personal business investment will divert the attention of the ordained priest or religious from their specific commitment as priests and religious.

390 Synod of Bishops – Special Assembly for Africa, *Instrumentum Laboris*, Vatican City, General Secretariat of the Synod of Bishops and Libreria Editrice Vaticana, 2003, n. 13.

for sharing, not to be rich among the poor masses."[391] This can put off not only the faithful and poor of the Church, but also the general public.

Vatican Council II Decree on the Ministry and Life of Priests, *Presbyterorum Ordinis*, recommends that: "Led by the Holy Spirit... priests as well as bishops should avoid (doing) anything that could put off poor people..."[392] From what we see in these examples, clericalism obscures transparency and accountability, both in pastoral and administrative activities, as well as personal moral accountability. From our questionnaire responses, we discovered that clericalism, in its varied manifestations, weakens the trust which the society have in the Church as an agency of Christian charity. Out of 287 responses, 103 (39%) said clericalism is a factor to dissaffection and withdrawal from ecclesial life. The difficulty which remains is that, in Nebbi Catholic Diocese, the Church is sometimes too easily associated with the person of the ordained priest.

4.2.2. Accountability

Accountability in the Church basically refers to transparency both in pastoral and administrative activities. It is an important factor to strengthening ecclesial life. According to Patrick Ryan, "Accountability is about taking responsibility for how we exercise our ecclesial ministry."[393] This involves a number of elements, each of which is as closely important as another, as presented below:

Reason	***Rating (how strong)***				
	Good	*Fair*	*Poor*	*Very poor*	***Total***
Leaders' personal moral accountability	52	59	104	72	287
Spirituality / Prayer life	64	97	77	36	**264**
Pastoral accountability	53	82	98	17	**250**
Administration accountability	49	79	103	27	**258**
Project planning accountability	33	57	124	70	**284**

391 *Acts of the First Diocesan Synod of Nebbi Diocese*, p. 15.

392 Vatican Council II, Decree on the Ministry and Life of Priests *Presbyterorum Ordinis*, n. 17 § 5: *AAS* 58 (1966), p. 1018. Text cited as in Norman P. Tanner (ed.), *Decrees of the Ecumenical Councils,* Vol. 2: *Trent to Vatican II,* London, Sheed & Ward, 1990, p. 1065.

393 Patrick Ryan, "Developing Creative Leadership Skills" in Patrick Ryan (ed.), *New Strategies for a New Evangelization in Africa*, Nairobi, Paulines Publications Africa, 2002, p. 95.

Project implementation and follow-up	27	40	119	68	**234**
Project management and follow-up	36	82	121	47	**286**
Policy making and reviewing	19	54	130	60	**263**
Policy implementation and follow-up	40	56	126	23	**245**
Financial management	45	58	98	42	**243**
Human resource management (placement)	57	61	81	67	266
Physical asset management (church property)	47	62	93	43	**245**
Strategic follow-up of implemented tasks	28	47	86	73	**234**
Meeting: attendance and participation	53	63	82	58	**256**
Communication: conveying information	59	99	47	30	**235**

Figure 6: Regarding accountability in church life and activities

The figure above shows that accountability goes into every aspect of the Church's mission; it entails faithful commitment. What must be borne in mind is the sensitivity it evokes, as shown by the ratings: good, fair, poor, very poor. According to Fr. Agwokotho, accountability is to be viewed in different dimensions; in the number of ways it affects church life. The main areas of concern include: personal moral responsibility, handling of finance, physical projects, administration, management, and pastoral ministry.[394]

Jonsen uses the term accountability synonymously with the stronger term responsibility. He clarifies that it does not only concern being answerable for one's behavior but that the deeper understanding refers to commitment to a solemn promise; performing one's part reliably in a promised engagement within a common undertaking. He writes that, "In this sense, responsible persons are not only those who are uncoerced and aware of the nature of their action and its consequences; they are also persons who demonstrate a certain stable or habitual attitudes to their relationships with other persons... Responsible persons conscientiously and consciously commit themselves to a task or form of life

394 Fr. Alfred Agwokotho, interviewed by the researcher, at Paidha, 6th June 2008, has been helpful in the identification of the elements of accountability and how they work differently.

and readily accept accountability for its success and failure."[395] This understanding underlines trustworthiness and transparency in acting upon common purposes.

Christian responsibility basically pertains to bearing witness to Gospel values. The 1993 *Instrumentum Laboris* of the Synod of Bishops for Africa states that: "The first form of proclamation is the witness of a truly Christian life – by individuals and community – in response to the demands and values of the Gospel."[396] This means that responsibility is vital to the internal life of the Church and the image it portrays of itself in the contingent society. How then does this relate to individualism and how relevant is it to the life of the Church and its apostolate? This question investigates how individuals or groups carry out their tasks in pastoral and administrative activities.

4.2.2.1. Personal Moral Responsibility

Personal moral responsibility is when we are true to objective values, transparent and exemplary in our commitment. It is a practical resource to Christian witnessing, the possibility of radiating the Gospel message. This has been empasised by Pope Paul VI in his address to the council of the Laity, where he states that, "Modern man listens more willingly to witness than to teachers, and if he does listen to teachers, it is because they are witnesses."[397] He continues with the same expression, as a mission statement, in his Apostolic Exhortation, *Evangelii Nuntiandi*, where he focuses on making evangelisation possible in the modern society.[398] In this understanding, personal moral responsibility lies in the testimony of life.

The same point has been re-emphasised by Pope John Paul II in his Encyclical Letter, *Redemptoris Missio*, where he writes: "People today put more trust in witness than in teachers, in experience than in teaching, and in life and action than in theories...The first form of witness is the very life of the missionary, of the Christian family, and of the ecclesial community, which reveal a new way of living."[399] His central point is that every believer is to consider if s/he is honestly accountable to God and truly working in the vineyard of the

395 Albert R. Jonsen, "Responsibility," in *NDCE*, p. 547.

396 Synod of Bishops – Special Assembly for Africa, *Instrumentum Laboris*, Vatican City, General Secretariat of the Synod of Bishops and Libreria Editrice Vaticana, 1993, n. 15.

397 Paul VI, Address to the Members of the *Concilium de Laicis* (2 October 1974): *AAS* 66 (1974), p. 568.

398 Idem, Apostolic Exhortaion *Evangelii Nuntiandi* (8 December 1975), 1st reprint, Nairobi, Paulines Publications Africa, 2000, n. 41: *AAS* 68 (1976), p. 31.

399 John Paul II, Encyclical Letter *Redemptoris Missio*, Nairobi, Paulines Publication Africa, 1991, n. 42: *AAS* 83 (1991), p. 289.

Lord.[400] Responsibility in the Church has to do with the witness we give by our way of life as Christians.

The Arua Diocese *Bulletin* addresses the question of personal moral accountability where it states: "The Church leaders shall be transparent to the Christians. They shall avoid scandalous behaviour that can attract investigation by the media, both diocesan and beyond."[401] In our research (figure 6 above) 176 out of 287 (61%) questionnaire responses mentioned poor personal moral conduct shown by some Church leaders. In oral interview, 73 (64%) out of 113 respondents counselled that church leaders at every level need to respect their name, which represents the name of the Church. Fr. Anwangkani remarked that the respect people have towards priests deserves a sincere response.[402] He explained this in the context of the changed image of the priesthood and consecrated persons during the war situation in northern Uganda, when priests and the religious took refuge together with their people and shared in the same condition.

4.2.2.2. Financial Responsibility

This regards how Church moneys are handled. The report of the Lay Apostolate, as recorded in the First Diocesan Synod document, mentions: "Lack of accountability, budget and reports."[403] This suggests that the parish priest does not involve the parish finance committee in discussing and handling finance.

The NGO staff the researcher interviewed at Nebbi acknowledged that the Church is the best and unparalleled interface for them to reach down to the people; but they commented that some Church leaders need to be more honest with accounting for money and materials entrusted in their hands to help the poor. They noted that in some parishes the specified income generating project is not visible; and the money or materials given are not accounted for. In some cases they discover that the same project is being funded by more than one charity organisation.[404] A parish youth group showed this researcher a letter from a charity organisation telling them that their request would not be granted because the same organisation had given money for the same parish through

400 Idem, Apostolic Exhortation *Christifideles Laici,* 1st reprint, Nairobi, Paulines Publications Africa, 1998, n. 2 § 4: *AAS* 81(1989), p. 394.

401 Arua Diocese, *Bulletin*, December 2008, p. 3. This bulletin reflects the resolutions of the Diocesan Pastoral Council.

402 Fr. Charles Anwangkani, interviewed by the researcher, at Rhino Camp, 30 May 2008.

403 *Acts of the First Diocesan Synod of Nebbi Catholic Diocese*, p. 31.

404 Dr. Lakwonyero Alfred, Director of AFARD, Nebbi Office, interviewed by the researcher, at Nebbi, 23 May 2008.

the parish priest who did not give any account.[405] These reports show lack of transparency in handling finance.

4.2.2.3. Project Responsibility

This refers to the identification, planning, implementation and on-going evaluation of Church projects whether they are fixed assets like land, buildings; or income generating projects. Out of 287 questionnaire responses, 146 (51%) made a general comment that the question of Church projects is a practical area where priests need to involve parishioners (represented by the parish council) and technical experts to identify, discuss and test the applicability of projects under the guidance of priests. Projects started by the priest without involving parishioners have proved a failure after the transfer or death of that individual priest. Three priests said that it is the experience of indigenous priests who took over parishes from missionaries.[406] Fr. Odokodit explained that the aim of Church projects is to promote self-support and to challenge the Christian communities. When they are not involved, this leads to a logical dependency; so they expect help from their leaders.[407]

4.2.2.4. Administration Responsibility

Administration accountability refers to handling personnel and offices; and how general Church affairs are organised and run. In the *Acts of the First Diocesan Synod of Nebbi Catholic Diocese*, the report of the diocesan priests indicates poor accountability with regard to administration: "We need to work in collaboration in running the Diocese... Trust and cooperation should be applied in posting people (priests) in various stations or positions. Dialogue should be used as a sign of cooperation."[408]

In the same document the report of catechists mentions: "The policy of transfer which sometimes makes catechists to be extremely mobile…The persons concerned (Parish Priests) should ponder the advantages and disadvantages of such policy of transfer… Relationship between clergy and catechists should be encouraged so that the latter (may) be given freedom to find his/her

405 The youth interviewed preferred to remain anonymous. The researcher respects their view.

406 Fr. Cornelius Odubi, interviewed by the researcher, at Panyimur, 5 June 2008; Fr. Primo Mananu, interviewed by the researcher, at Zeu, 8 June 2008; Fr. William Jupalwonga, interviewed by the researcher, at Parombo, 24 June 2008.

407 Fr. John Hercules Odokodit, interviewed by the researcher, at Nebbi, 23 May 2008.

408 *Acts of the First Diocesan Synod of Nebbi Catholic Diocese*, p. 23.

place in the Church."[409] These reports indicate that there are some ambiguities and irregularities regarding church administration in the diocese.

4.2.2.5. Management Responsibility

This refers to how resources of the Church are allocated for the right purposes. These resources may include persons, physical goods or finance. The youth report in the diocesan synod Act mentions: "No proper inventories in the Diocesan Youth Office."[410] However, this appears to be a general situation. In our field study we found out that most parishes lack an inventory. According to the Vicar General, this situation goes back to the time the missionaries handed over the parishes to diocesan priests.[411] Fr. Mananu pointed out that lack of inventory obscures transparency in handing over an office; it creates difficulty for the incoming leader/s.[412]

An inventory is a guideline document describing the Church's goods. In *A Dictionary of Canon Law*, the importance of the inventory is explained thus: "Before administrators begin their function they are to prepare and sign an accurate and clear inventory of immovable property, movable objects, whether precious or of some cultural value, or other goods, with their description and appraisal; any inventory already done is to be reviewed."[413] The inventory helps the leader to know about and handle Church property. The lack of an inventory creates inconsistency and difficulty in measuring the areas of strength and what might need to be improved. This means that every new leader will have no clear reference but to start in their own way, which makes it difficult for the parishioners to adjust to such a quick change.

Robert Kennedy writes that: "In the absence of a thorough, authenticated, and up-to-date inventory, serious conflicts can arise between individual administrators (such as pastors) and their successors over which assets belong personally to the administrator and which to the juridic person."[414] This is better understood when the distinction is clearly drawn between *moral* and *juridic persons* in the Church and how these two function:

409 Ibid., p. 36.

410 Ibid., p. 39.

411 Fr. Richard Lino Opio, interviewed by the researcher, at Nebbi, 23 June 2008.

412 Fr. Primo Mananu, interviewed by the researcher, at Zeu, 8 June 2008.

413 Burke (Compiler), *A Dictionary of Canon Law*, p. 360.

414 Robert T. Kennedy, "Commentary on Book V: The Temporary Goods of the Church [cc. 1254-1310]" in John P. Beal, James A. Corriden, Thomas J. Green (eds.), *New Commentary on the Code of Canon Law*, Commissioned by The Canon Law Society of America, Bangalore, Theological Publications in India, 2003, p. 1485.

> A moral person is a group or succession of natural persons who are united by a common purpose... conceived of as a single entity... what we refer to when we speak of a team... "they," "them," theirs."... Analogously, a moral person may also be understood as an accumulation or mass of material goods or assets which have been set aside for a common purpose... Since such a moral person is a collectivity, it may properly be referred to in the plural: "those."... A juridic person, on the other hand, is an artificial person, distinct from all natural persons or material goods, constituted by competent ecclesiastical authority for an apostolic purpose, with a capacity for continuous existence and with canonical rights and duties like those of a natural person (e.g., to own property, enter into contracts, sue or be sued) conferred upon it by law or by the authority which constitutes it... It is not a group or collectivity and may properly be referred to only in the impersonal singular: "it."[415]

From this it is clear that management accountability requires correct, up-to-date guidelines.

4.2.2.6. Pastoral Responsibility

This is about how pastoral activities are to be carried out effectively. It involves identifying pastoral strategies, planning, implementation and on-going evaluation. Our study discovered a weak pastoral accountability where the parish priest or leader tends to center much of activity on them alone. The 2006 annual report of Nebbi Catholic Diocese Pastoral Coordinator says:

> The spirit of working together with others is still low. Most of the time when planning, we do not even involve our close collaborators. We want to involve them to implement what we did not involve them in planning. How can that plan succeed? Some parish priests and heads of commissions plan alone and even the reports they give are just a one man's report. There is too little transparency and sharing of information with our colleagues, especially with regard to money. We must learn to plan, monitor and evaluate together as a Small Christian Community, together as a Chapel, together as a Zone, together as a Parish, together as a Deanery and then together as a Diocese.[416]

He remarks that such an individualistic spirit makes the implementation of pastoral plans and ecclesial activities impossible.[417]

---

415 Ibid., pp. 154-155.

416 Fr. Richard Lino Opio, "The Annual Report of the Diocesan Pastoral Coordinator's Office of Nebbi Catholic Diocese for the Year 2006 and Proposed Plans for the Year 2007," 23rd January 2007, p. 11.

417 Ibid., p. 10.

Insensitivity to pastoral accountability can lead to abuse of office. This is illustrated from the way leaders carry out their duties, especially in the manner they relate to those whom they are to serve. From questionnaire responses, 69 (out of 287) mentioned the denying or withholding of Holy Communion due to disagreement between a priest and certain individuals (including catechists, Sisters and group leaders). Personal disagreements have sometimes led to forming different groups behind individuals with conflicting points of view. In some cases it has led to the removal of the tabernacle from the Eucharistic Centre.[418] Bishop Luluga mentioned another case involving two priests of the diocese who started their own "church" which they called "Reformed Catholic Church." From our questionnaire responses, 31 out of 286 (11%) showed awareness of this group, whose action they called *apoka-poka*, division; *yeco pacu*, tearing the home, *lalu pacu*, scattering the home. The Bishop advised the faithful to refrain from participation in that split.[419]

Another case leading to abuse of office was connected with conflict of priorities. Missionary priests interviewed by the researcher remarked that money donated from external sources, designated specifically for liturgy, was not used for that purpose despite the dire need for song books, Missals, Lectionaries and Bible translations that await publication.[420] These reports show that there is no proper pastoral accountability. From this we may ask: What might be causing, or provoking, or accentuating individualism?

4.3. Factors Causing or Provoking or Accentuating Individualism

It is difficult to assign the cause of individualism to a single factor. These factors may be internal or external. The main factors identified in our study are presented below:

Reason	Rating: strength or intensity				
	Very strong	Strong	Moderate	Negligible	Total
Poverty – economic hardship	48	80	63	91	**282**
Influence from urban life	60	93	74	46	**273**

418 Padel Zone Council, interviewed by the researcher, at Padel, 22 June 2008.

419 Bishop Martin Luluga, interviewed by the researcher, at Nebbi, 27 May 2008. The researcher was unable to interview the priests concerned, who started this move.

420 Fr. Felice Centis and Fr. Mario Zecca, interviewed by the researcher, at Angal, 25 May 2008.

Social encounter and mixture	51	97	102	31	**271**
Influence of school life	80	103	79	18	**280**
Personal human rights and freedom	31	49	68	136	**284**
Materialistic liberalism	34	50	72	82	**238**
Influence of mass media	62	89	56	32	**239**
Generation conflict	27	56	78	107	**266**
Emerging Christian denominations	59	61	74	93	**287**
Weak family life	27	44	81	124	**276**
Weak pastoral planning	59	64	81	55	**256**
Weak seminary / novitiate formation	73	62	92	41	268

Figure 7: Factors causing, provoking, or accentuating individualism

The information above seeks to measure the intensity of each reason given as a likely cause to individualism. Respondents argued differently. Those under category *very strong*, *strong*, and *moderate* admit the reality of such a factor although in varrying degress. Those who say it is negligible admit that such a factor exists but argue that it must not be a reason to weaken the spirit of building ecclesial communion. This information can be evaluated together with responses from oral interviews. Of the 113 orally interviewed, 96 (85%) generally commented that these factors must be met with courage; they cannot justify individualism in the the diocese. This suggests that there is the good will to promote ecclesial communion. Nevertheless, these factors cannot be overlooked.

4.3.1. Weak Pastoral Planning

By pastoral planning reference is here made to informative and practical guidelines like the directory, inventory and diocesan policy book. These tools help to clarify ways of being accountable in the Church both in pastoral and practical administration. Upira, a parish council member, remarked that it is difficult to serve community purposes without the instruments of team action.[421] Effective team action depends upon strategic planning, which involves a clear mission statement or working policy, goal, strategies, objectives, action

421 Fabiano Upira, interviewed by the researcher, at Parombo, 1 June 2008.

plan and the means to achieve them. It is pastoral planning that gives direction and regulates relationships among persons, procedures of action, the handling of property and finances, according to the specified mission of the diocese or parish.

Schoneke observes that these elements are basic for effective strategic pastoral planning. He clarifies that: (a) A *mission statement* is a clear statement about the main purpose of the group or organisation or programme, the vision, and the values that motivate us. It answers the question: What are we here for? A good mission statement is the fruit of the common reflection and discussion of the whole group; (b) *A goal* describes the benefits, changes, and improvements that our action should bring about. It focuses on what we are trying to achieve; (c) A *strategy* shows the various ways and methods that we believe will help us to fulfill our mission and achieve our goals. All the ways and methods chosen are to provide the possilities of arriving at what it to be achieved; (d) *Objectives* express what quantifiable results or outcomes or benefits we expect to realise in a given time. They focus on what each strategy will achieve; (e) *An Action Plan* determines who will do what, when, and how. It focuses on what activities or interventions each strategy calls for; (f) *Means*, in terms of personnel, finance and material, need to be estimated and budgeted. The question here is: What resources will we need to achieve our objectives? Schoneke concludes that: "If such a planning process is done together with those who will carry it out, it will generate a strong motivation in each member and improve team spirit."[422]

From here we can see that without a clear strategic pastoral planning, accountability is flawed and inverted; individuals are left to choose a course of action which might not well articulate the vision and mission of the diocese. Kato writes that, "Absence of a clear pastoral plan that gives priority to evangelization in allocating human power, equipment and financial resources to direct evangelization ministry, affects evangelization."[423] From what we have seen here one can deduce that weak pastoral planning creates a gap that may provoke individualism in the Church.

422 Wolfgang Schoneke, "Pastoral Planning: New Responses to Changed Situations," in Patrick Ryan (ed.), *New Strategies for a New Evangelization*, Nairobi, Paulines Publications Africa, 2002, p. 133.

423 Joseph Bitole Kato, "Evangelization in Africa: Twelve Years after the *Ecclesia in Africa*," in *AFER*, Vol. 50, Nr. 1&2 (March-June 2008), p. 130.

4.3.2. Materialism

Materialism refers to how the use of material goods influences our choice, decision and relationships. In his book, *Does Morality Change?* Fagan observes that material goods can significantly change human life.[424] This is due to the vast majority of goods we use in daily life, which challenges the preservation of traditional and commonly held values. Materialism therefore can provoke or accentuate individualism. Is materialism contributing to individualism in Nebbi Catholic Diocese?

Fr. Emilio made the remark: "Materialism is subtly taking us, both elderly and young priests and religious alike."[425] The effect of this among priests and the religious is that it has set a tension between those who have their private resources and those who do not have. The central question here is the preoccupation with self-care which sometimes results into absence from pastoral work or commitment to common life. It is in this context that the Apostolic Nuncio to Uganda expressed his concern in a Letter addressed to all Catholic Bishops and Religious Houses in Uganda:

> The Apostolic Nunciature is willing to help those Priests, Religious Brothers and Sisters who need to travel to Italy and apply for Entrance Visa to the Italian Embassy through issuance of its recommended letter. Recently, however, some particular cases called my attention. Some people approached the Nunciature to request a recommendation letter to visit some friends in Italy or for tourism, sometimes even without the knowledge of their own Bishop... In my opinion, normally the priests should not be absent from their own parishes for such a long period (Cf. Can. 533 par 1 and 2)... From now on, a recommendation letter will be given only to those Priests, Religious Brothers and Sisters who need to go to Italy for serious and justifiable religious reasons...[426]

The problem of materialism is a curious one: Why, and how, should materialism become a matter of concern with regard to the internal life of the Church? What brings it about?

---

424 Seán Fagan, *Does Morality Change?* Dublin, Gill & Macmillan, 1997, pp. 16-17.

425 Fr. Emilio Onegwa, interviewed by the researcher, at Nyapea, 7 June 2008.

426 Paul Tschang In-Nam, "To All Catholic Bishops and Religious Superiors in Uganda," File, N. 650/08, Apostolic Nunciature in Uganda, Kampala, 8 July 2008. The same Letter was published in Tororo Archdiocese, for which see, *From the Desk of the Archbishop, Archdiocese of Tororo*, "To the Clergy, Religious and Laity of the Archdiocese of Tororo," D/C/08, August 2008, pp. 1-2.

4.3.3. Poverty

Poverty has been explained in the context of the general economic situation, which exerts pressure especially with regard to handling finances and Church property. The annual report of Nebbi Diocesan Pastoral Coordinator for 2006 mentions the problem of "little and late finances."[427] This situation makes it difficult to give precise accounts due to various needs to be met. Some parishes are generally poor; and the priests working in such situations have to fend for themselves. An example from our field finding was in Rhino Camp parish, covering an area of 111 Km^2, served by two young priests posted immediately after their ordination; without means of transport; no parish hall; poor house for their residence. Both Fr. Anwangkani and Fr. Oromcan commented that the spirit of solidarity and charity among diocesan priests is poor; those in poor parishes have to struggle on their own.[428]

The report of the Apostles of Jesus, recorded in the Acts of Nebbi Catholic Diocese Synod, states: "As the first male African Missionary Congregation founded on African soil, the Apostles of Jesus share the sad background of African society: poverty... We end up being tossed, consumed and helpless with the famous slogan of 'survival for the fittest.'"[429] However, Fr. Onencan (member of the Apostles of Jesus) argued the slogan of 'survival for the fittest' away in comparison with the life of the poorest people in their homesteads sharing the smallest of their resources and living happily.[430] Nevertheless, poverty poses a significant difficulty for priests working in such conditions. It forces them to fend for themselves. It is, thus, a potential factor which seems to provoke individualism. Reference to the traditional communitarian spirit and lifestyle seem to suggest another factor that might provoke or accentuate individualism.

4.3.4. Certain Aspects of Western Culture and Lifestyle

This is more of an external factor, mainly through the school, mass media, business, mobility and emerging religious groups (usually liberal in their style of communicating the teaching of Gospel message). These factors are men-

427 Fr. Richard Lino Opio, "The Annual Report of the Diocesan Pastoral Coordinator's Office of Nebbi Catholic Diocese for the Year 2006 and Proposed Plans for the Year 2007," 23 January 2007, p. 11.

428 Fr. Albert Oromcan and Fr. Charles Anwangkani, interviewed by the researcher, at Rhino Camp, 30 May 2008.

429 *Acts of the First Diocesan Synod of Nebbi Catholic Diocese*, p. 26.

430 Fr. Wilbert Onencan Alimundu, interviewed by the researcher, at Urusi, 2 June 2008. He insisted that a good working relationship in the parish will encourage parishioners to support their priests from their local resources how-ever little their contribution might be.

tioned in the Youth report, recorded in the diocesan synod document, all of which lead to imitating social models that impinge upon traditional values. The report says: "There is moral degeneration resulting into early pregnancy, abortion and contraceptives."[431] The major problem arising from this is mainly due to the liberal lifestyle that those aspects of Western culture propose, encapsulating freedom of indifference. Pinckaers describes *freedom of indifference* in relation to free will: the ability to take decisions independently from motives; implying the power to choose between contraries.[432]

Bujo discusses "western culture" with reference to European and North American industrial mentality and lifestyle. He argues that the influence of Western culture erodes the African morality based on ancestral foundations. This affects the cultural, social, political, economic as well as religious life.[433] In our study we shall limit ourselves to the cultural and religious aspects. From our questionnaire responses, 217 (75%) out of 287 said that the traditional values that held people together are waning in the face of overwhelming social changes. This has a significant impact on the individual who is confronted, and often over-flooded, with choices to make between clashing models. We can depict the situation as shown below:

Alur traditional communitarian values	Aspects of Western culture
1. Family, homestead, clan relationships.	1. School, open society as places of social encounter.
2. Parents, elders, uncles, aunts, peers.	2. Civil servants, school teachers, colleagues.
3. Council of elders, experience, wisdom.	3. Democracy, personal rights, court of law.
4. Cultural, religious, moral values.	4. Scientific experimentation, proof, pragmatism.
5. Cultural, religious, moral instruction.	5. Formal, liberal education.
6. Folk stories, proverbs, parables, riddles.	6. Mass media, classroom learning, debate.
7. Ancestors, tradition, culture, custom.	7. Heroes, heroines, inventors, discoverers.

Figure 8: Comparison between Alur traditional communitarian values and aspects of Western culture

431 *Acts of the First Diocesan synod of Nebbi Catholic Diocese*, p. 39.

432 Servais Pinckaers, *The Sources of Christian Ethics*, T & T Clark, Edinburgh 1995, pp. 351-352.

433 Bénézet Bujo, *The Ethical Dimension of Community: The African Model and the Dialogue Between North and South*, Nairobi, Paulines Publications Africa, 1977, pp. 15-23.

From this we can see that the traditional communitarian values that serve as filters to behaviours are peeling off as younger generations take on new social models.

4.3.5. Emerging Christian Denominations

By emerging Christian denominations reference is made to the evangelical church groups or organisations (we could not establish their exact number during our field study). These are identified by distinctive but sometimes confusing names. This phenomenon is in some way closely connected with what we have just said about certain aspects of Western culture. These different groups are generally understood in Nebbi to be offshoots of the Anglican Church (Church of Uganda, commonly known as Protestants). Our study enquires whether their activity might contribute to individualism; and what impact this might have on the internal life of Nebbi Catholic Church.

In Nebbi Catholic Diocese, there are officially acknowledged groups, associations, clubs and movements. However, there is a clear distinction between them and the different new Christian denominations. This situation of emerging Christian groups (sects or sect-like) poses the problem of sectarianism – that is, divisiveness – which runs parallel to the mainstream Churches. The Youth report in the diocesan synod Acts directly mentions that: "Most of our youth are taken up by the sects."[434] In the responses to our questionnaire, 194 out of 287 (67%, figure 7 above) stated that the increase of new Christian denominations is affecting Church communion due to their pronounced emphasis on freedom in the Holy Spirit (namely, freedom from Church authority), personal conversion and relationship with Christ, prophetic vision and prophesying.

These groups make intensive use of mass media programmes and material promises with strong appeal especially to young people and people living in modest conditions. A similar voice to this problem was given by Archbishop Mathias Ssekamanya, President of the Uganda Bishops' Conference, during his *ad limina* visit in Rome.[435] In our view, the actual problem lies in the responsive naivety of imbibing the liberal Western lifestyle shrouded in these religious claims. Nonetheless, it has a strong impact on the religious conscience, how people will understand religion and live by it. McManners in his study of the increasing number of Christian denominations remarks that: when religion

434 *Acts of the First Synod of Nebbi Catholic Diocese*, "Report of the Youth," p. 39. We were not able to establish the number of Catholics who have crossed to sects.

435 Archbishop Mathias Ssekamanya, President of the Episcopal Conference of Uganda, as reported in *Catholic Information Service for Africa (CISA)*, 5th March 2010.

becomes personalised and individualised faith is reduced to personal preference.[436]

A study of the evangelical churches in Eldoret (Kenya) carried out by Ochieng Ong'ondo may help us to understand the difficulty that these different groups pose to evangelisation and the unity of the Church. His study shows an unhealthy conflict created by them that cannot promote true ecclesial growth. His central point regards the cluster of confusing names that these groups take to justify their multiplied presence and mission. He argues that these evangelical groups can make a fruitful contribution to Christianity when they collaborate in the one goal of evangelisation instead of creating divisive factions.[437] Here again comes the critical moral dilemma of the freedom of indifference with which the individual is faced. Indifference cannot help to build church communion. An apt reflection, by Chibuko Patrick, can help us to discern the subtlety of individualism, infiltrating even through such emerging forms of Christian churches, due to the human factor that it carries with it. In his article on the Church (in Africa) and the challenge of individualisation, he argues that the erroneous understanding of the individual as the center of human progress and achievement eventually becomes insensitive to God and fellow humans. This denies charity. Advancing the primacy of the individual yields self-interest; this is incompatible with an understanding of the Church as communion.[438]

The *Lineamenta* to the second Synod of Bishops for Africa acknowledges that: "In Africa today, a significant role is being exercised by some spiritual movements and living ecclesial communities, providing a source of hope for the Church... Spiritual movements are also centres from which the Gospel emanates into the world of and its realities... Africa should profit from the spiritual movements... Africa should also be equipped to form and propagate them in the whole Church as a sign of its spiritual maturity..."[439] However, the mind of the synod reflected in this document is for a spirituality which is oriented towards building the ecclesial community for service to the world, that is, they are to be instruments for reconciliation, justice and peace in Africa. This com-

436 John McManners, "Enlightenment: Secular and Christian (1600 – 1800)" in John McManners (ed.), *The Oxford Illustrated History of Christianity*, reissued, Oxford, Oxford University Press, 2002, pp. 277-278. In this article (pp. 277-309), McManners illustrates how religion can turn the individual in on himself/herself.

437 Charles Ochieng' Ong'ondo, "Communicative Conflicts in the Nomenclature of Evangelical Organizations," in *AFER*, vol. 48, Nr. 3 (September 2006), 157-173.

438 Patrick C. Chibuko, "The Church and the Challenge of Individualization: An Ecumenical Reflection," in *AFER*, vol. 49, Nr. 3 & 4 (2007), pp. 265-267.

439 Synod of Bishops – II Special Assembly for Africa, *Lineamenta: The Church in Africa in Service to Reconciliation, Justice and Peace*, Nairobi, Paulines Publications Africa, 2006, n. 91.

mendation is to strengthen ecclesial growth, which is different from what we have said of the evangelical groups.

Pope John Paul II links groups, associations, organisations and movements in the Church with its apostolate and unity. He appreciates the presence of different forms of participation in the Church. His understanding is that they are ways of enriching the unity and ministries of the Church according to the different gifts of the Holy Spirit. In the Apostolic Exhortation on the Vocation and Mission of the Laity, *Christifideles Laici*, he writes about group forms of participation. His conclusion is that: "...the right of the lay faithful to form groups is essentially in relation to the Church's life of communion and to her mission."[440] Again in the Apostolic Letter *Tertio Millennio Adveniente*, he encourages the different forms of participation in the Church by the laity; but he still bases it on the ecclesiology of communion.[441]

In their Pastoral Letter, *Test the Spirits*, the Catholic Bishops of Uganda address all the faithful on cults, sects and "religious" groups. They appreciate the existence of the different forms of participation in the Church; but they caution the faithful from joining such dubious groupings which claim direct divine authority: "As Pastors of the People of God, we have constantly reminded the faithful to avoid "religious" groups, which do not conform to the teaching of the Church."[442] One specific group that has been active in Nebbi Diocese is the Marian Workers of the Laity whose doctrines are based on messages from "visionaries" and "seers." The Bishop of the diocese cautioned the faithful about them and banned their activities in the diocese, after their refusal to submit to the Church's teachings.

4.3.6. Influence of Liberal School Education

We have noted that Church schools in Uganda follow the government curriculum. Liberal subjects like political science are taught in secondary schools and higher institutions of learning. These subjects deal with issues of democracy and human rights. However, they are not quite favourable to African traditional morality as the models of self-knowledge and relationship change. Besides, the government campaign on education emphasises sciences as core subjects; arts subjects, including religious education, are optional. However, it is the arts subjects, those that deal with humanities and religious education that serve to instill moral values and general human maturity.

440 *CfL*, n. 29 § 8: *AAS* 81 (1989), p. 446.

441 *TMA*, n. 36 § 5: *AAS* 87 (1995), p. 28.

442 Catholic Bishops of Uganda, Pastoral Letter *Test the Spirits: Cults, Sects and "Religious" Groups*, Kisubi, Marianum Press, 2000, p. 4.

Bishop Joseph of Karamoja Diocese, Province of the Anglican Church of Uganda, expressed concern over external pressure from donors that weighs upon government policy making, which in consequence affects the moral life of its people. In reaction to a bill proposed in the Parliament of Uganda, advocating for the 'human rights' of homosexuals (gays and lesbians) he remarks that, "Our children are ignorant of the vice; but gays and their sympathizers want to appeal to their psyche, to their consciousness that they be infected too. They are spreading it in our institutions of learning. They want to condition every penny that comes to our government or churches or Non-Governmental Organisations."[443]

In his book, *Manipulation*, Häring shows how the school can easily become a vulnerable place that can only freeze the freedom of learners. This is especially when the process of learning is not dialogical so as to enable learners to become critical in distinguishing between values and dis-values. He writes: "If we ask why manipulation is such a complex and dangerous problem, then we must turn first to the field of learning and education… Education is the market-place of the various ideologies and of those who put their trust chiefly in manipulating others."[444] Häring concludes that: "Either learning is dialogue or it prepares the road for an oppressive and manipulative culture."[445]

In many ways, the impact of school education is felt in the family as in the Church. Parents feel inferior and defenseless before their children who argue with strong reasons for their rights to think and act differently. Educated women appeal to family planning, their rights and dignity.[446] Traditionally marriage has been a communal affair; today sexuality is learnt at school, in magazines and mass media. Young people decide by themselves whom to marry. Today society operates by professions in different fields of learning and specialisation, which also affects Church life. In the past the Church would send a priest for specialisation according to its needs; today a priest chooses to undertake a study according to his preference. This free choice is positively expressive of

443 Bishop Joseph Abura, "Today's Vices have been Turned into Virtues," in *CISA*, Issue No. 135, Wednesday, November 25, 2009, p. 4.

444 Bernard Häring, *Manipulation: Ethical Boundaries of Medical, Behavioural & Genetic Manipulation*, Slough, St. Paul Publications, 1975, pp. 13-14. Häring notes that the term *manipulation*, as used in behavioural science, has a negative connotation, where a person subtly or explicitly controls another.

445 Ibid., p. 15.

446 Jean-Marie Nsambu writes, "Africa Needs Feminist Leaders" in *Leadership*, Nr. 469, March 2009, pp. 30-31. This is after his interview with Sylvia Tamale, a feminist legal theorist; at the time, Dean of Law at Makerere University. The topic of discussion centres on the Uganda Domestic Bill, an attempt by Ugandan elite women, seeking that women in the home must live with dignity whether they are married or not.

self-determination but it can as well go out of control in the name of freedom, in the nuance of *free will*, to do what one can and wishes to do even if the result may not be constructive to the community.

4.3.7. Seminary Formation

This regards the impact of seminary life on candidates to the ordained priesthood. Two senior priests argued that a major cause of clericalism is seminary formation. From their experience, they mentioned the missionary factor as it affected them. Msgr. Ongom explained that many candidates to the priesthood did not develop fully their emotional capability to manage relationships among themselves and with the public. This orientation made them to remain anonymous throughout their formation.[447] The reason for this is a strict disciplinarian approach to formation of priests. Fr. Onegwa argued that missionaries had good intentions but they did not prepare indigenous priests to stand on their own and to face realities that lie ahead. This orientation has produced a generation of priests with dependency mentality and inferiority feelings.[448] A disciplinarian approach in seminary training is a factor to shaping candidates who will remain calm but anonymous to their teachers and spiritual guides in order to get through to ordination. Such an approach to produce 'virtuous and approved men' seems to reflect what Kohlberg has called in his study, a "bag of virtues approach." He writes that: "The objection of the psychologist to the bag of virtues is that there are no such things. Virtues and vices are labels by which people award praise or blame to others, but the way people use praise and blame toward others are not the ways they think when making moral decisions themselves."[449] Commenting on Kohlberg's critique of a wrong virtue approach to formation, Schindler observes that it can only deform character and cultivate individualism.[450]

Other factors emerge in the new situation when African seminaries are to prepare African priests. One factor is a wrong orientation towards the priesthood. Fr. Opio, the Pastoral Coordinator of Nebbi Catholic Diocese, observed that in the seminaries there is a tendency for seminarians to develop a false hope of becoming influential ruler-figures. This has repercussions in their life

447 Msgr. Ludovico Ongom, interviewed by the researcher, at Akanyu, 5 June 2008.

448 Fr. Emilio Onegwa, interviewed by the researcher, at Nyapea, 7 June 2008.

449 Lawrence Kohlberg, *The Philosophy of Moral Development*, Vol. 1: *Essays on Moral Development*, San Francisco, Harper and Row, 1981, p. 34. Lawrence Kohlberg (1927-1987) was professor at Harvard University (USA). He made a contribution in developing theories of human development in children, adolescents and adults.

450 Schindler, *Ethics: The Social Dimension – Individualism and the Catholic Church*, pp. 83-85.

as priests.[451] The second factor is a weak human formation. To this, Bishop Luluga pointed out that seminary academic orientation gives more attention to passing examinations in all the subjects; important courses that would address practical life skills on time management, sexuality, relationship, team action, basic administration and management are not well covered.[452]

What conscience of the priesthood does seminary training create? This question has been touched on by Rwiza in his book, where he observes that: "The current formation of priests as well as that of religious men and women tends to create a class apart, separated from the life of the people and from their problems, challenges and sufferings."[453] What emerges from this is detachment from contingent realities. We can deduce that seminary training has a significant impress on the life of future priests and the religious in the way they will serve the Church.

4.4. Assessment

From what we have discussed above, we can identify three concerns that arise from individualism: identity crisis, self-justification, and false personalism.

4.4.1. Identity Crisis

According to Moltmann, a false vision of self-identity weakens integral personal unity and the overall community identity without which personal identity cannot be fully understood. On the one hand, there is the 'ego' problem which reduces self-identity to the realms of having. In this way a person becomes an object: the body one has, the social position, the power one has to control events, activities or other persons. On the other hand, the 'I' is equated with being: the state one finds oneself in. The darkness in this is that a person only counts on the basis of materiality or condition of life: sex, health or the status one has.[454] Moltmann argues that this leads to 'self-substantiation' by which one tends towards exalting one's own being while deprecating others.

---

451 Fr. Richard Opio, interviewed by the researcher, at Nebbi, 23 June 2008.

452 Bishop Martin Luluga, interviewed by the researcher, at Nebbi, 23 June 2008.

453 Rwiza, *Formation of Christian Conscience in Modern Africa*, p. 128.

454 Moltmann, *The Church in the Power of the Spirit*, pp. 186-187, gives a good exposition.

4.4.2. Self-justification

Individualism is a misdirected love of oneself; it advances self-justification, which only weakens integral personal fulfillment. In their co-authored book, *Fulfillment in Christ*, Grisez and Shaw describe individualism as an attitude of going it alone;[455] an attitude that is opposed to community team spirit which works on the basis of common commitment.[456] Self-justification numbs community spirit, distorts personal resourcefulness and initiative; and denies the integral personal fulfillment of the individual. In his book, *The Way of the Lord Jesus*, Grisez writes that: "Individuals are not made for fulfillment in isolation; they are made for some form of common life and for fulfillment there."[457] In this understanding, "...individualism is not consistent with a will toward integral fulfillment which requires a fellowship of persons and sharing of goods."[458]

4.4.3. False Personalism

A third problem concerns false personalism. Muelder explains that: "Personalists affirm self-conscious experience to be the nonreducible synoptic key to reality and define value as of, by, and for persons-in-community. Person is the ontological ultimate, and personality is the explanatory principle."[459] This understanding poses some difficulties: the first is that of self-conscious experience and how this relates to commonly held values. Secondly, the question of the person as an 'ontological ultimate' may slip into absolutising the individual as all by oneself detached from others. Thirdly, personality may become an idealistic yardstick of measuring the worth of the person. Nevertheless, a positive approach to personalism brings to unity both the subjective and objective understanding of the person as someone in relation with others, the world and ultimately with God as the Creator of every personal existence and of all perceptible realities.

In his Letter to Families, *Nuntius*, Pope John Paul II addresses the antithesis that lies between individualism and personalism. He notes that this tension emerges not only on the level of theory, but even more on that of *ethos*: "The "ethos" of personalism is altruistic: it moves the person to become a gift for

455 Germain Grisez and Russell Shaw, *Fulfillment in Christ*, p. 88.

456 Ibid., p. 62.

457 Germain Grisez, *The Way of the Lord Jesus,* Vol. 1: *Christian Moral Principles*, Quincy, Franciscan Press, 1997, Chapter 24-A, n. 7, p. 576.

458 Ibid., Chapter 8-B, n. 1, p. 206.

459 Walter G. Muelder, "Personalism," in *NDCE*, p. 469.

others and to discover the joy of giving himself."[460] He makes the distinction that personalism is bound up with the civilisation of love; while individualism remains egocentric (centered on oneself) and selfish; and thus, it is directly and radically opposed to the civilisation of love.[461] He further clarifies that individualism operates not only at the individual level but takes on a social expression as it affects the family, group, community or the larger society.

It is important to understand the word *ethos*, a transliteration of the Greek word for *custom* or *character*. Lovin clarifies that the word *ethos* refers to "characteristic values, beliefs, and practices of a social group or a culture."[462] It is the pulse of community moral spirit. This means that if individualism plays on *ethos*, it can manifest itself in the attitudes and aspirations of the community of persons. Although *ethos* is constituted by pervasive beliefs and values that are not often questioned within the ethos, it is subject to normative ethical reflection on the basis of choices and decisions to be made. Therefore, if individualism expresses selfishness, its gravity, density and intensity must be assessed in how this can affect and shape the life of the ecclesial community and its mission of bearing witness to the Gospel message.

Conclusion

This chapter has discussed the problem of individualism under four perspectives: its notion, expressive forms, factors causing or accentuating it, and an assessment to weigh its impact. From its notion we have seen that individualism is a falsification of self-love, which is subtly pervasive; nevertheless, it remains incompatible with commonly held values. It dissociates the individual from the matrix of the community, and yet, it subversively pours into the community.

We have shown that individualism finds expression in a number of ways. This weakens not only personal moral accountability but also affects the life of the Church as an institution. In the assessment, we have specified three questions that need attention: the problem of self-identity, a distortion which brings with it identity crisis. This leads to the second problem of self-justification by which, in seeking self-advantage, one sacrifices others and the institution to which s/he belongs. Identity crisis and self-justification lead to the third problem of false personalism, a wrong vision of being oneself, a distortion of self-perception, depriving the individual of the possibility of self-fulfillment

460 *Nuntius*, n. 14: *AAS* 86 (1994), p. 894.

461 Ibid.

462 Robin W. Lovin, "Ethos," in *NDCE*, p. 208.

which can only be achieved in community. What remains difficult is that individualism can turn the individual against community, that is, it blurs common vision which in turn works to weaken or hinder common growth. In chapter five, we shall attempt to respond to the problem of the individual in view of Christian personality.

CHAPTER FIVE
The Individual in the Light of Christian Anthropology

Introduction

In Chapter Four, we underlined that individualism is a distortion of self-love; a love misdirected in the heart; and the wrong vision of the self. This chapter is an attempt to clarify the understanding of the individual in the light of Christian anthropology. It is an attempt to provide moral theological explanations about the individual as a member of the Church, the subject of God's Self-Revelation in Christ, through his Incarnation and work of Salvation. Focusing on this point of reflection the chapter discusses Christian personhood, the rightful autonomy of the individual, the individual as an embodied moral subject, who is capable of self-realisation, with a moral historicity, and must strive to be responsible, and to responsibly participate in the social reality of the Church.

5.1. Christian Personhood

The question of the individual is important in reflecting upon community. In his book, *Catholicsm*, McBrien explains the concept of Christian anthropology by the term *personalism*, which "...stresses the importance of the individual human being, or person, in reaching moral decisions."[463]

Grundy avers that, "The Bible offers no systematic view of the individual human constitution; indications that do appear are incidental to the interrelationships that entail thinking, feeling, and willing."[464] Nevertheless, recent developments in Church teaching have paid attention to the question of the human person, with reference to God's definitive Self-Revelation in Christ. Thus, the foundation of Christian anthropology is based in the mystery of Revelation and Salvation. A clear picture of understanding the human person in the light of Christ has been clarified in the document of Vatican Council II on the Church in the Modern World, *Gaudium et Spes*. It states: "For by his incarnation the Son of God united himself in some sense with every human being. He

463 McBrien, *Catholicism*, p. 1252.

464 Robert H. Grundy, "Human Being," in *HBD*, p. 411.

labored with human hands, thought with a human mind, acted with a human will, and loved with a human heart."[465]

The human person has been the focus of Pope John Paul II's first Encyclical Letter, *Redemptor Hominis*. He makes a Christological paradigm shift in theological anthropology, with a change of vocabulary from *soul* to *man*, where the term 'man' is used in the neutral sense, referring to the human person as such. He writes: "We are not dealing here with man in the abstract, but with the real, concrete, historical man. We are dealing with each individual since each one is included in the mystery of Redemption and through this mystery Christ has united himself with each one forever."[466]

He continues this reflection in other successive documents. In the Encyclical Letter *Centesimus Annus*, he maintains that a correct vision of the human person is the starting point and most fundamental issue at the centre of Catholic social doctrine. He writes: "...it will be necessary to keep in mind that the main thread and, in a certain sense, the guiding principle...of all of the Church's social doctrine, is a *correct view of the human person* and of his unique value..."[467]

In the Encyclical Letter on Faith and Reason, *Fides et Ratio*, the Pope asks: "I ask *everyone* to look more deeply at man, whom Christ has saved in the mystery of his love, and at the same time at the human being's unceasing search for truth and meaning. Different philosophical systems have lured people into believing that they are their own absolute master, able to decide their own destiny and future in complete autonomy, trusting only in themselves and their powers..."[468] He maintains that: "The chief purpose of theology is to *provide an understanding of Revelation and the content of faith*;"[469] which is even a stronger concern for moral theology.[470] He clarifies that all men and women are by nature philosophers and have their own philosophies by which they direct their lives. However, this does not neglect their particular religious traditions.[471]

465 *GS*, n. 22 § 2: *AAS* 58 (1966), p. 1042.

466 *RH*, n. 13: *AAS* 71 (1979), p. 283; idem., Encyclical Letter *Centesimus Annus*, Vatican Polyglot English translation, Vatican City, Libreria Editrice Vaticana, 1991, n. 53: *AAS* 83 (1991), p. 859.

467 *CA*, n. 11 § 3: *AAS* 83 (1991), p. 807, italicised emphases as in the original.

468 Idem., Encyclical Letter *Fides et Ratio*, Vatican Polyglot translation Vatican City, Libreria Editrice Vaticana, 1998, n. 107: *AAS* 91 (1999), p. 87.

469 *FR*, n. 93; cf. n. 99: *AAS* 91 (1999), p. 78; 82-83.

470 Ibid., n. 68 and 98: *AAS* 91 (1991), p. 58; 81-82.

471 Ibid., n. 64: *AAS* 91 (1991), p. 55.

Therefore, both philosophy and religion seek "*the truth of the person* – what the person is and what the person reveals from deep within."[472]

In his book, *L'Antropologia Cristiana tra modernità e Postmodernità*, a reflection on Christian anthropology in the context of modernity and post-modernity, Sanna makes an elaboration on the Encyclical, *Fides et Ratio*. The problem he confronts is the philosophical distortion which extols the primacy of reason to the defect of atomising the individual. His central point is that only an anthropology which has God for its foundation will enrich the vision and meaning of human existence.[473] This following discussion intends to respond to the cultural, affective, work, and political factors causing or accentuating individualism as we have highlighted in Chapter Four.

5.2. Rightful Autonomy

In his book, *Reason Informed by Faith*, Richard Gula clarifies that individuality involves *autonomy*, meaning that the individual has a personal uniqueness, fundamental originality and equality within the matrix of community existence. S/he lives among others, sharing interests in everything human; but with differing degrees of acting, of seeing the world and values. S/he has unique dispositions, intensity of affection or sensitivity and intention.[474] This legitimacy of individuality does not mean antinomy as individualism would propose. The content of Christian autonomy acknowledges God for its foundation, that is, personal individuality shares a unique aspect of God's autonomy.

Böckle cautions that moral autonomy is a grey spot that can subtly lead to sinning. He writes that, "It is, however, the source of radical temptation and the ground of the possibility of self-alienation, self-contradiction and sin."[475] The

472 Ibid., n. 32: *AAS* 91 (1991), p. 30.

473 Ignazio Sanna, *L'Antropologia Cristiana tra Modernità e Postmodernità*, Brescia, Queriniana, 2001, p. 255, writes, "L'antropologia ricentrata in Dio come suo ultimo fondamento... può essere considerata allo stesso tempo come tramonto di una visione debole ed aurora di una visione forte dell'esistenza umana" (*an anthropology centred on God as its ultimate foundation...can be considered at the same time the sunset of a weak vision and the dawning of a strong vision of human existence*), English translation ours.

474 Gula, *Reason Informed by Faith*, p. 71f.

475 Franz Böckle, *Fundamental Moral Theology*, English translation by N. D. Smith, New York, Pueblo Publishing Company, 1980, p. 63. Böckle's approach is dialogical. He tries to be respectful of insights from all human and social sciences for the need to improve social order. Despite the citation we have taken, the conclusion he makes on autonomous ethics is somewhat opaque and presents a moral dilemma: "On the one hand, freedom implies total dependence, insofar as man is offered the possibility of deciding in favor of freedom as a gift (creation as grace). On the other hand, however, it is also total independence, insofar as man finds himself confronted with the absolute self as a self-centered being. He can only gain himself

English word *autonomy* derives from Greek *autos*, 'self' and *nomos*, 'norm, law.' It entails moral maturity and integrity by which one directs one's life responsibly.

The question of moral autonomy has been clarified by Pope John Paul II in the Encyclical Letter, *Veritatis Splendor*, where he explains that true moral autonomy consists in man's dominion over himself.[476] It does not mean that the individual's consciousness is an absolute in itself: "Man's genuine moral autonomy in no way means the rejection but rather the acceptance of the moral law, of God's command... Human freedom and God's law meet and are called to intersect..."[477] He uses a technical language of "theonomy" or "participated theonomy" referring to a vertical transcendence which lies at the heart of every love, a gift of grace by which the human person is enabled to exercise a full measure of personal freedom, which alone can perfect the spiritual nature of the human person.[478] The Pope links up moral autonomy with the question of freedom, one's capacity to realise practical knowledge in accordance with moral truth. Cessario comments that: "The Holy Father reserves the term *freedom* to characterize the person who not only knows what the moral law teaches, but who also is able to render moral truth incarnate in his or her actions."[479] Autonomy does not turn someone in on oneself; it is not self-absorption but rather signifies being responsible.

5.3. An Embodied Moral Subject

This implies responsible self-determination and freedom, in a chain of relationships, lived in community with other persons and the material world. As McBrien explains, one is a moral subject "...insofar as the person is conscious, interrelates with others, and freely determines who and what he or she will become."[480] The term *embodied* is proposed by Gula to render a more unitary

---

when he is left to himself. He can only have power over himself when he is responsible for himself. This antinomy is not a real contradiction so long as God's and man's personalities are not placed on the same level" (p. 63). See his discussion: "The theological justification on moral autonomy" (p. 46-63).

476 *VS*, nn. 38-41: *AAS* 85 (1993), pp. 1164-1166.

477 Ibid., n. 41: *AAS* 85 (1993), pp. 1165-1166.

478 Cf. Romanus Cessario, "Moral Absolutes in the Civilization of Love" in J. A. DiNoia and Romanus Cessario (eds.), *Veritatis Splendor and the Renewal of Moral Theology*, Princeton, Scepter Publishers, 1999, p. 199.

479 *loc. cit.*

480 McBrien, p. 1257.

usage instead of *body and soul*.[481] The human person is part of the material world marked with limitations and ambiguities, tensions and conflicts; and yet embodying the spiritual reality which makes them self-transcending by a unique call from above.[482] *Embodied* also means that the individual is not self-sufficient both in the bodily and spiritual dimensions. The spiritual nature "Pertains to an attitude and style which reflects an attentiveness to the presence and action of God within us and in the world around us."[483] This understanding shows that the individual remains incomplete, and even incomprehensible, on their own. It is in community that s/he can find self-realisation.

5.4. Self-realisation

According to Lobo, human personality involves *self-realisation*, given one's potentiality, capability and the possibilities surrounding him or her.[484] However, both self-realisation and autonomy involve a correct self-knowing and self-loving in the wide spectrum of relational possibilities. Self-realisation comes from true and well-ordered love of oneself which, in turn, opens the individual to love others. Noonan argues that the general principles such as "Never do to others what you would not wish them to do to you" and "Do to others as you would have them do to you," point to the love of oneself which motivates us to love others as ourselves.[485]

Thus, it is impossible to love others if self-love is not properly cultivated. In some sense, individualism displays lack of self-love by which someone remains cold to the love which is self-giving. This shows that self-realisation is impossible without self-love. Pope John Paul II writes that: "…there are in the life of a human being many more truths which are simply believed than truths which are acquired by way of personal verification."[486]

5.5. An Historical Subject

Moral historicity signifies progress and direction, which consists in a process of learning, internalising and appropriating common values. Gula clarifies that it is a dynamic integration of the past into the person we are becoming so

---

481 Gula, p. 69.

482 Lobo, *Christian Living According to Vatican II*, p. 93.

483 McBrien, p. 1257.

484 Lobo, p. 93f.

485 John P. Noonan, *General and Special Ethics*, Chicago, Loyola University Press, 1947, p. 146.

486 *FR*, n. 31: *AAS* 91 (1999), p. 29.

as to shape a future rather than settling into a static condition.[487] Moral historicity is an interplay between the spiritual and bodily aspects of the self which bear upon the continuing present. This means that one has to weigh what might result from one's present behaviour in the near and distant future.

Bujo brings out another image of moral historicity where he talks of a "morality of *memoria*"[488] in the same sense of integrating the past into the present with a focus into the future. Historicity is memorial, remembering, by which the individual becomes part of the larger, living tradition of the community. The historicity of the individual therefore means that s/he can grow in moral maturity by making use of values that have shaped the spirit and vision of the community over time; the lived experience which prolongs the belief system, tradition and practices of that community.

5.6. A Responsible Individual

We have already defined responsibility in Chapter Four under accountability. Here we would like to emphasise personal moral accountability in the face of commonly held values. Autonomy, embodiment, self-realisation and historicity call freedom to expression. Gula argues that although freedom is affected by contingent factors, this does not mean selling out to determinism which avoids responsibility on the rhetoric that we are who we are and act the way we do by heredity, culture or environment.[489] The human person is before and above these necessary factors. Everybody is endowed with potentialities, primary orientations and freedom which must find adequate expression and contribute to the building of communal life. Responsibility entails striving to uphold the given values, meanings and purposes that bind the individual to their community.

5.7. Personhood is Relational

Christian relationship has its foundation in the Trinitarian vision, which signifies reciprocity. The teaching of Vatican Council II, continued in the Catechism, maintains that God is the sole origin, continuity and fulfillment of human relationship:

---

487 Gula, p.70.

488 Bujo, *The Ethical Dimension of Community*, pp. 15-23; idem, *Foundations of an African Ethic*, p. 70.

489 Gula, p. 76.

> All men are called to the same end: God himself. There is a certain resemblance between the union of the Divine Persons and the fraternity that men and women are to establish among themselves in truth and love. Love of neighbour is inseparable from love of God.[490]

The individual therefore progresses in acquiring their potentialities and a variety of values in the world of relationships.[491]

Relational aptitude opens the individual from intrapersonal autonomy to an interpersonal dynamic. In his study of the African philosophy of life, Mbiti writes that: "Only in terms of other people does the individual become conscious of his own being, his own duties, his privileges and responsibility towards himself and towards other people."[492] Relating is realisable through participation, expressible in a conscious and dynamic self-involvement, in the acknowledgement of discernible values, meanings and purposes.

Pope John Paul II insists that: "Human beings are not made to be alone. They are born into a family and in a family they grow…From birth, therefore, they are immersed in traditions which give them not only a language and a cultural formation but also a range of truths in which they believe almost instinctively…"[493] This calls the individual to integrate wider dimensions and ways of internalising and appropriating the human values, meanings and purposes into their uniquely individual yet shared life.

5.8. The Individual as a Participant

The individual is a *participant* whose wholeness works in a multifaceted reality of relationships: with others, social structures, material world and ultimately God. In its Pastoral Constitution on the Church in the World, Vatican Council II explains that no individual, male or female, is self-sufficient: "… God did not create man a solitary being… For by his innermost nature man is a social being; and if he does not enter into relations with others he can neither live nor develop his gifts."[494] For this reason the Council teaches that: "Insofar as man by his very nature stands completely in need of society, he is and he ought to be the beginning, the subject and the object of all social

490 *GS*, n. 24 § 3: *AAS* 58 (1966), p. 1045; *CCC*, n. 1878.

491 *CCC*, n. 1880.

492 Mbiti, *African Religions and Philosophy*, p. 106.

493 *FR*, n. 31: *AAS* 91 (1999), p. 29.

494 *GS*, n. 12 § 4: *AAS* 58 (1966), p. 1034, text as in Flannery (ed.), *Vatican Council II*, Vol. I: *The Conciliar and Post Conciliar Documents*, Ninth printing, Dublin, Dominican Publications, 1992, pp. 913-914.

organization."[495] The proper place of participation of the individual is the ecclesial community, which is the fuller reality of its individual members.

Conclusion

We have illustrated in this chapter that the individual is fully an individual through the web of relationships that shape and define him/her. Catechesis must bring the believer to understand herself or himself as a centre of relationships in the new order of existence and identity revealed in Christ. We have clarified that Christian personality is defined by love of God and of neighbour. The individual is autonomous but this autonomy does not imply self-sufficiency; it means self-mastery. The individual is an embodied moral subject who attains self-realisation in a historical reality. We have noted that s/he is a responsible moral subject in a relational reality. Lastly, we saw that the individual is a participant in a community of persons and shared values. The Church is therefore a community of individuals with such an identity that characterises it as a communion of persons in the love of Christ. This introduces the following chapter, which pays attention to the building of ecclesial communion.

495 *Ibid.*, n. 25 § 1: *AAS* 58 (1966), p. 1045; *CCC*, n. 1879.

CHAPTER SIX
Towards the Building of Ecclesial Communion

Introduction

This chapter looks for ways by which individualism may be reversed or overcome, and communion upheld, in the Church. It asks: How will Nebbi Catholic Diocese build a strong and viable ecclesial communion? To respond fairly to this question the chapter will first clarify what is meant by ecclesial communion. from this it will to draw examples from the early Christian communities; historical developments through the Church Fathers; the social nature of the Church; models of the Church; the Church as a moral community. Lastly, we shall try to link this by presenting the models of morality as ways of informing the Christian moral conscience on ecclesial communion and the actions ensuing from it.

6.1. The Notion of Ecclesial Communion

By *ecclesial communion* reference is here made of that togetherness which pertains to, and remains characteristic of, the Church. This can be explained by the basic theological term of *community*, referring to two other closely linked concepts: group, and relationship. With regard to community as *group*, Löser clarifies that: "Community is the name given to the assembly of Christians in a place or in some other frame of reference. The church manifests itself concretely in a community gathered for prayer, witness, or service."[496] Although this understanding provides for ample pastoral opportunities, Löser cautions that:

> …it also brings some danger, inasmuch as more comprehensive ecclesial groupings may disappear from the consciousness of the faithful… membership in church and parish has ceased to be something taken for granted by society, while the personal decision of faith as well as the experiential unity of Christians that manifests itself in manifold relationships, have become the basis and support for communities. The territorial principle is indeed still at work, but it has lost its earlier unchallenged influence. "Basic communities," "personal

496 Werner Löser, "Community (Group)" in Wolfgang Beinert and Francis Schüssler Fiorenza (eds.), *Handbook of Catholic Theology*, New York, The Crossroad Publishing Company, 2000, p. 111.

communities," "religious communities," and other Christian groups and movements not infrequently compete with the parishes.[497]

The second notion of ecclesial community refers to *relationship*. In this perspective, Langemeyer explains that: "Community is formed by two or more persons who are linked to each other through a direct sharing of life. Where human persons only interact with one another as freely interchangeable representatives of various functions (role-bearers), one can no longer speak of community. Community in the theological sense has its origin and ground in an experience of salvation that stems from the initiative of God."[498] The ecclesial community becomes real when it expresses concrete life through mutual love, communal recognition and celebration. However, Langemeyer observes that:

> The psychological capability of the human person to share in the life of others, however, is limited. When the concept of community is extended to all Christians or indeed to all persons in the world, it can easily become an ideology, in that it inevitably masks the given institutional structures. Just as the love of neighbor in the sense that Jesus gave it referred to whoever is the neighbor (see Lk 12:27-37), Christian community is to be formed among those whom one encounters... For this reason the concept of community retains a critical function toward ecclesial structures: they exist in order to make community possible.[499]

The ecclesial community depicted here is not a mere sociological togetherness or an institutionalised cultural belonging. It reflects the Gospel spirit of unity in Christ. In this study we are referring to Nebbi Catholic Diocese as an ecclesial communion, comprising the different contexts and levels of smaller unit communities such as the deanery, parish, zone, chapel, SCCs; with the Christian family as the foundation to all these contexts. The diocese also includes other frames of ecclesial realities such as communities of consecrated persons (the religious), groups, clubs, associations, movements and institutions of the diocese's apostolate in the health and education sectors. How will ecclesial communion be built in this setting? We can attempt to respond to this question by drawing examples from the Bible and the Church tradition born from it.

497 Ibid., p. 112.

498 Georg Langemeyer, "Community (Relationship)" in *HCT*, pp. 112-113.

499 Ibid., 113-114.

6.2. Biblical Perception

It is difficult in the context of our study to explore in details what Scripture records, concerning the building of ecclesial communion. There are two areas we would like to highlight to illustrate this: Christ's example, and the practices that followed from it in the early Christian communities.

6.2.1. Jesus Christ and the Initial Christ-Community

Christianity takes its name from Jesus Christ. Did He form a community? If not, was he a lonesome figure? Then how would he proclaim the message of God's kingdom? If he formed a community, what would be the image of that community? In this enquiry, we may agree with the theological hypothesis that: Jesus proclaimed the kingdom; what came was the Church.[500] The Gospels have numerous illustrations which attest to how Jesus Christ formed an active community life in different contexts. In his public ministry, he first gathers a community of twelve companions with whom he shares his daily ordinary life (Mk. 3:13-19). Later there is mention of seventy-two others (Lk. 10:1f). There are women who accompany him in his ministry (Mk. 15:40-41); it is through a woman that he approaches the Samaritan village, many of whom come to believe in him on the testimony of this woman (Jn. 4). He makes company with sinners and tax collectors whom he wins over for God (Mk. 2:13-14). He welcomes children into the family of God (Mk. 10:13-16). He involves the people and sometimes makes use of their own resources in the miracles that he performs: at the multiplication of bread and fish (Mt. 14:13-21; 15:32-39); at the healing of the daughter of Jairus he asks the community to give her something to eat (Lk. 8:54-56). The numerous accounts of his healing show that those who are healed become witnesses and participants in the message of God's love.

For Jesus, those who listen to the word of God and act on it are his family, far beyond natural bonds (Mk. 3:31-35). According to Edward Mally, "Jesus does not deny his natural kinship but radically subordinates it to a higher bond of brotherhood. The reign of God makes demands on the personal commitment of a disciple, which must transcend at times all natural bonds of family or ethnic grouping."[501] In this account the ministry of Jesus is driven by the Holy

---

500 Joseph Cardinal Ratzinger, *Called to Communion: Understanding the Church Today*, translated by Adrian Walker, San Francisco, Ignatius Press, 1996, pp. 21-29, elaborates on the origin and essence of the Church centered on the person of Christ as the fulfilment of God's promise and the present action of God. The phrase referred to is on, p. 21.

501 Edward J. Mally, "The Gospel According to Mark," in Raymond E. Brown, Joseph A. Fitzmyer and Roland E. Murhpy (eds.), *The Jerome Biblical Commentary*, Vol. 2: *The New Testament and Topical Articles*, reprint, London, Geoffrey Chapman, 1972, p. 29b.

Spirit. His true family is in the Kingdom of God whose members are those who do the will of God. Christ's example of gathering people into the kingdom of God has a historical import for us today. It is not just informative but provides a glimpse into how ecclesial communion can be formed: its composition, with regard to those who are received to participate in its daily life; its inspiration and focus. The community Jesus builds around him cuts across all sectors of the society but it has its own distinctive character. The Church historian, Bokenkotter, writes that:

> Jesus not only preached the good news of the kingdom, he also gathered his followers into a fellowship. They often took their meals together, celebrating joyfully their new covenant with God while they anticipated the glorious banquet to come in the kingdom of heaven. He called them the light of the world, the city of God, the salt of the earth. They were a family whose common devotion to God's will united them far more intensely than any bonds of flesh and blood.[502]

This fellowship gives a deeper religious consciousness to the community gathered around Jesus. He did not build a structured community; he called people into God's family, the kingdom of God. He leaves us with examples of how this community is to grow according to his Spirit. Flusser, a Jewish scholar, remarks that in all Jewish religious history, it was Jesus, who declared publicly, for the first time, that the new age of salvation had already begun.[503]

The teaching and deeds of Jesus on community building can be summarised in three words: service, prayer life, and mission. *Service*: which he illustrates at the celebration of the Last Supper by washing the feet of his disciples and enjoins them to do likewise (Mk. 14: 22-25). From this we can see that service provides the possibility of reaching out to others; at the same time it enables us to express our hidden gifts and dormant capacities. *Common prayer*: which he instructs his followers to practice, in the gathering of which he is always present (Mt. 18:19-20). Here we learn that common prayer is not only an act of piety; it gathers believers together and helps them to express their life experiences in a prayerful mood. *Mission*: Jesus did not intend a self-closed community of his disciples. The conclusion of the Gospel according to St. Mathew makes an introduction to the missionary work that the apostles are to undertake. Jesus tells them to make disciples (Mt. 28:19). This suggests that ecclesial growth is possible from an important principle: making disciples.

502 Thomas Bokenkotter, *A Concise History of the Catholic Church*, New York, Doubleday, 1990, p. 10.

503 David Flusser, *Jesus*, New York, Herder & Herder, 1969, p. 90.

These points raise one question: How did the life and message of Jesus contribute to the building of ecclesial communion after his Ascension?

6.2.2. Early Christian Communities

In their 1979 study conference, the AMECEA bishops focused on the methods of implementing their pastoral priority of establishing SCCs. Two biblical texts guided their reflections: Acts 2:42-47 and Ephesians 4:11-13. We shall begin by looking at the first text. Their reflections on this text brought out the following: (a) the Christian community must have all the valuable elements of a human community, for it is simply a human community transformed by the Holy Spirit; (b) it must include physical and spiritual proximity; (c) it must pursue a common goal under a common leadership; (d) mutual trust and affection must exist among the members; (e) it must be based on God's Word, must be Eucharistic and apostolic, and truly caring.[504]

The following questions may help us to understand this text more deeply. Were early Christians individualistic? How would the Church exist and grow in such a spirit? Did early Christians form a community? Did they share their experiences together? How was it possible for them to prolong the mission of Christ? Did they practice their faith together? Did they work together? What can we learn from them that will help us to build a strong and viable ecclesial communion today? To respond to these questions we have to look back to the sources as recorded in the Acts of Apostles, which describes how the early Christians lived community life.

6.2.2.1. Illustration from the Acts of the Apostles

Three summaries about the first community of believers at Jerusalem can help us to have a better picture of how they practiced their faith in daily life.

Acts 1:12-14 describes the return of the Eleven Apostles to Jerusalem from the Mount of Olives, after the Ascension event. The text says that, "With one heart all these joined constantly in prayer, together with some women, including Mary the mother of Jesus, and with his brothers" (v. 14). From this summary, there emerge three factors that can lead to building ecclesial communion: heartfelt unity; togetherness; common prayer.

Acts 2:37-41 describes the first conversions which increased their group. These new converts remained faithful to four things: (a) the teaching of the apostles; (b) the fellowship; (c) the breaking of bread; (d) common prayers

504 AMECEA Bishops, *AMECEA Study Conference*, Zomba, Malawi, 13th – 16th August 1979, in *AFER*, Vol. 21, No. 5, October 1979, p. 261.

(vv. 42, 46). Here we can notice four marks of ecclesial communion, which brought about an important factor: the joy of faith, leading them to share their food gladly and generously (v. 46).

In Acts 4:32-35, the whole group of believers is united, heart and soul; they share their possessions by making contributions for those who are, or might be, in need. From these accounts, what becomes distinctive of their life is their devotion or perseverance, a wholehearted commitment which binds them together as a community. It is this example that made a deep impression on the people: they were filled with awe, that is, a reverential fear came upon them and led more to be converted to the Christian faith.

In his study of the *Acts*, González observes that the nascent Church at Jerusalem was able to form a viable community through the perseverance of the believers.[505] As we have noted above, there are four marks that made this possible. The first mark of ecclesial communion is catechesis or instruction about the life and deeds of Christ. The texts from the *Acts of Apostles* we have referred to above report that the converts were devoted to the teaching of the Apostles. This aspect of devotion points to learning and studying in order to appropriate the Gospel message and apostolic teaching passed on in the Scriptures. It is in this way that the Church communities can remain faithful and move deeper into the joy of faith. Small Christian communities must be encouraged to practice Bible reading and sharing. This will enable them to understand the Gospel message and apply it to their life situation. By contrast, our fieldwork has brought us to realise that "Catholics" are generally shy to study the Bible in their homes or communities and apply it to their life situations, in comparison with their counterparts in the "Protestants" or "Evangelicals" churches.

The second mark of ecclesial communion is *fellowship*. The Greek word used to describe Christian fellowship is *koinonia*, meaning association, participation; from *koinos*, common, communal; and *koinonos*, companion, partner, sharer; the verb form *synkoinoneo*, to participate in together with someone.[506] Christian fellowship is not just a good feeling that someone has with another as among friends although it includes this component; its deeper meaning lies in solidarity and compassion, which involve the sharing of feelings, goods, and actions. The notation of fellowship, *koinonia*, in Acts 2:44-45 signifies communion: they had all things in common. This does not mean that there was no private ownership or that they sold off everything they had and put the proceeds in a common fund. It describes the devotion they had to one another

505 Justo L. González, *Acts: The Gospel of the Holy Spirit*, Maryknoll, Orbis Books, 2001, p. 49-55.

506 *NIV*, p. 696.

and their readiness to make contributions to meet the needs of their members. Common possession is a point that can help the Church to address its economic life. In his study of Acts 4:32-35, González argues that: "Because in our churches economic matters are not discussed as often as it should be, a careful study of this text is important."[507]

The third mark of ecclesial communion is *the breaking of bread.* There are two acts involved: (a) the Eucharist, a memorial of the Last Supper which Jesus celebrated with his disciples. This expressed their vertical communion with the Lord; (b) *Agape*, a meal in which they celebrated a love-feast. This expressed their horizontal communion with one another. It does not mean that they always ate their food together but rather that their love feast brought them to the practice of charity by making material support to community members who are in need. *Agape* is charity, an act of glad and generous heart, motivated by love for God, which is shown to those in need; it is not to be confused with philanthropy which is a natural pity at the wretched situation of someone. *Agape* is solidarity and sharing which can help the Church in three ways: (a) to ward off injustice within it; (b) to improve its structures; (c) to build relationships – in the Christian family, SCC, chapel community, zone, parish, deanery and diocese.

The fourth mark of ecclesial communion is *common prayer*. The believers devoted themselves to worshipping God in the temple together. From this we can learn that common prayer in every small ecclesial community will strengthen its life of holiness and virtue. However, common prayer must help them to go beyond the thrust of "evangelism" which sometimes digresses into activism or emotional obsession. We have already shown this difficulty as posed by the evangelicals which is attracting a number of Catholics. The second aspect of worship is the Eucharistic celebration, which is the centre of all the Church's prayer life. In Nebbi Catholic Diocese, the establishment of Eucharistic Centres with the service of catechists and other extraordinary ministers of the Eucharist has made it possible for the faithful to experience the importance of Holy Communion.

What we said here is that devotion to apostolic teaching (through learning and study of Scripture), fellowship (as solidarity and sharing), breaking of bread (as celebration of love feast, charity and social justice in the Church), and common prayer (prayer meetings and Eucharistic celebration) are the four marks which can help Nebbi Catholic Diocese to build a strong and viable ecclesial communion. However, another aspect needs to come to light: the diocese must detect the various gifts of God's grace in its members.

507 González, *Acts: The Gospel of the Spirit*, p. 70.

6.2.2.2. Gifts of Grace and Ministry

Another important factor that contributed to ecclesial growth in the early Church was the exercise of the different gifts in ministries. To understand this it is important to ask what is meant by *ministry in the Church.* Löser defines ministry in the Church in terms of service to the community:

> By ministry in the church is meant the service of leadership in the community that is given to certain persons in the church. It is distinguished from the universal (or common) priesthood of the church and the faithful as a "special ministry" or the "ordained ministry" or, finally, the "hierarchical ministry", and is in the service of the former... The concept of ministry or office is not formally present in the New Testament, but the various elements that characterize it are ready (e.g. discipleship, apostolate, calling and sending, service, imposition of hands, etc.). In the Pastoral Letters the picture of ministry in the church is already taking clear shape.[508]

Reference to "service" raises some questions on both pastoral and practical issues. How is Nebbi Catholic Diocese mobilising its human resources in order to meet the various possibilities of service in the school, clinics, economic and social-cultural activities? Do all the faithful understand service in all its implications? Do they understand that they are the living mission of Christ?

O'Meara remarks that today ministry in the Church exists in a new situation than in the early Church:

> The word *diakonia*, ministry, in the NT sometimes means a particular kind of action (Rom 12:7), and sometimes it means the general term which includes all the serving and evangelistic roles in the community (Eph 4:12). A service of services, it flows forth from Christian life and community and then is channeled into various Christian presentations of the word and power of God's new covenant... Every ministry is grounded in charism; some charisms in each Christian lead to ministry. Diaconal charisms come to baptized men and women in various modalities during their lives.[509]

This new situation is due to the Church's meeting with realities in the world. In Nebbi Catholic Diocese we have noted that the society in which it exists presents four faces: *villagers* (commonly traditional); *elite* (generally literate and informed); *business people* (more exposed, free and mobile); *free organisations*, typified by NGOs (more liberal and independent associations). This may raise some helpful questions of reflection on service: How does the diocese understand its old and new structures? How does it understand and

508 Werner Löser, "Ministry in the Church," in *HCT*, p. 479.

509 Thomas F. O'Meara, "Ministry," in *NDT*, p. 658.

make use of the dynamics of evangelical vitality within it? How effectively is the diocese working to bring about unity in its exercise of service (*diakonia*)?

The Church's service flows from its charism. *Charism* (plural, *charismata*) is a Greek word used in the Scripture with reference to God's "gift/s of grace" in the Church. In his analysis, Wilfrid Harrington clarifies that these gifts are manifold and are given individually but meant for the integral growth of the ecclesial community.[510]

A detailed study is made by Robert Banks in his book, *Paul's Idea of Community*. He observes that only until recently, theological scholarship on St. Paul's writings had for long forgotten the important theology of "gift" which is the basic principle of St. Paul's approach to the dynamics of the Church. God's gifts of grace are manifold: "So Paul can comprehend virtually the whole of God's saving activities vis-à-vis humanity in terms of gift: the sonship, the glory, the covenants, the giving of the law, the worship and the promises, justification, faith, eternal life – even Christ himself... These charismata are the fundamental gifts of God and undergird whatever other presents may be given to those who are in Christ."[511] Thus, for St. Paul, all the gifts in the Church which individuals have are meant for the common good, the growth of the community to maturity. What concerns us is about the nature of these gifts and their use to build ecclesial communion. Banks makes six conclusions about the nature of gifts in the Church.[512]

Gifts are open-ended in character, depending on the nature of a community: large or small, or another frame of ecclesial reality. The way specific gifts work or are developed in one community is not the same in another.

Gifts are distributed individually but not evenly: each person has a unique gift but not all have the same gift; yet others have many gifts. However, although the different gifts may allow for democratic procedures, God's gifts do not suggest an egalitarian principle because even the same gift works with different intensities in different persons.

Gifts are ranked according to their benefits: this does not mean that overemphasis is to be placed on those which appear to be most extraordinary, like speaking in tongues or prophesying. What is meant is the effect that those gifts bring to ecclesial growth, like teaching, preaching or interpretation of scripture. One gift is not to be used to downplay another; they do not stand in opposition but enrich one another.

510 Wilfrid Harrington, "Charism," in *NDT*, pp. 180-183.

511 Robert J. Banks, *Paul's Idea of Community: The Early House Churches in Their Cultural Setting*, revised edition, 6th printing, Peabody, Hendrickson Publishers Inc., 2007, p. 92.

512 Ibid., pp. 94-98.

Gifts are both regular and occasional: what St. Paul refers to as "higher" gifts like those for teaching are regular in nature and provide the basis for a continual ministry. Besides, there are gifts which are occasional, like prophesying, which can also provide the basis for regular ministry.

God's Gift is both newness and renewal: in Christ the Christian is a new person, the old has passed away; everything is new (2 Cor. 5:17). Banks clarifies that: "Paul does not mean that the Christian is a completely different person. He is pointing to the radical change that takes place when a person genuinely encounters God in Christ."[513] Thus, the "newness" of Christian living refers to the work of the Holy Spirit who activates one's God-given, providential potentials to reach their full expressions by the service that someone performs in the Church.

Gifts work on appropriate occasions: grace is not static but continuous. Christians must seize every opportunity to exercise their gifts, more especially in their small communities; they cannot wait until they gather at the chapel, parish, diocesan or other frames of ecclesial community. St. Paul uses the word *body* in the most ordinary sense of the small community of Christians where the experience of being body is most contingent (cf. 1 Cor. 12:12-27; Rom. 12:4-6; Eph. 4:4, 12-16). It is in this body, the community, the local "all," where the gift/s of each member becomes evident. The small community is the place where every gift can be best developed. This leaves us with a question: How are these gifts to be exercised for building an effective ecclesial communion?

The topic of gifts and service in the Church was the second point of focus during the study conference of the AMECEA bishops that we have mentioned above. In their reflection on St. Paul's Letter to Ephesians 4:8, 11-13, they realised that in the Church: (a) everyone has a part to play; (b) every gift is given not for one's own private use but for building up the community; (c) every member, and especially those in authority, need to be sensitive to the gifts of the Spirit in the community; (d) cooperation and collaboration are key words; (e) Christians are to be made more aware about their unique vocation to service; (f) the whole community must be patient and humble in its growth to the fullness of Christ.[514] How is this to be exercised for ecclesial growth?

513 Ibid., p. 98.

514 AMECEA Bishops, *AMECEA Study Conference*, Zomba, Malawi, 13th – 16th August 1979, in *AFER*, Vol. 21, No. 5, October 1979, p. 261.

6.2.2.3. The Exercise of Gifts in the Church

The exercise of gifts in the Church is measured by their relevance and effectiveness. There are five basic ways in which this can be done:[515]

Every gift is to be used in a proportionate way: each gift is directed towards some particular effect, like teaching towards pastoral care, wisdom and understanding towards counsel or advice. Gifts bring about psychological and social harmony in the community. Every individual member must use their particular gift with moderation and balance to give room for others so that every other gift finds expression.

The use of a gift must be within an understandable expression: St. Paul illustrates this with the gift of speaking in tongues: "…if you do not use your tongue to produce speech that can be readily understood, how can anyone know what you are saying? You will be talking to the air" (1 Cor. 14:9). However good a gift might be it will bear no good fruit if it is not used fittingly. This also applies to programmes that may be introduced into specific community contexts. The best programme may not work if the community does not understand what benefits it might bring.

A gift must be used discernibly: a gift cannot be used indiscriminately without a critical assessment of what effect it might bring. The admonition of St. Paul in view of community life is helpful for us today much as it was for the first beneficiaries. He advises that everything must be tested (1 Thess. 5:21); whatever is said must be evaluated, even if its claim is prophetic (1 Cor. 14:29). The criteria of discernment and evaluation are that everything is to be tested on the basis of the original Gospel (Gal. 1:8); apostolic tradition (2 Thess. 2:15); common church practice, "as in all the churches of God's people" (1 Cor. 14:34a); lived experience (Phil. 3:16); the motivation that accompanies the gift, especially the theological virtues of love, faith and hope (1 Cor. 13); and the constructive character of the gift (1 Cor. 14:26).

Self-control: every individual believer is to make their contribution to the benefit of the community and has to pay attention to the contributions that others might as well make on the same subject in view. This needs listening and patience in order to bring harmony.

Loving attitude towards other members of community: love is what brings every gift in the Church to its best expression. It enables one to respect others and to appreciate what gifts they have. Love is open to the contributions of others. It is love, working together with faith, which measures the genuineness of every gift.

515 Ibid., pp. 101-104.

In summary, the use of gifts in the Church requires balance, their understandability, evaluation, orderliness, and love. It is the proper use of the different gifts in the Church that made ecclesial growth possible for early Christians. How has this continued in the Church? We can answer this question by looking at the historical developments that followed from this foundation: the original insights of early Christian communities.

6.3. Historical Development

How did Christians carry ecclesial communion forward after the first communities? We can attempt to illustrate this from two sources: the *Didachē* or Teaching of the Twelve Apostles, and the writings of selected Church Fathers.

6.3.1. The Didachē [516]

The *Didachē*, also referred to as *The Teaching of the Twelve Apostles*, is a short manual, a handbook, on Christian morals and Church practice. It comes immediately after and outside the Gospels, Acts of Apostles and the Pastoral Letters. The precise date of its writing is not certain but the translation we cite here suspects that it was written between 60 and 150 AD. There are four main points in this text that are helpful for building ecclesial communion.

Personal decision and commitment: the believer is to make a personal decision and choice. This is the central point of instruction to converts. What is of importance is the indicative catechetical method. The text begins by placing before the convert the two ways between which s/he is to freely choose:

> There are two Ways: a Way of Life and a Way of Death, and the difference between these two Ways is great. The Way of life is this: Thou shalt love first the Lord thy Creator, and secondly thy neighbour as thyself; and thou shalt do nothing to any man that thou wouldst not wish done to thyself.[517]

Piety: believers are encouraged to lead a life of holiness, which grows by observing the precepts of Christ. This consists in a prayerful life performed in common, participating in the celebration of the Eucharist and receiving Holy Communion.[518]

516 Cf. Betty Radice (ed.), *Early Christian Writings: The Apostolic Fathers*, translation by Maxwell Staniforth, revised by Andrew Louth, London, Penguin Books, 1987, p. 198 note 1, suggests two titles: (1) The Teaching of the Twelve Apostles, (b) The Lord's Teaching to the Gentiles by the Twelve Apostles.

517 Ibid., 1:1, p. 191.

518 Ibid., 2:8-10, pp. 194-195.

Charity: the believer is admonished to observe self-restraint and to be well disposed in all relationships. S/he is to practice generosity towards those who are in need: "Never turn away the needy…If you and he are participators in things immortal, how much so in things that are mortal?"[519] Charity builds moral cohesion; it heals us of every individualsic tinge and brings us closer to one another both in spiritual and material things.

Church support: first this regards the attitude which ordinary community members are to have towards those who serve the cause of the Gospel. The text also cautions them to have a critical and discerning mind on matters of faith; they are not to take for granted everyone or group who claims to serve the cause of the Gospel.[520] Secondly, it regards material contribution for leaders of the community, such as teachers and prophets.

How did these practices from the early Christian communities continue to our day? The writings of the Church Fathers are a helpful reference for us. By Church Fathers we are referring to the immediate succesors of the Apostles and those who followed after them.

6.3.2. Church Fathers

The designation "Father of the Church" appears in the account of the martyrdom of Polycarp: "That father-figure of the Christians!"[521] According to Tixeront:

> The title *Father of the Church*, which has its origin in the name "Father" given to bishops as early as the second century, was commonly used in the fifth century to designate the old ecclesiastical writers – originally bishops – who died in the faith and in communion with the Church. According to modern theologians, the title applies only to those writers who have the four following qualifications: orthodoxy of doctrine, holiness of life, ecclesiastical sanction, and antiquity. Practically, however, it is given to many others who do not possess the first three requisites.[522]

519 Ibid., 1:2-4, pp. 190-193.

520 Ibid., 2:11-13, pp.195-197. In our time this may help us to discern the motivations of the different sects or sect-like movements that seem to attract the easy and quick attention of common believers.

521 *The Martyrdom of Polycarp*, in Betty Radice (ed.), *Early Christian Writings*, p. 129. The cry: "That father-figure of the Christians!" came from the audience in the public arena at Smyrna which saw the martyrdom of Polycarp. However, it seems to suggest that the use of the title "Father" was already common among Christians at the time.

522 Joseph Tixeront, *A Handbook of Patrology*, authorised translation by S. A. Raemers, English edition based upon the Fourth French edition, St. Loius, MO, B. Herder Book Co., 1920, p. 2.

What distinguish them as *Fathers of the Church* are: orthodoxy, holiness, authenticity, and originality (reliable knowledge of and touch with Christian antiquity). Tixeront mentions figures like Tertullian, Origen, Eusebius of Caesarea and still many others in his collection. Bettenson divides them into two categories: the Early and Later Church Fathers.[523] The list of "Church Fathers" is extensive and is not the subject of our study. Our enquiry focuses on how their endeavours might meet some of the questions in the church life of our own time and place, and might help us to work for the building of ecclesial communion. We shall limit ourselves to the writings of Clement of Rome, Ignatius of Antioch, Cyprian of Carthage, Basil of Caesare, Augustine of Hippo and John Chrysostom of Constantinople. From our reading of their works, what is central to our investigation is the theme of unity that runs through all of them. We shall begin with the *Apostolic Fathers*: Bettenson writes that these are understood as the immediate successors and disciples of the Apostles.[524] In this group we limit ourselves to the writings of Clement of Rome and Ignatius of Antioch.

6.3.2.1. Clement of Rome

St. Clement, Bishop of Rome, was probably the third pope (88 – 97 AD) after St. Peter. In his First Pastoral Letter to the Corinthians (ca. 96) he confronts the problem of disunity. Clement emphasises the legitimacy of ecclesiastical authority; acting against it amounts to rejecting Christ. The situation in which he writes this Letter is that in the Church at Corinth the leaders who had served faithfully are now disregarded and dejected. The community is torn by strife due to envy and jealousy.[525] In this situation, Clement seeks to restore an organic unity in the Church by insisting on harmony and peace. Central to this is the Trinitarian principle: "Why must there be all this quarreling and bad blood, these feuds and dissensions among you? Have we not the same God, and the

523 Henry Bettenson (ed.), *The Early Christian Fathers*, 11th impression, Oxford, Oxford University Press, 1991, lists in this group Clement of Rome, Ignatius of Antioch, Justin Martyr, Irenaeus of Lyons, Tertullian of Carthage, Origen, Cyprian, and Athanasius; Idem., *The Later Christian Fathers*, 10th impression, Oxford, Oxford University Press, 1991, lists in this group Cyril of Jerusalem, Hilary of Portiers, Basil of Caesarea, Gregory of Nazianzus, Gregory of Nyssa, Theodore of Mopsuestia, John Chrysostom, Ambrose of Milan, Jerome, Augustine of Hippo, Cyril of Alexandria, and Leo the Great. These lists do not exhaust the full number of the Church Fathers but present only some of the exponent personalities.

524 Ibid., p. 1.

525 Clement of Rome, *First Epistle to the Corinthians*, ch. 3, in Radice (ed.), *Early Christian Writings*, p. 24.

same Christ? Is not the same Spirit of grace shed upon us all? Have we not all the same calling in Christ?"[526]

Clement mentions a score of actual problems that disunity in the Church can bring: it leads many astray; it creates and deepens disaffection in the community; it sets disrepute and bad image of the Church in the society; above all it dishonours the Trinity God who is the source of Christian unity; it signals a weakening or loss of faith itself.[527] He encourages humility of mind and obedience to God; and he recommends that ecclesial unity can only come about through: (a) common prayer, both in smaller and larger groups; (b) the practice of faith through good works which consists first of all in good example that can speak even to people in the contingent society; (c) co-operation for the common good; (d) devotion to one another through acts of love, which is the heart of all relationships in the Church.[528] For Clement, ecclesial unity is a visible witness to the unity and wholeness of Christ, which Christians must not disappoint. It is through them that Chirst will be known; it is through them that people who still do not believe in Christ might come to believe.

What we may learn from this situation is that dissension and disunity in the Church can arise when individuals or like-minded individuals advance their opinions or feelings without regard for the greater common good of the whole ecclesial community.

6.3.2.2. Ignatius of Antioch

Ignatius (ca. 35 – ca. 107) was bishop of Antioch in Syria, now Turkey, at that time under the Roman Empire. His time saw the persecution of Christians during the reign of the Roman Emperor Trajan (98 – 117 AD). He was arrested by Roman authorities and sent to Rome where he suffered a martyr's death. It was on his way to Rome, at different places, that he composed his Epistles to the Christian communities in Ephesus, Magnesia, Tralles, Rome, Philadelphia, Smyrna, and to Bishop Polycarp of Smyrna.[529] In all his Epistles, the central theme is unity, which must be upheld in both the spiritual and practical aspects of church life. For him unity is the only visbible strength of ecclesial life. In his Epistle to Polycarp, he writes: "Give thought especially to unity, for there is nothing more important than this."[530]

---

526 Ibid., ch. 46, in Radice (ed.), p. 42.

527 Ibid., ch. 1; ch. 46, in Radice (ed.), p. 23; p. 42.

528 Ibid., ch. 49-51, Radice (ed.), pp. 43f.

529 Cf. Radice (ed.), p. 55.

530 *The Epistle to Polycarp*, ch. 1, in Radice (ed.), p. 99.

The foundation of ecclesial unity is the Trinity, as illustrated in the Epistle to the Magnesians: "Do your utmost to stand firm in the precepts of the Lord and the Apostles, so that everything you do, worldy or spiritual, may go prosperously from beginning to end in faith and love, in the Son and Father and the Spirit, together with your most revered bishop and that beautifully woven spiritual chaplet, your clergy and godly minded deacons."[531] As shown in this text, it is important to note that ecclesial unity is not only Trinitarian; it is also apostolic and missionary for the reason that it prolongs the Church's Tradition as communicated by the Apostles, as well as the various practical Gospel-inspired activities of the Church.

In the Epistle to the Ephesians, unity is strengthened by the affection of charity that exists and is live among all the believers in the community. They must strive to build one single harmonious unity.[532] He teaches that, unity: (a) dispels error;[533] (b) is a sign, and at the same time the heart, of corporate faith that dispels hostility;[534] (c) fosters the discipline which is uniquely Christian, and which remains characteristic of Christian relationship with one another;[535] (c) purifies individual and communal conscience;[536] (d) deepens solidarity and dispels self-glorification. It is such a unity that bears testimony even to those who do not profess Christ as their Saviour.

In his Letter to the Smyrnaeans, Ignatius introduces for the first time the theological term, "*catholic church.*" By this he means wholeness: the Church is whole when it lives as a united body of Christ under the leadership of the bishop. This permits no split or factions within it. Ignatius writes: "Abjure all factions, for they are the beginning of evils. Follow your bishop... Where the bishop is to be seen, there let all his people be; just as wherever Jesus Christ is present, we have the Catholic Church..."[537] Although the tone is juridical, the bishop is understood as a symbol of ecclesial unity: he represents and acts on the name of Christ who represents the will of the Father. The insistence on unity intends warding off factions within the Church. We may understand "factions" as an expressive form of group individualism. Ignatius makes no mention of charism and ministry in the Church; his maxim is: do nothing with-

531 *The Epistle to the Magnesians*, ch. 13, in Radice (ed.), p. 74.

532 *The Epistle to the Romans*, ch. 5, in Radice (ed.), p. 62.

533 *The Epistle to the Ephesians*, ch. 6, in Radice (ed.), p. 63.

534 Ibid., ch. 13, in Radice (ed.), p. 64.

535 *The Epistle to the Magnesians*, ch. 1, in Radice (ed.), p. 71.

536 *The Epistle to the Trallians*, ch. 7, in Radice (ed.), p. 80.

537 *The Epistle to the Smyrnaeans*, ch. 8, in Radice (ed.), p. 103, cf. p. 57.

out the bishop and clergy.[538] He encourages common prayer and Eucharistic celebration over which it is the bishop or, in his absence, a priest or deacon is to preside. Throughout his Epistles, Ignatius mentions the bishop in the same context of unity. What remains central in his message is the concern for organic unity and harmony in the Church. We may discern that unity in the Church is a visible sign of maturity in faith.

6.3.2.3. Cyprian of Carthage

St. Cyprian (ca. 200 – 258 AD) was bishop of Carthage (ca. 248 – 258) in North Africa at a time when the Church there lived in a situation of feudalism (prolonged bitter quarrels among families, tribes or groups); persecution of Christians and opposition to the Christian faith; schism (bitter splits) within the Church. Chadwick recounts that in the year 250 AD, the Roman Emperor Decius (349 – 251) ordered a systematic persecution of Christians. This situation forced many Christians to denounce their faith publicly, others were imprisoned, and still, others were martyred; Bishop Cyprian himself had to go into hiding and could only communicate through Letters. In this period, January 250 – March 251, the bishops of Rome, Antioch and Jerusalem were martyred; the See of Rome was vacant. What arose from this situation was that at Rome rivaling factions elected two competing popes: Cornelius and Novatian; and at Carthage, the absence of Cyprian left believers to look to 'confessors' (Christians in prison) whom they believed to have had a unique possession of the Holy Spirit and thus their power of the 'keys' of salvation. Cyprian came back to public life after March 251 with the return of peace.[539] It is in this context that Cyprian strove to strengthen the moral life of believers, both clergy and laity; and to put into effect unity and order in the Church. Our enquiry is focused on the methodology which enabled him to uphold the integrity of the Church in such a situation.

We find in all his Epistles one important factor that can contribute to ecclesial communion, namely, *consultation*. His methodology of church governance (in matters both pastoral and administrative) is consultation with fellow bishops, the clergy and the laity in all matters of common interest. We may interpret what is implied by Cyprian as a *reverential dialogue*, which involves prayer, listening, discernment and deliberation. There are seven points we would like to highlight to illustrate how consultation can help to build ecclesial communion.

538 *The Epistle to the Magnesians*, ch. 6-7, in Radice (ed.), p. 72.

539 Henry Chadwick, *The Eary Church*, Vol. 1, revised edition, London, Penguin Books, 1993, pp. 118-124.

First, the root of consultation, according to him, lies in prayer, asking God for guidance. This is illiustrated in his Epistle to one, by the name of Florentius Pupianus, who had believed in a calumny leveled against Cyprian. To this Cyprian responds: "…first I should consult my Lord whether He would permit peace to be granted to you…"[540] The value of consultation, according to this disposition, is that it checks against a judgment based on personal feelings towards another's opinion, good or bad.

Second, consultation enables us to become aware of the sensitivities due to custom or tradition: whether the matter in question has been the common practice in the place and how it has been handled; or whether it agrees with the common practice of the Church elsewhere. In response to Quintus, Bishop of Mauritania, who had asked his advice about the baptism given by schismatics or heretics, Cyprian refers him to consider whether such a practice is resonant with custom and tradition. The schismatics had adopted the baptismal practice of laying hands on the head of those being baptised, by which they say that those baptised thus have received the Holy Spirit, instead of using water for baptism. To this, Cyprian responds: "…we should not obstinately love our own opinions, but should rather adopt as our own those which at any time are usefully and wholesomely suggested by our brethren and colleagues, if they be true and lawful."[541] We may understand *schism*, split, as a form of irreconcilable group egoism against common practice.

Third, consultation helps to clarify a probable doubt in order to reach an agreeable decision. To the presbyters and deacons he writes: "…from the very first commencement of my episcopacy, I have made up my mind to do nothing on my own opinion, without your advice and without the consent of the people."[542] Here we find the parallel that exists between his approach and that of Ignatius of Antioch. While the approach of Ignatius is: Do nothing without the bishop; Cyprian's own rule is that the bishop is never to do anything of common interest without the clergy and the laity. We can learn that this approach checks against the self-bent pride that individualism advances.

540 St. Cyprian, *Epistle 68, To Florentius Pupianus, On Calumniators, ch. 9*, in Philip Schaff (ed.), *The Writings of the Fathers Down to AD 325, Ante-Nicene Fathers*, Vol. 5: *Hippolytus, Cypiran, Caius, Novatian, Appendix*, Grand Rapids, William B. Eerdmans Publishing Company, 1916, p. 375. We have used the electronic text under the same title: AFN05, *Fathers of the Third Century: Hippolytus, Cyprian, Caius, Novatian, Appedix*, Grand Rapids, MI, Christian Classics Ethereal Library, 2004, downloaded from website: http://www.ccel.org/ccel/schaff/anf05.toc.html (on 16 October 2012). References taken from this source will be indicated as ANF05.

541 Idem., *Epistle 70: To Quintus, Concerning the Baptism of Heretics*, ch. 3, in ANF05, p. 378.

542 *Epistle 5: To the Presbyters and Deacons*, ANF05, p. 283.

Fourth, consultation brings the ecclesial community to act together. In his Letter to the clergy regarding the re-admission of the lapsed, Cyprian admonishes them to act in common consultation as church leaders, and to involve the laity of good standing, on such a common pastoral interest.[543] He clarifies that acting together is not only modest but also a matter of discipline. It does not only help to clarify any probable doubt but it also helps to avoid doctrinal error. This is illustrated in another Letter which he wrote to presbyters and deacons, where he talks of withholding his decision even in a matter of urgency. He writes: "Now I have read the letter of the whole body of confessors, which they wish to be made known by me to all my colleagues... which matter, as it awaits the counsel and judgment of all of us, I do not dare to prejudge, and so to assume a common cause for my own decision."[544] In doing so, Cyprian seems to make a classic example of essential humility: placing even his best judgement before the judgement of others. The lesson he offers is moral responsibility (being accountable) to the community instead of going it alone.

The fifth benefit of consultation is that it leads to clarifying matters that might cause confusion, conflict, or disquiet in the community. In his Letter to the presbyters and deacons in Rome, he writes: "To the presbyters and deacons also was not wanting the vigour of the priesthood; so that some, too little mindful of discipline, and hasty, with rash precipitation, who had already begun to communicate with the lapsed, were restrained by my interpolation. Among the people, moreover, I have done what I could to quiet their minds, and have instructed them to maintain ecclesiastical discipline."[545] Here, we can understand that clarification heals the community of gossip (unverifiable and contentious communication which causes confusion and suspicion in the community).

Sixth, consultation ensures mature judgment according to the discipline of faith. In his Letter to the people, Cyprian calls all members of the community to think and discuss together, patiently, wisely and to seek religious solutions to matters that affect not only the common life of believers but of the Church as such. As in the address to the clergy, he admonishes the laity to avoid light-mindedness: they are not to take rash decisions which leave difficult matters half-solved or unresolved. This is to ensure that they arrive at a mature judgment according to the Lord's discipline.[546] The question of good judgment is of vital importance in the life of every ecclesial context. We may learn from this

543 *Epistle 13: To the Clergy*, ANF05, p. 294.

544 *Epistle 17: To the Presbyters and Deacons*, ANF05, p. 297.

545 *Epistle 14: To the Presbyters and Deacons Assembled in Rome,* ch. 2, ANF05, p. 295.

546 *Epistle 11: To the People*, ANF05, p. 292.

that, often times, things go wrong due to poor or wrong judgment, or a judgment made in haste.

Seventh, consultation creates trust and confidence, creative freedom, openness and transparency in accountability, particularly through the flow of communication by which members are informed about events and activities of the community, even when a decision has been made without involving the whole body of believers. This is shown in Cyprian's Epistle to the clergy (elders and deacons) and the people after he had raised Aurelius, a confessor, to the office of Reader. He makes the following account in which he declares the criteria of his assessment about the candidate:

> Cyprian to the elders and deacons, and to the whole people, greeting. In ordinations of the clergy, beloved brethren, we usually consult you beforehand, and weigh the character and deserts of individuals, with the general advice. But human testimonies must not be waited for when the divine approval precedes. Aurelius, our brother, an illustrious youth, already approved by the Lord, and dear to God, in years still very young, but, in the praise of virtue and of faith, advanced; inferior in the natural abilities of his age, but superior in the honour *he has merited,*—has contended here in a double conflict, having twice confessed and twice been glorious in the victory of his confession, both when he conquered in the course and was banished, and when at length he fought in a severer conflict, he was triumphant and victorious in the battle of suffering.[547]

From Cyprian's methodology of consultation, we may conclude that it is through such an approach that all the members of the ecclesial community can be positively and creatively involved and challenged to be responsible for the internal life of the Church. Cyprian does not downplay the place of the bishop, as a figure of unity; but he ecourages all members of the Church to proactively take part in the life and action of the Church, each according to their capability and due place in the community. Cyprian seems to bring out a humble but noble mind in matters of church authority and practice.

6.3.2.4. Basil of Caesarea

St. Basil (330 – 379 AD) also called Basil the Great, was the bishop of Caesarea in Cappadocia (370 – 379 AD). Bettenson writes that he was born into a deeply Christian family. His father was a rhetorician. He also took the same career and trained in the best schools at his home town of Caesarea, at Constantinople, and at Athens.[548] He, however, abandoned this career. He vis-

547 *Epistle 32: To the Clergy and People: About the Ordination of Aurelius as a Reader,* ch. 1, ANF05, p. 312.

548 Bettenson, *The Later Church Fathers*, p. 7.

ited monastic communities in Egypt, Syria and Mesopotamia. His experience moved him to give out his property for the aid of poor people. He withdrew into solitude and started a hermitage. This attracted disciples around him and the establishment grew into a community.

However, in 370, Basil was elected Bishop of Caesarea, the metropolis of Cappadocia. He found himself faced with two problems. Chadwick recalls that: (a) in 372, the civil government divided Cappadocia into two provinces, which left Basil with a small metropolitan area and he had to assert his jurisdiction over the lost territory; (b) the legacy of the controversy of the past, which had led to the Council of Nicea in 325, made each bishop cautious and suspicious of heresy towards all his colleagues, a situation in which everyone is afraid of everyone![549]

Our enquiry pays attention to how Basil worked to keep the Church united. We may understand his contribution more deeply by looking at the monastic aspect as a factor to ecclesial communion. It may help us to study what possibilities there are by which all the faithful (the clergy, religious, and laity) might fit in and work together within the diocesan framework in different ways and new situations; how the diocese may make programmes that will integrate all in its life and activities. St. Basil did not desire eremitic solitude as he had encountered it in the desert: a complete detachment, a flight which abandons the world to its sinful fate. He preferred a form of social monastic lifestyle. He saw that community life helps the individual to practice better the Christian virtues. His monastic Rule for monks can contribute towards the building of ecclesial communion in a number of ways. Question and Response 7 from his *Longer Rule* illustrates, in general, his teaching about ecclesial communion.[550] We may draw out the following summary:

Community life answers to the basic human question of complementarity: Basil argues that for bodily wants, the individual is insufficient on their own; we need each other to provide for necessities. Seclusion leaves one like a part of the body which cannot function on its own. Reverence to the love of Christ does not permit Christians to seek their personal advantage alone (cf. 1 Cor. 13:5). Moreover, love for Christ must inspire every Christian to look for the salvation of others as well (cf. 1 Cor. 10: 33).

Mutual and community support: no one in isolation recognises their own defects, since they have no one else to correct them.

Overcoming self-satisfaction: solitary life yields to self-satisfaction; the individual has no one else to test their work. Even in works of love, one may

549 Chadwick, *The Early Church*, p. 148.

550 St. Basil, *The Longer Rules*, English translation by Sr. Monica M. Wagner, New York, Father of the Church Inc., 1950, pp. 248-252.

convince onself that s/he has accomplished God's commandments but this is to be tested by the judgment of others and the community.

Community life helps believers to practice Christian virtues and imitation of Christ: solitariness, isolation from others, can be individualistic and repulsive to the command of love and can give rise to pride. It is in the community that we can practice humility as there is someone else who might be more superior to us, or more knowledgeable than ourselves; we can practice compassion as there are others to whom we give care and love; we can practice patience as we have others to oppose our wishes or opinions.

Community life enables us to act on our gifts and talents: namely, our search for consolation from the word of God in the Bible or professional knowledge may remain theoretical and fruitless if they are not tested by community experience. It is the relation with one another and interrelation within the larger community that calls out our potentialities and dormant capacities to action. St. Paul admonishes Christians that they shall be justified not as mere hearers but doers of the word of God (cf. Rom. 2:13). Basil makes reference to Christ, who was not content with just preaching the Gospel about God's kingdom but girded himself and washed the feet of his disciples in person. He then asks practical questions: Whom, therefore, will you wash? Whom will you care for? In comparison with whom will you be the lowest, if you live alone? For Basil, the community is the method of traveling together on the journey of faith towards perfection and fulfillment. It helps us to learn, to love, and to grow to maturity. He encouraged the monks to practice charity: for this purpose he brought monastic life into the heart of the city where there are the poor, the needy, the homeless and the sick. He is counted as the Father of Eastern monasticism; but much more, as the legislator of social monasticism.

The example of St. Basil might have something to offer which can be effective for building ecclesial communion. Of interest to our enquiry is his methodology of welding together the monastic and apostolic aspects into one, for the common good of the Church. For him these two are inseparable: prayer and work define the life of every Christian. Basil understands that God has given us two states of holiness: marriage and virginity. The same law that enjoins Christians to love God more than father, mother, children, oneself, and possession, is as binding in the married state as in the celibate: both respond to discipleship.[551] It is on this conviction that he founded the monastic community as a nucleus of the diocesan structure.

551 Schaff (ed.), NPNF2-08, *Basil: Letters and Select Works*, Grand Rapids, MI, Christian ClassicsEthereal Library, Created, 2003-09-28, URL: http://www.ccel.org/ccel/schaff/npnf208.html (accessed, 19 October 2012), p. 64.

In his Apostolic Letter, *Patres Ecclesiae* (Fathers of the Church) Pope John Paul II writes that: "For this reason many people think that the essential structure of the life of the Church, monasticism, was established, for all time, mainly by St. Basil; or that, at least, it was not defined in its more specific nature without his decisive contribution."[552] Following the same reflection, Pope Benedict XVI adds:

> Indeed, Basil created a very special monasticism: it was not closed to the community of the local Church but instead was open to it. His monks belonged to the particular Church; they were her life-giving nucleus and, going before the other faithful in the following of Christ and not only in faith, showed a strong attachment to him – love for him – especially through charitable acts. These monks, who ran schools and hospitals, were at the service of the poor and thus demonstrated the integrity of Christian life.[553]

From this we may conclude that St. Basil's example can help us to study what available opportunities we might have in order to strengthen ecclesial communion in our own time and place, particularly by bringing together the contemplative and apostolic gifts to a common whole. According to Basil, the perfection of solitariness (what goes on within oneself in contemplation) comes about through prayer, work (service), and relationships.[554]

6.3.2.5. Augustine of Hippo

St. Augustine (354 – 430 AD) was born at Thagaste in Numidia (now in the country of Algeria). After his studies he was professor of rhetoric at Carthage (374), Rome (383), and Milan (384). He had desired to become provincial governor but his conversion to the Christian faith (386; baptised in 387) changed his course of direction significanlty. In 388 he returned to Thagaste and founded a monastic community. In 391 he was ordained priest at Hippo, to where his ascetic community was transferred. In 395 he became co-adjutor to Bishop Valerius whom he later succeded after his death.[555]

It is important to recall that in North Africa, as we have said above with reference to St. Cyprian, there was the problem of the persecution of Christians

552 John Paul II, Apostolic Letter *Patres Ecclesiae*, n. 2: *AAS* 72 (1980), p. 6; see also *L'Osservatore Romano*, English edition, 25 February 1980, p. 6.

553 Benedict XVI, General Audience *Saint Basil (1)*, Wednesday, 4 July 2007, Vatican City, Libreria Editrice Vaticana, 2007. Electronic text downloaded from URL: http://www.vatican.va/holy_father/benedict_xvi/audiences/2007/documents/hf_ben-xvi_aud_20070704_en.html (accessed, 19 October 2012), p.1.

554 St. Basil, *Letter II: On the Perfection of the Life of Solitariness*, NPNF2-08, p. 290-293.

555 Cf. Chadwick, *The Early Church*, p. 216.

which left a scar on the internal life of the Church itself. Chadwick describes the context in which Augustine found himself thus: "At Hippo Augustine directly faced, in a way that was new to him, the pain of Christian division... The city was split between the two rival communities of North Africa, Donatist and Catholic, and each body treasured the memory of every injury..."[556] The Donatists, led by one, Donatus, had their own rite, and were ridiculous of the Catholics whom they considered to have blemished the Church of its moral and ritual purity.[557] However, the question lies in how, in our own time, we are to respond to problems that come from outside but impinge on the internal life and integrity of the Church as the body of believers. In our reflection, we are not going to talk about Augustine's theological wealth but shall try to highlight what can contribute towards ecclesial communion.

The focus of Augustine is the unicity and wholeness of the Church. His exposition on Psalm 149 talks of the Church as a community of new charity, that goes beyond and perfects cultural defects; a community of saints, whose lives bear fruit to the glory of God; it is Catholic, as opposed to divisiveness which weakens communion; it is a community of concord, and not confusion; a community of good example that appeals to the moral conscience of the society, which will make them able to find the Gospel message of salvation truthful and convincing.[558]

He explains the catholicity of the Church by analysing the Greek words *kath' holon* to mean "according to the whole," drawing from the Ascension conversation between Jesus and his disciples: "Has the time come for you to restore the kingdom to Israel? ...You will receive power of the Holy Spirit... you will be my witnesses...to earth's remotest end" (Act 1:7-8).[559] Again, he plays on the initials of the word ADAM to explain the Church's catholicity as God's action:

> He shall gather together His elect from the four winds (Mark 13:27). He gathers all His elect from the four winds: therefore from the whole world. For Adam... signifies in Greek, the whole world; for there are four letters, A, D, A, and M. But as the Greeks speak, the four quarters of the world have these initial letters.

556 Ibid., p. 219.

557 Ibid., pp. 219-225.

558 St. Augustine, *Exposition on the Book of Psalms: Psalm 149*, in Philip Schaff (ed.), *A Select Library of Nicene and Post-Nicene Fathers*, First Series, Vol. 8: *Augustine: Expositions on the Book of Psalms*, Fourth printing, Peabody, Hendrickson Publishers, 2004, pp. 677-681.

559 St. Augustine, *Response to the Letters of Petilian, the Donatist*, Book II, Ch. 38 § 91, in Philip Schaff (ed.), *A Select Library of Nicene and Post-Nicene Fathers of the Christian Church*, First Series, Vol. 4: *Augustine: The Writings Against the Manichaeans, and Against the Donatists*, Fourth printing, Peabody, Hendrikson Publishers, 2004, pp. 554-555.

> They call the East, *Anatole*; the West, *Dusis*; the North, *Arctus*; and the South, *Mesembria*, and these letters spell Adam. Adam therefore has been scattered over the whole world. He was in one place, and fell... broken small, he filled the whole world: but the mercy of God gathered together the fragments from every side, and forged them by the fire of love, and made one what was broken.[560]

By this Augustine is striving to remove the wound of sectarianism in the Church and the pride of regionalism being fanned among believers. The Church is *catholic* wherever *Christ* is proclaimed and believed in. Conflicting opinions, whether personal, theological, cultural, must not be brought to split the unicity that the Church deserves. From his writings we may make the following summary to highlight the points that might contribute to the building of ecclesial communion.

The communitarian nature of the human person: Augustine finds the truth of the human person in the light of Christian faith. Although s/he is not consubstantial with the Trinity, there is a trace of the Trinity in the nature of the human person. S/he is intrinsically communitarian but incomplete without others. This becomes clearer through love which opens the individual to relationship.[561] The Divine purpose for one's personal existence intends the unicity of the human family:

> And therefore God created only one single man, not, certainly, that he might be a solitary, bereft of all society, but by this means the unity of society and the bond of concord might be more effectually commended to him, men being bound together not only by similarity of nature, but by family affection. And indeed He did not even create the woman that was to be given him as wife, as he created the man, but created her out of the man, that the whole human race might derive from one man.[562]

For Christians, this unicity is brought to practice and experience in the Church, where the individual shares in the fullness of Christ: through ministry and mutual edification. This will lead to perfecting one another. It is in this way that believers grow in the knowledge of God. For Augustine belonging in the Church is interpersonal and must help Christians to be healed of all differences of opinion, gifts or male-female difference – all are one in Christ:

---

560 St. Augustine, *Exposition on the Book of Psalms: Psalm 91* §15, in Schaff (ed.), *Nicene and Post-Nicene Fathers*, First Series, Vol. 8, *Augustine: Expositions on the Book of Psalms*, p. 474.

561 Idem., *The City of God: Book 11, Ch. 26*, in *ibid.*, Vol. 2, p. 220.

562 Ibid., *Book 12, Ch. 21*, in *ibid.*, p. 241.

> As, therefore, there is a measure of the fullness of the whole body which is made up of all its parts, and it is of this measure it is said, "To the measure of the age of the fullness of Christ." This fullness he spoke of also in the place where he says of Christ, "And gave Him to be the Head over all things to the Church, which is His body, the fullness of Him that fills all in all. But even if this should be referred to the form in which each one shall rise, what should hinder us from applying to the woman what is expressly said of the man, understanding both sexes to be included under the same general term "man"? For certainly in the saying, "Blessed is he who fears the Lord," women also who fear the Lord are included."[563]

Good pastorship contributes to ecclesial communion: In his Sermon on the Gospel of St. John, leveled against the Donatists, whom he calls heretics, Augustine rejects the easy inclination of limiting the Church to regional or sectarian interests. The text in question is about the pastorship of Christ: "I am the good shepherd" (Jn. 10:14). Augustine argues that Christ's pastorship cannot divide the Church. On the contrary, it is the primary factor to ecclesial communion. He illustrates this, with a blend of authority and humility, in his Sermon on the anniversary of his ordination, where he says:

> Where I'm terrified by what I am for you, I am given comfort by what I am with you. For you I am a bishop, with you, after all, I am a Christian. The first is the name of an office undertaken, the second a name of grace; that one means danger, this one salvation. Finally, as if in the open sea, I am being tossed about by the stormy activity involved in that one; but as I recall by whose blood I have been redeemed, I enter a safe harbor in the tranquil recollection of this one; and thus while toiling away at my own proper office, I take my rest in the marvelous benefit conferred on all of us in common.[564]

For Augustine pastorship in the Church is not of a personal making; it is the pastorship of Christ, meant for the common good of the Church. He translates unity as charity, namely, the affection that must exist among leaders in the Church. This charity must grow among pastors themselves and with the whole body of believers. It is in this way that the ecclesial community will experience true unity.[565] What, then, is the essence of ecclesial unity?

---

563 Ibid., *Book 22, Ch. 18*, in *ibid.*, p. 497.

564 John E. Rotelle (ed.), *The Works of Saint Augustine: A Translation for the 21st Century*, translation and notes by Edmund Hill, Brooklyn, NY, New City Press, 1997, p. 292.

565 St. Augustine, *Sermon 88:3*, in Schaff (ed.), *A Select Library of the Christian Church: Nicene and Post-Nicene Fathers*, First Series, Vol. 6: *Augustin: Sermon on the Mount, Harmony of the Gospels, Homilies on the Gospels*, 4th printing, Peabody, Hendrickson Publishers, 2004, pp. 523-527.

Ecclesial unity: deriving from Christ's Baptism, Eucharist, Passion, charity, and joy.

The Baptism of Christ: ecclesial communion is born from and sustained by the Baptism of Christ, which is imparted to every believer in the working of the Holy Spirit.[566] The Christian Baptism is both gift and responsibility to the communion that Christ brings. This means that all believers are called, in the spirit of Christ, to contribute to the growth of the Church, much as they share in the same Baptism into Christ.

The Eucharist: the virtue of unity is apprehended in the Eucharist (cf. Mt. 6:6) where Christians are to look to one another in the Body of Christ as a new order of existence.[567] In the Eucharist is brought about the unity of all the saints, namely, of all believers. It is in the Eucharist that the Holy Spirit is continually imparting unity into the lives of believers, each one and all together.[568] The intensity and density of the Eucharist for ecclesial life is such that the one is in the whole and the whole in the individual. This is with reference to Christ as the center of Christian unity, and the Church as the Body of Christ. First, Christ, as Son, is one with the Father by his Divine nature, and united with the Father by Will. Second, Christ unites himself with every human person, and more so, believers in him, in his human nature. The unity of believers in the Church is therefore unity with Christ who is one with the Father. This entails concord and harmony among Christians, that is, they must strive to be of one mind and one heart. Their unity reflects and bears witness to the Trinity.[569]

The Passion of Christ: Christian believers are to see that they share the passion of Christ who desires to bring every member to fullness in the same Body. It is unity which holds this body together.[570] Augustine illustrates the *passion* of Christ with "the troubled water" into which people with infirmities descend and get well again (Jn. 5:1-18). By celebrating the mysteries of Christ, Christians are united with him in his Passion which continues to heal us of our coldness and infirmities in which we are isolated.

Charity: Augustine writes that one who abandons unity violates charity, and whoever violates charity, whatever great gifts such a believer has, amounts to no avail. Charity is the vitality of ecclesial communion.[571] It is not enough to know Christ; but to do what his love demands. The Spirit that Christ gives is a

566 *Tractate 6*:6, in Schaff (ed.), *Nicene and Post-Nicene Fathers*, First Series, Vol. 7, p. 41.

567 *Sermon 7*, in Schaff (ed.), *Nicene and Post-Nicene Fathers*, First Series, Vol. 6, p. 282.

568 *Tractate 26*: 13-17, in Schaff (ed.), Vol. 7, pp. 172-173.

569 *On the Trinity,* Book 4, Ch. 7-9, in *ibid.*, Vol. 3, pp. 75-76.

570 *Tractate 17*, in *ibid.*, pp. 111-114.

571 *Sermon 38:21*, in *ibid.*, Vol. 6, p. 386.

Spirit of charity.[572] Hence, whoever grows cold in charity is enfeebled in that Body of Christ, the ecclesial community.[573] In his definition of the virtuous life Augustine teaches that it is charity that will enable Christians to perfect all the human virtues and lead to a truly happy life:

> As to virtue leading to a happy life, I hold virtue to be nothing else than perfect love of God. For the fourfold division of virtue I regard as taken from the four forms of love... temperance is love giving itself entirely to that which is loved; fortitude is love readily bearing all things for the sake of the loved object; justice is love serving only the loved object, and therefore ruling rightly; prudence is love distinguishing with sagacity between what hinders it and what helps it.[574]

Charity is the life of the Church. Here *charity* is Christ, in whom the Church, and believer, rests in troubled times. To live by charity is to live in Christ and with Christ. It is only charity which can hold the unity of the Church and give it a living tradition – keeping its memory of faith alive, giving the present a vivid expression, and looking to the future with unfading hope. Without charity the ecclesial community will fail to know its true spirit and character. It is charity which brings the other two theological virtues of faith and hope into a living reality in countless ways.

Charity involves good moral life that does not only give a good name to the individual but also keeps the name of the Church in respect, and above all, the name of Christ will be honoured due to the witness the believer bears to Him by their sincere way of life. It also involves encouragement and support in moral, spiritual, intellectual, emotional as well as material benefits. Moreover, a life of charity is meaningful in the good example and acts of love in social commitment which speaks to the general society in which the Church lives. Lastly, in acts of charity Christ lives and acts in every believer.

Joy: the Church is a community of joy and praise to God. Christians are living members in the Church as Body of Christ. This brings out the concept of ecclesial communion as existing-with-one-another and existing-for-one-another in that Body. Augustine illustrates in his book, *Confessions*, that Christian joy is not materialist, nor merely intellectual, nor sensual pleasure; it consists in the truth that faith and contemplation of God can afford.[575] Its vibrancy is again defined by charity. Augustine draws a clear distinction between false joy and true joy. False joy is wanton, deceptive, full of pride and self-praise. Christians

572 *Tractate 27*:4-6, in *ibid.*, Vol.7, pp. 175-176.

573 *Sermon 87:1*, in *ibid.*, Vol. 6, p. 517.

574 *Of the Morals of the Catholic Church,* Ch. 15: 25, in *ibid.*, Vol. 4, p. 48.

575 *Confessions*, Book 10, Ch. 20-23, in Schaff (ed.), *Nicene and Post-Nicene Fathers*, First Series, Vol. 1, pp. 150-152; cf. Book 4, Ch. 15, pp. 75-77.

are to find true joy in God because God is the source and center of all values that truly frees the heart of all deception.[576] Christian joy is filled with creative freedom and self-giving love.[577]

In his book, *City of God*, Augustine is referring to the Church as that city of God, whose truth and joy goes beyond that which philosophers ponder. The truth and joy that human reasoning discovers finds satisfaction in the religious and reverential fear of God. Christian truth discerns the eternal values of our thoughts, actions and words. This is what defines the Church as both human and Christian and it is this contemplative self-awareness which will guide the believer to live a truly virtuous life.[578]

6.3.2.6. John Chrysostom

John was born in Antioch between 344 and 354 (or about 349 AD) into a noble Christian family. He received the best education that Antioch could offer in philosophy, rhetoric and theology. About the year 375 he became a monk, living in a hermitage outside the city of Antioch. In 381 he returned to Antioch and was ordained deacon; and priest in 386. John preferred pastoral work over hermitage. He served as a special assistant to the bishop in temporal care and spiritual instruction of the poor Christians of the city. In the years 386–397 he was a preacher at Antioch. In 397 the archbishop of Constantinople died; and John was consecrated as the metropolitan bishop in 398 (until 404 AD).[579]

John was a preacher, for which he was called *Chrysostom*, golden mouthed, and his contribution is through his sermons. We may understand the context in which he worked as one marred by intrigues, both internal and external. Everett Fergusson summarises it in the following manner:

> He was unsuited for the intrigues and pressures of Constantinople. His efforts to raise the moral climate of the capital met strong opposition. His enemies joined forces: the Empress Eudoxia, stung by his attacks on sin in high places; local clergy who found John too strict; and Theophilus, patriarch of Alexandria, jealous of a churchman from Antioch at the capital.[580]

---

576 *Confessions, Book 2, Chap. 4: 12-14*, in *ibid.*, Vol. 1, pp. 58-59.

577 *Ibid., Book 6,* Ch. *6:9*, in *ibid.*, pp. 93-94.

578 *City of God*, Book 19, Ch. 3-4, in *ibid.*, Vol. 2, pp. 400-403.

579 Chadwick, *The Early Church*, pp. 186-191.

580 Everett Ferguson, "John Chrysostom," in *A Lion Handbook: The History of Christianity*, Berkhamsted, Lion Publishing, 1977, p. 191.

What seems to lie at the heart of John's pastoral concern is expressed in his radical stand on the Christian faith. Four points are particularly important for ecclesial communion.

Faith as conscience: In Homily 20, on the Epistle to the Romans, "Do you have faith; have it to yourself" (Rom. 14:22), John Chrysostom understands faith as conscience, that is, a principle of personal moral responsibility, above all to God.[581] He sees the danger of fulfilling Christianity merely as a custom. In Homily 10, on the Epistle to the Hebrews, he says: "...if we have no fear, but fulfill our Christianity as a custom, and for form's sake..."[582] By this, as argued in the rest of the homily, what he means is that the depth of the believer's intimate reverential humility to God will be shown in what visible fruit it brings. Christians must not feel proud of belonging to the Church as an institution; as if being in the Church would cheaply mean being of the Church. Believers are to ponder what their faith entails in all its implications: they are to practice what they believe.

The Church is a spiritual school: where the assembly here gathered learns the arts of Christ, the way of Christ, his will and intentions. What is learnt here must lead to action: "This place is a spiritual school. Wherefore also there is but one thing aimed at, duly to perform the things that have been spoken..."[583] In this school, there are two factors that bring about ecclesial unity: the word of God proclaimed, and the Eucharist celebrated.[584] Chrysostom likens preaching to school learning: the word proclaimed is to bring listeners closer to Christ, to shape and to strengthen their relationship both in the family and with neighbours. In Homily 24, on 1 Corinthians, he says of the Eucharist:

> The Body of Christ: not many bodies, but one body. For as the bread consisting of many grains is made one, so that the grains no where appear; they exist indeed, but their difference is not seen by reason of their conjunction; so are we conjoined both with each other and with Christ: there not being one body for you, and one for thy neighbor to be nourished by, but the very same for all.[585]

581 St. John Chrysostom, *Homily 26*, "Epistle to the Romans 14:22" in Philip Schaff (ed.), *Nicene and Post-Nicene Fathers*, First Series, Vol. 11: *Chrysostom: Homilies on the Acts of the Apostles and the Epistle to the Romans*, 4th pringing, Peabody, Hendrickson Publishers, 2004, p. 531.

582 *Homily 10: 1*, "Hebrews 6:7, 8" in Philip Schaff (ed.), *Nicene and Post-Nicene Fathers*, First Series, Vol. 14: *Chrysostom: Homilies on the Gospel of Saint John and the Epistle to the Hebrews*, 4th printing, Peabody, Hendrickson Publishers, 2004, p. 414.

583 *Homily 17:6* "Mathew 5:27, 28" in Philip Schaff (ed.), *Nicene and Post-Nicene Fathers*, First Series, Vol. 10: *Chrysostom: Homilies on the Gospel of Saint Mathew*, 4th printing, Peabody, Hendrickson Publishers, 2004, p. 122b.

584 *Homily 11:9* "Mathew 3:7" in *ibid*., p. 73.

585 *Homily 24:4* "1 Corinthians 10:13" in Philip Schaff (ed.), *Nicene and Post-Nicene Fathers*, First Series, Vol. 12: *Chrysostom: Homilies on First and Second Corinthians*, Fourth printing, Peabody, Hendrickson Publishers, 2004, p. 140.

Charity is the action of faith: acts of charity make faith visible and expressible. John was aware of the prevalent cultural, social, economic and religious problems in his society. He knew the divide between the wealthy and the poor. He condemned every abuse in these areas. For him, charity is both the attitude one must have toward others as well as material contribution to alleviate their hardships. Christians must set an example. In Homily 50, on the Gospel of Mathew, he asks his listeners to celebrate the mysteries of Christ in the Church building and go out to meet him in the actual situations outside: in the poor, the hungry, the naked – all who are at the margins of life:

> Do you wish to honor the body of Christ? Do not neglect him when he is naked. Do not honor him here inside with silken robes but neglect him outside when he is perishing of cold and nakedness… The one who said, "This is my body", and established the fact by his word, is also the one who said, "You saw me hungry and did not give me to eat", and "As much as you did not do for one of these least ones, you did not do to me" (cf. Mt. 25:31-46). The body of Christ in the Eucharist has no need of garments but of a pure soul; the body of Christ outside needs much care… God has no need of golden vessels but of golden souls… in saying this, I am not hindering you from making such votive offerings as these. I am insisting that, along with these and before these, you give alms. He accepts the former but is much more pleased with the latter… Consider this with regard to Christ when he comes by as a beggar or a stranger needing shelter… Do not decorate this house and neglect your suffering brother. He is more truly a temple than this building.[586]

Christians are to use all their talents and gifts to the effects of salvation. Chrysostom uses the example of the unwise virgins to illustrate that spiritual perfection can lead to self-glory (chaste, discreet, self-controlled only to oneself) if it is not tested by works of charity. In Homily 20, on the Acts of the Apostles, he says: "Nothing is more frigid than a Christian who cares not for the salvation of others."[587] In this particular aspect no Christian can plead poverty or innocence; and no one is to be left ignorant.

Integral growth of the individual: to build a strong ecclesial communion individuals are to be educated properly to be good Christians. The human growth of the Church is based in the growth of its individual members. In Homily 80, on the Gospel of St. Mathew, he compares the three phases of human growth

586 *Homily 50:4* "Mathew 14:23-24" in *ibid.*, Vol. 10, p. 313. For the sake of readability, we have used the English translation as offered by Pier Franco Beatrice, *Introduction to the Fathers of the Church*, Vicenza, Edizioni Istituto San Gaetano, 1987, pp. 333-334.

587 *Homily 20,* "Acts 9: 10, 12" in Schaff (ed.), *Nicene and Post-Nicene Fathers,* First Series, Vol. 11, p. 133b. For the sake of readability, we have used the translation given by Pier Franco Beatrice, *op. cit.* p. 330.

with the sea in the vast ocean: infancy, adolescence and adulthood.[588] This involves the physical, intellectual and moral growth by which one is opened to relationships. In Homily 3, on the Gospel of St. John, Chrysostom finds the Johannine theology, "In the beginning was the Word," suitable for the Christian formation to full human growth. At the phase, of *infancy*, parents and teachers must guide them to learn the basic human and religious values. Childhood is a tender age at which "...what children hear is impressed as a seal on the wax of their mind. Besides, it is then that their life begins to incline to vice or virtue... "[589] The second phase, of *adolescence*, is faced with violent winds of wild passions and conflicting choices to make.[590] It is a delicate age full of fancies; they need not only correction but proper guidance which will lead them to see their worth as persons beyond their bodily nature and its inclinations: "Let us then send forth on them the fire of the Spirit, and burn up these wicked desires..."[591] The youth cannot be left to their own conscience: "But God has provided many other instructors for us besides conscience; namely, fathers for children...Thus fathers and teachers take the young in hand, and bring them into order..."[592] The third phase is *adulthood*, when a man and a woman found a family; where the duties of family abound. This phase is likened to the sea of covetousness, which stands against temperance and moderation in relating with other people and in the use of things. Chrysostom says of the Christian family: "It is a type of the Church, and of Christ."[593] If they have a child, there is a trinitarian communion, where the three become one: "And the child is a sort of bridge, so that the three become one flesh, the child connecting, on either side, each to other."[594] The Christian family is therefore a trinitarian community that gives strength to the larger ecclesial reality, and there it also finds its fuller reality of communion.

588 *Homily 81:5* "Mathew 26:17-18" in *idem.*, Vol. 10, p. 490.

589 *Homily 3:1* "John 1:1" in *idem.*, Vol. 14, p. 10.

590 *Homily 59:7*, "Mathew18:7" in *idem.*, Vol. 10, p. 370b-371.

591 *Homily 49:5*, "Mathew 14:13" in *ibid.*, p. 309.

592 *Homily 13:10-11*, "Concerning Statues" in Philip Schaff (ed.), *Nicene and Post-Nicene Fathers,* First Series, Vol. 9: *Chrysostom: On the Priesthood, Ascetic Treatises, Select Homilies and Letters, Homilies on the Statues*, Fourth printing, Peabody, Hendrickson Publishers, 2004, p. 429.

593 *Homily 12*, "Colossians 4:12-13" in Philip Schaff (ed.), *Nicene and Post-Nicene Fathers,* First Series, Vol. 13: *Chrysostom: Homilies on Galatians, Ephesians, Philippians, Colossians, Thessalonians, Timothy, Titus, and Philemon*, Fourth printing, Peabody, Hendrickson Publishers, 2004, p. 318b.

594 Ibid., p. 319a.

Summary

From the writings of the Church Fathers we can conclude that ecclesial communion depends on the spirit of unity, which comes about through personal commitment, common prayer, charity, church support drawn from local sources, overcoming selfishness, good pastorship, proclamation of the word of God, mutual support, well-founded faith, the integral growth of the person, and the testimony of faith by getting involved in the realities of life. A careful reading of the Church Fathers brings out an important point: the social nature of the Church into which every member is made a part.

6.4. The Social Nature of the Church

The intention of this presentation is to bring the believers to understand themselves both as human (discussed in Chapter Two) as well as Christian (highlighted in Chapters Three and Five) in a specific setting (presented in Chapter One) which will help them to overcome the allurements of individualism (Chapter Four). It asks the following questions: What is the understanding of all Christian believers in Nebbi Catholic Diocese about the social nature of the Church in their own place? How does this Church give them a sense of belonging? How do they bring the communitarian values that we have highlighted into real life at every ecclesial reality? The following paragraphs will try to answer these questions.

In his reading of the Fathers of the Church, Henry de Lubac explains the social nature of the Church as: Jesus Christ spread abroad and communicated to all peoples on earth, denoting a spiritual nature.[595] In the Church humanity is therefore organically one by its Divine structure:

> Men, women, children, profoundly divided in nationality, race, language, walk of life, work, knowledge, rank or means...all these she recreates in the Spirit. On all in the same measure she imprints a Divine character. All receive of her a single nature which cannot be divided and by reason of which their many and deep differences can no longer be held in account. By it all are brought up and united in a truly Catholic manner...[596]

He continues to expound that the Church as 'People of God' signifies: the whole world chosen from the whole world.[597] The Church is the fruit of the earth and cannot shrink back from existence with it; and yet its character is

595 De Lubac, *Catholicism*, p. 46-61.

596 Ibid., p. 53-54.

597 Ibid., p. 295.

both human and divine. This does not lead to idiosyncrasy that would congeal in syncretism, which thrives on absorbing elements that would weaken the validity of faith. The Church considers the fact that Christianity has used human cultural elements, literature, art and thought patterns to explain the mysteries of faith. The Incarnation affirms the Divine source of Christianity but also sets the earthly stage in humanity which is perceptible to humans.[598] For de Lubac, catholicity is both grace and challenge for the Church to find within itself the possibility for a larger context of becoming, according to its character as a people gathered together for wholeness. It is a wholeness that builds up at the guidance of the Holy Spirit but not through naiveté, syncretism or liberalism. De Lubac further expounds a pneumatic undesrtanding, focusing on the Pentecost event as a bestowal of the Holy Spirit, a way by which God reestablishes mutual comprehension among people, since each will understand in their own language the truth which is to reunite them to their fellows. The different tongues that the Spirit evokes signify belonging to one another in a rich diversity. The gathering of the Church therefore means that God's goodness is acted out in the individual for the whole and vice-versa.

The point in view is that a correct understanding of the Church's catholicity will help to make clear the sense of ecclesial communion and promote its growth. We are using the word *catholicity* not in the institutional sense although this is implied, but rather in the constitutive sense of communion, the wholeness of Christ, which every believer embodies and contributes to the life of the Church. This begins to find expression in the individual, widening through the Christian family, into the SCC, chapel, zone, parish, deanery and diocese, as well as in the other contexts and frames of ecclesial realities (such as groups, movements, associations and institutions). Every member is thus *catholic* in the sense that s/he embodies Christ's wholeness. However, this wholeness is not selfish; it is impossible if individuals are not actively committed to the building up of ecclesial communion.

In *A New Dictionary of Theology*, the term *catholic* is defined as "…the quality of being universal, complete or all-embracing."[599] The *Catechism* understands the word *catholic* to mean 'universal' or 'wholeness' with reference to Christ's presence in and with the Church;[600] and the universal mission to bring salvation to the entire human race.[601] The main characteristic of the Church's catholicity lies in unity. It is in this context that every particular or

598 Ibid., pp. 299-301.

599 Donald J. Georgen, "Catholicity" in *NDT*, p. 172; cf. Monica K. Hellwig, "Catholicism," in *ibid*., p. 167f.

600 *CCC*, n. 830.

601 Ibid., n. 831.

local Church is defined as *catholic*, inasmuch as its life and action enriches the common effort of all its members for the realisation of Christ's wholeness.[602] Francis Sullivan argues that although the word *catholic* is absent in the Scriptures the concept is nonetheless implied. He defines *catholic* to mean 'universal,' denoting communion of mind and heart, unity, togetherness, joint effort.[603]

We have seen above that St. Ignatius of Antioch was the first to introduce the term *catholic* with regard to the Church. After him St. Cyril, Bishop of Jerusalem (ca. 315 – 387 AD) provided a more cosmological definition of the Church's catholicity:

> It is called catholic because it extends to over all the world, from one end of the earth to the other; and because it reaches universally and completely one and all the doctrines which ought to come to people's knowledge concerning things both visible and invisible, heavenly and earthly; and because it brings into subjection to godliness the race of humankind, governors and governed, learned and unlearned…[604]

Vatican Council II, in its Dogmatic Constitution on the Church, *Lumen Gentium*, understands the Church as the light of the nations, for which it is the universal sacrament of salvation. This theology is developed in view of the eschatological nature of the pilgrim Church on earth in union with the heavenly Church.[605] Grillmeier clarifies that the analogy of sacrament is here made in relation to Christ and how his Spirit inspires and shapes the Church. Just as the eternal Son of God assumed only one individual body for the ransom of humanity, so the Spirit of Christ works through the social structure of the Catholic Church (*socialis compago*) as the organ of salvation for the world. In this way the Church develops a special pneumatic life of its own in all the forms which are proper to it as a social structure in the Spirit.[606] The proper

602 Ibid., n. 832-835.

603 Francis A. Sullivan, *The Church We Believe In: One, Holy, Catholic and Apostolic*, New York, Paulist Press, 1988, p. 84. The word *catholic* is derived from two Greek root words, *kath (*from *kata)*, 'according to' and *holou*, 'the whole.' The basic meaning lies in the adjective, *holou*, 'universal.'

604 St. Cyril, *Catechetical Lectures: Lecture XVIII: 23*, in Philip Schaff (ed.), *A Select Library of Nicene and Post-Nicene Fathers of the Christian Church*, Second Series, Vol. VII, *St. Cyril of Jerusalem and St. Gregory Nazianzen*, Grand Rapids, William B. Eerdmans Publishing Company, 1989, p. 139-140.

605 Vatican Council II, Dogmatic Constitution on the Church *Lumen Gentium*, n. 48: *AAS* 57 (1965), p. 53-54. See Walter M. Abbott and Joseph Gallagher (eds.), *The Documents of Vatican II*, p. 78.

606 Aloys Grillmeier, "Dogmatic Constitution on the Church, Chapter 1: The Mystery of the Church," in Herribert Vorgrimler (ed.), *Commentary on the Documents of Vatican II*, New York, Herder and Herder, 1967, p. 149.

understanding of catholicity therefore does not match Christianity with any single cultural, political, economic or civilisation models although it acknowledges these entities for the ordering of society. Syncretistic allusion would compromise the destiny of the Church and would make it great from a thrifty society or cultural humours, or scanty from a weaker one. How can the social nature of the Church find expression in Nebbi Catholic Diocese? How can its wholeness be strengthened? In what follows we shall make use of the models of the Church to illustrate the different possibilities that can be applied for a deeper understanding of the Church as communion. The purpose is to offer a variety of possible ways by which Nebbi Catholic Diocese can deepen its self-understanding; to become more self-propagating, self-administering and self-supporting.

6.5. Models of the Church

We would understand church model in a simple language as a clear, perceptible and practicable representation which can serve to build a strong, active and life-giving ecclesial communion. It is an approach of deepening the Church's self-understanding with regard to its life and activities. From this understanding, our study asks: What church model would help Nebbi Catholic Diocese to build a strong ecclesial life? Our study would prefer the model of the *church as home*. But before we come to this, we shall first acknowledge that the diocese can make use of the different images to enrich its ecclesial life and activity.

Vatican Council II Dogmatic Constitution on the Church, *Lumen Gentium*, offers images or models which present the Church both as a mystical and constitutive reality. The former is variously called: sheepfold of Christ, field and vineyard of God, building or temple of God, Mother;[607] Body of Christ, and Bride.[608] The latter is likened to community of faith, hope and charity,[609] People of God,[610] and hierarchical.[611] Our search question is: What do we mean by *model* and what is its relevance to understanding the Church?

607 *LG*, 6: *AAS* 57 (1965), pp. 8-9.

608 Ibid., 7: *AAS* 57 (1965), pp. 10-11.

609 Ibid., 8: *AAS* 57 (1965), pp. 11-12.

610 Ibid., 9-17: *AAS* 57 (1965), pp. 12-21.

611 Ibid., 18-29: *AAS* 57 (1965), pp. 21-30.

6.5.1. Theological Meaning of Church Model

Theologians have developed such terms as model, image, symbol, metaphor or paradigm in trying to bring out an understanding of the Church which is closer to life, especially with regard to its functioning and cognition. Snyder explains that a model is a relatively simple construction found useful and illuminating for dealing with realities which are more complex and differentiated.[612] What this means is that a *model* is generally a conceptual or symbolic representation in an attempt to depict and express reality as a whole or in part.

A vivid description is given by Minear. According to him, good models put life and dynamism into an existing structure or system. He illustrates this with the Church's self-understanding:

> Its self-understanding, its inner cohesion, its *esprit de corps*, derives from a dominant image of itself, even though that image remains inarticulately imbedded in subconscious strata. If an inauthentic image dominates its consciousness, there will first be subtle signs of malaise, followed by more overt tokens of communal deterioration. If an authentic image is recognised at the verbal level but denied in practice, there will also follow sure disintegration of the ligaments of corporate life.[613]

The expression: *esprit de corps*, in the French language, means a feeling of devotion to, and pride in, the group to which one belongs. With regard to the Church, this means that every individual is happy with and devoted to the community.

Dulles took the first step after Vatican Council II to develop five models of the Church: institution, mystical communion, sacrament, herald, servant. His seminal work was published in 1974. In it the central point is that the Church is "the communion of minds and hearts through sharing in the same divine life."[614] His later work, *Models of the Church*, acknowledges the three traditional biblical images: people of God, body of Christ, temple of the Holy Spirit;[615] but adds a sixth model of the Church as community of disciples, as the summation of the first five models. The central point in this latter work is

612 Howard A. Snyder, *Models of the Kingdom*, Nashville, Abingdon Press, 1991, p. 20.

613 Paul Minear, *Images of the Church in the New Testament*, Philadelphia, Westminster Press, 1960, p. 24. What catches attention is the French phrase *esprit de corps*, signifying a deeply felt sense of belonging, the joy of being a member, part of the group or institution, in which one becomes more fully aware of one's identity and personhood. Equally so is the community's cumulative strength drawn from its individual, participant members.

614 A. Dulles, *The Dimensions of the Church: A Postconciliar Reflection*, New York, Doubleday, 1974, p. 5.

615 Idem, *Models of the Church*, expanded edition, New York, Image Books, 2002, p. 213.

that, in order to win acceptance, these images must resonate with the experience of the faithful. Models of the Church are therefore to motivate action, to be translated into life.

6.5.2. The Church as Institution

This model acknowledges that the Church needs to be structured as an organised community, with recognised officials to direct and guide it, to preside over worship, to determine the limits of dissent, and to represent the community in an official manner. However, by itself, it can turn into institutionalism, which tends to become rigid, doctrinaire and conformist, with a marked concept of structures, official authority and obedience to rules. This can turn the institution into a rigid hierarchical Church with no room for democratic expression among the faithful. It can also promote clericalism with the emphasis that bishops are the source of power and initiative. In this way it kills initiative among the laity since they cannot do so before it is approved by Church leaders. Authority becomes more important than service. This leaves especially the laity passive; and thus Church management is entirely left in the hands of the bishop and priests.

Dulles notes that the institutional vision "defines the Church primarily in terms of its visible structures, especially the rights and powers of its officers."[616] This does not imply that the institution has no value; it means "the institutional elements in the Church must be justified by their capacity to express or strengthen the Church as a community of life, witness, and service, a community that reconciles and unites in the grace of Christ."[617] In other words, Church structures must be seen as subordinate to and serve its communal life and commission. The problem of structure lies in an over-emphasis on hierarchy, what Congar has called hierarchology, by which the institution can slip into a machinery of hierarchical mediation.[618] This can downplay the spiritual or mystical aspect of the Church.

6.5.3. Mystical Communion

This model presents the Church as a New Covenant People of God, uniting the members to God by grace and among themselves in Christ. "The Church, from this point of view, is not in the first instance an institution or

---

616 Dulles, *Models of the Church*, p. 27.

617 Ibid., p. 37-38.

618 Yves Congar, *Lay People in the Church: A Study for a Theology of Laity*, English translation by D. Attwater, Westminster, Newman, 1957, p. 45.

a visibly organized society. Rather it is a communion of men, primarily interior but also expressed by external bonds of creed, worship and ecclesiastical fellowship."[619] Dulles notes that the term *koinonia* (communion) can be used ambiguously to cover both the sociological and mystical communion although it is not palpable that the two necessarily go together.[620] Church communion is not just a biological or sociological reality or a simplistic mutual fellowship among individuals; nor is it a family-like or friendly interpersonal relationship of like-minded believers, which remain at the horizontal level. The ties that bind Church communion are pneumatological, integrating both the vertical and horizontal dimensions into unity. It is a communion of grace, communicating God's Spirit and his gifts.[621] However, reference to the Holy Spirit as the 'life principle' of the Church must not lead to indiscriminate attribution of all the actions of the Church to the Holy Spirit. This would obscure the personal responsibility and freedom of the members, and would make the presence of sin and error in the Church difficult to explain, even on the corporate and official levels.

The blind spot of this model is an erroneous divinisation of the Church, which can: (a) arouse an unhealthy spirit of enthusiasm; (b) lead to false expectations in its search for religious experiences; (c) arouse impossible demands in its search for warm, familial relationships; (d) lead to loss of interest in the earthly life and thus loss of the sense of mission which is a task for striving for bettering human conditions. The remedy can be found in patience, faith, and concern for the greater and a more universal good.[622]

6.5.4. Sacrament

This model renders the Church as Christ's sacrament, an efficacious sign of grace, which produces or intensifies that of which it is a sign: God's favorable presence. But the sacrament of redemption is not complete in Jesus as a single individual; the reality signified achieves an existential depth, emerging into solid, tangible existence and expression in the community.[623] A sign is a testimony. The Church must strive to truly embody the grace it signifies: a community of love. The sacramental aspect must not induce an attitude of sterile aestheticism and an almost narcissistic self-contemplation that is incom-

619 Dulles, *Models of the Church*, pp. 47-48.

620 Ibid., p. 53.

621 Ibid., p. 49-50.

622 Ibid., p. 186.

623 Ibid., p. 58-59.

patible with a full Christian commitment to social and ethical values.[624] This understanding must increase in the believers an awareness of critical existence: striving to communicate Christ.

God's grace is through the Church for the world, not to be manipulated. It commits the Church and therein all believers to bring salvation to maturity: (a) through cooperation in the collective salvation of the world by taking part, each according to their calling; (b) by the impact of our whole Christian life, to cooperate in the individual salvation of those who are outside the Church. As sacrament the Church is a life-giving communion, working for the sanctification and salvation of the world. Lawler and Shanahan argue that "…from the beginning, the Church that is the sacrament of Christ in the world is perceived not as a crowd of passive spectators but as a communion of active participants."[625]

In synthesis, the purpose of the Church as sacrament is to bring people together; just as Christ brings people to God. Sacraments are of themselves social in nature: no one can anoint or baptise oneself. Therefore, by its teaching and example the Church must be seen as the presence of God.

6.5.5. Herald **or** *Kerygmatic*

The Church is a herald, acting as God's messenger; in other words it is kerygmatic, that is, proclaiming God's saving love and justice to the human world. Dulles writes that this model "…emphasises faith and proclamation over interpersonal relations and mystical communion… it looks upon the Church as a herald – one who receives an official message with the commission to pass it on."[626] The focus on proclamation constantly calls for renewal and reformation.

The herald model has its strength and weakness. It has its strength in the biblical vision and the communitarian understanding of the Church as People of God. Its weakness is that it is not incarnational enough; it can become too pietist, pessimistic and quietist. This vision neglects the possibilities of human effort in the establishment of a better human society in this life; and the duty of Christians to take part in social action and the public arena. The remedy is to be found in the incarnation of faith in life and action through service.[627]

624 Ibid., p. 67.

625 Michael G. Lawler and Thomas J. Shanahan, *Church: A Spirited Communion*, Collegeville, Minnesota, The Liturgical Press, 1995, p. 50.

626 Dulles, *Models of the Church*, p. 67-68.

627 Ibid., p. 186.

6.5.6. Servant

This approach highlights service as an essential characteristic of the Church's life and mission. Service gives life and dynamism in the Church and enables it to move outside itself towards society. Vatican Council II document, *Gaudium et Spes*, clarifies that the Church is not only Mother and Teacher but also servant. This document recommends that the Church has to learn from accomplishments made in the world and make itself relevant. Following the mission of Christ who came to serve and not to be served; so is the Church to seek and to find meaning in serving the world by fostering unity among people.[628] We can discern that the rationale (internal logic) of this service: unity among people.

Service was the main concern of the Synod of Bishops in 1971 under the theme: *Justice in the World.* In its document the Synod states that, "The Christian lives under the interior law of liberty, which is a permanent call to us to turn away from self-sufficiency to confidence in God and from concern for self to a sincere love of neighbour. Thus takes place his genuine liberation and the gift of himself for the freedom of others."[629] From this statement we may understand the mind of the synod, that service is one way of doing justice, doing what is right before God, of improving relationships among God's people. Through service the Church seeks ways of acting out God's justice towards his people.

Dulles calls this model "secular-dialogic" in the sense that the world (secular reality) is the theological place where the Church discerns the signs of the time; and thus enters into dialogue with it by translating the biblical message and Christian tradition in such realities. This approach therefore brings the Church to "...consider itself as part of the total human family, sharing the same concerns as the rest of men."[630] It places the Church in the continuing mission of Christ through service and example. In the example of Christ who was a man for others, so the Church practices to be a community for others. It encourages every one of its members to internalise this spirit and reach out to others as a witness to Christ. Dulles argues that the servant model must bring about in the Church a spiritual renewal; overcoming its "corporate egoism" and offering to society a credible prophetic Gospel message. This means that

628 *GS*, n. 3: *AAS* 58 (1966), p. 1027.

629 Synod of Bishops, *Justice in the World*, Vatican City, Libreria Editrice Vaticana, 1971, n. 33; cf. Austin Flannery (ed.), *Vatican Council II – Vatican Collection*, Vol. 2: *More Post Conciliar Documents*, New York, Costello Publishing Company, 1982, p. 701-702.

630 Dulles, *Models of the Church*, p. 84.

the Church does not close in on itself; but carries out its mission by paying attention to social concerns.

This approach has its strengths and limitations. Its core strength lies in its emphasis on serving others. It must naturally strengthen service within the Church itself; but, this spirit of service provides also an ecumenical field for the Church to work together with other Christian denominations, other religions, cultural institutions, charity organisations and the civil authorities and institutions – for the good of the human society. Practical areas of involvement will include topics like justice and peace, unity, conflict resolution, human rights, gender issues, and community building.

Nebbi Catholic Diocese can translate this in the context of its own human realities, as already expressed in its First Synod document, where it identifies three key avenues for service: (a) Ministries, especially the non-ordained, most of which has not been much excercised in our Diocese; (b) Christian commitment in society today; (c) Self-reliance, as a goal of development.[631]

The servant approach provides rich possibilities for service; but Dulles argues that it has some weaknesses which need to be clarified.[632] He observes that the concept of service must be carefully nuanced in a way that it keeps alive the distinctive identity and mission of the Church. It is to be interpreted in light of the Kingdom of God, personalised in Christ. Not to know Christ and put one's faith in him is not to know the Kingdom of God; this is a serious failure of understanding the Christian message. The Church is not to be likened to a volunteer group or free association performing generous activities. Its service is Gospel-inspired and does not uncritically take on a completely secular or socio-cultural pattern; nor does it terminate in a completely this-worldly view of salvation. True service includes the ministry of word and sacrament. The New Testament term for service, *diakonia*, has all types of ministries including preaching, sacraments and temporal help. All offices in the Church are forms of service. Emphasis on service alone may tend to dissolve too much of what is distinctive to Christianity. The Church's service towards the world rarely bears much resemblance with that which is advocated by those who hold this model. Service has to be separated from the preaching of Jesus as the Lord who gives life. The Church must always look to Christ the Servant-Saviour and his kingdom, which penetrates, but transcends, the earthly reality. Salvation is not fully realised in the world.[633]

631 *Acts of the First Diocesan Synod of Nebbi Catholic Diocese*, pp. 7-8.

632 Dulles, *Models of the Church*, pp. 91-94.

633 Ibid., p. 187.

6.5.7. Community of Disciples

The discipleship model is a wide, inclusive and flexible notion, having potentialities for a comprehensive ecclesiology. Dulles writes that: "It precludes the impression that the ecclesial communion exists merely for the sake of mutual gratification or support."[634] Discipleship creates awareness about the values and purposes that build up the Church: empowerment for Christian mission, initiation into a deeper significance of Jesus' teaching, breaking of old ties and attachment to the person of Jesus, election to a community opposed to the standards of the world, self-emptying love in imitation of Christ, assimilation to God, hope in the victory of Christ, single-minded commitment, and solidarity in the suffering of Christ.[635]

In its Decree on the Ministry and Life of Priests, *Presbyterorum Ordinis*, Vatican Council II teaches that discipleship underscores fidelity to Christ, which characterises the life of faith: both clergy and laity share the same status of discipleship.[636] Fidelity to Christ and to one another creates a spirit of confidence and cooperation. This serves as an antidote to the problem of clericalism in the Church. Corporate discipleship functions as 'body' and enables organic growth in a spirit of faith and affiliation with a praying community. Besides, in the contemporary social context, corporate discipleship enables Christians to become more aware of the needs and opportunities of the day.

Christian discipleship is demanding; it cannot be taken merely as a contrast society in opposition to a sinful world. Such an attitude would blur the Church's catholicity with the impression that Christianity forms a reclusive enclave of those who believe in Christ and reject the sinful world. Adeyemo observes that the spirit of communitarian discipleship as offered in the New Testament is weakening today. He writes that:

> Discipleship in the NT sense is rare today because of the preaching of cheap grace. Abuse of the concept has given rise to false cults and privatization of faith. The very size of modern churches also works against any sense of community... To make an impact on African society today, the church must return to the Bible and rediscover the NT concept and practice of discipleship.[637]

The phrase "false cults and privatization of faith" can be interpreted to mean that faith is treated as a personal possession where individuals or like-

634 Ibid., p. 198.

635 Ibid., p. 203.

636 Vatican Council II, *Presbyterorum Ordinis*, n. 9: *AAS* 58 (1966), pp. 1005-1006.

637 Tokunboh Adeyemo, "Discipleship," in *Africa Bible Ccommentary*, p. 1249.

minded groups act as they prefer without due regard for the integral vision and growth of the Church as a communion of believers, both local and universal.

6.5.8. Church-as-Family

This model, church as family of God, was expressly preferred by the Assembly of the Synod of Bishops for Africa in 1994.[638] The rationale for this is that the family model is an ecclesiology that comes closer to the African reality. This model can help us to come out of individualism by placing the individual in the family context where we practice to integrate community values. It is in the family that the individual learns the foundational communitarian values through interpersonal relationships.

Earlier, Pope John Paul II, in his Apostolic Exhortation on catechesis, *Catechesi Tradendae*, used the binomial family-home preferably focusing on the parish, which he defines as "…a fraternal and welcoming family home, where those who have been baptised and confirmed become aware of forming the People of God."[639] He clarifies that, "The parish is not principally a structure, a territory, or a building, but rather, the family of God, a fellowship affair with a unifying spirit, a familial and welcoming home, the community of the faithful."[640] He further clarifies that the parish is a place in the world for the community of believers to gather together as a sign and instrument of the vocation of all to communion. The Church is meant "…to be a house of welcome to all and a place of service to all."[641]

This ecclesiology has been promoted by Vatican Council II where it provides vivid biblical illustrations of the Church as family of God. (a) It is a Gospel *command* for unity: "In his (Jesus') preaching he explicitly commanded God's children to behave towards each other as sisters and brothers."[642] (b) It is a *faith conviction* by which "…the Church believes that through its individual members and as a whole it can contribute to making the human family and its history more human."[643] (c) It is founded on Christ's grace and thus a *mission* for the Church: "The union of the human family is greatly strengthened and brought to completion by the unity of the family of God's children which is

638 *Proposition 8*, in AFJN, p. 89.

639 *CT*, n. 67 § 3, in Austin Flannery (ed.), *Vatican Council II*, Vol. 2: *More Post Conciliar Documents*, p. 804: *AAS* 71 (1979), p. 1333.

640 *CfL*, n. 26: *AAS* 81 (1989), p. 438.

641 Ibid., n. 27: *AAS* 81 (1989), p. 442.

642 *GS*, n. 32 § 3: *AAS* 58 (1966), p. 1051.

643 Ibid., n. 40 § 3: *AAS* 58 (1966), p. 1058.

based on Christ."[644] (d) It is *constitutive* of the life of the Church as an institution: "More often the Church is called God's building… This building is called by various names: God's household (1 Tim. 3:15), in which his family lives… 'God's dwelling with his human beings'…"[645] (e) It is *Trinitarian*, implying the strongest bond of unity. The New Testament tells us that God lives and works in an inseparable community of three identifiable Divine Persons: Father, Son and Holy Spirit (2 Cor. 13:13; Mt 28:19b). These illustrations show that the Church, depicted as *family*, is a Church of communion.

However, the family model cannot be taken uncritically. The 'family' ecclesiology can bear a subtle but systematic potential for individualism (in the institutional context). In the traditional African context, the family reality is typically hierarchical; in it the father figure is more dominant at most, leaving marginal space for women and youth participation in social-cultural roles and process of decision. Waliggo has observed that: "The theology of church-as-family is a double-edged sword. It can be used profitably but it may also lead to benign paternalism. We must be careful not to end up again with a pyramid structure of the Church instead of the circular one of communion."[646] Reference to *paternalism* presents male dominance and father figure over women and youth in the process of decision making. The situation portrays a form of an institutionalised individualism. Another critical observation of the family model is made by Bishop Sarpong, where he draws clear parallels between the Church and the African family:

> … as one studies the African Family closely one becomes aware of ambiguities. In that family system there is a complex mixing of good and evil, of positive and negative possibilities. For all the excellent qualities that could stand in good stead for the Church, therefore, the African Family could be counter productive to the Christian cause if not well-directed. It could negate the Christian insistence on such cardinal virtues as love for all, justice, peace, humility, compassion, all virtues and values in which Christianity finds its very raison d'être.[647]

The Synod of Bishops for Africa in 1994 expressed an awareness of this reality where they cite an example within the Church that, "A certain idea of the Church produced a type of lay person who was too passive."[648] Even if the church-as-family can complement other models of the Church, we may discern

644 Ibid., n. 42 § 1: *AAS* 58 (1966), p. 1060; cf. LG, n. 9: *AAS* 57 (1965), pp. 12-15.

645 *LG*, n. 6 § 3: *AAS* 57 (1965), p. 6.

646 John Mary Waliggo, "The Synod of Hope at a time of Crisis in Africa," in AFJN, p. 208.

647 Peter K. Sarpong, *Dear Nana: Letters to My Ancestor*, Takoradi-Ghana, Franciscan Publications, 1998, p. 117.

648 AFJN, "Message of the Synod," p. 84, n. 57.

that Nebbi Catholic diocese may not benefit at best with this alone. It needs to move from the family image to that of the Small Christian Community for a larger ecclesial community context.

6.5.9. The Small Christian Community (SCC)

Can the SCC model help to build ecclesial communion? Can it help to correct the problem of individualism in the Church? Reference to the SCC in this study bears in mind such values as family, fraternity, solidarity, Trinitarian spirit, communion, togetherness and Christ-centeredness; all of which are incompatible with individualism.

The SCC complements and strengthens the ecclesiology of church-as-family. The image is depicted by Sanon as: "…church communion, the church family, the church fraternity."[649] The SCC has three essential concepts: (a) *Trinitarian*: resting on and living from the Communion of God the Father, the Son and the Holy Spirit in a relational dynamic; (b) *Christ-centred*: in his mission of salvation, Christ formed and lived in a Small Community with twelve companions (Mk. 3:13-19; Lk. 6:12-16; Mt. 10:1-4); after Christ's Ascension those in Jerusalem who believed the preaching of the Apostles formed the first SCC (Acts 2:42-47); (c) *Pneumatological* foundation, the Holy Spirit: Christ promised an Advocate as the Teacher of his community, to guide them into the truth of faith (Jn. 14:26; 15:26-27; 16:7-8, 13). The event of Pentecost shows that the Holy Spirit gives inspiration (Acts 2:1-4f), defines the spirit of life according to faith (Rom. 8:1-13) and gives different gifts for ecclesial growth (1 Cor. 12). Our enquiry is how the SCC might serve to build a strong and viable ecclesial communion.

The 1994 Special Assembly of the Synod of Bishops for Africa realised that: "The Church-as-Family cannot reach its full potential unless it is broken up into communities which are small enough to permit close human relations."[650] Following this Synod, in his Post-Synodal Apostolic Exhortation on the Church in Africa, *Ecclesia in Africa*, Pope John Paul II depicts the SCC as a vital Christian community, a community of life, where the practice of living Christ's love must become natural to Christians.[651] By this he means that these communities put life into the Church. In what follows, we shall give a brief highlight on the processes that led the Bishops in the AMECEA Region to choose the SCC as a model for the Church in Africa.

---

649 Anselme T. Sanon, "The church is Communion, Family, and Brotherhood," in *L'Osservatore Romano*, Weekly Edition, n. 17, April 27, 1994, p. 14.

650 AFJN, *Proposition* 9.

651 *EA*, n. 89: *AAS* 88 (1996), p. 56.

In their 1973 study conference, the Bishops chose the SCC as a pastoral priority to express the ecclesial reality at the most basic level possible, in order to bring about an effective evangelisation. They understood that in this way the Church can become really "local." By this they meant that the SCC approach must enable the Church to become self-ministering and self-propagating.[652] Their focus was that the SCC approach is one that can make the Church truly incarnated in the life experiences of the people, as expressly stated:

> While the Church of Christ is universal, it is a communion of small local Christian Churches, communities of Christians rooted in their own society... Thus the Church, like Christ himself, becomes incarnated in the life of the people. She is led by local people, meets and answers local needs and problems, and finds within herself the resources needed for her life and mission.[653]

The point is further propounded by Bishop Kalilombe, basing his argument on the rationale of the New Testament ecclesiology as lived by early Christian communities. That is, the Church of Christ subsists in a communion of local Churches. This has the benefit of expressing veritable oneness in a face-to-face relationship with some everyday unifying factors that will call Christian witnessing to be realised in the lived experience of believers. Besides, the SCC approach will contribute to restructuring the Church from the more administrative-focused parish and diocesan set-up.[654]

In 1976, the Bishops reaffirmed the same pastoral strategy, maintaining that, basing on lived realities, these communities reflect the natural family model, informed by faith. In their understanding, all other ecclesial groups based on common interests or common tasks should be seen as supplementary to these natural groups.[655] They preferred the family model because of the prominent role the family has in the African society.[656] On this background, Sr. Nwagwu writes that the goal of the Church in Africa is to be a:

---

652 AMECEA Bishops, "Planning for the Church in East Africa in the 1980's: Record of the AMECEA Study Conference held at St. Thomas Aquinas Seminary, Nairobi, 14-21 December 1973," in *AFER*, Vol. 16, Nr. 1&2, 1974, p. 10.

653 Ibid., p. 9.

654 *Ibid.*, p. 60.

655 AMECEA Bishops, "Building Christian Communities in Eastern Africa," in *AFER*, Vol. 18, Nr. 5, 1976.

656 Synod of Bishops – Special Assembly for Africa, *The Church in Africa and Her Evangelising Mission towards the Year 2000: Instrumentum Laboris*, Vatican City, General Secretariat for the Synod of Bishops and Libreria Editrice Vaticana, 1993, n. 25; AFJN, "Message of the Synod: Synod Documents," p. 89, *Propositions 8-9*, title; also pp. 78-79, n. 28, 31; cf. p. 72, n. 3.

> Christ-centered, vibrant and people-oriented church where the African sense of family is experienced and lived by all. The ideal African family is based on the extended family system where members are united in a common ancestry which gives each person his or her identity. It is also a center of passing on traditions and culture as well as a place where reconciliation and healing of wounds are facilitated. The church in Africa must therefore become a family in the African sense where the family is an oasis of rest, security and identity.[657]

The Bishops believe that the creation of small communities at the human level can promote communitarian life: "In such communities, which are cells of the Church-as-Family, one is formed to live concretely and authentically the experience of fraternity."[658] We can understand that promoting the spirit of fraternity is one way of eradicating individualism in the Church; fraternity is incompatible with the self-bent spirit that individualism engenders.

A more methodological study has been carried out in South Africa. Basing on the Bishops' option for SCCs, his parish pastoral experience and study, Anselm Prior writes that: "Small communities also seem to be the most effective means of making the gospel message truly relevant to African traditions."[659] A methodology in its regard has been developed by the LUMKO Institute in South Africa, which identifies five stages of ecclesial growth. The LUMKO booklet on SCCs clearly points out the: "Contrasts between Individualism and Small Christian Communities."[660] It offers a historical, developmental survey that can help the community to see where it has come from, assess where it is, and where it is going.[661]

The first stage is the *provided-for church*. The dominant person is the parish priest who organises everything and offers the laity all the necessary means of salvation. This is the role described in the 1917 Code of Canon Law as a *right* of the laity: they are to receive spiritual goods and strong help for their salvation from the ordained priests (Can. 682).

The second stage is *a pastoral church* in which the laity play the role of *helpers*, working alongside the priest through a shared leadership, rather than

657 Mary Gerald Nwagwu, "Communion and Self-Reliance: Signs of Church as God's Family in Africa," in *AFER*, Vol. 42, Nos. 1&2 (2000), p. 23.

658 AFJN, "Message of the Synod: Synod Documents," p. 78, n. 28.

659 Anselm Prior, *Towards a Community Church*, Gemiston, Lumko Publications, 1991, p. 7.

660 Nebbi Catholic Diocese, Pastoral Coordinator's Office, *Small Christian Communities in Nebbi Catholic Diocese: A Pastoral Priority as the Way for Effective and Efficient Evangelization Today*, Nebbi, Catholic Press, 2003, p. 15. "Programme C: The Contrast between Individualism and Small Christian Communities," is based on the LUMKO Programme for developing a shared ministry.

661 Anselm Prior (ed.), *Towards a Community Church*, 2nd edition, *The Training for Ministries Series*, Nr. 28T, Natal, LUMKO Publications, 1997, p. 17-27.

carrying their own responsibility. Although Vatican Council II introduced the pastoral council as a legal entity (can. 536), they are only *optional*, depending on whether the Bishop wants them in the diocese or not. Moreover, the members of these councils have only a *consultative,* but not a decisive, vote.

The third stage is *the awakening church* at which more lay people are involved in church life. The tension here is that of power struggle: who decides? The issue of power and control arises. This may become exclusivist as power is placed totally in the hands of the ordained priests, mainly the Bishops and the Parish Priest (the curate, as an assistant to the Parish priest, also has no decision power; just as the laity are).

The fourth stage is the *task-group church:* the stage of *social action* where the laity take responsibility at their best both within and beyond the confines of the congregation. It is a Church both at worship and in the service of others.

The fifth stage is the *communion of communities*: where SCCs become part of the parish structure. One of them is a member of the Parish Council. In this way the activities of the SCC connect them to the parish Church. This energises and enables every particular small community to participate more consciously in the universality of the Church through the parish and diocesan communion. The SCC has four operative marks for its dynamism.

The four marks of SCCs: (a) Meeting of members in their homes, as sodalities, rotating the hosting family, once a week or a fortnight; (b) Gospel sharing enables members to express common experiences; (c) Looking to one another's needs in the locality which they want to put into practice, based on "doing to Christ" through the community members or their neighbourhoods; (d) Practice of universality (catholicity) through inter-community visits and activities; taking turns in preparing and leading Sunday liturgy; scheduled meetings to discuss and work together as a team; each community represented at Parish Pastoral Council.[662]

The evaluation of Healey on the SCC practice in the AMECEA region demonstrates that the SCC can be instrumental for Nebbi Catholic Diocese in overcoming individualism. It has the advantage of shaping the moral life of believers and fostering a spirit of listening to one another, planning together, setting workable strategies and implementing tasks through team action, continually assessing the implemented tasks and looking for the way forward together. The design and setting of the SCC is to make every community self-reliant and, in this way, self-actualising. It can be applied in every ecclesial framework: in the Christian homestead setting, school, seminary, or place of work. It is a way of enabling the faithful to theologise in their own life situation and context. That is, through experience, the laity will become theologians of life where they are.

662 Prior, *Towards a Community Church*, pp. 42-43.

They will be able to *translate* the gospel message into their ordinary and daily experiences. Furthermore, the SCC will help to nurture vocations to the priesthood and religious communities of consecrated persons.[663] The SCC must lead the diocesan church to understand itself and promote an ecclesiology of the church as home, a homely communion.

6.5.10. Home

From our field study an understanding of the Church as home is more expressive of the lived experience of the people in Nebbi. The Church must be *homely* in the family, in the SCC, in the parish, in the deanary, in its diocesan functions and other ecclesial contexts. This approach will bring about integral ecclesial growth, built upon the two footholds of fraternity and friendship. *Fraternity* signifies an interminable oneness, consistent unity, that stays and holds people together even in times of conflicts and tensions. *Friendship* signifies freedom and openness with one another, such as reflected in Christ's example, how he related to people during his salvific mission on earth, through word and deed. In other words, fraternity and friendship are the two hinges about which practical relationship in the Church, at all its levels and dimensions, will rest and move. This will help the Church to understand itself as a home born of and sustained by the spirit of togetherness, solidarity and inseparability: born in the unifying Spirit of God. In this way, the Church assumes a *new culture*, which defines God's people in Christ, through the Spirit, as a *new people*.

St. Paul's "no more" metaphor provides a helpful theological reflection that can guide us in building up the Church as home. In his Letter to the Galatians he writes: "There can be neither Jew nor Greek, there can be neither slave nor free man, there can be neither male nor female – for you are all one in Christ Jesus" (Gal. 3: 28). Commenting on this verse, Callan writes that "... religiously no differences exist, national or social, but all form one moral and mystical body with Christ their head."[664] From this we can draw three insights: (a) no more "Jew or Greek" can help us to appreciate the meaning and richness of faith-identity, which will help us to overcome any form of division among believers; (b) no more "slave or free" points to openness and acceptance for the deepening of ecclesial life through involvement and participation; (c) no more "male or female" takes its foundation in creation as 'man and woman' and should help Christians to address gender imbalance. It is upon this social un-

663 Healey, *Building the Church as Family of God*, pp. 89-100.

664 Charles J. Callan, *The Epstles of St. Paul – With Introductions and Commentary for Priests and Students:* Vol. I: *Romans, First and Second Corinthians, Galatians*, New York, Joseph F. Wagner (Inc.), 1922, p. 627.

derstanding of justification in the freedom of faith, that individuals and groups must find meaning and strength as one people – Alur saying: *wan aciel*, we are one – in Christ. The Christian faith message should always appeal to the free social identity in Christ's justification. It is a Christian culture of real human life in which people address one another with recognition, regard, respect and gratritude, offering that finest touch of a well disposed inner loving. In this spirit, our former cultural, social or sexual realities are not seen as privileges; but they provide for mutual strength and growth. In other words, the diocese must strive to build a living communion of saints called together by the word of God and guided in its life and activities by the internal wisdom of this word.

Theologically, this approach has a biblical foundation. In the writing of St. Paul, the Church is a community where people are not anonymous or aliens to one another (Eph. 2:19-22). To see the Church as home is to find in it a communion which is both spiritually and humanly engaging; such a communion in which one learns and strives to become fully human and truly Christian. A home is more than ethnicity; it is more than boundary; it is wholeness in every aspect. This understanding will help us to translate catholicity (*kath holos*, according to the whole) into the lived experience of the faithful.

We have already noted that in Nebbi Catholic Diocese, individualism in the Church is understood as tearing, splitting or scattering the home. Building the Church as home intends welding together the different models we have discussed above into a Church truly planted, which remains, in the place; a Church which is itself at home among the people of the place; a Church in which everyone is at home; a Church which all the believers will know and experience and love as *pacu mwa*, our home, and *thúwá*, homeland, where we belong and live. Those various models of the Church are vital elements to making it a home; a truly living institution; the sacrament of sanctification; evangeliser; servant; communion; body of Christ; family of God; and people of God. Nebbi Catholic Diocese may need to build such a Church which is truly home to all its members; a church of the soil – with its roots there; a Church which is truly one, catholic, missionary, and universal; a church of salvation and human progress both in the spiritual and material aspects; a church that knows its needs and pulls its efforts together in response. The Church built as home is one which becomes more conscious of itself as a Church which is gathering the people into one; a Church which is striving to become self-propagating, self-ministering and self-supporting.

On the human side it is resonant with the tradition of the people in Nebbi. Building the Church as *home* intends inclusive rootedness and growth of such a Church incarnated in the human realities of the place, truly implanted. Such appellatives of belonging provide clear explaination: *judongo pacu*, elders of the home; *mego pacu*, mothers of the home; *nyithindho pacu*, children of the home; *nya-pacu*, daughter of the home; *wo-pacu*, son of the home. These appeals have an important moral meaning to persons in the community, signifying faithful commitment to upholding the values upon which the home stands; one must do one's part deservingly of their name and see its fruit in the achievement that the community reaches.

In this way Nebbi Catholic Diocese will not only be at home in the place but also a home to the people of God there; it will not just embody, preserve and carry forward the kinship, chiefship and religious values but will enrich and perfect them with Christian values. This will enable the diocese to live and act as a moral community.

6.6. The Church as a Moral Community

The deeper sense of being *Christian*, of being *church*, of being *catholic*, of *mystical communion* with God and with one another in the Church, and of being a *sacramental* reality – all this must influence the life of every believer and must be translated into a visible life that can contribute to building up and strengthening the Church as a true, living communion. We shall develop this by looking at the Church as a moral community. In their co-authored book, *Bible and Ethics*, Birch and Rasmussen identify three ways by which the Church functions as a moral community: (a) shaping moral identity; (b) communicating moral tradition; (c) a community of moral deliberation.

The Church as shaper of moral identity: by which is meant that the Christian moral life works through fellowship, as early Christians practiced. It is in the community that the individual's relational capacities like sensitivity, empathy, secularity, trust and courage are nurtured. "The Christian has no enduring identity *as Christian* apart from the Church. Thus the Church is the necessary context for relating the Christian's moral life to his or her identity *as Christian*."[665] In other words, the Church is a school of love where the individual moves from self-story into community-story by internalising community values and aspirations, meanings and purposes.

The Church as bearer of moral tradition: meaning that the Church functions as the place and agent of Christian moral tradition by providing the material and setting for character-formation and decision-making.[666] Gula has tried to clarify the question of moral tradition in the Church by making a connection

665 Bruce C. Birch and Larry L Rasmussen, *Bible and Ethics in the Christian Life*, Minneapolis, Augsburg Publishing House, 1976, pp. 127-132, citation on p. 132, italic emphases in the original.

666 Ibid., pp. 132-136.

between the magisterial teachings with the personal conscience of believers in specific moral decisions. He writes that, "Most of the attention given to the role of the church in moral life focuses on the magisterium providing moral instruction on specific issues in the form of norms or laws in order to inform consciences and to guide the process of making decision."[667] The authoritative teaching of the Church must strengthen the moral life of believers, namely, the moral tradition must be a living reality in their lives. Every committed believer embodies and shares in the Church's moral tradition with different kinds of responsibilities. Thus, the moral tradition is in: (a) the lay faithful through family life, the Church's social activities in church-founded or church-sponsored institutions and the public arena; (b) theologians and pastoral ministers by their interpretative function at different levels and fields of involvement; (c) the hierarchy who act in a more official manner to proclaim the apostolic tradition through their documents and pronouncements – they speak *for* the Church.[668]

The Church as a community of moral deliberation, referring to public opinion in the Church. This considers that the Church is both a necessary and decisive community for the Christian moral life. The central question is about Christian character and conduct; and the life of the Church as God's People.[669] This involves listening, in order to learn, through consultation and dialogue which will enable moral discourse in a setting of public scrutiny and accountability in order to bring about a fuller understanding of what their concerns are.

The question of *public opinion* in the Church has received authoritative recognition. It was first used in relation to the Church by Pope Pius XII (1939-1958) where he says:

> Public opinion is part of the legacy of any normal society constituted of human beings… We wish to add a word about public opinion in the Church, in those matters that are open to free discussion. The expression of such opinion comes as a surprise only to those who do not know the Catholic Church, or who have a false opinion of it. For the Church, too, is a living organism, and an important element would be missing from its life were it to be without expression of public opinion. The blame for this shortcoming would lie with its shepherds and faithful.[670]

The importance of public opinion in the Church was again emphasised at Vatican Council II (fifteen years after Pope Pius XII's declaration) in its document, *Gaudium et Spes*, where it states: "It should be recognised that the

667 Gula, *op. cit.*, p. 199.

668 Ibid., pp. 202-206.

669 Birch and Rasmussen, *op. cit.*, pp. 136-141.

670 *L'Osservatore Romano*, February 18, 1950.

faithful, clerical as well as lay, have a just freedom of inquiry, of thought and of humble and courageous expression in those matters in which they enjoy competence."[671]

In 1971 the Holy See published an Instruction on Social Communication, *Communio et Progressio*. About public opinion in the Church the document says:

> Since the Church is a living body, she needs public opinion in order to sustain a giving and taking between her members. Without this she cannot advance in thought and action... Catholics should be fully aware of the real freedom to speak their minds which stems from a "feeling for the faith" and from love... Those who exercise authority in the Church will take care to ensure that there is responsible exchange of freely held and expressed opinion among the people of God... Since the development of public opinion within the Church is essential, individual Catholics have the right to all the information they need to play their active role in the life of the Church... The normal flow of life and the smooth functioning of government within the Church require a steady two-way flow of information between ecclesiastical authorities at all levels and as organised groups. This applies to the whole world.[672]

Commenting on public opinion in the Church Quinn remarks that: "Public opinion and criticism which it implies are necessary for Church authority to carry its responsibilities. Church leaders... have to know the hopes and dreams of the people, what their problems are, what they find difficult and why."[673] This raises a question to reflect upon: How will Christians critically explore and reflect upon their basic commitments and convictions in order to translate faith into choices, decisions and actions? We can respond to this question by looking at the models of morality as possibilities of forming conscience and deepening the sense of being responsible for working to build up the ecclesial community.

---

671 *GS*, n. 62: *AAS* 58 (1966), p. 1084. We have used the wording as in Norman P. Tanner (ed.), *Decrees of the Ecumenical Councils*, Vol. 2: *Trent - Vatican II*, London, Sheed & Ward Limited, 1990, p. 1113.

672 "Pastoral Instruction on the Means of Social Communication," n. 115-117, 119, 120, in Austin Flannery (ed.), *Vatican Council II*, Vol. 1: *The Conciliar and Post Conciliar Documents*, pp. 330-332.

673 John R. Quinn, *The Reform of the Papacy: The Costly Call to Christian Unity*, New York, The Crossroad Publishing Company, 1999, pp. 63-64.

6.7. Models of Morality

Models of the Church can remain abstract ideals if they do not shape its moral life and enable its conscious growth in the relational spirit of communion. In its examination of conscience, the 1994 Synod of Bishops for Africa makes the following statement:

> The churches in Africa are also aware that, insofar as their own internal affairs are concerned, justice is not always respected with regard to those men and women who are at their service. If the Church should give witness to justice, she recognizes that whoever dares to speak to others about justice should also strive to be just in their eyes. It is necessary therefore to examine with care the procedures, the possessions, and the life style of the Church.[674]

Building Church communion requires implementing the identified Church models and structures into practical life.

We have already noted that the Alur traditional values that shaped its moral life are now affected by social-cultural changes. The Church has to respond to this situation with models of morality that can appeal to the moral conscience of believers and of the general society, in order to cultivate and strengthen a communitarian spirit. We are indebted to two moral theologians, Harrington and Fagan, whose thoughts on the models of morality give lucid illustratrations. Both of them approach the question of Christian morality in view of the changes in society which impinge on the moral life. These changes equally resonate in the Church. In his book, *What is Morality?* Harrington identifies five models that present morality as law, inner conviction, personal growth, love, social transformation.[675] In his book, *Does Morality Change?* Fagan proposes seven approaches to the shaping of the moral life, presenting morality as: law (legal approach), love and discipleship, liberation, inner conviction, relationship and growth, experiencing others, and personal growth.[676] Both these agree with the Church models highlighted above. Their approach seeks to rethink the Church's moral teaching in light of contemporary social-cultural realities. From the models they develop, we shall add our own: that of *indwelling* or *immanence* which we feel brings to life the other models.

The legal model understands law as a path of life: which serves to guide, encourage and convince believers about values that safeguard the common

---

674 AFJN, p. 81, n. 43. The Bishops address their audience as "Dear Brothers and Sisters in Christ." p. 72.

675 Donal Harrington, *What is Morality? The Light Through Different Windows*, Dublin, The Columba Press, 1996.

676 Seán Fagan, *Does Morality Change?* 1997.

good of the community and society for their viability and sustenance. This is an objective approach, not based on what one would wish to be or do or think but on the nature of things as they are. Its aim is to promote virtue, appreciation, respect and love among members.[677]

In the context of Nebbi Catholic Diocese, we have cited in Chapter Two one traditional practice of its people as *dipo pa judongo* (council of elders) which discuses, and *vura* (a general assembly) which disseminates, matters pertaining to community life and welfare. It bears the same context of what Bujo calls *palaver* in his advocacy for an African ecclesiology of the council of elders, not as a hierarchical or logical law-making body but a participation in the "common inheritance of the Lord" through experience and wisdom.[678] Its methodology is dialogical, conducted in a common gathering which discusses community matters, not for the sake of intellectual excellence but to express the community's experience.[679] In its preparatory document, *Instrumentum Laboris* (2009), the Second Special Assembly of the Synod of Bishops for Africa cites palaver as a useful traditional tool for building up community life. It asks: "What has the Church learned from the experiences of diocesan synods, days of recollection for clergy and forums for lay faithful and Small Christian Communities?"[680]

The legal model has its weakness. Care must be taken of this approach does not keep people out of the Church. Nevertheless, a wise use of palaver checks against legalism with its accent on duty and uncritical obedience, a sanction-laden approach: heaven or hell, benefit or burden, reward or punishment. The legal approach must be strenthend with love.

The love model: based on creative love, which is the law of Christ.[681] Christian love is self-giving and incarnatoric, transcending and perfecting cultural standards. Harrington writes: "Moral consciousness is about 'we' rather than

677 Harrington, *What is Morality?* pp. 11-13; Fagan, *Does Morality Change?* pp. 35-36.

678 Bénézet Bujo, "On the Road toward an African Ecclesiology: Reflections on the Synod," in AFJN, *The African Synod: Documents, Reflections, Perspectives*, p. 146. For Bujo, 'palaver' is a predominant methodology that covers the full range of topics on morality. See his *The Ethical Dimension of Community*, pp. 58-89; *Foundations of an African Ethic*, pp. 45-54, 143-150.

679 Cf. Juvénal Ilunga Muya, "Bénézet Bujo: The Awakening of a Systematic and Authentically African Thought" in Bénézet Bujo and Juvénal Ilunga Muya (eds.), *African Theology: The Contribution of the Pioneers*, Vol. 1, Nairobi, Paulines Publications Africa, 2003, p. 108-109.

680 Synod of Bishops II – Special Assembly for Africa, *The Church in Service to Reconciliation, Justice and Peace: Instrumentum Laboris*, n. 88, also n. 8.

681 Harrington, p. 16-17; Fagan, p. 36-37. Love as the foundation of Christian moral life is the central theme of Bernard Häring's three-volume work. See his *Free and Faithful in Christ*, Vol. 1, pp. 1-6.

just 'I'. It is our awareness of the relationship, where we see living in terms of 'we' – as when Paul said that 'It is no longer I who live but it is Christ who lives in me' (Gal 2:20)."[682] This model checks against the impasse of a structured hierarchy of existence with its emphasis on 'call and response' which sets a moral tension of 'communion *against* isolation.' The love model can help the Church to overcome, for example, male-female and paternalistic bias which tends to relegate or sideline women and youth to passiveness. The love model can be questioned for its softness. But, on the contrary, Christian love is a discipleship love which commits us to promote the good of persons in whom our love for God is tested. Christian love says: the same heart with which we love God is the same heart with which we love one another. This is the moral assessment of Christian loving.

The discipleship model: denotes two things in the Christian moral life. Subjectively, it refers to the intimate personal relationship that one has with Christ. Objectively, it is lived in the faith community.[683] In the ecclesiological aspect, Dulles considers discipleship as a possibility for the Church to adopt a lifestyle practiced by the first disciples of Jesus.[684] He argues that this model is not resonant with an individualistic ecclesiology. Discipleship does not intend isolation of the individual, group or institution in a locked-up, mystical world detached from contingent realities of life; it means commitment for social concerns.

The liberation or *social transformation model*: explains the moral life not just as a matter of personal piety but rather poised for social concerns, involving the administration of justice, distribution of resources and improving social structures.[685] This approach can help the Church to continuously study, revise and update its structures, which will enable it to strengthen its inner life and respond to its contingent society. Christian love is not a confinement; it is open to communion in Christ's self-giving to all and for all. However, the blind side of this model lies in its objective-personalist approach which is preoccupied with topics like freedom, conscience and authority. The way forward can be found in being attentive to facts through sensitivity and reasonableness. Liberation is not selective or categorical and does not mean relativising the truth of faith.

The inner conviction model: has to do with truthful life informed by faith in Christ; what *Gaudium et Spes* calls "inner law."[686] It signifies personal moral

682 Harrington, p. 175.

683 Ibid., p. 16-17; Fagan, pp. 36-37.

684 Dulles, *Models of the Church*, pp. 195-217.

685 Harrington, pp. 17-19; Fagan, pp. 37-38.

686 *GS*, n. 16: *AAS* 58 (1966), p. 1037.

responsibility not only to Christ but also to the present community. Inner conviction underscores integrity and authenticity, fidelity and inner light of true self, and the consistency between knowing and doing. Integrity means that one is not pressured into action from outside, nor acting at selfish humours. The problem with this model is that it tends to over-emphasise topics like conscience, joy *against* disappointment or self-contradiction. This can melt down into a too subjective-personalist preoccupation that can easily slip into individualistic atomisation. The corrective can be found through fidelity to Christ and to one's community.[687] Bujo observes that the individual's moral consciousness is a participation in the web of community existence: "the individual cannot avoid reflecting on how his ethical actions affect the community."[688] Inner conviction is not self-contemplation as individualism tends to suggest; rather inner conviction opens us to share our joy in relationship.

The relationship model, based on the Trinitarian foundation, helps Christians to grow together as persons by experiencing one another. This leads to personal growth: *personal* in the matrix of community identity and *personal* as a specific individual. Relationship develops true self-acceptance, self-transcendence and a fuller self-identity.[689]

The relationship model links with the model of Church as *family*. As reflected in the document of the 1994 Special Assembly of the Synod of Bishops, it raises the challenge of relationship within the Church:

> Belonging to Christ puts differences in origin aside and brings people together as brothers and sisters in one family of the sons and daughters of God. Since this is the case, Christ's disciples are called upon to transform their differences, based on tribes, ethnic groups, races or social class, which oftentimes impede togetherness. In doing so, they will show that the bond created by the waters of Baptism is stronger than blood-ties (cf. *Gal* 3: 27-28). Because the image of the Church as Family is founded on the fatherhood of God, it highlights the African family-values of solidarity, sharing, respect for others, hospitality, togetherness, etc.[690]

This understanding can help the diocese to evaluate the cultural values of the local people. However, an exaggeration of personal or group growth can melt down into self-centredness or group egoism and thereby undue self-justi-

687 Harrington, pp. 13-14; Fagan, pp. 38-39.

688 Bénézet Bujo, *Foundations of an African Ethic*, p. 125. Here Bujo argues against the tendency to objectify individual conscience as a guiding inner moral light: the individual conscience takes shape in the community (pp. 124-130). This means that the community has a noticeable role in the question of 'inner conviction.'

689 Fagan, pp. 41-45; Harrington, pp. 14-16.

690 AFJN, n. 87, 88.

fication as opposed to self-determination. The corrective can be found in practicing the theological virtues of relating to God – faith, love and hope; and the human relational virtues of prudence, temperance, fortitude and justice which together serve to regulate relationships.

The model of immanence or *indwelling*: refers to openness and availability, which can enable members of the Church to work together. An objection against this model would be that availability would make someone vulnerable by being over-exposed in relationship. However, the fear of being exposed leads to procrastination and postponing what is to be done at the proper time. On the contrary, Christian loving means becoming all for all, becoming, so to speak, 'charity personified.' Two biblical personalities illustrate this point: (i) the person of Abraham, becoming a universal blessing (Gen. 12:1-12); (ii) the person of Paul: becoming all things for all people – different personalities, background settings and conditions of life, women, children and men (1 Cor. 9:19-23). The approach in this model is incarnatoric, dialogical and adaptive. In our view, a spirit of immanence is most suitable for the SCC ecclesiology; it can foster the community's moral growth.

Conclusion

In this chapter we have discussed ways of building ecclesial communion. We started by clarifying the notion of ecclesial communion. Here we discovered that the term communion can be explained by its cognate, community. This helped us to trace the images of ecclesial communion back to Jesus Christ, looking at how he formed a community of followers around him. We further saw that Jesus left his followers who continued as a unified community. This led us to notice that early Christians practiced community life which enabled them to bear witness to God's love as Christ had taught them. A strong factor to their communion was perseverance, through common prayer, charity and the teaching of the Apostles. The Didachē continues to show how Christians practiced common life through regulated prayer, charity and church support.

From the writings of the Church Fathers one emphasis runs through: unity. Here we saw that ecclesial communion is strengthened by consultation, acts of charity, prayer life, good pastorship, a deeper understanding of Baptism by which they are made one in Christ, and the Eucharist by which they become one Body and one life-blood in Christ.

This led us to develop an understanding that the Church has a social nature, that is, communitarian both by Divine constitution and in its human ordering. We have tried to illustrate that this can be expressed in different ways, as the exposition on the models or images of the Church suggests. These models do not only help to deepen our understanding of the Church but also provide possibilities of working for a greater wholeness. The most important is that these models can only be realised in the lived experience of the faithful, particularly when the Church becomes more a place of *kinship* in Christ, of life and service. This will make the Church more lively, relevant and effective place of love, a home.

We have further shown that the Church is a moral community, insofar as it acts as a shaper of moral identity, bearer of moral tradition, and a community of moral deliberation. We have expounded the preceding point by reflecting on the models of morality. The intention of proposing these models is the formation of the conscience of believers in order to make them responsible for the Church both personally and as a community; and to apply them to their lived experience. The following chapter will make some moral theological recommendations in view of what we have presented in chapters one to six.

CHAPTER SEVEN
Moral Theological Recommendations

Introduction

In order to respond to the problem of individualism in Nebbi Catholic Diocese our study proposes three main areas that deserve close attention: the use of the Word of God, formation, and collaboration. The aim of this recommendation is to achieve community spirit which will help all the faithful – priests, the religious, catechists and other pastoral agents, the different groups, SCCs, families and individuals – to work together with conviction and dedication in the building up of a strong and viable ecclesial communion. The prime resource of formation to inspire and sustain ecclesial life is the Word of God as communicated in Sacred Scripture.

7.1. The Word of God

Can the Word of God help Nebbi Catholic Diocese to overcome individualism, and build a strong and viable ecclesial communion? Evaluating the strength of evangelisation in Africa twelve years since the publication of Pope John Paul II's Post-Synodal Apostolic Exhortation, *Ecclesia in Africa*, Kato remarks that, "The ignorance of scripture among some Catholics as compared to other Christian Churches, must be challenged and henceforth rectified."[691] We have already noted that in Nebbi Catholic Diocese, the Catholic laity are shy in the use of the Bible in comparison to their counterparts in the "Protestant" or "Evangelical" Churches. To respond to this situation, there are three factors we are looking at: the role of the Word of God in the life of the Church, the use of the Bible, and its role in the moral life of believers.

7.1.1. The Importance of the Word of God in the Life of the Church

Although the Bible cannot be taken as a ready reckoner for every emerging moral problem, its role in the life of faith cannot be downplayed. Vatican Council II, in its Dogmatic Constitution on Divine Revelation, *Dei Verbum*, teaches that the Word of God has a perennial value for the life of the Church as for every believer. This document distinguishes between "natural" revelation

691 Joseph Bitole Kato, "Evangelization in Africa: Twelve Years After the *Ecclesia in Africa*," in *AFER*, Vol. 50, Nr. 1&2 (March-June 2008), p. 130.

and Divine Revelation: the former can lead to discovering God's ways displayed in nature; the latter culminates in the Incarnation which communicates God's personal utterance in the person and life of Christ. Commenting on articles 3 and 6 of the document, Walter writes that: "The first sentence in Art. 3 refers to so-called "natural" revelation: the indications of God's nature and activity to be gathered from the existence of created things."[692] The Word of God is the possibility of transmitting God's Divine Revelation as above "natural" revelation. The Council teaches that without recourse to Scripture the Christian religion and life of the Church is bound to weaken and lose its vigour.[693]

The role of the Word of God in the life and mission of the Church was the theme of the Twelfth Ordinary General Assembly of the Synod of Bishops. The *Lineamenta* to this Synod states that the Word of God nourishes the life and activity of the Church: (a) in the celebration of the liturgy; (b) in evangelisation and catechesis; (c) in exegesis and theology; (d) in the life of the believer.[694]

Following this Synod, Pope Benedict XVI published his Post-Synodal Apostolic Exhortation, *Verbum Domini*, in which he emphasises the need to rediscover the importance of God's Word in the life of the Church as a constant wellspring of newness and renewal: "...I express my hope that the word of God will be ever more fully at the heart of every ecclesial activity."[695] We may understand that one way to do this is to place the Scripture in the hands of all believers, especially those who have little access to it. This needs a concerted effort of all pastoral agents, reaching down to Christian homesteads, the school and other frames of ecclesial communities. How then will the Word of God be used effectively to build ecclesial communion?

7.1.2. The Use of the Bible

A good use of the Bible as the Word of God has much benefit for ecclesial life. This calls for an adequate catechesis on the use of the Bible as the Word of God. In his book, *The Craft of Theology*, Avery Dulles highlights ten theologi-

692 Vatican Council II, Dogmatic Constitution on Divine Revelation *Dei Verbum*, nn. 6-13: *AAS* 58 (1966), pp. 819-824. Cf. Walter W. Abbott and Joseph Gallagher (eds.), *The Documents of Vatican II*, p. 112, footnote 4.

693 *DV*, n. 21: *AAS* 58 (1966), pp. 827-828. Cf. Austin Flannery (ed.), *Vatican Council II*, Vol. 1, p. 762.

694 Synod of Bishops, XII Ordinary General Assembly, *The Word of God in the Life and Mission of the Church: Lineamenta*, Nairobi, Paulines Publications Africa, 2007, nn. 20-24.

695 Benedict XVI, Post-Synodal Apostolic Exhortation *Verbum Domini* (On the Word of God in the Life and Mission of the Church), Vatican City, Libreria Editrice Vaticana, 2010. n. 1: *AAS* 102 (2010), p. 2.

cal approaches to using the Bible, which can bring vitality into the Church. We are indebted to him for his reflections as summarised here below.[696]

There is the *doctrinal approach*, which finds in the Bible the mysteries of faith. However, while it serves to confirm the fundamentals of faith, Dulles observes that it can easily take a fundamentalist and conservative bend which overlooks the historical context in which the message was composed and the audience addressed. It is also selective on certain biblical references from which the reader/s may draw conclusions to support personal positions or those of their particular Church. This can remain insensitive to universal ecclesial concepts or practices.

Secondly, is the *biblical theology* method which appreciates variety and the unity of Scripture, linking the Old Testament with the New Testament. It corrects and supplements the doctrinal method by providing different themes which enrich the reading and intepreptation of the Bible to life's realities. While this is true it has the blindspot of dwelling on cultural or abstract expressions. It can also set antagonisms between one culture and another. Both these can eventually lead to moving away from the central Gospel message of God's love for and salvation of His people from the darkness of sin.

The third use of the Bible is *spiritual exegesis*, an approach that seeks to find out the spiritual meaning of biblical language that brings a living continuity with the story, metaphors and expressions used in the Bible. It is a way of encountering the Trinity through the Scripture: the Father showing love and compassion towards God's people; Christ always present in His community; the Holy Spirit giving life and sustaining the community that believes in Christ. However, it is to be noted that an exaggeration of enthusiasm for spiritual meaning of the Scripture can digress into far-fetched interpretations which may impose personal or group experiences on the Word of God.

Fourth, is *Word theology*, an approach that understands Christ as the living Word of God who continues to communicate himself through the written word as a continuing event of God's Self-revelation in human history. The Bible is the story that not only tells but also mediates an encounter with Christ, the personal and living Word of God. This use of scripture cautions us not to impose on God our own meanings which might be saturated with our peculiar interpretation or experience.

The fifth use of the Bible is the *existential hermaneutics and proclamation*, which seeks to bring out the significance of self-understanding. Biblical *hermeneutics* has to do with the search for meaning. This may help to affirm personal identity inspired by faith in the light of God's Word. However, this ap-

696 Avery Dulles, *The Craft of Theology: From Symbol to System*, New Expanded Edition, New York, The Crossroad Publishing Company, 2000, pp. 69-85.

proach to using the Bible also lies close to the weakness of narrowing the Word of God down to existential categories of 'what God speaks to me, my personal response and relationship with God.' This has the subtlety of centering too much on oneself, a self-justification which sets opposition to the supernatural.

The sixth use of the Bible is the *experiential-expressive*, which can serve to correct the over-emphasis that is placed on the individual. It looks back to the experience of early Christian communities and tries to bring the divine grace of faith to intelligible expression. It seeks to be in touch with Jesus' original *Abba*-experience and the disciples' Easter-experience. The limitation of this approach lies in the dilemma of "experience" itself. Dulles observes that, "To classify any experience as "religious" is a matter of interpretation, and the interpretation is inevitably dependent on social and historical factors."[697]

The seventh approach to using the Bible is the *authorial intention*, a literal reading of the Bible to find in it the intended meaning as written down by the inspired author. The search for the original literal meaning in the Bible makes the contribution of correcting misinterpretations that might have arisen in the course of translations and editions of the Bible. However, while this approach has the merit of paying attention to originality, the following reservations may not be overlooked. First, many texts in the Bible have no direct original author; the present text as we read it might have passed through many hands. Dulles comments that, "The so-called author is simply a redactor of an oral tradition or fragmentary documents that originated and grew anonymously. For other texts, which presumably have an author, we cannot identify the place and time of composition."[698] The second problem is that the same text may mean differently to different readers. Thirdly, the full meaning of a biblical text takes into consideration the context/s in which it has been handed down, together with the perspectives of the readers.

Another use of the Bible is the *historical reconstruction*, a critical reading of the Bible with the focus on finding what meaning there is that comes before the texts came to be written. It searches for the earliest sources with the intention of making a reliable historical reconstruction of biblical narrative. With regard to the New Testament, it seeks to find the Jesus of history behind the texts themselves. Its intention is to add variety in the ways of deepening the believers' understanding of the Gospel stories. It can serve to correct the experiential approach which emphasises more a direct experience with transcendence. However, the reconstruction approach has the bias of tending to predertermine what might happen one after the other as a historical sequence. The presuppositions of the historian may lean on weak imaginations which are

697 Ibid., p. 78.

698 Ibid., p. 79.

incompatible with the Christian story. This presents the difficulty of weakening faith or sound theology of the Bible.

The ninth helpful use of Sacred Scripture pays attention to the *narrative theology* or *cultural-lingusitic approach*, which holds that the Bible primarily consists of stories which communicate God's way of dealing with humanity. The narrative approach seeks to avoid forcing on the Bible contemporary social images which can only obscure the intention and content of the biblical message of salvation. It presents to the reader the interaction of persons and events. The merit of the cultural-linguistic approach is not to make a crucial distinction between biblical passages that are, or not, historically or scientifically exact. It provides a good interpretative possibility of dialogue which can help believers to understand God's Word with regard to their cultural values and realities of life. To our assessment this usage may be a profitable practice for Bible reading and sharing in the SCC and other frames of ecclesial groups. However, this approach must not remain in the telling of biblical stories only; it must explore the implications of those stories to bear upon Christian commitment in social or charitable activities; it must understand the Trinity as a living God in the collaborative efforts of building ecclesial communion; it must bear upon the moral life of the individual as much as of the ecclesial community: in the family, SCC, groups, parish, deanary, diocese.

The tenth possibility of using Sacred Scripture is the *liberation theology* approach, which uses the Bible in the context of the existing social situation – mainly relating to the condition of the poor and oppressed. While this reading of the Bible calls attention to critical social and political realities it is not without theological difficulties. Its theme of 'liberation' is mainly political liberation which fails to work out an objective and systematic procedure to overcome the structures of oppression. It proposes 'social commitment' but reads the Bible with partiality, dwelling on selective phrases or themes to support its agenda of liberation. Dulles writes that, "...these theologians consciously adopt a partiality based on commitment to the poor and the oppressed. In light of that commitment they adopt a "hermeneutics of suspicion," contesting all readings of Scripture that do not favor their own social orientation. Conversely, they select in the Bible passages that confirm their own preferences."[699] What we can learn from this use of the Bible is its accent on social justice. Nevertheless, it needs to appreciate the other methods of reading the Bible as we have highlighted above.

Our central focus on the use of the Bible is to place the Word of God in the hands of the faithful, so that it may inspire ecclesial communion and activities

699 Ibid., p. 84.

that will sustain it. A good use of the Bible as the Book of the Church does not only inspire faith but also contributes to a specifically Christian moral life.

7.1.3. Scripture and Christian Moral life

Medes illustrates the importance of Scripture in the context of modern situations. From his reflection we can highlight the following points. (a) The Bible offers moral direction in various forms, including prescriptions, general principles, examples and stories. (b) Modern life presents problems not covered in the specific prescriptions of Scripture; and this calls for humility and diligence in evaluating these problems in a way that is rationally comprehensible without compromising the authority of Scripture. (c) The Bible's moral teachings are relevant, in a general sense, to all modern problems. The positive intent of the Decalogue, the law of love, and the goal of justice inform the moral agent in significant, if general, ways. (d) The application of biblical guidance to moral problems requires a careful analysis of the facts of the case. It involves openness to dialogue in order to provide insights from Scripture that can enlighten our understanding and critical evaluation of arising issues. This helps to avoid abuse or unquestioned use of Scripture as though it were a formular book. (e) In the crucible of life's moral challenges, we are not excused by the Bible from the agonies of decision making. Here lies the importance of praying with the Scripture for spiritual wisdom.[700]

The importance of the Word of God in the Life of the Church, the proper use of the Bible, and its relevance in the Christian moral life provide the possibility for an integral Christian formation that will lead to a healthy ecclesial life.

7.2. Integral Formation

Formation is here taken to cover the whole arrangement and process of how all the faithful of the diocese are informed, and thus formed, to become more conscious of being the members of the Church as a living community in the spiritual, moral and practical dimensions. The focus on formation is to produce members who are convinced, who have a team spirit, dedicated and responsible. It must enable them to appreciate that each one is a steward, namely, a responsible caretaker of God's gifts of grace, designated for the growth of their ecclesial community.

In our fieldwork, 193 (67%) out of 287 respondents strongly recommended that formation deserves the greatest attention; it is necessary for all the faithful:

700 L. B. Medes, "Ethics: Modern Problems," in *ISBE*, Vol. 2, pp. 192-193.

laity, religious and priests. This has to begin with the individual where personal conversion and appropriation of values begin.[701] One respondent, Upira, remarked that formation does not just mean going to school. It is about how the spirit and meaning of life grows in each person. It must make every believer consciously involved and accountable in the life of the Church. "We are all responsible for our Church."[702] However, becoming a responsible person in the ecclesial community requires proper formation.

7.2.1. Church Teaching on Formation

In this exposition we shall not go into a historical narrative on formation but shall limit ourselves to recent Church teaching, especially in the light of Vatican Council II. In its document, *Gaudium et Spes*, the Council states that the individual is to be carefully educated to become a responsible social participant. The reason for a careful education of the individual is to enable them to discharge with greater exactness the obligations of their conscience toward themselves and the various groups to which they belong.[703]

The Catholic Bishops of Uganda have not been silent on the question of formation. In their Pastoral Letter, *With a New Heart and a New Spirit*, they write that: "Moral rehabilitation is a task that must begin with individuals..."[704] This Pastoral Letter is addressed to all the clergy, religious, Christ's faithful, men and women of good will, for a fundamental renewal of attitude after the military regime of the 1970s which had plunged the country into violence and revenge. The National Resistance Army (NRA) had come into power, and this Letter was a response to the new changes this government brought.[705] Katongole describes the situation of that time, that: "...a culture of violence, corruption, and individualism seems to have become the "normal" way of life in Uganda."[706] It is in this context that the bishops saw the individual as the primary subject of formation, to make of him/her a responsible moral agent,

701 Sr. Saveria Fwathum, interviewed by the researcher, at Pakwach, 4 June 2008 and Sr. Nataline Kareo, interviewed by the researcher, at Paidha, 6 June 2008, both insisted that the result of weak formation is visible in the poor concern for the common good of the Church and the poor relationship among priests, religious and parishioners, evident in the diocese in many ways.

702 Fabiano Upira, interviewed by the researcher, at Parombo, 1 June 2008.

703 *GS*, n. 31: *AAS* 58 (1966), p. 1050.

704 Catholic Bishops of Uganda, Pastoral Letter *With a New Heart and a New Spirit*, Kampala, St. Paul Publications Africa, 1986, n. 43.

705 Ibid., n. 4.

706 Katongole, *A Future for Africa: Critical Essays in Christian Social Imagination*, p. xii.

in order to re-form and renew the society.[707] From the foregoing, we could say that Christian formation with the aim of instilling the values of community life deserves a close attention. It is through formation that believers will know their responsibility in the Church and in the society.

7.2.2. Leadership Training

In Chapter Four we saw that weak leadership has a negative impact on the internal life of the Church as well as its public image. Christian formation is to make of every believer a true agent of evangelisation. As Mejía argues, it must lead to personal conviction and witness of life.[708] This holds true more especially for those in leadership whose role is to guide the community.

The Catholic Bishops of Uganda, in their Pastoral Letter, *Be My Witnesses*, on the vocation and mission of women in the Church and in Society, express the concern that:

> Leadership is a fruit of a well-prepared education program. Leadership education should be given to women and men on their role in the family, small community, parish, diocese and national level. It should bring out the values of responsibility, initiative, creativity, influencing people, motivating them and the courage to face problems and find solutions to them.[709]

The Church needs well prepared leaders who understand community concerns and can shoulder its burdens. Perrin Jassy clarifies that: "Leadership is not a personal gift but a relationship between two partners, leader and follower, who complement each other."[710] She distinguishes between *emergent leadership*, which arises to meet *felt needs*; and *planned leadership*, which anticipates the needs of the local population. Leadership works according to the value system that upholds a community or group in a given context; its viability is based on relationship and complementarity. On the one hand, *emergent leaders* arise from the group and coordinate the satisfaction of their followers' *felt needs*. On the other hand, *planned leaders* are *sent* in response to the *felt needs of a sending agency* to coordinate the satisfaction of *anticipated needs* in

707 Catholic Bishops of Uganda, Pastoral Letter *With a New Heart and a New Spirit*, n. 78.

708 Rodrigo Mejía, "Conditions for Promoting Justice and Peace: An Integrated New Evangelisation," in Patrick Ryan, (ed.), *New Strategies for a New Evangelization in Africa*, Paulines Publications Africa, 2002, p. 54f.

709 Catholic Bishops of Uganda, Pastoral Letter *Be My Witnesses: The Vocation and Mission of Women in the Church and Society Today*, Kampala, Catholic Secretariat, August 1996, n. 39.

710 Marie-France Perrin Jassy, *Leadership*, Eldoret, AMECEA Gaba Publications, Spearhead Nos. 153-154, 1st reprint, 2001, pp. ix.

a receiving group from which they expect to draw their followers.[711] Because leadership is not a personal gift, there is the need to equip leaders with necessary skills through adequate training. This will help to transcend "the wall of intuition" in order to meet the felt needs of the community.[712] It is clear from this to see that good leadership in the Church must begin from its foundation in the family and expand to the institutional apex.

7.2.3. Christian Family Catechesis

The Christian family needs a deeper catechesis. In its understanding of the Church as Light to the Peoples, Vatican Council II, in the document, *Lumen Gentium*, defines the family as a *domestic* or *small church*, the *primary vital cell of society*, where parents are the first teachers to their children; where everyone learns through giving and receiving knowledge.[713] In this light we can say that a promising cure or reversal of individualism in the Church begins in the family, by integrating human and Gospel values to strengthen a communitarian spirit.

In the document on the Church's Missionary Activity, *Ad Gentes Divinitus*, Vatican Council II teaches that the existence of good Christian families is one of the indicators of the maturity of local churches: "...by living a true Christian life families should become seminaries for lay apostles and indeed of priestly and religious vocations."[714] Basing on this teaching, the Pontifical Council for Culture adds that the family is the cradle of life and love, the source of culture and school of humanity, deserving proper family education.[715]

The Catechism teaches that: "The family is the *original cell of social life*."[716] By forming the family, the Church is making a twofold contribution: building itself up as well as the society because: "Authority, stability and a life of relationships within the family constitute the foundations for freedom, security and fraternity."[717] Forming the family therefore means forming the con-

---

711 Ibid., p. 68, italics emphases hers.

712 Ibid., p. 119.

713 *LG*, n. 11: *AAS* 57 (1965), p. 16; this has remained the official Church teaching in other documents as well, cf. *AA, n.* 11: *AAS* 58 (1966), p. 848; *FC*, nn. 17-18: *AAS* 74 (1982), pp. 100-101.

714 *AGD,* n. 19: *AAS* 58 (1966), p. 969.

715 Pontifical Council for Culture, *Towards a Pastoral Approach to Culture*, Nairobi, Paulines Publications Africa, 1999, nn. 14-15.

716 *CCC*, n. 2207.

717 Ibid.

science of every individual, who is the center of human relationships.[718] It is in the family that the most intimate, vivid and fundamental expression of a truly human relationship is lived, which opens every individual to all extended family relationships.[719] It is in the family that one knows and can feel the sense and need for sharing, solidarity, fraternity and being neighbor.[720] In other words, life in the family is a 'life-love covenant' where husband and wife are united, together with their children (if they have them). The Church sees in this life-love communion a point of reference, expressive of God's plan for humanity.[721] It is the family that provides home for the development of personal qualities, rights, initiatives and sense of responsibility.[722]

In his Apostolic Exhortation on the Christian family, *Familiaris Consortio*, Pope John Paul II calls the family the soul of both civil society and the Church.[723] It is a natural community, the basis of social life and human relationships; a school of deeper humanity, particularly because it guards and transmits virtue and values. Life in the family reveals God's love through education, upbringing, discipline, moral and religious training.[724] It is to be understood beyond sociological, biological, historical or cultural entity. It is spiritual with its origin in God's self-same love.[725] Strengthening the family through good formation contributes, in hope, for the future: "The future of humanity passes by way of the family."[726] The Pope refers to the Holy Family of Nazareth as the model for a good Christian family: St. Joseph as a "just man" and the Blessed Virgin Mary as Mother *par excellence*. This affirms that parents are the primary educators and pastors to their children, for which their leadership role has a perennial value.

Pope John Paul II continues to emphasise, in his Message for World Day of Peace, that: "The family plays a primary role in the important task of forming consciences. Parents have a grave duty to help their children to seek the truth from their earliest years…"[727] This acknowledges that: (a) the family institu-

718 Ibid., n. 2212.

719 Ibid., n. 2208.

720 Ibid., n. 2224.

721 Ibid., nn. 371-373.

722 *GS*, n. 25: *AAS* 58 (1966), pp. 1045-1046; *CCC*, n. 1882.

723 *FC*, n. 18, 21: *AAS* 74 (1982), p. 100, 104.

724 Ibid., n. 14: *AAS* (1982), pp. 96-97.

725 Ibid., nn. 42-42: *AAS* 74 (1982), p. 134.

726 Ibid., n. 86: *AAS* 74 (1981), p. 188.

727 John Paul II, Message for the World Day of Peace (1 January 1991), *If You Want Peace, Respect the Conscience of Every Person*, Rome, Libreria Editrice Vaticana, 1990, III.

tion is the human foundation of good leadership; (b) centre of human education prior to any other intelligible human institution; (c) parents are the immediate stewards (entrusted with the care) of God's gifts in the family institution.

An important place of formation apart from the family is the school. A vital point of consideration regards the question of parenting: the role which Christian parents are to play in accompanying their children in the school environment. According to Takahikire, parenting is a major concern of educationists today. He defines parenting as: "...the way parents exert their influence on a child through care and home education. This involves the imparting of skills that can later be transferred to the school environment."[728] This means that parents must be equipped with skills in leading the family, combining cultural wisdom with Christian leadership models.

However, the Christian formation has a deeper spiritual meaning by which we can understand parenting; even in the school environment it carries the mark of an evangelising mission for Christian parents.[729] Pope John Paul II writes that: "By virtue of their ministry of educating, parents are, through the witness of their life, the first heralds of the Gospel for their children... they are begetters not only of bodily life but also of the life that through the Spirit's renewal flows from the Cross and Resurrection of Christ."[730]

The Congregation for the Doctrine of the Faith has given more light on the role of the Christian family as promoters of a just world by the way and spirit in which they impart Gospel values to their children. In its Letter to the Bishops of the Catholic Church, it writes that it is in the family that:

> ...the features of a people take shape; it is here that its members acquire basic teachings. They learn to love inasmuch as they are unconditionally loved, they learn respect for others inasmuch as they are respected, they learn to know the face of God inasmuch as they receive a first revelation of it from a father and a mother full of attention in their regard. Whenever these fundamental experiences are lacking, society as a whole suffers violence and becomes in turn the progenitor of more violence.[731]

---

728 Peter Takahikire, "The Role of Parenting in Education," in Amanuel A. Teklemarian and Winston Jumba Akala (eds.), *Effective Schools for 21st Century in Africa*, Nairobi, CUEA Press, 2011, p. 59.

729 *EN*, n. 71: *AAS* 68 (1976), pp. 60-61.

730 *FC*, n. 39 § 4: *AAS* 74 (1982), p. 131.

731 Congregation for the Doctrine of the Faith, *Letter to the Bishops of the Catholic Church on the Collaboration of Men and Women in the Church and in the World*, Rome, Libreria Editrice Vaticana, 2004, n. 13: *AAS* 96 (2004), p. 682.

In their Pastoral Letter, *Let Your Light Shine*, the Catholic Bishops of Uganda notice that it is in the family that Christianity has found the greatest obstacle to authentic gospel living. They detect that the success of a strong Christian life is judged by the quality of the Christian families that the Church has formed.[732] They call upon Church leaders at every level to strengthen family catechesis; and Christian families to evangelise each other and reach out to evangelise society.

They notice that a fruitful formation of Christian families needs examining the real problems that confront them and to strive to effectively respond to them. The second Special Assembly of Bishops for Africa calls attention to resting the Church on its true human foundation: the family. It considers the family as the primary place for education. The participants expressly state that:

> …there is the urgent need to re-define the family as the "Domestic Church" and the primary place for education in love, reconciliation, justice and peace. In this way, Christian families would become the solid foundation of vibrant Ecclesial Communities that would in turn form "family communities" into true schools of evangelization.[733]

Proposition 38 mentions the "capital importance" of the family to both the Church and society. It recommends an integral implementation of a pastoral programme that can safeguard the family from disturbing contemporary social pressures and ideologies that trivialise family values.[734]

In his Post-Synodal Apostolic Exhortation *Africae Munus*, Pope Benedict VI has expressed that it is the family which makes the best setting for learning and applying the culture of a true human living. He encourages Christian families to practice a spirituality that brings Christ into the heart of everyday life: "I therefore strongly encourage families to draw inspiration and strength from the sacrament of the Eucharist, so as to live the radical newness brought by Christ into the heart of everyday life, leading each person to a radiant witness in his or her working environment and in the whole of society."[735] It is therefore from strong Christian families that strong and viable Christian communities can be built.

---

732 Catholic Bishops of Uganda, Pastoral Letter *Let Your Light Shine*, Kisubi, Marianum Press, 1992, n. 43.

733 Synod of Bishops – II Special Assembly for Africa, *Relatio Post Disceptationem*, section on "The Family" § 2, Permalink: http://www.zenit.org/article-27196?l=english Code: ZE09101404 - 2009-10-14 (downloaded, 16 october 2009).

734 *Proposition 38*, electronic text downloaded from Permalink: http://www.zenit.org/article-27386?l=english Code: ZE09102910 – 2009-10-29 (downloaded, 1 November 2009).

735 *AM*, n. 44.

7.2.4. Building Viable Small Christian Communities

The Christian family is insufficient without its extended relationship, in the SCC context. In Nebbi Catholic Diocese, the SCC is commonly called *Ungú Pacu pa JuKristo*, Christian homestead. It is a place of catechesis and community building through the exercise of regulated Bible reading, reflection and life application. In our field study, 203 (out of 287) questionnaire responses recommended the SCC approach as a simple and clear method of evangelisation. Their reasons are summarised below:

(1) The SCC is easy to organise and manage, taking into account the closeness of members in each community who know and understand themselves well; who know and understand their problems better and can support one another in daily matters;

(2) The SCC approach provides the ground for dialogue and integration with the people's traditional and Christian values;

(3) The SCC challenges and enables Christians to take up tasks in their own contexts within the common unity. That is, this method creates a self-defining consciousness at the level of the smallest community of believers that motivates a sense of being church, which will lead to taking their own responsibility at their level;

(4) The diocese is strong only when it stands on a firm ground for its viability, and that is the SCC. The diocese can particularly look at these basic communities in the simple and clear picture of the family as the fundament from which it is born, which it must love to strengthen and promote;

(5) The SCC inculcates and builds a sense of autonomy and authenticity necessary to strengthen ecclesial unity in the chapel, zone, parish, deanery and diocese. The cumulative strength of the Church derives from and must be sought in the SCC. In his study entitled: *Towards a Theology of Inculturation*, Shorter observes that it is this cumulative influence of basic communities which will transform the Church;[736]

(6) The SCC provides the opportunity for an easier coordination of activities and insemination of information: conducive for articulating both administrative and pastoral activities. This is akin to the African practice of neighbour-communication, by which every member is a messenger to neighbour and thus accountable for the information conveyed, respecting its originality, content and testifying to the authority that issues it;

(7) The SCC facilitates involvement in the small and manageable activities, which enlist the effort of every member. Two elderly catechists the researcher

736 Aylward Shorter, *Toward a Theology of Inculturation*, Eugene, Wipf & Stock Publishers, 1999, p. 267.

interviewed used the term 'bite-size' in the metaphor of the eating habit where one bites each time a quantity of food that one can chew and swallow without difficulty;[737]

(8) Based on experience, the SCC has a greater advantage of discernment in vocation promotion to the priesthood or religious life. Our interview with members from ten SCCs (one randomly selected in a parish) brought us to understand the important role of the local community in recommending their son or daughter to the seminary or convent. Besides, the researcher interviewed eleven major, and nine minor, seminarians who generally supported this truth of vocation promotion by the family and SCC. In both interviews, the model of traditional marriage was used: the community is proud of their son/daughter who marries into another clan; such as they know will raise their name there;[738]

(9) The SCC is like the African clan, encompassing the nuclear family, homestead, village and the kinship continuum. In this sense, the SCC is where believers can define their true identity that opens them to the wider ecclesial community of the parish. The parish, in turn, becomes a wider door for a universal relationship. This agrees with the conviction of the Special Assembly of Bishops for Africa, which connects the African clan structure and ecclesial communion:

> Small Christian Communities... bring together several families from an area of the town or village within the parish territory. The advantage of such communities is that they give Christians a sense of belonging and a sense of being united in a common purpose. The family and clan structure of traditional African society makes these Small Christian Communities particularly appropriate.[739]

In his Encyclical Letter *Redemptoris Missio*, Pope John Paul II recognises SCCs as "...good centers for Christian formation...an instrument of formation and evangelisation, and a solid starting point for a new society based on a "civilisation of love.""[740] The SCC sets the stage for catholicity through experience and growth in the spirit of Christian communion that transcends and enriches every specific family.

---

737 Catechist Vincensio Ubat of Mungujakisa Chapel and Catechist Luciano Udota of Rero Chapel, both interviewed by the researcher, at the specified chapel centers, 30 June 2008.

738 The researcher met selected SCCs, with the help of catechists: Nyapea, Paidha, Nebbi, Angal, Urusi, Panyimur, Parombo, Pakwach, Uleppi and Rhino Camp. We are indebted to 6 members of the Association of the Parents of Priests and Religious whom we met at Paidha, 6 June 2008, with the arrangement of Paula Ani-Rwoth, a helpful field assistant.

739 Synod of Bishops – Special Assembly for Africa, *The Church in Africa and her Evangelizing Mission Towards the Year 2000: Instrumentum Laboris*, Vatican City, Libreria Editrice Vaticana, 1993, n. 45.

740 *RM*, n. 51: *AAS* 83 (1991), p. 298; *FC*, nn. 36-39: *AAS* 74 (1982), pp. 126-131.

In their pastoral implementation strategy, the Bishops in the AMECEA region deliberated that: "Creative pastoral approaches are needed today to adequately respond to the life situations of our people and communities. Better methods must be devised to incarnate the Gospel message into the local customs and traditions of our people, e.g., feasts and celebrations performed at different stages of… life."[741] They explain that the SCC interprets, in Christian language, what the traditional African setting knows in terms of extended family relationships. They continue to expound that: "The African notion of extended family forms a good atmosphere for Christian community. Groups based on common interests or common tasks should be seen as supplementary to these natural groups."[742] This strategy gives priority to the SCC over other movements and associations in the Church because every member of such groups belongs to a specific SCC. In the SCC the believers develop an intense vitality of a truly Christian community life, becoming more aware of its true needs in its own environment.[743]

At their Plenary Study Conference, the Bishops in the AMECEA region noted that: "In the SCC every member is able to make full use of the gifts of the Holy Spirit. The role of the ordained minister is to organise, encourage and coordinate the various gifts of the Spirit."[744] At the same Conference, Bishop Ndingi proposed a "complementary priesthood" which enlists the efforts of both the laity and ordained ministers.[745] From his familiarity with the Bishops' SCC theological developments, Joseph Healey clarifies that: "The emphasis is on a grassroots Church, where there is a bottom-up rather than a top-down approach."[746] What is central in these observations is that the SCC

741 AMECEA Bishops, "Conclusions on Implementation Strategies," *Conclusion 1*, in *AFER*, Vol. 18, Nr. 5 (1976), p. 253.

742 Ibid., *Conclusion 2*.

743 Cf., Elochukwu E. Uzukwu, *A Listening Church: Autonomy and Communion in African Churches*, p. 112-119, gives a good synthesis.

744 AMECEA Bishops, Plenary Study Conference held at Zomba, Malawi, 13-16 August 1979, "Communities Called Church," in *AFER*, Vol. 6 (1979), p. 265.

745 Bishop Raphael Ndingi, "Implementing AMECEA's Pastoral Priority: Plenary Presentation Paper," in *AFER*, vol. 21 (1979), p. 287.

746 Joseph G. Healey, *A Fifth Gospel: The Experience of Black Christian Values*, Maryknoll, Orbis Books, 1981, p. 39. Joseph Healey is a Maryknoll Missionary priest from USA with a long experience in Africa. He served as Social Communications Secretary of AMECEA for six years (1968-74) and had a long missionary experience in Tanzania, the insights of which he writes in this book (p. 9). It is important to note that in his encounter with the experience in Tanzania, he calls the SCC the "village" church (p. 37), that is, a church setting simple enough for the people, which can enable them to practice their Christian faith in their own familiar human context.

approach challenges and engages lay people to become truly responsible for their Church.

Pfaff, during the 1989 Uganda Theological Week, argued that the SCC makes the Church the people of God, which can heal the divide between the hierarchy and the laity by fostering instead a spirit of co-responsibility.[747] A parallel view appears in the study of Shorter where he observes that establishing the SCC must not slip into paternalism by transmitting hierarchical structures that would again relegate the laity to coldness.[748] The African Bishops are aware of this difficulty. The Message of the first Special Assembly of the Synod of Bishops for Africa rejects the kind of ecclesiology which leaves the laity passive; they recommend that all pastors are to develop a pastoral programme in which the laity can rediscover their proper place and importance in the Church.[749]

The central point for formation in the SCC is to equip its members with necessary skills and means to enable growth at that level. The definition of the SCC as "the body of the faithful," developed by Archbishop J. Lebulu of Arusha Archdiocese (Tanzania) with the aim of restructuring the diocese, makes the Church people-of-God focused, where priest, religious, and laity together form an organic body.[750] It is important to note that the term 'faithful' is used to include the clergy, religious and laity. This brings about and nurtures reciprocal confidence and trust, which will strengthen ecclesial growth.

747 Franz Pfaff, "People's Participation in Development," in Joseph Therese Agbasiere and Boniface K. Zabajungu (eds.), *Church Contribution to Integral Development: A New Vision*, Fourth Uganda Theological Week: African Theology in Progress, Vol. 2, Spearhead, Nr. 108-109 (1989), p. 164.

748 Aylward Shorter, *The Church in the African City*, London, Geoffrey Chapman, 1991, p. 102f. Shorter's case study focuses on the SCC in the city context. However, the content of his argument is relevant to the growth of the SCC even in the countryside diocese. His point is that the SCC must not transmit existing hierarchical structure which again would leave believers passive listeners or observers.

749 AFJN, "Message," n. 57.

750 Archbishop Josephat Louis Lebulu, Arusha Arch-diocese, North-eastern Tanzania, took this approach in his pastoral action plan to restructure the diocese in line with the ecclesiology which conceives the Church as a communion of communions. See elaboration in Elochukwu E. Uzukwu, *A Listening Church*, p. 115. Uzukwu published his book when Bishop Lebulu was the Ordinary of Same Diocese (Bishop of Same Diocese, February1979 – November 1998; Arusha Diocese (Bishop, November 1998 – Archbishop, March 1999 – ...). See website: http://www.gcatholic.org/dioceses/diocese/arus0.htm

7.2.5. Promoting Child Apostolate

In this category we are referring to those from three to about nine years of age. Vatican Council II document, *Gaudium et Spes*, states that: "Children should be educated in such a way that on reaching adulthood they can exercise full responsibility in following their calling..."[751] The motive for educating children is to promote marriage and family life, which must be the concern of all. This rationale is clarified in the opening sentence of the same article where it states that: "The family is a school for a richer humanity."[752] Both the Church and the society cannot have any true human future without children.

In Uganda, Catholic children fall under the *Pontifical Missionary of Holy Childhood*, commonly called "Saint Kizito" (in Nebbi Catholic Diocese it is called, *Lwak pa Kizito Maleng*, Companions of St. Kizito). The Uganda National Office of the Catholic Church for child apostolate published a handbook with guidelines for animators to help them.[753] The aim is to make them missionaries to fellow children, as their motto states: *children helping children*; and their slogan: *Jesus is our friend, let us love one another*. It is a programme which helps children to learn Gospel values through the virtues of service, recreation, and practicing to lead themselves under the guidance of their animators.

The point on forming children was argued by Sr. Ifechukwu at the second Synod of Bishops for Africa. Her thesis is that a planned programme for youth activities in the Universities will be a continuation of this work started at primary and secondary levels. This programmatic foundation will make it easier when candidates for religious life and the priesthood are drawn from the society in the next ten years.[754]

7.2.6. Developing the Youth

Youth ministry deserves an increased attention. David Wong defines youth as "…a transition between childhood and adulthood."[755] To develop the

751 *GS*, n. 52: *AAS* 58 (1966), p. 1073. Text as in Norman P. Tanner (ed.), *Decrees of the Ecumenical Councils,* Vol. 2: *Trent-Vatican II*, p. 1105.

752 *Loc. cit.*

753 Pontifical Society of Missionary Holy Childhood – Uganda, *The Missionary Society of St. Kizito*, Kampala, National Office of Missionary Holy Childhood, 2003.

754 Sr. Maria Ifechukwu Udorah, Superior General of the Daughters of Divine Love, Enugu (Nigeria), Interventions of Auditors at 12th Congregation, Permalink: http://www.zenit.org/article-27179?l=english Code: ZE09101302 (downloaded, 13 October 2009), p. 4.

755 David Wong, *Notes on Evangelising the Youth Today*, Hawaii, Maui Haggai Institute, 2000, p.1.

youth means to direct their resourcefulness through skill and capacity building, growth in creative freedom through self-discipline, creativity, responsible choices and decisions which must channel their potentialities and energies to fruitful community building activities.

What Getui says of the situation in Kenya is true of our study findings in Nebbi: The African traditional family setup, with its strong kinship ties, can no longer play an effective role in educating their children due to various changes and influences.[756] In this context the school has become an important place for youth formation where parents and the Church can join hands. Developing the youth must take account of contemporaneous realities. The Church must have specially trained youth animators; it must plan and budget on the youth ministry. Our respondent, Fr. Ohuro, a secondary school chaplain, remarked that the Church needs to have a strategic plan and spend money on youth ministry: "On a non-existent budget, the chaplain must come up with folk stories for the youth, which is to compete with television shows that are produced by professionals at a cost of millions of Shillings. The Church will continue fighting a losing battle."[757] It is helpful to design youth programmes that include: (a) recreational activities; (b) debates on cultural and religious values; (c) acting biblical and life stories; (d) annual essays on culture and Bible knowledge prepared by the diocesan education office to be distributed to parishes and schools; (e) forming and encouraging youth groups, clubs and movements.

7.2.7. Empowering Women

In the Decree on Lay Apostolate, *Apostolicam Actuositatem*, Vatican Council II acknowledges that: "Since in our time women have an ever more active role in the whole life of society, it is very important that they participate more widely also in the various fields of the Church's apostolate."[758] In its closing adderss to women, the Council expresses that:

> As you know, the Church is proud to have glorified and liberated the woman, and in the course of the centuries, in diversity of characters, to have brought into relief her basic equality with man. But the hour is coming, in fact has come,

756 M. N. Getui, "The Family, the Church and the Development of Youth" in Jesse N. K. Mugambi and Laurenti Magesa (eds.), *The Church in African Christianity: Innovative Essays in Ecclesiology*, Nairobi, Initiatives Publishers, 1990, p. 84.

757 Fr. Ohuro Charles, interviewed by the researcher, at Angal, 23 May 2008. He pointed out that the Catholic youth are getting flooded with confusing life models in the school, trading centres and through the media of social communication. The media is one reason for which they are attracted to Pentecostals.

758 *AA*, n. 9: *AAS* 58 (1966), p. 846.

> when the vocation of woman is being achieved in its fullness, the hour in which woman acquires in the world an influence, an effect, and a power never hitherto achieved. That is why, at this moment when the human race is undergoing so deep a transformation, women imbued with the spirit of the gospel can do so much to aid humanity in not falling.[759]

In the Uganda context women have received the Church's official recognition as well. In 1992 the annual study theme of the Catholic Bishops of Uganda was: *The Role of Catholic Women in the Church, the Family and Society*. This was organised and facilitated by women leaders. In response to their contributions the Bishops published a Pastoral Letter with the title: *Be My Witnesses*. In it they directly mention the formation of women as a pastoral priority:

> Education has been chosen by women leaders as the priority for the empowerment of all women. We support this priority. We appeal to all parents, to government and, above all, to our pastoral agents to put emphasis on the education of girls at all levels. We want to see well organized awareness courses for both men and women, which are designed to give gender sensitization to all, development education and call to active participation in all socio-economic and political fields. It is through education that women will succeed to achieve self-confidence and reject any feeling of inferiority complex. Through education men will learn to abandon the unwarranted, unjust and oppressive male superiority complex.[760]

The two Synods of Bishops for Africa have both continued to acknowledge the importance of women in the Church and its apostolate. The *Instrumentum Laboris* to the 1994 Synod deplores the tendency by which women are regarded as inferior to men "even in the Church."[761] In its *Proposition 48*, the Synod states that: "It is imperative that women be included in appropriate levels of decision making in the Church and that the Church establishes ministries for women and intensify efforts toward their formation."[762]

The Second Special Assembly of the Synod of Bishops for Africa mentions women 20 times.[763] Like the First Synod, it decries the meager recognition

759 Vatican Council II, "Closing Messages of the Council: To Women (December 8, 1965)," text as in Walter M. Abbott and Joseph Gallagher (eds.), *The Documents of Vatican II*, p. 733; *AAS* 58 (1966), p. 13-14.

760 Catholic Bishops of Uganda, Pastoral Letter *Be My Witnesses: The Vocation and Mission of Women in Church and Society Today*, Kisubi, Marianum Press, 1996, n. 37.

761 Synod of Bishops – Special Assembly for Africa, *Instrumentum Laboris*, Vatican City, General Secretariat of the Synod of Bishops and Libreria Editrice Vaticana, 1993, n. 120.

762 AFJN, p. 103.

763 Zenit, *Keywords at the Africa Synod*, Permalink: http://www.zenit.org/article-27186?l=english Code: ZE09101309 – 2009-10-13 (downloaded, 14 October 2009).

of women both in the society and Church based on social-cultural reasons. *Proposition 47* recommends a "greater integration of women into the Church structures and decision-making processes."[764] In her intervention at the same Synod, as an auditor, Barbara Pandolfi remarks that the role of the African woman as a pillar in the society is done in a hidden manner, unofficial and unknown, marked with difficulty and prejudice. She argues that:

> If the first fracture in mankind, caused by sin, was that between man and woman, one of the signs of peace and reconciliation, perhaps, could be given by the promotion of an authentic joint responsibility and of an effective acknowledgement of equal dignity between men and women, beyond all domination and discrimination. Perhaps the moment has arrived that woman, often, traditionally subjected by man, may truly stand, in all areas of social and ecclesial life, facing man, in dialogue with him. In this sense the Gospel may become an authentic force for change.[765]

Empowering women would involve: (a) forums through seminars and workshops for both women and men, where they can share ideas on topics like bride price, power sharing and collaboration in cultural, religious, social and economic activities; (b) in the same frame of forum, it is helpful to encourage Bible sharing, with selected themes which highlight Jesus' attitude towards women as a key to discerning their rightful roles in the Church and in the society; (c) the Church also has opportunities of collaborating with other institutions in adult literacy campaigns for women in the villages.

7.2.8. Encouraging Lay Apostolate

If Church leaders wish to evaluate the success of their pastoral input, they are to look at how the lay faithful are progressing in a Christ-like life. This is the focus of St. Paul's pastoral letters (cf. 1 Tim. 3:2; Ti. 1:9) where he refers to the function of the bishop or elder as a teacher. Grassi, reading St. Paul's Letter to the Ephesians, observes that: "The epistles rarely employ the title "Son of God" (cf. Rom. 1:4; Gal. 2:20). When they do, it denotes Jesus Christ as man. Here, knowledge of the Son of God means acquiring the image of the perfect man, who reaches maturity in Christ by living the type of human life that was characteristic of Jesus as Son of God."[766] In this understanding, for-

764 Zenit, "Africa Synod Propositions 41-50," Permalink: http//www.zenit.org/article-27389?l=english Code: ZE09103001 – 2009-10-30 (downloaded, 2 November 2009).

765 Zenit, "Intervention of Auditors at 12th General Congregation, 13 October 2009," Permalink: http://www.zenit.org/article-27179?l=english Code: ZE0910132 (downloaded, 15 October 2009).

766 Joseph A. Grassi, "The Letter to the Ephesians," in *JBC*, p. 347b.

mation intends a full-grown adulthood in faith. In the Letter to the Ephesians, the Greek word *anēr* is used to mean 'full-grown adulthood' (4:13) in contrast to childhood or immaturity in the faith. Commenting on this verse, Kobelski writes that: "The emphasis of the Gk *anēr* in this context is not on maleness but on adulthood... This adulthood is measured in relation to "the stature of the fullness of Christ.""[767]

Vatican Council II, in its Dogmatic Constitution on the Church, *Lumen Gentium*, understands the term "laity" to mean "all the faithful except those in holy orders and those in a religious state sanctioned by the Church. These faithful are by baptism made one body with Christ and are established among the People of God."[768] The document continues to state that: "By divine institution Holy Church is structured and governed with a wonderful diversity."[769] Emphasis is placed on apostolate where the Council acknowledges that: "The lay apostolate, however, is a participation in the saving mission of the Church itself."[770] Abbott comments that this understanding corrected some earlier conceptions which had been limited to the cooperation of the laity in the apostolic tasks reserved to the hierarchy. He writes that: "The present document, as well as the Decree on the Apostolate of the Laity, makes it clear that while *laymen* may laudably assist in the hierarchical apostolate as collaborators, the term "lay apostolate" refers primarily to apostolic tasks pertaining to the laity as such."[771] The Council further clarifies that: (a) the faithful who by Baptism are incorporated into Christ and integrated into the People of God, are made sharers in their particular way in the priestly, prophetic and kingly office of Christ and have their own part to play in the mission of the whole Christian people in the Church and in the world;[772] (b) as priests, the faithful consecrate the world itself to God;[773] (c) as prophets, they are involved directly in the ordinary circumstances of the world, evangelising by their way of life and example;[774] (iv) their participation in Christ's king-

767 Paul J. Kobelski, "The Letter to the Ephesians," in *NJBC*, p. 889b.

768 *LG*, n. 31, footnote 163 in Walter M. Abbott and Joseph Gallagher (eds.), *The Documents of Vatican II*, p. 57, states that the definition of "laity" is given "positively, in terms of their baptism and their active role in the People of God." Albert C. Outler, commenting on this understanding says that: "The Constitution on the Church serves as the doctrinal foundation for the more practical concerns of the Decree of the Apostolate on the Laity" (p. 104).

769 *LG*, n. 32: *AAS* 57 (1965), p. 38.

770 Ibid., n. 33: *AAS* 57 (1965), p. 39.

771 Abbot and Gallagher (eds.), p. 59, footnote 167. Italic, *laymen*, ours, understood in an inclusive sense: implying both women and men.

772 *LG*, n. 31 § 1: *AAS* 57 (1965), p. 37; also *CCC*, n. 897.

773 Ibid., n. 34: *AAS* 57 (1965), pp. 39-40; also *CCC*, n. 901.

774 Ibid., n. 35 §§ 1-2: AAS 57 (1966), p. 40; also *CCC*, n. 905.

ship has the efficacy of remedying the institutions and conditions that serve as inducements to sin, through the promotion of justice and thus by their action enriching culture and human work with a moral value.[775]

In its Decree on the Apostolate of the Laity, *Apostolicam Actuosiatatem*, the Council acknowledges the indispensable apostolate of the laity which derives from their Christian vocation. The Council understands it as an unmistakable work of the Holy Spirit, making the laity conscious of their own responsibility, and inspiring them to serve Christ and the Church.[776] Abbott comments that the term *apostolate*, as used with reference to the laity, superseded the attempt to call it *participation* by some of the Council Fathers.[777] Emphasis is laid on a holistic formation with a focus on the common good, based on moral principles and the social teaching of the Church. This is because: (a) "The apostolate of the laity derives from their Christian vocation, and the Church can never be without it."[778] (b) "Their activity is so necessary within Church communities that without it the apostolate of the pastors is generally unable to achieve its full effectiveness."[779]

In his Apostolic Exhortation on the vocation and mission of the laity, *Christifideles Laici*, Pope John Paul II writes that: "The fundamental objective of the formation of the lay faithful is an ever-clearer discovery of one's vocation and the ever-greater willingness to live it so as to fulfill one's mission… However, to act in fidelity to God's will requires a *capability* for acting and *the developing of that capability*."[780] Looking at formation as a process of maturation, he insists that: "…there comes the possibility, indeed the necessity, of total and ongoing formation of the lay faithful…"[781] He maintains that by virtue of Baptism the laity share in the priestly, prophetic-teaching and kingly offices of Christ. This is their vocation and ministry in the world, for which they are, like Christ, anointed.[782] For this reason, it is not permissible for anyone to remain idle.[783] He calls to mind: "It must be asked how many Christians really know and put into practice the principles of the Church's social doctrine."[784] He had

775 Ibid., n. 36 § 3: AAS 57 (1965), p. 42; *also CCC*, n. 909.

776 *AA*, n. 1 § 3: *AAS* 58 (1966), p. 838.

777 Abbott and Gallagher (eds.), *The Documents of Vatican II*, p. 489, note 1.

778 *AA*, n. 1: *AAS* 58 (1966), p. 837.

779 *AA*, n. 10 *AAS* 58 (1966), p. 846; *LG*, n. 33: *AAS* 57 (1965), p. 39; also *CCC*, n. 900.

780 *CfL*, n. 58: *AAS* 81(1989), p. 508, Italic emphasis in the original.

781 Ibid., n. 57: *AAS* 81 (1989), p. 507.

782 Ibid., n. 14: *AAS* 81 (1989), pp. 409-413.

783 Ibid., n. 3 § 2: *AAS* 81 (1989), p. 398.

784 *TMA*, n. 36 § 4: *AAS* 87 (1995), p. 28.

earlier emphasised the same point in his address to the Indian Bishops that: "The mission of training the faithful to respect and proclaim the Gospel falls to parents, teachers and catechists of today. For this reason, a fundamental task of every bishop is to ensure that he has well-trained laity equipped and ready to be teachers of the faith."[785]

The two Synods of Bishops for Africa have acknowledged the important role of the laity. The *Instrumentum Laboris*, in preparation for the Synod of Bishops of 1994, states that: "In everyday life the laity are in constant touch with the world and sometimes know it better."[786] The Synod of 2009 repeats the same point, clarifying that the laity are salt and light in the world. With this they higliht three central points: (a) to give them adequate formation; (b) to involve them consciously and proactively; (c) to make them responsible for their Church.[787]

The Catholic Bishops of Uganda are explicit on the formation of the laity. In their 1986 Pastoral Letter, *With a New Heart and a New Spirit*, they write: "Initiatives should be taken to form the laity, and especially lay Christian leaders at parish, diocesan, and national level, and to make them aware of their responsibilities in the Church."[788] Formation must enable them to be involved in the Church's apostolate with conviction and consciously. Writing on the contribution of the laity in the work of evangelisation in Uganda, Kato advocates for a deepened interest in their continued involvement. He argues that: "The apostolate of the laity is the same apostolate of the Apostles and of Christ's Church. It is the same apostolate of bishops, priests, deacons and religious."[789]

7.2.9. Adequate Catechist Training

Vatican Council II document on Missionary Activity, *Ad Gentes Divinitus*, article 3, mentions the important role of catechists and auxiliary catechists, for which they need proper training. Six recommendations are noteworthy: (a) they are true co-workers of the priestly order; (b) diocesan and regional

785 Idem, Address to Indian Bishops of the Latin Rite, *Allocution III* (27 June 2003), n. 3: *AAS* 96 (2004), p. 17.

786 Special Assembly of the Synod of Bishops for Africa, *Instrumentum Laboris*, 1993, n. 34.

787 Second Special Assembly of the Synod of Bishops for Africa, *Proposition* 37, electronic text from Zenit, "Africa Synod Propositions 31-40," Permalink: http://www.zenit.org/article-27386?l=english Code: ZE0102910 – 2009-10-29 (downloaded, 1 November 2009).

788 Catholic Bishops of Uganda, Pastoral Letter *With a New Heart and a New Spirit*, Kampala, St. Paul Publications Africa, 1986, n. 91.

789 Joseph Bitole Kato, *Awakening the Laity: Ugandan Pastoral Approach*, Spearhead Nos. 161-163, Eldoret, AMECEA Gaba Publications, 2003, p. 96.

training centres are to be set up for them; (c) these institutes are entrusted to the Sacred Congregation for the Propagation of the Faith (now the Congregation for the Evangelisation of Peoples) to provide aid to them; (d) they are to receive a thorough training in doctrine, spirituality, Bible, catechetical method and pastoral practice; (e) after completion of their training they are to receive canonical mission in a public liturgical celebration, by which their authority is recognised among the faithful; (f) full-time catechists are to be given a decent standard of living and social security through a just salary.[790]

In its document, *Guide for Catechists*, the Congregation for the Evangelisation of Peoples mentions the need for specialised catechists.[791] It adds that there is need for animators of catechetical activity with responsibility at diocesan level, in regions and in parishes.[792] The training is to develop their proficiency in relational qualities including dialogue, communication, disposition to collaboration, willingness to act as a guide, serenity in judgment, understanding and realism, giving consolation and hope.[793]

In its opening report before discussions, the First Special Assembly of the Synod of Bishops for Africa mentions that: "…catechists form a special category of honor among the laity… The Church in Africa and Madagascar would be at a great loss without their collaboration."[794] This was reaffirmed in *Proposition 13* which continues to recommend adequate formation of catechists as the nature of their work requires.[795] Pope John Paul II takes the point in his Post-Synodal Exhortation following this synod and recommends that: "Both Bishops and priests are to have their catechists at heart, seeing to it that they are guaranteed suitable living and working conditions so that they carry out their mission properly. In the midst of the Christian community the catechists' responsibility is to be acknowledged and held in respect."[796]

The same point was repeated by the second Synod of Bishops for Africa in 2009. The *Instrumentum Laboris* to this Synod states that: "Catechists… will

---

790 *AGD*, n. 17: *AAS* 58 (1966), pp. 967-968.

791 Congregation for the Evangelisation of Peoples, *Guide for Catechists: Document of Vocational, Formative and Promotional Orientation of Catechists in the Territories Dependent on the Congregation for the Evangelisation of Peoples,* Vatican City, Libreria Editrice Vaticana, 1993, n. 5.

792 Ibid., n. 5.

793 Ibid., n. 21.

794 Hyacinthe Thiandoum, *Relatio Ante disceptationem: The Gospel, Inculturation and Dialogue*, n. 12, URL: http://www.ewtn.com/new_evangelization/africa/synod/relatio.htm (downloaded, 12 October 2010).

795 AFJN, *The African Synod*, p. 91.

796 *EA*, n. 91: *AAS* 88 (1996), p. 57.

make a better contribution, if they are given a sound scriptural and doctrinal formation as well as a just compensation, so that they can care for their families in a dignified way and provide a proper education for their children."[797] In its *Proposition 44*, the Synod recommends that catechists need "...a solid formation and material support which is necessary for them to effectively assume their role as spiritual guides."[798] Following this synod, Pope Benedict XVI confirms the fundamental and deeper contribution catechists have made in evangelisation and inculturation in Africa. It is a role that cannot be closed in the past but continues in the present and looks to the future. He then urges bishops and priests to be concerned for the human, intellectual, doctrinal, moral, spiritual and pastoral formation of catechists. They are to pay attention to the living conditions of catechists and to ensure that they live a dignified life. Catechists must not just wait for the heavenly recompense without any material support for what they truly need.[799]

In its document, *General Directory for Catechists*, the Congregation for the Clergy outlines the strategic pastoral needs for which catechists must receive specialised training: (a) catechists in small rural populations deprived of the constant presence of a priest; (b) catechists for young people; (c) catechist for adults – these two categories of catechists promote initiatory and continuing catechesis; (d) catechists for children and adolescents whose work is to prepare them in basic catechism, Penitence, First Holy Communion and Confirmation; (e) catechists for pre-sacramental encounter, whose task it is to instruct parents on their responsibility in accompanying their children approaching First Holy Communion and Marriage; (f) catechists for other special pastoral needs.[800]

Such a focus on formation needs an approach that enters into the real situation and experience of the people among whom these future catechists will work. In our field study we obtained the following two recommendations at Angal Catechist Centre.[801] (a) A Life-application technique, combining insights from cultural and biblical stories, must be designed and included in the

797 Synod of Bishops – II Special Assembly for Africa, *The Church in Africa in Service to Reconciliation, Justice and Peace: Instrumentum: Instrumentum Laboris*, Vatican City, The Secretariat of the Synod of Bishops and Libreria Editrice Vaticana, 2009, n. 116.

798 Zenit, "Africa Synod Propositions 41-50," Permalink: http://www.zenit.org/article-27389?l=english Code: ZE09103001 - 2009-10-30 (downloaded, 2 November 2009); cf. *CISA*, Issue No. 122, Monday, November 2, 2009, electronic text downloaded from website: http://www.cisanewsafrica.org

799 *AM*, nn. 125-126.

800 *GDC*, p. 160.

801 Vincent Aguda and Anthony Orombi, interviewed by the researcher, at Angal, 26 June 2008.

syllabus for teaching, especially drama and group discussions on marriage and family life, polygamy, children, elders, homestead and neighbourhood relationships; (b) A basic course on pastoral counseling, which must prepare catechists to listen to the people they are to serve. The question of pastoral counseling needs some elaboration.

In his study entitled, *Pastoral Counselling in Africa*, Kiriswa writes that: "Pastoral counseling works within a religious framework, utilizing insights and principles derived from the disciplines of theology and behavioral sciences in working with individuals, couples, families, groups and social systems toward the achievement of wholeness and health."[802] The focus of pastoral counseling is to enable the faithful to grow in the theological virtues. Giardini clarifies this point by drawing the parallelism that exists between humanistic counseling which promotes maturation of the person; and Christian counseling which fosters the conversion and sanctification of the faithful. He writes: "Now, as the natural gaps in self-knowledge, self-acceptance, and self-love are filled through the process of personal maturation which is promoted by humanistic counseling, so the imperfect forms of supernatural self-knowledge, self-acceptance and self-love are perfected by the process of religious conversion and fostered by Christian counseling."[803]

In his intervention at the First Synod of Bishops for Africa, Bishop Bakyenga of Mbarara diocese (Uganda) noted that there are several main areas that the Church should emphasise. With regard to catechists, he posed the question: "...there is need for more involvement and sharing of lay people in the priest's ministry. Would catechists be allowed to administer anointing of the sick, especially as they are nearest to the sick people? Could they also witness at marriages (can. 1112)?"[804] This question has been passed over in silence at both the First and Second Synods on Africa. In our field study, the question referring to anointing of the sick was presented by catechists and Christian communities (in a parish) as a major pastoral concern and difficulty. The catechists are to fill a form and present it to the parish priest who then files them and follows the list by order of dates, conditions of the sick, homestead, and other factors, as illustrated below:

802 Benjamin Kiriswa, *Pastoral Counselling: An Integrated Model*, Spearhead NOs. 156-157, Eldoret, AMECEA Gaba Publications, 2002, p. 4.

803 Fabio Giardini, *Counseling: Humanistic and Christian*, Rome, Millennium, 1997, p. 237.

804 Paul Bakyenga, "Interventions" in AFJN, p. 112. To this date, Bakyenga is serving as secretary of the Uganda Episcopal Conference.

Lwongo Padri pi Sacramento mi Wiro Jatwo	***Calling the Priest for the Sacrament of Anointing the Sick***
1. Nying Jatwo..............................	Name of the sick person....................
2. Pacu pa...................................	Home of......................................
3. Jatwo ulwongo sacramento?...........	Has the sick asked for anointing? ....
3. Awene?	When? ....
4. Kit kwo pare..............................	His/her way of life..........................
5. Ébedo katwoyo pi kare ma rukani?.....	For how long has s/he been sick? ....
6. Ébed é maku sacramento ungo? .... (Kwo pare ubedo kwo mi sacramento?...)	Has s/he not been receiving the sacraments?.............................. (Did s/he live a sacramental life?..........)

Figure 9: A form for visiting the sick by the Priest

This situation leaves a number of the faithful dying without the sacrament of anointing, and Holy Communion, even if they had asked for it. From our questionnaire responses, 131 (45%) out of 287 mentioned that it is a gesture of the rejection of its members by the Catholic Church.

In his Post-Synodal Apostolic Exhortation, *Africae Munus*, Pope Benedict XVI asks the Catholic Bishops in Africa to find the causes that are leading Catholics to cross over to the syncretistic movements and sects. He calls to mind that: "The Church's theology and pastoral care must determine the causes of this phenomenon, not only to stem the haemorrhage of the faithful from the parishes to the sects, but also in order to lay the foundations of a suitable pastoral response to the attraction that these movements and sects exert."[805] From what we have just said, one strong reason for doing so is what they have called 'rejection.' In our questionnaire, 98 (34%) responses out of 287 mentioned that this is one reason why Catholics are crossing over to the sects, which they call "*both,*" meaning "liberation" and *bedo agonya*, "being free, freedom." We may discern that the problem seems to lie in how pastoral approach is set in responding to such sensitive spiritual needs of the people.

7.2.10. Formation of Seminarians and Religious Novices[806]

What is said here of priestly formation applies to religious formation as well; both are preparing for a lifelong commitment of service in the Church

805 *AM*, n. 91.

806 Sr. Saveria Fwathum, interviewed by the researcher, at Nyapea, 4 June 2008, particularly emphasised the importance of integral formation for the candidate to religious life as well as the ordained ministry; cf. Little Sisters of Mary Immaculate of Gulu, *Chapter Documents 2007:*

and its apostolate. The Decree of the Second Vatican Council on Priestly Formation, *Optatam Totius*, gives five basic reasons for which training towards the ordained priesthood deserves a sensitive attention: (a) the permanent nature of the office priests assume from the effect of their ordination, animated by the "spirit of Christ;"[807] (b) the Christ-priesthood is not of a civil religion nor does it follow after the pattern of a particular human path of life (culture) although it is incarnated in these human principles; (c) the vital role priests play in directing the laity;[808] (d) their way of life (power of example) has significant influence both on the ecclesial community and the wider society; (e) they need a formation with a good coverage in the humanities which will lead them to enter into the mystery of Christian salvation.[809] As stated in *Gaudium et Spes*, this means that the education of future priests must be responsive to, and integrate, contemporary realities and local situations.[810]

In his reflection, *Crossing the Threshold of Hope*, Pope John Paul II alludes to the rise in priestly and religious vocations in Africa (and Asia) as one of the touchstones of this threshold of the Church's hope.[811] This raises some practical questions: What kind of priests for the Church in Africa? What should priestly formation look for? What is to be achieved? What teaching method is there designed for teaching them?

Both the First and Second Synods of Bishops for Africa recommend the selection of candidates to be done carefully, even to involve the family and SCC.[812] During the First Synod, Bishop Bakyenga made the following observation in his intervention:

> ...leadership should first be proven in the local community. The training of priests in the local community and the evaluation of candidates by the local community where they work should be taken seriously. A number of priests are not good leaders and yet they are put at the head of communities and they feel

Seventh General Chapter, Gulu, December 2007. This Chapter chose formation (human, intellectual, spiritual, pastoral) as a key to renewing and deepening the zeal for community life and apostolate that can respond to real local situations.

807 *Op. Tot.*, Preface: *AAS* 58 (1966), p. 713.

808 Footnote 1, in Abbott and Gallagher (eds.), *The Documents of Vatican II*, p. 437; Flannery (ed.), *Vatican Council II*, Vol. 1, p. 707, note 1; Tanner, *Decrees of the Ecumenical Councils*, Vol. 2, p. 947.

809 *Op. Tot.*, n. 14-17: *AAS* 58 (1966), pp. 722-725.

810 *GS*, n. 62: *AAS* 58 (1966), pp. 1082-1084.

811 John Paul II, *Crossing the Threshold of Hope*, p. 111-112.

812 AFJN, *The African Synod*, p. 93; Synod of Bishops – II Special Assembly for Africa, *Proposition 40*, Permalink: http://www.zenit.org/article-27386?1=english Code: ZE09102910 - 2009-10-29.

ill at ease. To remedy this, candidates for priesthood should be approved first by the community, before being ordained.[813]

According to Bishop Ndingi discernment and selection of candidates to future priests and novices to religious life must involve the Parish Pastoral Council. He recommends that: "No candidate should be accepted for priestly formation in the major seminary, unless the Parish Pastoral Council has been consulted, and has given its views and consent... Selection should be made after careful observance of the candidate over a reasonable time, and under different circumstances. The role of the Vocation Committee and the Pastoral Council does not end, once the candidate has been admitted to the major seminary or novitiate, but should continue, right up to ordination or religious profession."[814]

Formation has been Pope John Paul II's concern in his Apostolic Exhortation, *Pastores Dabo Vobis* (I Will Give You Shepherds). He emphasises four areas in the formation of candidates to the ordained priesthood: human, spiritual, intellectual, pastoral, qualities which future priests need to internalise and appropriate in the course of their training.[815]

(1) Human formation is foundational, intending three aptitudes in the candidate.

(a) Relational attitude: formation must instill in the candidate a spirit of communion, that is, one who is open to others: fellow priests, the bishop, the consecrated religious and laity. They are to ponder that the priest is chosen from among the people to act on their behalf in their relationship with God (cf. Heb. 5:1).[816] The ordained priesthood is centered on Christ and carried out in his name. In his catechesis on the priesthood, he clarifies that:

> There is no further need or possibility of other priests in addition to or alongside the one Mediator, Christ (cf. Heb. 7:24-28), the point of union and reconciliation between mankind and God (cf. Heb. 9:15; Rom. 5:15-19; 1 Tim. 2:5), the Word made flesh, full of grace (cf. Jn. 1:1-18), the true and definitive *hiereús*, or Priest (Heb. 5:6; 10:21), who on earth "took away sin by his sacrifice" (Heb. 9:26) and continues to make intercession for his faithful (cf. Heb. 7:25), until

813 Paul Bakyenga, "Interventions," in *AFJN*, p. 112.

814 Raphael S. Ndingi Mwana 'a Nzeki, "Vocation and Formation of Priests," in *AFER*, Vol. 32, Nr. 1 (February 1990), p. 23.

815 John Paul II, Post-Synodal Apostolic Exhortation *Pastores Dabo Vobis* (I Will Give You Shepherds, 25 March 1992), 2nd reprint, Nairobi, Paulines Publications Africa, 1998: *AAS* 84 (1992), pp. 657-804.

816 Ibid., n. 43: *AAS* 84 (1992), pp. 731-733.

they attain the heavenly inheritance won and promised by him. No one else in the new covenant is *hiereús* in the same sense.[817]

(b) Affective maturity: by which the candidate must understand that it is love that builds up community life. This is particularly important in view of the commitment to celibacy. Affective growth is to bring out a lively and personal relationship to Christ, which must in turn find expression in a serene friendship and strong brotherliness with all; [818]

(c) Freedom for self-giving: a convinced and heartfelt obedience to the truth and meaning of one's own being, leading to sincere self-giving as the way and fundamental content of authentic self-realisation. It entails self-mastery, striving to "overcome the different forms of selfishness and individualism" which diminish one's true freedom;[819]

(d) *Education of the moral conscience,* by which the candidate is to develop a deep sense of personal moral accountability in face of the obligations that the ordained ministry demands. This is what will make the priest's moral command effective on those he serves.

(2) Spiritual formation must make of the candidate: (a) *a man of prayer,* developed through the practice of *lectio divina*, regular praying of the Divine Office, celebration of the Eucharist and participation in the celebration of the sacraments; (b) *a man of community character,* to develop a conscious, self-defining identity of *being* and *acting* as a priest in communion with the Trinity and a trustful attachment to the Church;[820] (c) *a man of charity,* which lies in self-giving. Charity involves a conscious sensitivity, enabling him to identify with, and minister to, all in the example of Christ. It is particularly important to the celibate nature of the ordained priesthood (and religious life).[821]

A house of formation must nurture a spirituality and atmosphere of communion. As recommended in *Optatam Totius*, a strong human factor is the cultivation of the strictest communitarian spirit of harmony and behaviour that must exist in the seminary or formation house (among formators, teaching staff and administrators): "Among themselves and with their students they should

817 Cf. James P. Socias (compiler), *Priesthood in the Third Millennium: Addresses of Pope John Paul II 1993*, Princeton, Scepter Publishers, 1994, p. 18. This book is a collection of 18 General Audiences of the Pope's Catechesis on the Ordained Priesthood (*Presbyterate*), Wednesday, 31 March until Wednesday, 29 September 1993.

818 *PdV*, n. 44: *AAS* 84 (1992), pp. 733-736.

819 Ibid., n. 44 § 6: *AAS* 84 (1992), p. 736.

820 Ibid., n. 45-46: *AAS* 84 (1992), pp. 736-740.

821 Ibid., n. 49 ('and religious life,' ours): *AAS* 84 (1992), pp. 745-746.

constitute the kind of family which answers the Lord's Prayer "that they may be one" (Jn. 17:10)."[822]

(3) Intellectual formation must bring out in the candidate three features. (a) *A critical mind* rigorously trained to discern the mysteries of faith. Academic study must engage the student to seek the truth of faith as a revealed truth with a unifying force for the common good;[823] (b) *Objective judgment*, the task of philosophical training (the humanities), which must acquaint the student with the different currents of thought and help him to transcend self-centred thinking. Pope John Paul II calls this a formation in "the cult of truth,"[824] the focus of which is to prepare the candidate to be truthful, sincere and honest in judgment; (c) *A believer*, that is, the candidate must understand the Church and partake of its life as "a community of faith."[825] This is the task of theological training through which teachers in the seminary must strive to prepare future priests for ecclesial communion.[826]

The second Synod of Bishops for Africa directly mentions the word "education" 76 times.[827] Based on this, Pope Benedict XVI takes the world of education in Africa as an important gateway to entering into a critical analysis of, and dialogue with, the contemporaneous social-cultural reality in the continent. He places it in the hands of the Bishops to consider the need for raising the intellectual capacity in the Church as much as in the society. He writes:

> In order to make a solid and proper contribution to African society, it is indispensable that students be taught the Church's social doctrine. This will help the Church in Africa serenely to prepare a pastoral plan which speaks to the heart of Africans… Once again, it is up to bishops to support a pastoral outreach to the life of the intellect and reason so as to foster a habit of dialogue and critical analysis within the society and in the Church.[828]

From this we may understand that intellectual life is also a vocation, quite demanding, which calls considerable attention in its own regard for the good

---

822 *Op. Tot.*, n. 5: *AAS* 58 (1966), p. 717.

823 Congregation for the Doctrine of the Faith, Instruction on the Ecclesial Vocation of the Theologian *Donum Veritatis*, Dublin, Veritas Publications, 1990, nn. 1-5: *AAS* 82 (24 May 1990), pp. 1550-1552.

824 *PdV*, n. 52: *AAS* 84 (1992), p. 750.

825 Ibid., n. 53: *AAS* 84 (1992), p. 752.

826 Ibid., n. 57: AAS 84 (1992), p. 757-759.

827 Zenit, *Keywords at the Africa Synod*, Permalink: http://www.zenit.org/article-27186?l=english Code: ZE09101309 – 2009-10-13 (accessed, 14 October 2009).

828 *AM*, n. 137.

of the Church and society. The following observations are therefore helpful to promote a strong seminary formation: (a) The seminary institution needs teachers with suitable academic qualification, exemplary life, and concern for the good of the Church;[829] (b) The academic dean of the seminary must be appointed a person of good knowledge, human and spiritual experience, capable of coordinating academic activities as recommended in canon law. Commenting on canon 239 of the Code of Canon Law, which talks about the chief personnel of the seminary, Cunningham writes that: "Often the rector will appoint an academic dean or dean of the faculty who chairs the cooperative efforts of the teaching staff."[830] (c) The seminarian himself must show progress in academic, moral, spiritual and relational capabilities.[831]

Seminary formation must not only produce pastors but also scholars. This point has been highlighted by Pope Benedict XVI in his Address at Yaoundé to the members of the Special Council for Africa of the Synod of Bishops. He specifically calls attention to the re-awakening of the spirit of scholarship where he expresses that:

> This century will perhaps permit, by God's grace, the rebirth, on your continent, albeit certainly under a different and new form, of the prestigious School of Alexandria. Why could we not hope that Africans today and the universal Church might thereby be furnished with great theologians and spiritual masters capable of contributing to the sanctification of those who dwell in this continent and throughout the Church?[832]

(4) Pastoral formation is the synthesis of the various disciplines taught in the seminary. This is to develop in the candidate the following characteristics: (a) *A pastor* in communion with the charity of Christ who is teacher, priest and shepherd, to share the sentiments and behaviour of Christ in a spirit of friendship that pays attention to social-cultural realities in order to win people for God;[833] (b) *A servant* to the community as defined by the three stages of service (lector, acolyte, deacon) that the candidate passes through. This is to foster the experience of service, by which they prepare to be a visible sign of the solici-

829 *Op. Tot.*, n. 5: *AAS* 58 (1966), p. 716-717.

830 Richard G. Cunningham, "Sacred Ministers or Clerics [cc. 232-293] – Chapter 1: The Formation of Clerics [cc. 232-264]" in John P. Beal, James A. Corriden, Thomas J. Green (eds.), *New Commentary on the Code of Canon Law*, Bangalore, Theological Publications in India, 2003, p. 311a.

831 *Op. Tot.*, n. 6: *AAS* 58 (1966), pp. 717-718.

832 Benedict XVI, *Address to Members of the Special Council for Africa of the Synod of Bishops*, Yaoundé, 19 March 2009: *AAS* 101 (2009), p. 312.

833 *PdV*, n. 57: *AAS* 85 (1992), pp. 757-759.

tude of the Church who is Mother and Teacher; acting in the community with a pastoral authority (a sensitivity) which sets aside all attitudes of superiority or of exercising a power if it is not simply that which is justified by pastoral charity;[834] (c) *A person with team spirit* in the awareness that the Church is a missionary communion. This must make them open and available to all the possibilities for the proclamation of the Gospel.[835]

In his recommendation following the Second Synod of Bishops for Africa, Pope Benedict XVI states that the synod calls for: "...transforming theology into pastoral care, namely into a very concrete pastoral ministry in which the great perspectives found in sacred Scripture and Tradition find application in the activity of bishops and priests in specific times and places."[836] From this reflection we may understand that the formation of the candidate to the ordained priesthood and to the consecrated religious life should involve the following factors:

(a) The candidate must show interest and growth in the Christian and human virtues. Pieper clarifies that human or natural virtue is not just a tame respectability or uprightness but the enhancement of the human person in a way befitting of their nature; the realisation of the person's potentiality for being; the steadfastness of their orientation towards the realisation of their nature. And, theologically, virtue is the ennobling of human nature that entirely surpasses what one can be of oneself; it is a steadfast orientation towards a fulfillment and beatitude that are not owed to the natural human person; it is a grace-filled participation in divine nature which comes to human beings through Christ;[837]

(b) The seminary or novitiate syllabus (teaching programme) must be designed to prepare candidates for an in-depth evangelisation. In its Decree on Priestly Formation, *Optatam Totius*, Vatican Council II clarifies that doctrinal training is not just a mere communication of ideas; it is a genuine and deep formation of candidates, for which teaching methods for lectures, discussions and seminars must be designed to promote a learning;[838]

(c) The *pastoral cycle* approach proposed by pastoral theologians is a good methodology of an actual translation or life-application which works from seeing, discursing, acting, implementing and evaluating together as an ecclesial community. In this way the candidate is being prepared to be able to make a

834 Ibid., n. 58: *AAS* 85 (1992), pp. 759-761, citation on p. 760.

835 Ibid., n. 59: *AAS* 85 (1992), pp. 761-762.

836 *AM*, n. 10. Here, reference is made to an earlier address to the Roman Curia, for which see, Benedict XVI, *Address to the Roman Curia* (21 December 2009): *AAS* 102 (2010), p. 35.

837 Joseph Pieper, *Faith, Hope, Love*, San Francisco, Ignatius Press, 1997, p. 99.

838 *Op. Tot.*, n. 17: *AAS* 58 (1966), pp. 724-725.

theological evaluation that connects what is happening in life with faith. According to Mejía, this approach is the interplay between the Word of God and human experience;[839]

(d) In the same connection seminary lessons must not dwell only on doctrinaire deductive methods; it must make ample use of an inductive methodology which is akin to the African approach to life. Mejía clarifies that the deductive method has been used in classical theology, deriving guidelines for faith and morals from Biblical texts. However, developments in theology have also appreciated the inductive method which takes into consideration the cultural background and the human experience of those reading the Word of God. We may therefore discern that the integration of both the deductive and inductive models can enrich formation: the inductive translates the deductive into lived experience.

(e) Besides, formation needs to make of candidates persons with good judgement, capable of taking certain decisions at demanding and critical moments. They are going to become interpreters of the gospel message in a human world which is increasingly becoming more complex. An important point that the pastoral cycle does not seem to mention clearly is that of *translation*, which calls for careful judgement by which the interpreter will reach to the heart of people in simple but convincing style, mindful of their sensitivity, how they think, how they look at the world, the way they react or respond.

7.2.11. Permanent and On-going Formation

Formation does not end with basic catechesis as for the common believer; nor in the classroom as for those in religious and clerical training. Pope John Paul II explains that formation is both permanent and on-going. It is permanent inasmuch as it must leave an indelible conviction in the life of the believer. It is on-going insofar as conviction must be continually in touch with contingent and contemporaneous realities.

Vatican Council II teaches that the life of faith must take on a permanent intimate union with Christ. This is to lead all believers into a continuous exercise of faith, hope and love, making them participants in both the spiritual and the temporal-secular life and activities of the Church.[840] Pope John Paul II, clarifies that this permanence applies to the: (a) *laity*, in their untiring com-

839 Rodrigo Mejía, "Pastoral Theology and the Pastoral Cycle: The Methodology and Dynamics of the Pastoral Cycle," in Patrick Ryan (ed.), *New Strategies for a New Evangelization in Africa*, Nairobi, Paulines, 2002, pp. 122- 143. An update in Frans Wijsen, Peter Henriot, Rodrigo Mejía (eds.), *The Pastoral Cycle Revisited: A Critical Quest for Truth and Transformation*, Nairobi, Paulines, 2006, pp. 251-253.

840 *AA*, n. 4: *AAS* 58 (1966), pp. 840-842.

mitment to Christ;[841] (b) *ordained priests*, in faithfulness to the grace received, trust in God's faithfulness to the Church, cooperating in the action of God;[842] (c) *bishop*, following Christ, and uniting the community.[843]

However, this permanence is not static; it is on-going, in the following manner: (a) to keep in touch with theological questions in contemporaneous contexts bishops, religious and priests need special seminar and workshop programmes. This is to continue and to deepen what has been learnt earlier on, which now may need adaptation, updating and modifications in face of ongoing pastoral realities; (b) the emotional aspect needs attention as well. The study of Coate, in her book, *Clergy Stress*, illustrates that ministers of the Gospel suffer a lot of emotional fatigue or stress due to various factors combined with the workload they meet in their ministry;[844] (c) the laity are to be reinvigorated through discussions on topics which can challenge them with insights that connect faith with daily living.

7.3. Collaboration in Ecclesial Activities

We may here use the English word *collaboration* synonymously with another word, *cooperation*, both referring to concurrence in some work, a joint activity, joining of efforts, working or acting together to the same end.[845] In his Encyclical Letter on the mission of the Church, *Redemptoris Missio*, Pope John Paul II understands collaboration as "...a united effort in confronting great questions of common concern, with due regard for the competence proper to each authority and structure."[846] The same notion of "...a closer working relationship..." has been made by Pope Benedict XVI in his Post-Synodal Apostolic Exhortation on the Word of God in the life and mission of the Church, *Verbum Domini*, where he encourages cooperation among pastors, exegetes and theologians. The focus of collaboration in both explications is ecclesial communion. From our questionnaire responses, collaboration has been ex-

---

841 *CfL*, n. 59: *AAS* 81 (1989), p. 509.

842 *PdV*, n. 2; 70: *AAS* 84 (1992), p. 659; 789.

843 *PaG*, n. 24: *AAS* 96 (2004), p. 857.

844 Mary Anne Coate, *Clergy Stress: The Hidden Conflicts in Ministry*, 2nd Impression, London, SPCK, 1989. This work needs to be read in its entirety. Coate is a clinical psychologist (and deputy training coordinator at the Westminster Pastoral Foundation, the time she published this work).

845 The verb, *collaborate*, deriving from Latin, *collaborare* (*com-*, with; *laborare*, to work); *co-operate*, from Latin, *cooperari* (*co-*, with, together with; *operari*, from *opus*, *operis*, work) to work together in a common effort for the same cause.

846 *RM*, n. 75: *AAS* 83 (1991), p. 323.

pressed in the words *diko cing* (joining hands), *ribo cing* (uniting hands), by which is meant "joining efforts."[847]

The Second Vatican Council Decree on the Missionary Activity of the Church, *Ad Gentes Divinitus*, teaches that formation is to foster communitarian and collaborative habits of the mind cultivated, uplifted and nourished by the spiritual life.[848] Here the Council encourages that: "Since Christ's faithful have different gifts, they should collaborate in the service of the gospel, each in accordance with their opportunities, ability, charism and ministry…"[849] This is because the apostolate exercised by the individual "…is the origin and condition of the whole lay apostolate, even in its organised expression, and admits no substitute."[850]

Pope John Paul II has made emphasis on collaboration in the mission of the Church. In his Apostolic Exhortation on the Laity, he explicitly states that his intention is: "…to stir and promote a deeper awareness among all the faithful of the gift and responsibility they share, both as a group and as individuals, in the communion and mission of the Church."[851] He insists that every individual is called to a form of participation;[852] and must therefore be consciously engaged in the life of the Church because each Christian is: (a) an individual; (b) unique and irreplaceable; (c) a member, who belongs; (d) called personally; (e) entrusted with a unique task which cannot be done by another and which is to be fulfilled for the good of all.[853] The individual is a participant who increases the resourceful convergence of communal efforts, expressible through the various groups which bring to life the different apostolic charisms.[854]

Cardinal Kasper has made a critical study on collaboration in his book, *Leadership in the Church*, especially in view of the task of leading the ecclesial community.[855] In this book he reports of his travel experience of the young local churches in the so-called third world countries where he encountered an

---

847 Out of 287 responses, 109 recommended "*collaboration*" as a possible way of warding off individualism in the Church.

848 *AGD*, n. 25: *AAS* 58 (1966), p. 976.

849 Ibid., n. 28: *AAS* 58 (1966), p. 979.

850 *AA*, n. 16: *AAS* 58 (1966), p. 851.

851 *CfL*, n. 2 § 13: *AAS* 81 (1989), p. 397.

852 Ibid., n. 54: *AAS* 81 (1989), pp. 500-502.

853 Ibid., n. 28: *AAS* 81 (1989), p. 442.

854 Ibid., n. 29: *AAS* 81 (1989). pp. 443-446.

855 Walter Cardinal Kaspar, *Leadership in the Church: How Traditional Roles Can Serve the Christian Community Today*, translation by Brian McNeil, New York, The Crossroad Publishing Company, 2003, pp. 45-75.

increased commitment of lay service in the Church. The following points are particularly relevant to this present study:

(a) The Church cannot be taken as purely charismatic or purely democratic. Its structure, as in the early Church, is regulated by defined ministries;[856]

(b) It is helpful for the Church to promote the form that is close at many points to Jesus' original vision of the kingdom of God, that is, to the *communio*-ecclesiology of Scripture and the patristic age, and to the intentions of the Second Vatican Council, rather than the form so familiar as from the last 150 years;[857]

(c) In the Christological tradition, the ordained priesthood is a witness to Jesus, and represents Christ's handing on of himself, an office of reconciling God with his people. This representative office does not take the place of an absent Lord; but rather it allows Christ to speak as one who is genuinely present. The responsibility of the ordained ministry is therefore neither exclusive nor universal; it is inherently related to other Christians, which it must complete and strengthen;[858]

(e) The ordained priest, as Christ's representative, is a sign of something that he himself cannot effect. Thus, where connection of laity public opinion is missing, office-bearers become a caricature of themselves, as "shepherds who merely pasture their own selves" (cf. Ez. 34:2). Walter argues that: "Vatican II puts an end to obsessive concentration on the clergy; urging pastors to listen to the laity, in the hope of the new intimacy on both sides."[859] The ordained priest, as a pastor, must be open to inspiration, and sometimes to criticism from others in the Church;

(f) According to Kasper, "As a spiritual service, community leadership cannot be exercised in an autocratic manner; it must collaborate with the other ministries and with the entire community, and it is in this context that the term "cooperative pastoral care" has been coined."[860]

(e) Collaboration by lay persons in tasks of community leadership does not mean that they are taking the place of the priest:

> Thanks to their own *missio*, the laity can assume the exercise of particular tasks (*munia*) that are more closely linked with the ministries (*officia*) of the pastors, in teaching, in liturgical actions, and in pastoral work (*cura animarum*). In this

856 Ibid., p. 50.

857 Ibid., pp. 73-74.

858 Ibid., pp. 49-55.

859 Ibid., p. 62; reference is made to *Lumen Gentium*, n. 37 and *Presbyterorum Ordinis*, n. 9.

860 Ibid., p. 66-67.

context, the council speaks of a *cooperatio* in the exercise of specific ministries that, however, does not entail a *participatio* in the hierarchical ministry itself.[861]

Another specific reference to collaboration regards the apostolate of the Religious institutes whose presence is acknowledged in the diocese. Hill and Dunn clarify that apart from the office of the ordained priest;[862] other offices, for example, director of religious education, tribunal collegial judge, chancellor and finance officer, can be entrusted to a non-ordained person.[863] Besides, apostolic activities such as schools, health care centers and other social works can be entrusted to the religious. It is important here to understand what is meant by ecclesiastical office in Church law. Richard Hill clarifies that it is any function which has been conferred with stability for a spiritual purpose.[864] These offices can be of Divine Law, such as held by the Pope, and the bishop in a diocese. They can also be of church law, such as held by the Vicar General, Episcopal Vicar and Chancellor.[865] Capable and reliable religious may be entrusted with such offices within the diocesan structure. Canon Law recommends that any provisions of an ecclesiatical office should be made in written agreement between the two juridic persons: the diocese and the religious institute, acting through their canonical representatives, the Bishop or his delegate and the legitimate religious superior.[866] Canon 681 § 2 states that: "In these cases, the diocesan bishop and the competent superior of the religious institute are to draw up a written agreement which, among other things, is to define expressly and accurately those things which pertain to the work to be accomplished, the members to be devoted to it, and economic matters."[867]

861 Ibid., pp. 69-70; cf. *LG*, n. 33; *AA*, n. 24.

862 Richard A. Hill, "The Apostolate of Institutes: Canons 673-683," in Jordan Hite, Sharon Holland and Daniel Ward (eds.), *A Handbook on Canons 573-746: Religious Institutes, Secular Institutes, Societies of Apostolic Life*, Collegeville, Minnesota, Liturgical Press, 1985, p. 214.

863 Beverly K. Dunn, "Apostolate," in Catherine Darcy, Michael Joyce, Robert Kaslyn and Margaret Sullivan (eds.), *Procedural Handbook for Institutes of Consecrated Life and Societies of Apostolic Life,* Washington, Canon Law Society of America, 2001, 176.

864 Richard A. Hill, "The Apostolate of Institutes: Canons 673-683" in Jordan Hite, Sharon Holland and Daniel Ward (eds.), *A Handbook of Canons 573-746*, p. 214.

865 Anthony Pinheiro, "Bishop-Religious Relationship in the Apostolic Activities of the Diocese According to the Code of Canon Law, (cc. 678 §3-683)" Doctoral Dissertation, Roma, Pontificia Universita Lateranense, 1986, p. 77; see also CIC, Can. 145 §1.

866 Richard A. Hill, "Complementary Competencies: Bishop, Superiors and Apostolates" in Patrick J. Cogan (ed.), *Selected Issues in Religious law: Bulletin on Issues of Religious Law 1985-1995*, Washington, D.C.: Canon Law Society of America, 1997, p. 39.

867 *Code of Canon Law,* Latin-English Edition, New English translation, prepared under the auspices of the Canon Law Society of America, 1st printing, Washington, DC, Canon Law Society of America, 1999, p. 222.

In Nebbi Catholic Diocese the Religious expressed the concern for collaboration in apostolic works such as school education and health services, but also pastoral activities. Our questionnaire reports recommended the role of the religious as important.[868] In order to realise this, the following points were proposed: (a) To organise regular joint meetings for diocesan priests and consecrated persons working in the diocese, with the intention of encouraging dialogue and sharing of ideas; (b) To sensitise all the faithful, both laity and clergy, on the specific place of the religious in the diocese. This can be done by organising workshops on topics of *team spirit* and *teamwork* for all agents of evangelisation in the diocese, including diocesan priests, the religious; leaders of groups, movements and associations; (c) To introduce the religious to ecclesial communities at all levels in the diocese; (d) Every priest must read and understand the constitution of all the religious institutes working in the diocese, which will help him to know their charism and what they are expected to offer in the diocese; (e) The priest is not to assign other tasks to the religious, nor the religious to assume roles which fall outside what is written in the contract; (f) Every religious institute working in the diocese must have a written copy of the diocesan policy which will help them to know what is expected of them.

From the foregoing, we can understand collaboration in the Church as the joining of efforts in working together for the growth of the ecclesial community. In our assessment, it involves the important factor of subsidiarity with the aim of achieving the common good of the Church, which benefits both the individual member and the community.

7.3.1. Subsidiarity

Subsidiarity has to do with trust and reciprocal support. The basic connotation of *subsidiarity* derives from its etymology, the Latin word, *subsidium*, "help, aid, assistance, support, completion." It was proposed for the first time by Pope Pius XI in his Encyclical Letter *Quadragesimo Anno*, as the right approach to reconstructing social order and organic harmony in the society. He writes that:

> ...it is wrong to withdraw from the individual and commit to the community at large what private enterprise and industry can accomplish, so, too, it is an injustice, a grave evil and a disturbance of right order for a larger and higher organisation to arrogate to itself functions which can be performed efficiently by smaller and lower bodies... Of its very nature the true aim of all social activity

868 From our questionnaire responses, 178 out of 287 recommended the role of the religious as important in the diocese. This figure seems to suggest that their role in the diocese is still little known.

should be to help individual members of the social body, but never to destroy or absorb them.[869]

The principle is based on that of charity and the common good against the pressure of state collectivism. It is intended for the right ordering of society. The state or larger society is to safeguard the personal initiative and freedom of its individual members or groups and to guarantee the necessary means to preserve the common good. The higher institution or authority must leave to the lower what can be done just as well or even better at that lower level; but the larger or higher authority must genuinely support the lesser where need arises in order to realise or complete their initiatives.

On this background, Pope John Paul II, in his Encyclical Letter, *Centesimus Annus*, writes that: "...a community of higher order should not interfere in the internal life of a community of a lower order, depriving the latter of its functions, but rather should support it in case of need and help to coordinate its activity with the activities of the rest of society, always with a view to the common good."[870]

Schonecke observes that the same principle can inspire the way the Church plans its activities; to improve its structures and internal working by promoting the strength of its individual members, groups and localities. He writes that:

> The church proposes this principle for the organisation of society... But if the church is not only a divine institution but also a human society, this principle should inspire the way we plan actions... In practical terms it would mean that whatever can be achieved in the SCCs should not be taken over by the parish. But services and functions that the SCCs is not able to provide must be taken up by the parish. The same would apply to the relationship between parish and diocese, local church and universal church... If we take the teaching of the Vatican Council and orientations of the African Synod serious, we would need to rethink our pastoral plans in the light of the principle of subsidiarity and restore to the "lesser and subordinate bodies" (read SCCs and parishes) all the responsibilities they can handle without endangering the common good and the unity of the church.[871]

According to Schonecke, the practice of subsidiarity in the Church can serve to overcome the problem of clericalism within it. He argues that clerical-

869 Pius XI, Encyclical Letter *Quadragesimo Anno* (On Social Reconstruction), Vatican Polyglot translation, Boston, St. Paul Editions, II: 5, p. 40: *AAS* 23 (1931), p. 203.

870 *CA*, n. 48 § 4: *AAS* 83 (1991), p. 854.

871 Wolfgang Schoneke, "Pastoral Planning: New Responses to Changed Situations" in Patrick Ryan (ed.), *New Strategies for a New Evangelization in Africa*, Nairobi, Paulines Publications Africa, 2002, pp. 134-135.

ism stands against the principle of subsidiarity, to the detriment of the vitality of Christian life and communities. From this reflection we can deduce that the principle of subsidiarity can help Nebbi Catholic Diocese in organising and strengthening its internal life and activities. However, it is not merely to evaluate and improve ecclesial structure; individual members and groups must be made aware that this principle asks of them their best efforts which can reinvigorate the Church as everyone makes their contribution to the common ecclesial good.

7.3.2. Common Good

By common good is here meant what works to the good or wellbeing of all. It calls for the spirit of commitment that we are to have in mind and heart, by which we appreciate and work to promote the intelligible community values and concerns. Vatican Council II defines common good as "...the sum total of social condition, which allow people, either as groups or as individuals, to reach their fulfillment more fully and more easily."[872] Based on this definition, the *Compendium of the Social Doctrine of the Church* clarifies that: "The common good, in fact, can be understood as the social and community dimension of the moral good."[873] It is primarily a "moral good" of the relational spirit that unites members of a community or society. It it this moral good that leads to and bears fruit in the physical common goods. How does this help to build ecclesial communion?

Underlying the concept of common good are interdependence and collaboration by which every individual participates in the life of the community. Gremillion writes that: "In Church teaching, the common good is not the glib phrase of a political campaign. It forms the bedrock of Catholic social doctrine, more fundamental than property, because its goal and measure is the human person and his perfection."[874] The Christian gist of common good has an eschatological content: the ultimate fulfillment of every individual and all. As Benetollo Ottorino explains, it is *ultimate* because it points to God who is the ultimate Common Good of humankind as God's family.[875]

872 *GS*, n. 26: *AAS* 58 (1966), p. 1046

873 Pontifical Council for Justice and Peace, *Compendium of the Social Doctrine of the Church*, n. 164 § 2.

874 Joseph Gremillion, *The Gospel of Peace and Justice: Catholic Social Teaching since Pope John*, Maryknoll, Orbis Books, 1976, p. 33.

875 Vincenzo Benetollo Ottorino, *Morale e Società: Princìpi di Etica Sociale*, Bologna, Edizioni Studio Domenicano, 1999, pp. 41- 51.

A practical interpretation of common good has been expressed by Pope Benedict XVI in his Post-Synodal Apostolic Exhortation, *Africae Munus* (Africa's Commitment). He links common good to the various gifts working for the common strength and growth of the Church. He writes: "One can never be a Christian alone. The gifts given by the Lord to each – bishops, priests, deacons, and religious, catechists and lay people – must all contribute to harmony, communion and peace in the Church herself and in society."[876] The question of common good in the Church is therefore to bring all the human and material resources for its common growth.

Conclusion

In this chapter we have proposed three factors that need close attention: the Word of God, integral formation, and collaboration in ecclesial activities. We have shown that the Word of God gives inspiration and vision to ecclesial life and all its activities. We have discussed the variety of ways Scripture can be used to bring out its richness and depth for the life of the Church.

Secondly, we have tried to illustrate that formation is an important factor in building ecclesial communion inasmuch as it brings about love for the Church, personal conviction and commitment, team spirit and responsibility to community values. It must enable every believer to become deeply aware that God's grace works uniquely in each one to the benefit of the ecclesial community. We have also noted that formation is not just permanent but ongoing at all levels and in every dimension. This needs designing a life-application methodology which reflects contingent and contemporaneous realities. The family, SCC, school, church groups, clubs, movements, religious communities and church offices are such places for harnessing the efforts of every member. Our thesis here is that the Church needs convinced believers (clergy, religious, laity) and formation must make them aware that their ecclesial community cannot grow from outside, without them. It is only a well articulated formation programme that will make this conviction true.

Thirdly, we have said that collaboration helps to bring together the different gifts, talents and efforts of every member of the ecclesial community into real life. This works by bearing in mind the principle of subsidiarity, and the common good of the Church which everyone is to appreciate and work for.

---

876 *AM*, n. 97.

GENERAL CONCLUSION

In this study we have attempted to show the contrast between individualism as a self-bent spirit and the communitarian spirit which promotes communal life. Our case study was carried out in Nebbi Catholic Diocese in North-Western Uganda. This has helped us to look at the problem more closely. The following questions guided our field research: Is there individualism in Nebbi Catholic Diocese? Can it be verified? If so, how does it affect the internal life of the Church as the People of God? What image of the Church does it portray before the society which the Church strives to shape after its image of the family of God? How can the Church be a home if everyone would stand away from others?

We saw that the spread of the faith in Nebbi Catholic Diocese registered the efforts of catechists and particular members of the common laity. The study paid attention to the mission method used in the implanting of the Church, especially the three approaches of mission station catechumenate, school education, and Christian homestead communities. This helped us to follow its development to the present stage, with a focus on how the Church became a centralised parish Church for the coordination of pastoral and administrative activities. We have also looked at external factors. First, the Government policy which nationalised all schools: this has contributed significantly to the weakening of the Church's moral authority over the school; in turn, it has weakened religious education which had emphasised moral formation. Secondly, while aware of the acknowledgement of movements in the Church for its spiritual growth, we have, nevertheless, seen that the presence of different Christian denominations has posed the challenge of religious freedom, which leads in some way to the freedom to choose between the different churches: this has a direct impact on the family and SCCs as its individual members can make their personal choice of which denomination to adhere to. Thirdly, the traditional lifestyle is continually weakening due to social-cultural changes through factors like mobility, school life, the mass media and business.

Our field study and the sources cited in this work have helped us to highlight the traditional communitarian values of the Alur people. We found out that the basic values of kinship, Chiefship and religious practices are resonant with other neighbouring peoples in the same diocese. To deepen its work of evangelisation the diocese may need to carry out more research on those identified values and to assess how they have adjusted to new situations. Besides, a critical study of their customs will not only deepen the Church's understanding of the people but also it will help to discover a proper methodology to follow in the process of inculturation, that is, the insertion of Gospel values into the life of the people in a spirit of respectful dialogue.

Our discussion on Christian communitarian values intended to draw attention to the sources of the Church's life and embedded values to which it can always refer for its spiritual, moral and practical life. These sources are helpful to the Church not only for its self-awareness and self-definition; but they are also possibilities of addressing itself to the society which it strives to evangelise by proposing Gospel values. We have illustrated that these values have an invaluable moral content for the life of the Church and every believer. We have tried to explain that the Church is not just an institution; it is a moral community shaped by divine law and the values that characterise it as specifically Christian.

We further attempted to show that individualism finds expression in the Church in a number of ways and with different intensities. Its biggest problem is its subversive subtlety. It poses a moral problem insofar as it hinders progress both in the Church's pastoral and administrative activities. It weakens responsibility (that creative and faithful commitment to the building of the ecclesial community) in a number of ways. Nevertheless, the factors provoking or accentuating individualism are at the same time strong invitations for finding appropriate ways of strengthening the spirit of communion.

We have seen that there are many possibilities that can serve to the building up of ecclesial communion for spiritual, moral, as well as practical benefits. The different models of the Church that we have discussed provide the various intelligible ways which are mutually enriching for deepening our understanding of the Church. In our assessment, all of those different models must lead to making the Church a home, where everyone is truly at home in it. There are also models of morality that can help us to interpret those church models into practical life. The models of morality are tools for the continuous formation of the Christian conscience for the growth of the Church as a communion of disciples working together to the same cause and end.

To respond to the problem of individualism in the Church, we sought to explain, in the light of Christian anthropology, that the individual is relational and finds self-definition as person in relation with others. The human person has a legitimate autonomy but this means self-mastery which appreciates objective values. We said that the human person is an embodied moral subject, signifying responsibility. Again, we noted that s/he is capable of self-realisation but within the community matrix. Moreover, s/he is a historical subject, shaped in the social-cultural realities, meaning that s/he is in a continuous process of becoming by internalising the hierarchy of community values that surround her/

him. The individual is therefore relational and achieves personal fulfillment through a wide spectrum of relationships. Finally, the individual is a participant, that is, s/he reaches a true self-realisation by taking part in the life of the community.

In our recommendations we cited different sources. A significant problem, from our findings, regards weak leadership at different levels and contexts of ecclesial communities. This can only be rectified through formation which is not just to supply information; it must be a life-application method designed to foster relational attitudes and personal maturity. From the different church documents we have cited in this work there emerges the image of the Church as missionary. This raises the question of participation in that missionary work: Have all the faithful (not just laity) been challenged enough? Have they understood what being "missionary" might mean, even in their own environment? Are they 'proud' to be the builders of their ecclesial communion from their own human resources? Can the strength of life in Nebbi Catholic Diocese come from outside without its own members, in their different capacities, taking responsibility for their ecclesial community?

Another outstanding problem regards the question of pastoral planning, and with it, implementation and evaluation. The process of planning an action is more important than having the action because that action can only come from what is already there. Who are involved in the process of planning Church activities? Who are the beneficiaries? Who implement/s? Who evaluates? Who decides precise actions? Perhaps the Trinitarian portrait may need to be taken up in an attempt to studying the possibilities that might be helpful in strengthening ecclesial communion. Such an approach might help Nebbi Catholic Diocese to evaluate the progress that it makes, both in pastoral and administrative matters.

In our assessment, what deserves the greatest attention is the change of heart, from self-absorption to community interest and concern. Insensitivity or hardness of heart to the indentified common ecclesial values will only paralyse its life and growth. Without sincere change of heart, the diocese can only remain an institution without spirit and life.

From our field finding we are convinced that an honest study on the problem of individualism in the diocese can provide a practical approach to understanding the various other problems that might emerge from the actions of its individual members or groups of like-minded individuals in the different contexts they belong and act in the Church. Ours is only a case study. More research could be done, for example, on church administration in view of handling both human and material resources responsibly for the growth of its life as family-of-God; on what impact formation programmes may have on the life of the individual and the church community; on how the diocesan structural set-up might affect the consciousness of its members and thus shape the way they will relate and handle relationship towards one another, among groups, and towards authority; on how leadership roles might inspire cooperation in ecclesial life and activities; how they show interest in pastoral and administrative matters of the diocese.

It is our hope that this study has given some clue about individualism in the Church in Africa, even if it is only a case study. We hope that the recommendations made here may stimulate deeper reflection on what possibilities there might be which will help in working to build a strong and viable ecclesial communion. We also hope that this study may contribute to further academic research on the moral problem posed by individualism elsewhere in the Church in Africa.

BIBLIOGRAPHY

Bible

The Interlinear NIV Parallel New Testament in Greek and English, translated by Alfred Marshal, Michigan, Zondervan Publishing House, 1998.

The New Greek-English Interlinear New Testament, translated by Robert K. Brown and Philip W. Comfort, edited by J. D. Douglas, Illinois, Tyndale House Publishers, Inc., 1990.

The New Jerusalem Bible, London, Darton, Longman & Todd Ltd., 1985.

Official Church Documents

(a) General Ecumenical Councils

COUNCIL OF NICEA: I – 325 A.D., "The Profession of the Faith of the 318 Fathers," in TANNER, Norman, P. (ed.), *Decrees of the Ecumenical Councils*, Vol. 1: *Nicea – Lateran V*, London, Sheed & Ward Limited, 1990, p. 5.

COUNCIL OF CONSTANTINOPLE: I – 381 A.D., "The Exposition of the 150 Fathers," in TANNER, Norman, P. (ed.), *Decrees of the Ecumenical Councils*, Vol. 1: *Nicea – Lateran V*, London, Sheed & Ward Limited, 1990, p. 24.

VATICAN COUNCIL II, Dogmatic Constitution on the Church, *Lumen Gentium*, 21 November 1964: *Acta Apostolicae Sedis* 57 (1965), pp. 5-67.

__, Decree on Priestly Training, *Optatam Totius*, 28 October 1965: *Acta Apostolicae Sedis* 58 (1966), pp. 713-727.

__, Declaration on Christian Education, *Gravissimum Educationis*, 28 October 1965: *Acta Apostolicae Sedis* 58 (1966), pp. 728-739.

__, Dogmatic Constitution on Divine Revelation, *Dei Verbum*, 18th November 1965: *Acta Apostolicae Sedis* 58 (1966), pp. 817-830.

__, Decree on the Apostolate of the Laity, *Apostolicam Actuositatem*, 18 November 1965: *Acta Apostolicae Sedis* 58 (1966), pp. 837-864.

__, Decree on the Missionary Activity of the Church, *Ad Gentes Divinitus*, 7 December 1965: *Acta Apostolicae Sedis 58* (1966), pp. 947-990.

__, Decree on the Ministry and Life of Priests, *Presbyterorum Ordinis*, 7 December 1965: *Acta Apostolicae Sedis* 58 (1966), pp. 991-1024.

__, Pastoral Constitution on the Church in the Modern World, *Gaudium et Spes*, 7 December 1965: *Acta Apostolicae Sedis* 58 (1966), pp. 1025-1115.

__, Decree on Religious Freedom, *Dignitatis Humanae*, 7 December 1965: *Acta Apostolicae Sedis* 58 (1966), pp. 930-931.

(b) Papal Documents

BENEDICT XVI, Encyclical Letter *Deus Caritas Est* (God Is Love: On Christian Love), 25 December 2005, Nairobi, Paulines Publications Africa, 2005: *Acta Apostolicae Sedis* 98 (2006), pp. 217-252.

__, Post-Synodal Apostolic Exhortation *Sacramentum Caritatis* (The Sacrament of Charity), 22 February 2007, Nairobi, Paulines Publications Africa, 2007: *Acta Apostolicae Sedis* 99 (2007), pp. 104-180.

__, *Allocution VII: Address to Members of the Special Council for Africa of the Synod of Bishops,* Yaoundé, 19 March 2009: *Acta Apostolicae Sedis* 101 (2009), pp. 311-313.

__, Address to the Roman Curia, *Allocution II*, 21 December 2009: *Acta Apostolicae Sedis* 102 (2010), pp. 32-40.

__, Post-Synodal Apostolic Exhortation *Verbum Domini* (The Word of God in the Life and Mission of the Church), 30 September 2010, Nairobi, Paulines Publications Africa, 2010: *Acta Apostoliocae Sedis* 102 (2010), pp. 681-787.

__, Post-Synodal Apostolic Exhortation *Africae Munus* (Africa's Commitment), Nairobi, Paulines Publications Africa, 2011.

GIOVANNI PAOLO II, *Udienza Generale*, Mercoledì, 4 agosto 1993, Cità del Vaticano, Libreria Editrice Vaticana, 1993.

JOHN PAUL II, Encyclical Letter *Redemptor Hominis* (The Redeemer of Man), 4 March 1979, Boston, Pauline Books & Media: *Acta Apostolicae Sedis* 71 (1979), pp. 257-324.

__, Apostolic Exhortation *Catechesi Tradendae* (Catechesis Today), 16 October 1979, 2nd reprint, Nairobi, Paulines Publications Africa, 2001: *Acta Apostolicae Sedis* 71 (1979), pp. 1277-1340.

__, Apostolic Letter *Patres Ecclesiae*: *XVI Expleto Saeculo ab Obitu Sancti Basilii, Episcopi et Ecclesiae Doctoris*: AAS 72 (1980), pp. 5-23.

__, Apostolic Exhortation *Familiaris Consortio* (The Role of the Christian Family in the Modern World), 22 November 1981: *Acta Apostoliocae Sedis* 74 (1982), pp. 81-191.

__, *Address to Intellectuals, Students and University Personnel at Medellin*, Colombia, 5 July 1986, Rome, Libreria Editrice vaticana, 1986: *Acta Apostolicae Sedis* 97 (1987), pp. 95-100.

__, Encyclical Letter *Sollicitudo Rei Socialis* (On Social Concern), 30 December 1987: *Acta Apostolicae Sedis* 80 (1988), pp. 512-586.

__, Apostolic Exhortation *Christifideles Laici* (Vocation and Mission of the Lay Faithful), 30 December 1988, 1st reprint, Nairobi, Paulines Publications Africa, 1998: *Acta Apostolicae Sedis* 81 (1989), pp. 393-521.

__, Encyclical Letter *Centesimus Annus* (On the Hundredth Anniversary of *Rerum Novarum*), 1 May 1991, Vatican City, Libreria Editrice Vaticana: *Acta Apostolicae Sedis* 83 (1991), pp. 793-868.

__, Encyclical Letter *Redemptoris Missio* (Mission of the Redeemer), 7 December 1991: *Acta Apostolicae Sedis* 83 (1991), pp. 249-340.

__, Post-Synodal Apostolic Exhortation *Pastores Dabo Vobis* (I Will Give You Shepherds), 25 March 1992, 2nd reprint, Nairobi, Paulines Publications Africa, 1998: *Acta Apostolicae Sedis* 84 (1992), pp. 657-804.

__, Apostolic Constitution *Fidei Depositum* on the Publication of the Catechism of the Catholic Church Prepared Following the Second Vatican Ecumenical Council, 11 October 1992, Rome, Libreria Editrice Vaticana, 1992: *Acta Apostolicae Sedis* 86 (1994), pp. 113-121.

__, Letter to Families, *Nuntius* (On the Year of the Family), Rome, Vatican Press, 22 February 1994: *Acta Apostolicae Sedis* 86 (1994), pp. 868-925.

__, Apostolic Letter *Tertio Millennio Adveniente* (On Preparation for the Jubilee of the Year 2000), 10 November 1994, Boston, Pauline Books and Media, 1994: *Acta Apostolicae Sedis* 87 (1995), pp. 5-41.

__, Encyclical Letter *Evangelium Vitae* (The Gospel of Life: A Message of Hope), 25 March 1995, London, Fount, 1995: *Acta Apostolicae Sedis* 87 (1995), pp. 401-522.

__, Encyclical Letter *Ut Unum Sint* (May They Be One: On Commitment to Ecumenism), 25 May 1995, Boston, Pauline Books & Media: *Acta Apostolicae Sedis* 87 (1995), pp. 921-982.

__, Post-Synodal Apostolic Exhortation *Ecclesia in Africa* (The Church in Africa), 14 September 1995, Nairobi, Pauilines Publications Africa, 1995: *Acta Apostolicae Sedis* 88 (1996), pp. 5-82.

__, Encyclical Letter *Fides et Ratio* (On the Relationship Between Faith and Reason), 14 September 1998, Vatican City, Libreria Editrice Vaticana, 1998: *Acta Apostolicae Sedis* 91 (1999), pp. 5-88.

__, Apostolic Letter, *Novo Millennio Ineunte* (At the Close of the Great Jubilee of the Year 2000), 6 January 2001, Vatican City, Libreria Editrice Vaticana, 2001: *Acta Apostolicae Sedis* 93 (2001), pp. 266-309.

__, Encyclical Letter *Ecclesia de Eucharistia* (The Eucharist: Life of the Church), 17 April 2003, 1st reprint, Nairobi, Paulines Publications Africa, 2003: *Acta Apostolicae Sedis* 95 (2003), pp. 433-475.

__, Post-Synodal Apostolic Exhortation *Pastores Gregis* (Bishops: Shepherds of the Lord's Flock), 15 October 2003, Nairobi, Paulines Publications Africa, 2003: *Acta Apostolicae Sedis* 96 (2004), pp. 825-924.

PAUL VI, Encyclical Letter *Ecclesiam Suam* (Paths of the Church), 6 August 1964, Boston, Paulines Books & Media: *Acta Apostolicae Sedis* 56 (1964), pp. 609-659.

__, Motu Proprio *Africae Terrarum* (The Land of Africa), 29 October 1967: *Acta Apostolicae Sedis* 59 (1967), pp. 1073-1097.

__, Motu Proprio *The Credo* of the People of God *Solemni hac Liturgia,* 30 June 1968, in FLANNERY, Austin (ed.), *Vatican Council II*, Vol. 2: *More Post-Conciliar Documents*, New York, Costello Publishing Company, 1982, pp. 387-396: *Acta Apostolicae Sedis* 60 (1968), pp. 433-445.

__, *Allocution 9,* Address to the Episcopal Conference of Africa and Madagascar and to the People of Africa, Thursday, 31 July 1969: *Acta Apostolicae Sedis* 61 (1969), p. 573-578.

__, *Allocution 11,* Address to the Parliament of Uganda, Kampala, Friday, 1 August 1969: *Acta Apostolicae Sedis* 61(1969), p. 580-586.

PIUS XI, Encyclical Letter *Quadragesimo Anno* (On Social Reconstruction), 15 May 1931, Vatican Polyglot English translation, Boston, St. Paul Editions: *Acta Apostolicae Sedis* 23 (1931), pp. 991-1024.

PIUS XII, Encyclical Letter *Mystici Corporis* (On the Mystical Body of Christ and Our Union in It with Christ), 29 June 1943, Boston, St. Paul Books & Media, 1943: *Acta Apostolicae Sedis* 35 (1943), pp. 193-249.

(c) Pontifical Congregations, Commissions, Councils

CONGREGATION FOR THE EVANGELISATION OF PEOPLES, *Pastoral Guide for Diocesan Priests in Churches Dependent on the Congregation for the Evangelization of Peoples*, Vatican City, Libreia Editrice Vaticana, 1989.

__, *Guide for Catechists: Document of Vocational, Formative and Promotional Orientation of Catechists in the Territories Dependent on the Congre-*

gation for the Evangelisation of Peoples, Vatican City, Libreria Editrice Vaticana, 1993.

CONGREGATION FOR THE CLERGY, *General Directory for Catechesis*, Nairobi, Paulines Publications Africa, 1988.

INTERNATIONAL THEOLOGICAL COMMISSION, *Memory and Reconciliation: The Church and the Faults of the Past* (December 1999) – and – *Homily of John Paul II: Mass for the day of Pardon* (March 12, 2000), Boston, Pauline Books & Media, 2000.

PONTIFICAL COUNCIL FOR CULTURE, *Towards a Pastoral Approach to Culture*, Nairobi, Paulines Publications Africa, 1999.

PONTIFICAL COUNCIL FOR JUSTICE AND PEACE, *Compendium of the Social Doctrine of the Church*, Nairobi, Paulines Publications Africa, 2004.

(d) Synods of Bishops

EXTRAORDINARY SYNOD OF BISHOPS (Rome, 1985), *A Message to the People of God* and *The Final Report*, Washington, National Conference of Catholic Bishops (USA), 1986.

SYNOD OF BISHOPS, *Convenientes ex Universo* (*Justice in the World*), 30 November 1971, in FLANNERY, Austin (ed.), *Vatican Council II – Vatican Collection*, Vol. 2: *More Postconciliar Documents*, Northport, New York, Costello Publishing Company, pp. 696-710.

__, Special Assembly for Africa, *The Church in Africa and Her Evangelizing Mission Towards the Year 2000: Instrumentum Laboris*, Vatican City, General Secretariat of the Synod of Bishops and Libreria Editrice Vaticana, 1993.

__, II Special Assembly for Africa, *Lineamenta: The Church in Africa in Service to Reconciliation, Justice and Peace*, Nairobi, Paulines Publications Africa, 2006.

(e) Regional and Local Church

AMECEA BISHOPS, Record of the AMECEA Study Conference held at St. Thomas Aquinas Seminary – The AMECEA's 5th Triennial Meeting, Nairobi, 14-21 December 1973, *Planning for the Church in Eastern Africa in the 1980's*, published in *African Ecclesial Review*, Vol. 16, Nos. 1 & 2, 1974, pp. 5-256.

__, AMECEA Plenary, *Building Christian Communities in Eastern Africa*, published in *African Ecclesial Review*, Vol. 18, No. 5, 1976.

__, *AMECEA Plenary Study Conference*, Zomba, Malawi, 13th – 16th August 1979, published in *African Ecclesial Review*, Vol. 21, No. 5, October 1979, 257-316.

ARUA CATHOLIC DIOCESE, *Acts of the First Synod in Arua Diocese*, Kisubi, Marianum Press, 1990.

__, *Policy Book: A Pastoral Guide for Christian Communities*, 3rd printing, Arua, Arua Diocese Publications, 2000.

CATHOLIC BISHOPS OF UGANDA, Pastoral Letter *Shaping Our National Destiny*, Kisubi, Marianum Press, 1962.

__, Pastoral Letter *Celebrating Our Ancestors in the Faith – The Martyrs: Models of Christian Commitment*, Kampala, St. Paul Publications, 1984.

__, Pastoral Letter *With a New Heart and a New Spirit*, Kampala, St. Paul Publications, 1986.

__, Pastoral Letter *Let Your Light Shine*, Kisubi, Marianum Press, 1992.

__, Pastoral Letter *Be My Witnesses: The Vocation and Mission of Women in the Church and in Society Today*, Kisubi, Marianum Press, 1996.

__, Pastoral Letter *Test the Spirits: Cults, Sects and "Religious" Groups*, Kisubi, Marianum Press, 2000.

NEBBI CATHOLIC DIOCESE, *Acts of the First Diocesan Synod of Nebbi Catholic Diocese: Angal, 13th January – 24th January 2003*, Nebbi, Catholic Press, 2003.

SYMPOSIUM OF THE EPISCOPAL CONFERENCE OF AFRICA AND MADAGASCAR, The 12th Assembly of the Symposium Episcopal Conferences of Africa and Madagascar (SECAM), *Christ Our Peace: Church as Family of God, Place and Sacrament of Reconciliation, Forgiveness and Peace in Africa*, 30th September - 9th October, Rome, SECAM, 2000.

THE PONTIFICAL SOCIETY OF MISSIONARY HOLY CHILDHOOD – UGANDA, *The Missionary Society of St. Kizito: A Missionary Handbook for Children and Animators*, Kampala, The National Office of Missionary Holy Childhood, 2003.

TORORO ARCHDIOCESE, *From the Desk of the Archbishop, Archdiocese of Tororo*, "To the Clergy, Religious and Laity of the Archdiocese of Tororo," D/C/08, August 2008, pp. 1-2.

TSCHANG, IN-NAM, Paul, *Letter to All Catholic Bishops and Religious Superiors in Uganda,* File, N. 650/08, Kampala, Apostolic Nunciature in Uganda, 8 July 2008.

Dictionaries

BURKE, John (Compiler), *A Dictionary of Canon Law*, Revised edition, Ibadan City, Society of African Missions, 2006.

GOOD, Carter V. (ed.), *Dictionary of Education*, 2nd edition, New York, McGraw-Hill Book Company, 1959.

MCKENZIE John L., *Dictionary of the Bible*, New York, Macmillan Publishing Company, 1965.

VERBRUGGE Verlyn D. (ed.), *The NIV Theological Dictionary of the New Testament Words*, Michigan, Zondervan Publishing House Grand Rapids, 2000.

Books

ABBOT, Walter M. and GALLAGHER, Joseph (eds.), *The Documents of Vatican II*, London, Geoffrey Chapman, 1967.

ACCATTOLI, Luigi, *When a Pope Asks Forgiveness: The Mea Culpa's of John Paul II*, translated by Jordan Aumann, Boston, Pauline Books & Media, 1998.

ADLER, Mortimer J. (ed.), *Great Books of the Western World*, Vol. 44: TOCQUEVILLE, *Democracy in America*, translated by George Lawrence, Chicago, Encyclopedia Britannica, Inc., 2nd edition, Ninth Printing, 2007.

AFRICA FAITH & JUSTICE NETWORK, *The African Synod: Documents, Reflections, Perspectives*, Maryknoll, Orbis Books, 1996.

AGOSTONI, Tarcisio, *The Comboni Missionaries: An Outline History 1867-1997*, Comboni Missionaries, Rome 2003.

ALLEN, Joseph L., *Love and Conflict: A Covenantal Model for Christian Ethics*, Nashville, Abingdon Press, 1984.

ARMES, R., *Third World Film Making and the West*, Berkeley, University of California Press, 1978.

AYISI, Eric O., *An Introduction to the Study of African Culture*, reprint, Nairobi, East African Educational Publishers, 1997.

BANKS, Robert J., *Paul's Idea of Community: The Early House Churches in Their Cultural Setting*, Peabody, Hendrickson Publishers, 2007.

BANSIKIZA, Constance, *Restoring Moral Formation in Africa*, Spearhead Number 155, Eldoret, AMECEA Gaba Publications, 2001.

BASIL of Caesarea (St.), *The Longer Rules*, translated by Sr. Monica M. Wagner, New York, Father of the Church Inc., 1950.

BEATRICE, Pier Franco, *Introduction to the Fathers of the Church*, Vicenza, Edizioni Istituto San Gaetano, 1987.

BELLAH, Robert N., MADSEN, Richard, SULLIVAN, William M., SWIDDLER, Ann and M. Steven Tipton, *Habits of the Heart: Individualism and Commitment in American Life*, Berkerly, University of California Press, 1985.

BENETOLLO P. Vincenzo Ottorino, *Morale e Societá: Principi di Etica Sociale*, Bologna, Edizioni Studio Domenicani, 1999.

BETTENSON, Henry (ed.), *The Early Church Fathers*, 11th impression, Oxford, Oxford University Press, 1991.

__, *The Later Church Fathers*, 10th impression, Oxford, Oxford University Press, 1991.

BIRCH, Bruce C. and RASMUSSEN, Larry L., *Bible and Ethics in the Christian Life*, Minneapolis, Augsburg Publishing House, 1976.

BITOLE, Kato Joseph, *Awakening the laity: Ugandan Pastoral Approach*, Spearhead Numbers 161-163, Eldoret, AMECEA Gaba Publications, 2003.

BÖCKLE, Franz, *Fundamental Moral Theology*, English translation by N. D. Smith, New York, Pueblo Publishing Company, 1980.

BOHR, David, *Catholic Moral Tradition*, Huntington, Our Sunday Visitor, Inc., 1999.

BOKENKOTTER, Thomas, *A Concise History of the Catholic Church*, revised and expanded edition, New York, Doubleday, 1990.

BROWNING, Don S., *Equality and the Family: A Fundamental, Practical Theology of Children, Mothers, and Fathers in Modern Societies*, Grand Rapids, William B. Eerdmans Publishing Company, 2007.

BÜHLMANN, Walbert, *The Coming of the Third Church: An Analysis of the Present and Future of the Church*, Maryknoll, Orbis Books, 1978.

BUJO, Bénézet, *Do We Still Need the Ten Commandments?* Kampala, St. Paul Publications, 1980.

__, *African Christian Morality at the Age of Inculturation*, Nairobi, St. Paul Publications, 1990.

__, *The Ethical Dimension of Community: The African Model and the Dialogue Between North and South*, Nairobi, Paulines Publications Africa, 1998.

__, *Foundations of an African Ethic: Beyond the Universal Claims of Western Morality*, New York, The Crtossroad Publishing Company, 2001.

__, *Plea for Change of Models for Marriage*, Nairobi, Paulines Publications Africa, 2009.

BUJO, Bénézet and ILUNGA MUYA, Juvénal (eds.), *African Theology: The Contribution of the Pioneers*, Vol. 1, Nairobi, Paulines Publications Africa, 2003.

CALLAN, Charles J., *The Epistles of St. Paul – With Introductions and Commentary,* Vol. I: *Romans, First and Second Corinthians, Galatians*, New York, Joseph F. Wagner (Inc.), 1922.

CHIOCCHETTA, Pietro, *Daniel Comboni: Papers for Evangelization of Africa*, Bologna, Editrice Missionaria Italiana, 1982.

CHUKWU, Cletus N., *Introduction to Philosophy in an African Perspective*, Eldoret, Zapf Chancery, 2002.

CLAUSEN, John A. (ed.), *Socialization and Society*, Boston, Little Brown and Company, 1968.

CLAYTON, Richard R., *The Family, Marriage, and Social Change*, Lexington, D. C. Heath and Company, 1975.

CONGAR, Yves, *Lay People in the Church: A Study for a Theology of Laity*, English translation by D. Attwater, Westminster, Newman, 1957.

__, *I Believe in the Holy Spirit*, Vol. 2: *Lord and Giver of Life*, English translation by David Smith, New York, The Seabury Press, 1983.

__, *I Believe in the Holy Spirit*, Vol. 3: *The River of Life Flows in the East and in the West*, translated by David Smith, New York, The Seabury Press, 1983.

CONN, Walter, *Christian Conversion: A Developmental Interpretation of Autonomy and Surrender*, New York, Paulist Press, 1986.

CRAZZOLARA, Joseph Pasquale, *The Lwoo – Part I – Lwoo Migrations*, Verona, Editrice Nigrizia, 1950.

__, *The Lwoo – Part II – Lwoo Traditions*, Verona, Editrice Nigrizia, 1951.

__, *The Lwoo – Part III – Clans*, Verona, Editrice Nigrizia, 1954.

DE LUBAC, Henri, *The Splendor of the Church,* English translation by Micheal Mason, San Francisco, Ignatius Press, 1956.

__, *Catholicism: Christ and the Common Destiny of Man*, English translation by Lancelot C. Sheppard and Sister Elizabeth Englund, San Francisco, Ignatius Press, 1988.

DE VAUX, Roland, *Ancient Israel: Its Life and Institutions*, translated by John McHugh, Second edition, reprint, London, Darton, Longman and Todd Ltd., 1998.

DICKSON, Kwesi A. and Ellingworth Paul (eds.), *Biblical Revelation and African Beliefs*, London, Lutterworth Press, 1972.

DINOIA, J. A., and CESSARIO, Romanus (eds.), *Veritatis Splendor and the Renewal of Moral Theology*, Princeton, Scepter Publishers, 1999.

DONCEEL, J. F., *Philosophical Anthropology*, New York, Sheed and Ward, 1967.

D'SOUZA, Anthony, *Leadership: Trilogy on Leadership and Effective Management*, 6th reprint, Nairobi, Paulines Publications Africa, 2003.

DULLES, Avery, *The Dimensions of the Church: A Postconciliar Reflection*, New York, Doubleday, 1974.

__, *The Craft of Theology: From Symbol to System*, New Expanded Edition, New York, The Crossroad Publishing Company, 2000.

__, *Models of the Church*, Expanded Edition, New York, Doubleday, 2002.

DURKHEIM, Émile, *The Elementary Forms of the Religious Life*, New York, Free Press, 1912.

FAGAN, Seán, *Does Morality Change?* Dublin, Gill & Macmillan, 1997.

FLANNERY, Austin (ed.), *Vatican Council II,* Vol. 1: *The Conciliar and Post Conciliar Documents*, New revised edition, Dublin, Dominican Publications, 1992.

__, *Vatican Council II – Vatican Collection*, Vol. 2: *More Post Conciliar Documents*, Northport, New York, Costello Publishing Company, 1982.

FLYNN, Kieran, *Communities for the Kingdom: A Handbook for Small Christian Community Leaders*, Spearhead Nos. 181-182, Eldoret, AMECEA Gaba Publications, 2007.

GEERTZ, Clifford, *The Interpretation of Cultures*, New York, Basic Books, 1973.

GEYER, Francis Xaver, *Durch Sand, Sumpf und Wald: Missionsreisen in Zentral-Afrika*, Freiburg i. Br., Herdersche Verlagshandlung, 1914.

GERKIN, Charles V., *Widening the Horizons: Pastoral Responses to a Fragmented Society*, Philadelphia, The Westminster Press, 1986.

GIARDINI, Fabio, *Counseling: Humanistic and Christian*, Rome, Millennium, 1997.

GIBBONS, William J., *et al.* (eds.), *Encyclical of Pope John XXIII, Mater et Magistra: Christianity and Social Progress*, Study Club Edition, Glen Rock, Paulist Press, 1961.

GILLI, Aldo, *Daniel Comboni: The Man and His Message*, Bologna, EMI, 1980.

GIUSSANI, Luigi, *Why the Church?* Montreal, McGill-Queen's University, 2001.

GONZÁLEZ, Justo L., *Acts: The Gospel of the Spirit*, Marknoll, Orbis Books, 2001.

GREMILLION, Joseph, *The Gospel of Peace and Justice: Catholic Social Teaching since Pope John*, Maryknoll, Orbis Books, 1976.

GRISEZ, Germain and SHAW, Russell, *Beyond the New Morality: The Responsibility of Freedom*, 3rd edition, Notre Dame, University of Notre Dame Press, 1988.

__, *Fulfillment in Christ: A Summary of Christian Moral Principles*, Notre Dame, University of Notre Dame Press, 1991.

GRISEZ, Germain, *The Way of the Lord Jesus,* Vol. 1*: Christian Moral Principles*, Quincy, Franciscan Press, 1997.

GRUNLAN, Stephen A. and MAYERS Marvin K., *Cultural Anthropology: A Christian Perspective*, 2nd edition, Grand Rapids, Michigan, Zondervan Publishing House, 1988.

GULA, Richard M., *Reason Informed by Faith: Foundations of Catholic Morality*, New York, Paulist Press, 1989.

HÄRING, Bernard, *Manipulation: Ethical Boundaries of Medical, Behavioural & Genetic Manipulation*, Slough, St. Paul Publications, 1975.

__, *Free and Faithful in Christ: Moral Theology for Priests and Laity*, Vol. 1: *General Moral Theology*, reprint, Slough, St. Paul Publications, 1985.

__, *Evangelization Today*, rev. ed., Slough, St. Paul Publications, 1990.

HAPPEL, Stephen and WALTER, James J., *Conversion and Discipleship: A Catholic Foundation for Ethics and Doctrine*, Philadelphia, Fortress Press, 1986.

HARRINGTON, Donal, *What is Morality? The Light through Different Windows*, Dublin, The Columba Press, 1996.

HEALEY, Joseph G. and HINTON, Jeanne (eds.), *Small Christian Communities Today: Capturing the New Moment*, Nairobi, Paulines Publications Africa, 2006.

JASSY, Marie-France Perrin, *Leadership*, Spearhead Nos. 153-154, Eldoret, AMECEA Gaba Publications, 1st reprint, 2001.

JALOBO, Jacan Ngomlokojo, *Rituals of Religious Worship among the Traditional Alur*, Gulu, Catholic Press, 1985.

JEDIN, Hubert (ed.), *History of the Church*, vol. X: *The Church in the Modern Age*, translated by Anselm Biggs, London, Burns & Oates, 1981.

JOHN PAUL II (Pope), *Crossing the Threshold of Hope*, 5 October 1994, edited by Vittorio Messori, New York, Alfred A. Knopf, Inc., 1995.

KATONGOLE, Emmanuel M., *A Future for Africa: Critical Essays in Christian Social Imagination*, Scranton, The University of Scranton Press, 2005.

KASPER, Walter Cardinal, *Leadership in the Church: How Traditional Roles Can Serve the Christian Community Today*, translated by Brian McNeil, New York, The Crossroad Publishing Company, 2003.

KEATING, James (ed.), *Moral Theology: New Directions and Fundamental Issues*, New York, Paulist Press, 2004.

KIRISWA, Benjamin, *Pastoral Counselling: An Integrated Model*, Spearhead Nos. 156-157, Eldoret, AMECEA Gaba Publications, 2002.

KOHLBERG, Lawrence, *The Philosophy of Moral Development*, Volume 1: *Essays on Moral Development*, San Francisco, Harper and Row, 1981.

LACUGNA, Catherine Mowry, *God for Us: The Trinity and Christian Life*, New York, Harper San Francisco, 1993.

LOBO, George V., *Moral Theology Today: Christian Living According to Vatican II*, Bangalore, Theological Publications in India, 1999.

MACINTYRE, Alasdair, *After Virtue*, Notre Dame, Indiana, University of Notre Dame Press, 2008.

MAGESA, Laurenti, *African Religion: The moral Tradition of Abundant Life*, Nairobi, Paulines Publications Africa, 1998.

MAGUIRE, Daniel C., *The Moral Choice*, Garden City, Doubleday and Company, Inc., 1978.

MCBRIDE, Alfred, *Images of Christ: Ten Invitations to Intimacy*, Cincinnati, St. Anthony Messenger Press, 1993.

MCBRIEN, Richard P., *Catholicism: Study Edition*, New York, HarperSanFrancisco, 1981.

MCMANNERS, John (ed.), *The Oxford Illustrated History of Christianity*, Oxford, Oxford University Press, 1992.

MBITI, John Samuel, *African Religions and Philosophy*, Oxford, Heinemann, 2006.

__, *Introduction to African Religion*, 2nd edition, Nairobi, East African Educational Publishers, 2003.

MINEAR, Paul, *Images of the Church in the New Testament*, Philadelphia, Westminster Press, 1960.

MOLTMANN, Jürgen, *The Church in the Power of the Spirit: A Contribution to Messianic Ecclesiology*, London, SCM Press Ltd., 1998.

MUGO, E., *African Response to Western Christian Religion*, Nairobi, East African Literature Bureau, 1975.

MUGAMBI, Jesse N. K. and MAGESA, Laurenti (eds.), *The Church in African Christianity: Innovative Essays in Ecclesiology*, Nairobi, Initiatives Publishers, 1990.

MYERS, David G., *Social Psychology*, Boston, McGraw-Hill, 2008.

NAMWERA, Leonard, et al. (eds.), *Towards African Christian Liberation* (CHIEA Extension Programme, 1987-1988), Nairobi, St. Paul Publications Africa, 1990.

NIEBUHR, H. Richard, *The Responsible Self: An Essay in Christian Moral Philosophy*, New York, Harper & Row, 1963.

NISBET, Robert, *Prejudices: A Philosophical Dictionary*, Cambridge, Harvard University Press, 1982.

NOONAN, John P., *General and Special Ethics*, Chicago, Loyola University Press, 1947.

NKAFU, Nkemkia Martin, *African Vitalogy: A Step Forward in African Thinking*, Nairobi, Paulines Publications Africa, 1999.

O'CONNELL, Timothy E., *Principles for a Catholic Morality*, New York, Harper San Francisco, 1990.

OROBATOR, Agbonkhianmeghe E., *Theology Brewed in an African Pot: An Introduction to Christian Doctrine from an African Perspective*, Nairobi, Paulines Publications Africa, 2008.

OSABUTEU-AGUEDZE, Isaac D., *The Principles Underlying the African Religion and Philosophy*, Nairobi, Maillu Publishing House, 2002.

PIEPER, Joseph, *Faith, Hope, Love*, San Francisco, Ignatius Press, 1997.

PINCKAERS, Servais, *The Sources of Christian Ethics*, Edinburgh, T & T Clark, 1995.

PLATO, *Republic*, translated by Robin Waterfield, Oxford, Oxford University Press, 1993.

PRIOR, Anselm, *Towards a Community Church*, Gemiston, Lumko Publications, 1991.

__, (ed.), *Towards a Community Church*, 2nd edition, *The Training for Ministries Series*, Nr. 28T, Natal, LUMKO Publications, 1997.

QUINN, John R., *The Reform of the Papacy: The Costly Call to Christian Unity*, New York, The Crossroad Publishing Company, 1999.

RADICE, Betty (ed.), *Early Christian Writings: The Apostolic Fathers*, translated by Maxwell Staniforth, revised by Andrew Louth, reprint, London, Penguin Classics, 1987.

RATZINGER, Joseph Cardinal, *Called to Communion: Understanding the Church Today*, translated by Adrian Walter, San Francisco, Ignatius Press, 1996.

RICHARDSON, Cyril C., *Early Christian Fathers*, New York, Touchstone, 1996.

ROTELLE, John E. (ed.), *The Works of Saint Augustine: A Translation for the 21st Century*, translation and notes by Edmund Hill, Brooklyn, New City Press, 1997.

RWIZA, Richard N., *Formation of Christian Conscience in Modern Africa*, Nairobi, Paulines Publications Africa, 2001.

RYAN, Patrick (ed.), *New Strategies for a New Evangelization in Africa*, Nairobi, Paulines Publications Africa, 2002.

SANNA, Ignazio, *L'Antropologia Cristiana tra Modernità e Postmodernità*, Brescia, Queriniana, 2001.

SARPONG, Peter K., *Dear Nana: Letters to My Ancestor*, Takoradi-Ghana, Franciscan Publications, 1998.

SCHAFF, Philip (ed.), *A Select Library of the Christian Church: Nicene and Post-Nicene Fathers*, First Series, Vol. 1: *The Confessions and Letters of St. Augustine, With a Sketch of His Life and Work*, First Series, 4th printing, Peabody, Hendrickson Publishers, 2004.

__, *A Select Library of the Christian Church: Nicene and Post-Nicene Fathers*, First Series, Vol. 2: *Augustine: City of God, Christian Doctrine*, 4th printing, Peabody, Hendrickson Publishers, 2004.

__, *A Select Library of the Christian Church: Nicene and Post-Nicene Fathers*, First Series, Vol. 3: *Augustine: On the Holy Trinity, Doctrinal Treatises, Moral Treatises*, 4th printing, Peabody, Hendrickson Publishers, 2004.

__, *A Select Library of the Christian Church: Nicene and Post-Nicene Fathers*, First Series, Vol. 4: *Augustine: The Writings Against the Manichaeans, and Against the Donatists*, 4th printing, Peabody, Hendrickson Publishers, 2004.

__, *A Select Library of the Christian Church: Nicene and Post-Nicene Fathers*, First Series, Vol. 6: *Augustine: Sermon on the Mount, Harmony of the Gospels*, 4th printing, Peabody, Hendrickson Publishers, 2004.

__, *A Select Library of the Christian Church: Nicene and Post-Nicene Fathers*, First Series, Vol. 7: *Augustine: Homilies on the Gospel of John, Soliloquies*, 4th printing, Peabody, Hendrickson Publishers, 2004.

__, *A Select Library of the Christian Church: Nicene and Post-Nicene Fathers*, First Series, Vol. 8: *Augustine: Expositions on the Book of Psalms*, 4th printing, Peabody, Hendrickson Publishers, 2004.

__, *A Select Library of the Christian Church: Nicene and Post-Nicene Fathers*, First Series, Vol. 9: *Chrysostom: On the Priesthood, Ascetic Treatises, Select Homilies and Letters, Homilies on Statutes*, 4th printing, Peabody, Hendrickson Publishers, 2004.

__, *A Select Library of the Christian Church: Nicene and Post-Nicene Fathers*, First Series, Vol. 10: *Chrysostom: Homilies on the Gospel of Mathew*, 4th printing, Peabody, Hendrickson Publishers, 2004.

__, *A Select Library of the Christian Church: Nicene and Post-Nicene Fathers*, First Series, Vol. 11: *Chrysostom: Homilies on the Acts of the Apostles and the Epistle to the Romans*, 4th printing, Peabody, Hendrickson Publishers, 2004.

__, *A Select Library of the Christian Church: Nicene and Post-Nicene Fathers*, First Series, Vol. 12: *Chrysostom: Homilies on First and Second Corinthians*, 4th printing, Peabody, Hendrickson Publishers, 2004.

__, *A Select Library of the Christian Church: Nicene and Post-Nicene Fathers*, First Series, Vol. 13: *Chrysostom: Homilies on Galatians, Ephesians, Philippians, Colossians, Thessalonians, Timiothy, Titus, and Philemon*, 4th printing, Peabody, Hendrickson Publishers, 2004.

__, *A Select Library of the Christian Church: Nicene and Post-Nicene Fathers*, First Series, Vol. 14: *Chrysostom: Homilies on the Gospel of Saint John and then Epistle to the Hebrews*, 4th printing, Peabody, Hendrickson Publishers, 2004.

__, *A Select Library of the Christian Church: Nicene and Post-Nicene Fathers*, Second Series, Vol. 7: *St. Cyril of Jerusalem and St. Gregory Nazianzen*, Grand Rapids, William B. Eerdmans Publishing Company, 1989.

SCIMECCA, Joseph A., *Society and Freedom: An Introduction to Humanist Sociology*, 2nd edition, Chicago, Nelson-Hall Publishers, 1995.

SCHINDLER, Thomas F., *Ethics: The Social Dimension – Individualism and the Catholic Tradition*, Wilmington, Michael Glazier, 1989.

SCHREITER, Robert J. (ed.), *Faces of Jesus in Africa*, 8th printing, Maryknoll, Orbis Books, 2002.

SHORTER, Aylward and KATAZA, Eugene (eds.), *Missionaries to Yourselves: African Catechists Today*, London, Geoffrey Chapman, 1972.

SHORTER, Aylward, *African Christian Theology: Adaptation or Inculturation?* Maryknoll, Orbis Books, 1977.

__, *African Culture, an Overview: Social-Cultural Anthropology*, Nairobi, Paulines Publications Africa, 1998.

SNYDER, Howard A., *Models of the Kingdom*, Nashville, Abingdon Press, 1991.

SOCIAS, James P. (Compiler), *Priesthood in the Third Millennium: Addresses of Pope John Paul II 1993*, Princeton, Scepter Publishers, 1994.

SOCCIO, Douglas J., *Archetypes of Wisdom: An Introduction to Philosophy*, Belmont, Wadsworth Publishing Company, 1995.

SOFIELD, Loughlan, HAMMETT, Rosine and JULIANO, Carroll, *Building Community: Christian, Caring, Vital*, Notre Dame, Ave Maria Press, 1998.

SOUTHALL, Aidan William, *Alur Society: A Study in Process and Types of Domination*, Nairobi, Oxford University Press, 1953.

SPIAZZI, Raimondo, *Principi di Etica Sociale*, Bologna, Edizioni Studio Domenicani, 1990.

SULLIVAN, Francis A., *The Church We Believe In: One, Holy, Catholic and Apostolic*, New York, Paulist Press, 1988.

TANNER, Norman P. (ed.), *Decrees of the Ecumenical Councils*, Vol. 2: *Nicea I – Lateran V*, London, Sheed & Ward, 1990.

__, *Decrees of the Ecumenical Coucils*, Vol. 2: *Trent – Vatican II*, London, Sheed & Ward Limited, 1990.

TEKLEMARIAN, Amanuel A., and JUMBA AKALA, Winston (eds.), *Effective Schools for 21st Century in Africa*, Nairobi, CUEA Press, 2011.

TEMPELS, Placide, *Bantu Philosophy*, English edition from the French Version, *La Philosophie Bantoue* (1945), translated by A. Rubbens, Paris, Présence Africaine, 1959.

TIXERONT, Joseph, *A Handbook of Patrology*, English edition, authorized translation by S. A. Raemers, based upon the Fourth French edition, St. Louis, MO, B. Herder Book Co., 1920.

TYLOR, Edward Burnett, *Primitive Culture: Researches into the Development of Mythology, Philosophy, Religion, Art, and Custom,* London, John Murray, 1891.

UZUKWU, Elochukwu E., *A Listening Church: Autonomy and Communion in African Churches*, Maryknoll, Orbis Books, Maryknoll, 1996.

WADDINGTON, C. H., *The Ethical Machine*, The University of Chicago Press, Phoenix Book, 1967.

WALIGGO, John Mary, *Struggle for Equality: Women and Empowerment in Uganda*, Spearhead Numbers 158-160, Eldoret, AMECEA Gaba Publications, 2002.

WALIGGO John Mary, CROLLIUS, Ary Roest, NKÉRAMIHIGO, Théoneste, MUTISO-MBINDA, John, *Inculturation: Its Meaning and Urgency*, Kampala, St. Paul Publications Africa, 1986.

WIJSEN, Frans, HENRIOT Peter, MEJÍA Rodrigo (eds.), *The Pastoral Cycle Revisited: A Critical Quest for Truth and Transformation*, Nairobi, Paulines Publications Africa, 2006.

WONG, David, *Notes on Evangelising the Youth Today*, Hawaii, Maui Haggai Institute, 2000.

WORLD COUNCIL OF CHURCHES, The Bucharest Conference of the World Council of Churches on "Science and Technology for Human Development," June 1974, *Anticipation* 19, Geneva, November 1974.

ZWEIG, Paul, *The Heresy of Self-Love: A Study of Subversive Individualism*, New Jersey, Princeton University Press, Princeton, 1980.

Articles

(a) Articles in Bible Commentaries

ADEYEMO, Tokunboh, "Discipleship," in ADEYEMO, Tokunboh (ed.), *Africa Bible Commentary*, Nairobi, WordAlive Publishers, 2006, p. 1249.

ASSOHOTO, Barnabe and NGEWA, Samuel, "Commentary on the Book of Genesis," in ADEYEMO, Tokunboh (ed.), *Africa Bible Commentary*, Nairobi, WordAlive Publishers, 2006, pp. 10-84.

GRASSI, Joseph A., "The Letter to the Ephesians," in BROWN, Raymond E., FITZMYER Joseph A. and MURPHY Roland E. (eds.), *The Jerome Bibli-*

cal Commentary, Vol. 2: *The New Testament and Topical Articles*, reprint, London, Geoffrey Chapman, 1972, pp. 341-349.

FITZMYER, Joseph A., "The Letter to the Romans" in Brown, Raymond E., FITMYER, Joseph A., and MURPHY, Roland E. (eds.), *The Jerome Biblical Commentary*, Vol. 2: *The New Testament and Topical Articles*, reprint, London, Geoffrey Chapman, 1972, pp. 291-331.

KOBELSKI, Paul J., "The Letter to the Ephesians," in BROWN, Raymond E., FITZMYER Joseph A., and MURPHY, Roland E. (eds.), *The New Jerome Biblical Commentary*, Vol. 2: *The New Testament and Topical Articles*, New Jersey, Prentice Hall, 1990, pp. 883-890.

MCKENZIE, John L., "Aspects of Old Testament Thought," in BROWN Raymond E., FITZMYER, Joseph A., and MURPHY, Roland E. (eds.), *The Jerusalem Bible Commentary*, Vol. 2: *The New Testament and Topical Articles*, reprint, London, Geoffrey Chapman, 1972, pp. 734-767.

TURRO, James C., "1-2 Samuel," in Brown, Raymond E., Fitzmyer Joseph A., Murphy, Roland E. (eds.), *The Jerome Biblical Commentary*, Vol.1: *The Old Testament*, reprint, London, Geoffrey Chapman, 1972, pp. 163-178.

(b) Articles in Dictionaries

AMALORPAVADASS, D. S., "Church and Culture," in KOMONCHAK, Joseph A., COLLINS, Mary and LANE, Dermot A. (eds.), *The New Dictionary of Theology*, Dublin, Gill and Macmillan, 1990, pp. 201-206.

AMIOT, François, "Baptism," in LÉON-DUFOUR, Xavier (ed.), *Dictionary of Biblical Theology*, updated 2nd edition, reprint with revisions, Maryland, The Word Among Us Press, pp. 40-43.

BEINERT, Wolfgang, "Faith," in BEINERT, Wolfgang and SCHÜSSLER FIORENZA, Francis (eds.), *Handbook of Catholic Theology*, New York, The Crossroad Publishing Company, 2000, pp. 249-253.

BEST, Ernest, "Church," in ACHTEMEIER, Paul J. (Gen. ed.), *Harper's Bible Dictionary*, Bangalore, Theological Publications in India, 2002, pp. 168-170.

CHILDRESS, James F., "Autonomy," in MACQUARRIE, John and CHILDRESS, James (eds.), *A New Dictionary of Christian Ethics*, 6th impression, London, SCM Press Ltd., 1997, pp. 51-53.

CLARK, Henry, "Culture," in MACQUARRIE, John and CHILDRESS, James (eds.), *A New Dictionary of Christian Ethics*, 6th impression, London, SCM Press Ltd., 1997, pp. 140-142.

__, "Community," in MACQUARRIE, John and CHILDRESS, James (eds.), *A New Dictionary of Christian Ethics*, London, SCM Press Ltd., 1997, pp. 105-106.

GEORGEN, Donald J., "Catholicity," in KOMONCHAK Joseph A., COLLINS Mary and LANE Dermot A. (eds.), *New Dictionary of Theology*, Dublin, Gill and Macmillan, 1990, pp. 172-174.

GRUNDY, Robert H., "Human Being," in ACHTEMEIER, Paul J. (Gen. ed.), *Harper's Bible Dictionary*, Bangalore, Theological Publications in India, 2002, p. 411.

HARRINGTON, Wilfrid, "Charism," in KOMONCHAK Joseph A., COLLINS Mary and LANE Dermot A. (eds.), *New Dictionary of Theology*, Dublin, Gill and Macmillan, 1990, pp. 180-183.

HELLWIG, Monica K., "Catholicism," in KOMONCHAK Joseph A., COLLINS Mary and LANE Dermot A. (eds.), *New Dictionary of Theology*, Dublin, Gill and Macmillan, 1990, pp. 167-172.

JONSEN, Albert R., "Responsibility," in MACQUARRIE, John and CHILDRESS, James (eds.), *A New Dictionary of Christian Ethics*, Sixth impression, London, SCM Press Ltd., 1997, pp. 545-549.

LOVIN, Robin W., "Ethos," in MAQUARRIE, John and CHILDRESS, James (eds.), *A New Dictionary of Christian Ethics*, p. 208.

MATHALER, Berard L., "Creeds," in KOMONCHAK, Joseph A., Collins Mary and Lane Dermot A. (eds.), *The New Dictionary of Theology*, Dublin, Gill and Macmillan, 1990.

MUELDER, Walter G., "Personalism," in MACQUARRIE, John and CHILDRESS, James (eds.), *A New Dictionary of Christian Ethics*, 6th impression, London, SCM Press Ltd., 1997, p. 469.

O'DONNEL, John, "Faith," in KOMONCHAK, A. Joseph, COLLINS, Mary and LANE Dermot S. (eds.), *The New Dictionary of Theology*, Dublin, Gill and Macmillan, 1990, pp. 375-386.

O'MEARA, Thomas F., "Ministry" in KOMONCHAK, Joseph A., Collins Mary and Lane Dermot A. (eds.), *The New Dictionary of Theology*, Dublin, Gill and Macmillan, 1990, pp. 657-661.

PORTEOUS, N. W., "Soul," in BUTTRICK, George Arthur (ed.), *The Interpreter's Dictionary of the Bible: An Illustrated Encyclopedia,* Vol. 4: R – Z, 13th printing, Nashville, Abingdon Press, 1982, p. 428-429.

SMALLEY, William A., "Culture," in MACQUARRIE, John and CHILDRESS, James (eds.), *A New Dictionary of Christian Ethics*, London, SCM Press, 1997, pp. 142-143.

__, "Custom," in MACQUARRIE, John and CHILDRESS, James (eds.), *A New Dictionary of Christian Ethics*, London, SCM Press, 1997, pp. 142-143.

STACKHOUSE, Max A., "Sect," in MACQUARRIE, John and CHILDRESS, James (eds.), *A New Dictionary of Christian Ethics*, London, SCM Press Ltd., 1997, pp. 566-567.

STOUT, Jeffrey, "Tradition in Ethics," in MACQUARRIE, John and CHILDRESS, James (eds.), *A New Dictionary of Christian Ethics*, London, SCM Press Ltd., 1997, pp. 629-631.

(c) Articles in Encyclopedic Works

ALLAN, Davina, "Values," in MCLEISH, Kenneth (ed.), *Key Ideas in Human Thought*, New York, Facts on File, Inc., 1993, pp. 769-770.

__, "Church," in MCLEISH, Kenneth (ed.), *Key Ideas in Human Thought*, New York, Facts on File, Inc., 1993, p. 123.

BEINERT, Wolfgang, "Faith," in BEINERT Wolfgang and SCHÜSSLER, Fiorenza Francis (eds.), *Handbook of Catholic Theology*, New York, The Crossroad Publishing Company, 2000, pp. 249-253.

BIRKEY, A. J., "Ambition," in BROMILEY, Geoffrey W. (Gen. ed.), *The International Standard Bible Encyclopedia*, Vol. 1, Michigan, William B. Eerdmans Publishing Company, 1989, Volume 1, p. 110.

BROMILEY, Geoffrey W., "Baptism," in BROMILEY, Geoffrey W. (Gen. ed.), *The International Standard Bible Encyclopedia*, Vol. 1, Michigan, William B. Eerdmans Publishing Company, 1989, pp. 410-415.

__, "Church," in BROMILEY, Geoffrey W. (Gen. ed.), *The International Standard Bible Encyclopedia*, Vol. 1, Michigan, William B. Eerdmans Publishing Company, 1989, pp. 693-696.

GWIN, R. A. "Selfish; Selfishness," in BROMILEY, Geoffrey W. (Gen. ed.), *The International Standard Bible Encyclopedia*, Vol. 4, 1st printing, Michigan, William B. Eerdmans Publishing Company, 1989, p. 387.

KOCH, Günter, "Sacrament," in BEINERT Wolfgang and SCHÜSSLER, Fiorenza Francis (eds.), *Handbook of Catholic Theology*, New York, The Crossroad Publishing Company, 2000, pp. 605-609.

LANGEMEYER, Georg, "Community (Relationship)" in BEINERT, Wolfgang and SCHÜSSLER, Fiorenza Francis (eds.), *Handbook of Catholic Theology*, New York, The Crossroad Publishing Company, 2000, pp. 112-113.

LEHMAN, F. K., "Kinship," in *New Catholic Encyclopedia*, Vol. 8, Washington, D.C., The Catholic University of America, 1967, p. 202-204.

LÖSER, Werner, "Church," in BEINERT, Wolfgang and SCHÜSSLER, Fiorenza Francis (eds.), *Handbook of Catholic Theology*, New York, The Crossroad Publishing Company, 2000, p. 99-101.

__, "Community (Group)" in BEINERT, Wolfgang and SCHÜSSLER, Fiorenza Francis (eds.), *Handbook of Catholic Theology*, New York, The Crossroad Publishing Company, 2000, pp. 111-112.

__, "Ministry in the Church," in BEINERT, Wolfgang and SCHÜSSLER, Fiorenza Francis (eds.), *Handbook of Catholic Theology*, New York, The Crossroad Publishing Company, 2000, pp. 479-481.

MCDONALD, L. M., "Wanton," in BROMILEY, Geoffrey W. (ed.), *The International Standard Bible Encyclopedia*, Vol. 4, 1st printing, Michigan, William B. Eerdmans Publishing Company, 1988, p. 1013.

MURPHY, F. X., "Names, Christian," in *New Catholic Encyclopedia*, Vol. 10, New York, McGraw-Hill Book Company, 1967, pp. 201-203.

ORR, James and BROMILEY, Geoffrey W. "Christianity," in BROMILEY, Geoffrey W. (ed.), *The International Standard Bible Encyclopedia,* Vol. 1, Fully Revised, Michigan, William B. Eerdmans Publishing Company, 1989, pp. 657-663.

OSBORNE, Kenan B., "Individualism," in MCBRIEN, Richard P. (Gen. ed.), *The HarperCollins Encyclopedia of Catholicism*, 1st edition, New York, HarperCollins Publishers, 1995, p. 622b.

ROBECK, C. M., "Soul," in Geoffrey W. (ed.), *The International Standard Bible Encyclopedia*, Vol. 4, Fully Revised, reprint, Michigan, William B. Eerdmans Publishing Company, 1988, pp. 587-588.

SCHLETTE, Heinz Robert, "Individualism," in RAHNER, Karl (ed.), *Encyclopedia of Theology: The Concise Sacramentum Mundi*, New York, Crossroad, 1982, pp. 700-702.

SCHILDENBERGER, Johannes, "Covenant," in Johannes B. Bauer (ed.) *Encyclopedia of Biblical Theology*, second impression, London, Sheed Ward, 1976, pp. 140-146.

SMEDES, Lewis B., "Ethics: Modern Problems," in BROMILEY, Geoffrey W. (ed.), *The International Standard Bible Encyclopedia*, Vol. 2, reprint, Michigan, William B. Eerdmans Publishing Company, 1988, pp. 190-193.

SPLETT, Jörg, "Meaning," in RAHNER, Karl (ed.), *Encyclopedia of Theology: The Concise Sacramentum Mundi*, New York, Crossroad, 1982, pp. 945b-952a.

WHITE, Leslie A., "The Concept and Components of Culture," in *The New Encyclopedia Britannica*, Vol. 16, 15th edition, Chicago, Encyclopedia Britannica, Inc., 2005, pp. 974-881.

WOOD, A. S., "Antinomism," in BROMILEY, Geoffrey W. (ed.), *The International Standard Bible Encyclopedia,* Vol. 1, Fully Revised, Michigan, William B. Eerdmans Publishing Company, 1989, pp. 141-142.

(d) Articles on Church Documents

CUNNINGHAM, Richard G., "Sacred Ministers or Clerics [cc. 232-293] – Chapter 1: The Formation of Clerics [cc. 232-264]" in John P. Beal, James A. Corriden, Thomas J. Green (eds.), *New Commentary on the Code of Canon Law*, Bangalore, Theological Publications in India, 2003, pp. 304-328.

DUNN, Beverly K., "Apostolate," in DARCY, Catherine, JOYCE, Michael, KASLYN, Robert and SULLIVAN, Margaret (eds.), *Procedural Handbook for Institutes of Consecrated Life and Societies of Apostolic Life,* Washington, D.C.: Canon Law Society of America, 2001, 167-194.

GRILLMEIER, Aloys, "Dogmatic Constitution on the Church, Chapter 1: The Mystery of the Church," Article 1, in VORGRIMLER, Herribert (ed.), *Commentary on the Documents of Vatican II*, New York, Herder and Herder, 1967, pp. 138-152.

HILL, Richard A., "The Apostolate of Institutes: Canons 673-683" in HITE, Jordan, HOLLAND, Sharon and WARD Daniel (eds.), *A Handbook on Canons 573-746: Religious Institutes, Secular Institutes, Societies of Apostolic Life*, Collegeville, Minnesota: Liturgical Press, 1985, pp. 197-220.

KENNEDY, Robert T., "Book V: The Temporary Goods of the Church [cc. 1254-1310]" in BEAL, John P., CORIDEN, James A., GREEN, Thomas J. (eds.), *New Commentary on the Code of Canon Law*, Commissioned by The Canon Law Society of America, Study Edition, Bangalore, Theological Publications in India, 2003, pp. 1450-1525.

(e) Articles in General History

FERGUSON, Everett, "John Chrysostom," in *A Lion Handbook: The History of Christianity*, Berkhamsted, Lion Publishing, 1977, pp. 191-192.

MAZRUI, Ali A., "Towards the Year 2000" in MAZRUI Ali A. and WONDJI C. (eds.), *UNESCO General History of Africa*, Vol. VIII, Oxford, James Currey Ltd., 1999, pp. 905-934.

(f) Articles in Periodicals/Journals/Bulletins

CENTIS, Felice, "The Cross at Omach," Angal, Comboni Missionaries' Diamond Pamplet, 1985.

CHIBUKO, Patrick C., "The Church and the Challenge of Individualization: An Ecumenical Reflection," in *African Ecclesial Review*, Vol. 49, Nr. 3 & 4, (September – December 2007), pp. 254-283.

KATO BITOLE, Joseph, "Evangelization in Africa: Twelve Years after the Ecclesia in Africa," in *African Ecclesial Review*, Vol. 50, Nr. 1&2 (March-June 2008), pp. 115-131.

LONEMA, Fabien, "Structures of Participation in the Parish," in *African Christian Studies*, Vol. 26, Nr. 1 (March 2010), pp. 93-118.

MAGESA, Laurenti, "Involving All in Ministry: A Challenge to the Church of the Third Millenium," in *African Ecclesial Review*, Vol. 42, Nr. 1, February/April, 2000, pp. 2-15.

MUTUKA, Tarcisius, "Africa and the Return of Priestcraft – Book Review," in *African Ecclesial Review*, Vol. 35, Nr. 6 (August 1993), pp. 256-264.

NDINGI MWANA 'A NZEKI, Raphael S., "Vocation and Formation of Priests," in *African Ecclesial Review*, Vol. 32, Nr. 1 (February 1990), pp. 17-28.

NSAMBU, Jean-Marie, "Africa Needs Feminist Leaders" in *Leadership*, Nr. 469 (March 2009), pp. 30-31.

NWAGWU, Mary Gerald, "Communion and Self-Reliance: Signs of Church as God's Family in Africa," in *African Ecclesial Review*, Vol. 42, Nr. 1&2 (2000), pp. 23-25.

NWAIGBO, Ferdinand, "*Instrumentum Laboris*: The Holy Spirit and the Sings of the Times for the Second Synod for Africa," in *African Ecclesial Review*, Vol. 51, Nr. 4 (December 2009) & Vol. 52, Nr. 1 (March 2010), pp. 598-624.

NWATU, Felix, "Africa and the Return of Priestcraft," in *African Ecclesial Review*, Vol. 35, Nr. 4 (August 1993), pp. 240-251.

OCHIENG' ONG'ONDO, Charles, "Communicative Conflicts in the Nomenclature of Evangelical Organizations," in *African Ecclesial Review*, Vol. 48, Nr. 3 (2006), pp. 157-173.

ONYANGO AWINO, James, "Towards an Analytical African Theology: The Luo Concept of God as a Case in Point," in *African Ecclesial Review*, Vol. 36, Nr. 3 (June 1994), pp. 171-180.

PFAFF, Franz, "People's Participation in Development," in AGBASIERE, Joseph Therese and ZABAJUNGU, Boniface K. (eds.), *Church Contribution to Integral Development: A New Vision*, Fourth Uganda Theological Week: African Theology in Progress, Vol. 2, Spearhead 108-109 (1989), pp. 154-166.

SANON, Anselme T., "The Church is Communion, Family, and Brotherhood," in *L'Osservatore Romano*, Weekly Edition, Nr. 17 (April 27, 1994), p. 14.

SHORTER, Aylward, "Concepts of Social Justice in Traditional Africa," in *ATR Special Topics*, published in *Pro Dialogo Bulletin* 12 (1977), pp. 32-51.

Unpublished Works

DIPIO, Dominic, "Bishop Caesar Asili: A Gift to the Universal Church – a Biography." Preface by Msgr. Pierino Madrwa, Episcopal Vicar of Moyo Vicariate, Arua Diocese, 1996.

LA SALANDRA, Tonny, "The History of the Catholic Church in West Nile," Arua, 2003.

OGULA, Paul A., "The Impact of the Church on Education in Africa," Paper Presented at The 13th Interdisciplinary Theological Session, Faculty of Theology, Nairobi, The Catholic University of Eastern Africa, 2nd - 4th March 2011.

ONGOM, Qurine K., "An Integrative Approach to Christian Spiritual Direction with Reference to the Alur of Uganda," MA/Specialized Licentiate in Spirituality, CUEA, Nairobi, July 1993.

OPIO, Lino Ricahrd, "The Annual Report of the Diocesan Pastoral Coordinator's Office of Nebbi Catholic Diocese for the Year 2006 and Proposed Plans for the Year 2007," given at Angal Pastoral Centre, 23 January 2007.

PINHEIRO, Anthony, "Bishop-Religious Relationship in the Apostolic Activities of the Diocese According to the Code of Canon Law (cc. 678 §3-683)," Doctoral Dissertation, Roma, Pontificia Universitá Lateranense, 1986.

UKWONG MAYELE, Gabriel, "The Catholic Church among the Alur of North Western Uganda: A Pastoral Analysis of the Church's Work in the Light of Vatican II." A Masters/Licentiate Thesis Submitted to the Catholic Higher Institute of Eastern Africa (CHIEA), Nairobi 1986.

Electronic Sources

ABURA, Joseph (Bishop of Karamoja Diocese, Province of the Anglican Church of Uganda), “Today’s Vices Have Been Turned Into Virtues,” in *CISA*, Issue No. 135, Wednesday, November 25, 2009, downloaded from website: http://www.cisanewsafrica.org (accessed, 26 November 2009).

AYLWARD, Shorter, *ATR Special Topics: Concepts of Social Justice in Traditional Africa,* published in *Pro Dialogo Bulletin* 12 (1977), pp. 32-51, downloaded from website: http://www.afrikaworld.netafrel/atr-socialjustice.htm (accessed, 14 August 2011).

BURNETT TYLOR, Edward, *Primitive Culture: Researches into the Development of Mythology, Philosophy, Religion, Art, and Custom,* Vol. 1, London, John Murray, 1871. Digitalised by Google, original from: The University of Michigan, 2nd edition, 30 May 2006, downloaded from website: http://books.google.co.uk/books/about/Primitive_culture.html?id=AucLAAAAIAAJ&redir_esc=y (accessed, 3 September 2011).

GULU ARCHDIOCESE, *Newsletter of the Justice and Peace Commission of the Archdiocese of Gulu*, “Justice and Peace News,” Vol. 9, Nr. 1, January 2009, Gulu_JPC_Newsletter_Jan_2009.pdf (accessed, 3 May 2010).

JOHN PAUL II, *Letter to Families*, Provided by Courtesy of Eternal Word Television Network (EWTN), downloaded from website: http://www.ewtn.com/library/papaldoc/jp2famlt.htm (accessed, 29 October 2011).

LA SALANDRA Tonny, “The History of the Catholic Church in West Nile,” downloaded from website: http://www.aruadiocese.org/history.htm file location: http:aruadiocese.org/toni_la_salandra.pdf. (accessed, 11 June 2006).

NEBBI DISTRICT ADMINISTRATION OFFICE, “State of the Environment Report 2004,” Website: http://www.nemaug.org (accessed, 13 September 2008).

MENZIES, Allan (ed.), Christian Classics Ethereal Library, ANF03, *Latin Christianity: Its Founder, Tertullian*, Edinburgh, T&T Clark, 2006, downloaded from website: http://www.ccel.org/ccel/schaff/anf03.html (accessed, 18 April 2011).

MCCLAY, Wilfred M., “Individualism” in *First Principles*, ISI Web Journal, Intercollegiate Studies Institute, Wilmington, 03/13/08, downloaded from website: http://www.firstprinciplesjournal.aspx?article=144&loc=b&type=cbtp (accessed, 11 June 2010).

O'SHEA, Donagh, "Pentecost," downloaded from website: http://www.goodnews.ie/jacobswelljoie.shtml (accessed, 16 April 2010).

REPUBLIC OF UGANDA, *Constitution of the Republic of Uganda*, Entebbe, 1995, http://en.wikisource.org/wiki/Constitution_of_the_Republic_of_Uganda (accessed, 4 November 2009).

RYAN, John Augustine, "Individualism," in *The Catholic Encyclopedia,* Vol. 7, New York, Robert Appleton Company, 1910, downloaded from website: http://www.newadvent.org/cathen/07761a.htm (accessed, 13 June 2010).

SCHAFF, Philip (ed.), *NPNF2-08, Basil: Letters and Select Works*, Christian Classics Ethereal Library, created 2003-09-28, downloaded from URL: http://www.ccel.org/schaff/npnf208.html (accessed, 19 October 2012)

__, ANF05, *Fathers of the Third Century: Hippolytus, Cyprian, Caius, Novatian, Appendix*, Christian Classics Ethereal Library, created, 2004-07-04, URL: http://www.ccel.org/ccel/schaff/anf05.toc.html (accessed, 16 October 2012).

Sources on the Special Assembly of the Synod of Bishops for Africa

SPECIAL ASSEMBLY OF THE SYNOD OF BISHOPS FOR AFRICA (1994), *Relatio Ante Disceptationem (Report Before Discussion): The Gospel, Inculturation and Dialogue*, from: http://www.ewtn.com/new_evangelization/africa/synod/relatio.htm (accessed, 12 October 2010).

Zenit: Africa Synod Propositions (2009)

SECOND SPECIAL ASSEMBLY OF THE SYNOD OF BISHOPS FOR AFRICA (2009), *Relatio Post Disceptationem (*Report After Discussion*)*, Permalink: http://www.zenit.org/article-27196?l=english Code: ZE09101404 – 2009-10-14 (accessed, 16 October 2009).

__, *Propositions 11-20*, Permalink: http://www.zenit.org/article-27354?l= english Code: ZE09102702 – 2009-10-27 (accessed, 29 October 2009).

__, *Propositions 31-40*, Permalink: http://www.zenit.org/article-27386?l= english Code: ZE09102910 – 2009-10-29 (accessed, 1 November 2009).

__, *Propositions 41-50*, Permalink: http//www.zenit.org/article-27389?l= english Code: ZE09103001 – 2009-10-30 (accessed, 2 November 2009).

__, *Propositions 51-57*, Permalink: http//www.zenit.org/article-27411?l= english Code: ZE09103001 – 2009-11-02 (accessed, 5 November 2009).

__, *Keywords at the Africa Synod*, Permalink: http//www.zenit.org/article-27411?l=english Code: ZE09101309 – 2009-10-13 (accessed, 14 October 2009).

IFECHUKWU UDORAH, Sr. Maria, "Interventions of Auditors at 12th Congregation," Permalink: http://www.zenit.org/article-27179?l=english Code: ZE09101302 – 2009-10-13, pp. 4-5 (accessed, 15 October 2009).

PANDOLFI, Barbara, "Intervention of Auditors at 12th General Congregation, 13 October 2009," Permalink: http://www.zenit.org/article-27179?l= english Code: ZE0910132, pp. 3-4 (accessed, 15 October 2009).

APPENDIX 1
Questionnaire

Introduction

I am a doctoral student of moral theology at the Catholic University of Eastern Africa (CUEA) in Nairobi, Kenya. I am carrying out a field study on the problem of individualism in the Church. I have chosen Nebbi Catholic diocese as a case study. The proposed title for this research is: *The Moral Problem Posed by Individualism in the Church: A Case Study in Nebbi Catholic Diocese, North-Western Uganda*. This study is part of the requirement for an award of the doctoral degree in theology, in the department of moral theology. This field-work is only for academic purpose. Your contribution will lead to the results just indicated; for which I am thankful to you in advance. I kindly ask you to respond to the questions below. I assure you of my utmost confidentiality for any information that you will provide.

Instruction

The first part has closed-ended questions; just tick [√] in the bracket provided. The second part has open-ended questions; write your answers to show your views.

Section One: Demographic information

Gender: Female [ ] Male [ ]
Age: 10-19 [ ] 20-29 [ ] 21-29 [ ] 30-39 [ ] 40-49 [ ] 50-59 [ ] 60 and above [ ]
Education: Nil [ ] Primary [ ] Secondary [ ] Technical [ ] College/ Technical [ ]
Occupation: Peasant [ ] Small scale business [ ] Casual worker [ ] Employed [ ] Other___
Religious Affiliation: ATR [ ] Catholic [ ] Anglican [ ] Other Christian [ ] Islam [ ] Other_____

If Catholic:
(a) Pastoral Agent: Priest [ ] Deacon [ ] Nun [ ] Brother [ ] Catechist [ ]
(b) Lay Apostolate: tick here below next to your category

Parish Pastoral Council	Pontifical Missionary Society
Catholic Action	Parents of Religious and Priests Association
Christian Family Association	Catholic Women Association
Catechists Association	Catholic Women Clubs
Youth Group	Catholic Widows Council
Choir Group	Seven Sorrows of Our Lady
Seminarian	Legion of Mary Association
Altar Servers and Crusaders	Catholic Association for Professionals of Uganda
Ex-Sister	St. Vincent de Paul
Ex-Brother	Catholic Charismatic Renewal
Ex-seminarian	Other ....

Section Two: General Questions

Our description of individualism

We understand individualism as that spirit in which one is locked in on oneself with little or no regard for relational interest and sympathy. In this spirit one behaves or does things without caring about what others might think or say or do. It makes someone insensitive to commonly held values and matters of life which bind people together. It is self-dissociation from others.

Based on the above description, you are kindly asked to give your views in response to the questions that follow. This section has two parts: (a) and (b). Answer each part as explained.

(a) Regarding Traditional Values of Relationship

Based on the tradition of your people, give your views on the following questions. You can illustrate your answer with examples.

1. How would you define individualism in your own words? That is, what other words would you use to describe individualism, or words that relate to individualism?

....
....
....

2. What are the traditional values that have shaped a communitarian lifestyle among your people?

....
....
....

3. Could you say that someone was individualistic in his or her attitude, behaviour or action? Any visible ways which showed that a person behaved or acted in a selfish manner?

....
....
....

4. How did people react to a behaviour in which someone dissociated oneself from others?

....
....
....

5. What is the influence of the society today on the traditional communitarian values? Are those values still practiced today as in the past (twenty, thirty, forty, fifty years ago)?

....
....
....

6. What seem to be causing or provoking or accentuating individualism in your community?

....
....
....

7. Can the traditional communitarian values of your people help to reverse individualism?

....
....
....

(b) Regarding Life within the Church

Based on your faith conviction, what are your responses to the following questions? You can illustrate your answer with examples from what is happening.

1. (a) Can it be said that there is individualism in Nebbi Catholic Diocese?
   (b) Do you see any expressive forms of individualism?
   Yes [ ]　　　　　　No [ ]　　　　　　Not decided [ ]

2. If yes, in what ways do you see the spirit of individualism at work in your diocese?

....

....

....

3. What are your impressions about individualism in your diocese? What are the effects?

....

....

....

4. What is causing or provoking or accentuating individualism in the diocese?

....

....

....

5. What can be done to put this right?

....

....

....

Section Three: Qualifying Questions

Part One: Factors causing, provoking, or accentuating individualism in the Church

Reason	**Rating: strength or intensity**				
	Very strong	Strong	Moderate	Negligible	**Total**
Poverty – economic hardship					
Influence from urban life					
Social encounter and mixture					
Influence of school life					
Religious formation / orientation					
Personal human rights and freedom					
Materialistic liberalism					
Influence of mass media					
Generation conflict					
Other reasons	Rating: strength or intensity				
1…New Christian denominations					
2…Weak family life					
3………………………………	…………	…….	………..	…………	**……..**

Part Two: Expressive Forms of Individualism in the Church

Expression	Rating (how strong)				
	Very strong	Strong	Moderate	Minor	Total
No transparency in communicating					
Not together in planning projects					
Not together at implementing plans					
Rivalry among individuals and groups					

Favours in appointment and placement					
Sidelining by transfer or pondered neglect					
Mishandling (diverting, swindling) funds					
Mishandling assets (diverting elsewhere)					
Using (abuse of) office for personal gains					
Telling cover-up lies					
Threats, intimidation, silencing					
Poor or no accountability					
Personal projects from common resources					
One-man decision					
Clericalism: the priest is everything					
Syncretism: anonymous, double life					
Power struggle: want to dominate					
Stand-alone behaviour					
Over-employment: one man in many offices					
Opening busy or business-like outstations					
Other	......	......	......	......	**......**

Part Three: Regarding Accountability in Church Life and Activities

Reason	**Rating (how strong)**				
	Good	Fair	Poor	Very poor	**Total**
Leaders' personal moral accountability					
Spirituality / Prayer life					

Pastoral accountability					
Administration accountability					
Project planning accountability					
Project implementation and follow-up					
Project management and follow-up					
Policy making and reviewing					
Policy implementation and follow-up					
Financial management					
Human resource management (placement)					
Physical asset management (church property)					
Strategic follow-up of implemented tasks					
Meeting: attendance and participation					
Communication: conveying information					

Part Four: Regarding Relationship in the Church

Description	**Rating: how strong**				
	Good	Fair	Poor	Very poor	**Total**
Men towards women					
Women towards men					
Adults towards youth					
Youth towards adults					
Inter-group relationships					
Leader towards members					
Members towards leader					

Community, Groups towards catechists					
Groups towards priests					
Catechists towards community					
Catechists towards priests					
Priests among themselves					
Priests towards parish council					
Priests towards laity, groups					
Priests towards religious					
Priests towards seminarians					
Priests towards aspirants					
Religious towards priests					
Religious towards the community					
Religious among themselves					
Religious towards catechists					
Other................................	......	......	......	......	......

Appendix 2

General Questions for Oral Interviews

(1) Could we say that there is individualism to be found in Nebbi Catholic Diocese?
(2) Can the reality of individualism in the diocese be verified?
(3) How does individualism affect the internal life of the Church?
(4) How does individualism affect the Church's mission of evangelisation?
(5) What image does individualism portray of the Church in the contingent society?
(6) What might be causing, or provoking, or accentuating individualism in the diocese?
(8) Can this problem be reversed or overcome?
(9) What could be done in response to this problem?
(a) Can traditional Alur communitarian values help to reverse individualism in the diocese?
(b) Can Christian communitarian values help to reverse individualism in the diocese?

Appendix 3

List of Informants Interviewed in the Months of May-July 2008 (Name, Status, Place, Date)

1. Adaka Alba, Student Catechist, Angal Catechetical Centre, 26th June.
2. Adubango Ernest, Field Assistant, night study, Angal trading Centre, 13th-14th July.
3. Adubango George, School Teacher, Nyaravur Primary School, 28th June.
4. Aguda Vincent, Catechist Instructor, Angal Catechist Centre, 26th June.
5. Agwokotho Alfred, Diocesan Priest, Paidha Parish, 6th June.
6. Akelo Carolina, Elderly Mother, Panyimur Clan, 4th July.
7. Akina Donald, School Teacher, Parombo Primary School, 24th May.
8. Alicega Richard, School Teacher, Parombo Secondary School, 24th May.
9. Amandu John, Missionary Priest, Apostles of Jesus, Urusi Parish, 2nd June.
10. Ani-Rwoth Beatrice, Student Catechist, Angal Catechetical Centre, 26th June.
11. Ani-Rwoth Paula, School Teacher, Paidha Demostration Teachers' College, 6th June.
12. Anwangkani Charles, Diocesan Priest, Rhino-Camp Parish, 30th May.
13. Anyonga Stella, Secondary School student, Field Assistant, night study, Nyaravur Trading Centre, 10th July.
14. Arac Betty, interviewed with 10 other women in a group, Nyaravur, 28th May.
15. Atimango Lilian, Student Catechist, Angal Catechetical Centre, 26th June.
16. Atimango Margaret, Sister (Religious), Parombo, 10th May.
17. Atimango Mary, Sister (Religious), Parombo, 10th May.
18. Ayela David, Field Assistant, night study, Nebbi Trading Centre, 9th July.
19. Ayiocan Zita, Sister (Religious), Parombo, 10th May.
20. Bayo Abele, Student Catechist, Angal Catechetical Centre, Angal, 26th June.
21. Candia Stephen, School Teacher, Parombo Secondary School, Parombo, 24th May.

22. Centis Felice, Comboni Missionary Priest, Angal, 25th May.
23. Cwinya-ai Atya Richard, Civil Servant, Nyaravur, 26th May.
24. Fwathum Saveria, Sister (Religious), Pakwach, 4th June.
25. Jalbonyo Lemisio, Zone Pastoral Council Member, Padel, 28th June.
26. Jupalwonga William, Diocesan Preist, Parombo, 24th June.
27. Kareo Nataline, Sister, Paidha, 6th June.
28. Kertho William, School Teacher, Padel Primary School, Padel, 28th May.
29. Kwawun Nicholas, Diocesan Priest, Nyapea, 7th June.
30. Lakwonyero Alfred, (Dr., Human Resource Management), AFARD Director, Nebbi, 23rd May.
31. Lemb-Pacu Aventi, Member of Catholic Women Association, Parombo, 28 May.
32. Luluga Martin, Bishop of Nebbi Catholic Diocese, Nebbi, 27th May; 23rd June.
33. Mananu Dominico, Mbaru Clan Elder, Angal, 27th May.
34. Mananu Rufino, Padel Zone Pastoral Council member, Padel, 26th June.
35. Mungujakisa Ovoya Paul, Diocesan Priest, Nebbi, 27th May.
36. Ngabiroc Jenifer, Student Catechist, Angal Catechetical Centre, 26th June.
37. Ngomuling Geoffrey, Field Assistant, night study, Panyimur Trading Centre, 19th-20th July.
38. Nyirrac Stella, Secondary School Student, Field Assistant, night study, Nyaravur, 26th June.
39. Odokodit John Hercules, Diocesan Priest, Nebbi, 23rd May.
40. Odubi Cornelius, Diocesan Priest, Panyimur, 5th June.
41. Okweda Benedict, Diocesan Priest, 1st July.
42. Ombidi Charles, Paramount Chief of Panyimur Clan, Panyimur, 20th July.
43. Onega Etienne, Diocesan Priest, Monsignor, Akanyu, 5th June.
44. Onegwa Emilio, Diocesan Priest, Nyapea, 7th June.
45. Onencan Alimundu Wilbert, Missionary Priest, Apostles of Jesus, Urussi, 2nd June.
46. Ongom Ludovico, Diocesan Priest, Monsignor, Akanyu, 5th June.
47. Opio Richard Lino, Diocesan Pastoral Coordinator, 23rd June.

48. Oromcan Albert, Diocesan Priest, Rhino Camp, 30th May.
49. Owacgiuw Geoffrey, Diocesan Priest, Wadelai, 30th May.
50. Raleo Immaculate, Sister (Religious), Uleppi, 3rd June.
51. Rubangadit Moses, Field Assistant, night study, Wadelai Trading Centre, 24th July.
52. Susu Marcelina, Sister (Religious), Angal, 25th -26th June.
53. Tabu Peter, Student Catechist, Angal, 26th June.
54. Toli Alfred, Zone Head-Catechist, Wadelai, 30th May.
55. Ubat Vincensio, Catechist, Mungujakisa Chapel, 30th June.
56. Ucaki Donald, Ex-Seminarian, Parombo, 28th May; Field Assistant, night study, Parombo Trading Centre, 17th-18th July.
57. Ucama Elia, Clan Elder, Parombo, 26th May.
58. Ucama Juliano, Boro Clan Elder, Rero, 16th May.
59. Ucan Hilary, Headmaster, Parombo Primary School, 24th May.
60. Ucendi Donasiano, Elder, Jupa-Gilo, 6th July.
61. Ucida Nataline, Sister, Urusi, 2nd June.
62. Ucul Jenesio, Elder, Father of a Priest, Zeu Parish, 8th June.
63. Udaga Charles, Catechist, Rero Chapel, 3rd July.
64. Udiga Primo, Parent, Rero, 4th July.
65. Udokodit Alfred, Zone Head-Catechist, Padel, 28th June.
66. Udongtho Doreen, District Administration Councilor, Nebbi, 22nd June.
67. Udongtho Saverio, Parent, Parombo Chapel, 22nd June.
69. Udota Luciano, Catechist, Rero Chapel, 30th June.
69. Ugen Robert, Youth, Nyaravur, 28th May.
70. Ugen Richard, motor-cyclist, Field Assistant, night studies: Zeu Trading Centre, 3rd-4th July; Nyapea Trading Centre, 5th-6th July; Paidha Trading Centre, 7th-8th July.
71. Uguta Nyilak Emilia, Sister (Religious), Nyapea, together with 6 others, 7th June.
73. Ugwetha Regina, Elderly Mother, Boro Christian Community, Rero, 30 June.
73. Ujwiga Mark, Field Assistant, Acana Trading Centre, 28th July.
74. Ukathi, Cultural Elder, Alur Traditional Religion, Parombo, 26th May.
75. Ukec Alfred, Student Catechist, Angal Catechetical Centre, 26th June.

76. Ukeca Charles, Field Assistant, night study, Kasatu Trading Centre, 25th July; at Murusi trading centre, 26th July.
77. Ukelo Mukasa, Zone Council Member, Padel, 28th June.
78. Ukelo Peter, Zone Council Member, Padel, 28th June.
79. Ukok Anrea, Parent, Clan Elder, Panyimur, 4th July.
80. Ukumu John, Primary School Teacher, Nyaravur, 28th June.
81. Ukwir Amula, Medical Doctor, Kasatu, 25th July.
82. Ulama Jilbert, Zone Pastoral Council Member, Padel, 28th June.
83. Ulama Utali, Zone Pastoral Council Member, Padel, 28th June.
84. Ularker Kennedy, Primary School Teacher, Parombo, 24th May.
85. Ulul Gaspar, Parent, Zeu Parish, 8th June.
86. Umiya Peter, Student Catechist, Angal Catechetical Centre, 26th June.
87. Undoga David, Field Assistant, night study, Rhino-Camp Trading Centre, 11th-12th July.
88. Uneggiuw Peter, Field Assistant, Dei Trading Centre, 21st-22nd July.
89. Unencan George, Police Officer, Parombo Police Post, 27th June.
90. Unencan Vinansio, Student Catechist, Angal Catechetical Centre, 26th June.
91. Ungei Santo, Field Assistant, Urusi Trading Centre, 15th-16th July.
92. Unoba Mananu Charles, Ex Brother, Nyaravur, 26th May.
93. Unziga David, Seminarian, Wadelai, 30th May.
94. Upira Fabiano, Chapel Pastoral Council Member, Parombo, 1st June.
95. Upiyo Akile, Clan Elder, 29th-31st July.
96. Upiyo Edward, Zone Council Member, Padel, 28th June.
97. Upoki Angelo, Catechist, Makwera Chapel, 3rd July.
98. Uroca John, Catechist, Alala Chapel, 27th June.
99. Uroci Nicolas, Parent and businessman, Parombo Chapel, 22nd June.
100. Urombi Anthony, Catechist Instructor, Angal Catechetical Centre, 26th June.
101. Uronya Matilde, Elder, Panyimur Clan, Rero, 6th July.
102. Urunge John, retired Catechist, Padel, 28th June.
103. Uryem Richard, Census Officer, Nebbi, 29th May.
104. Utengi Marcelina, Sister (Religious), Nyapea, 7th June.

105. Uthembi James, Field Assistant, night study, Padel Trading Centre, 27th July.
106. Uthuba George, Chapel Pastoral Council Member, Parombo, 1st June.
107. Uwacgiu Joseph, Student Catechist, Angal Catechetical Centre, 26th June.
108. Uwaci Peter, Boro Clan Chief, Rero, 16th May.
109. Uyi-Rwot Alfred, Field Assistant, night study, Pakwach Trading Centre, 23rd July.
110. Uzunga Vittorio, Zone Pastoral Council Member, Padel, 28th June.
111. Wapokrwa Santos Constantine, Missionary Priest, Apostles of Jesus, Pakwach, 4th June.
112. Yoni-Rwoth Florence, Student Catechist, Angal Catechetical Centre, Angal, 26th June.
113. Zecca Mario, Comboni Missionary Priest, Angal, 25th May.

EOS-VERLAG ▪ THEOLOGISCHE REIHE

BAND 95

Michael Joe Okpalanozie

Christianity, Islam and African Traditional Religion in Nigeria
Conflicts and Challenges to Peaceful Co-existence

306 Seiten, € 29,95, ISBN 978-3-8306-7500-6

BAND 96

Xaver X. Kazimoto Komba

Die Selbsterhaltung der afrikanischen Kirche.
Eine sozio-theologische Analyse der heutigen „Kleinen christlichen Gemeinschaften“, dargestellt am Beispiel der Ortskirche von Tansania

292 Seiten, € 29,95, ISBN 978-3-8306-7540-2

BAND 97

Paul Obiechefu Nwandu

Religious Education in the Diocese of Ahiara (Nigeria) and in the Archidiocese of Munich and Freising (Germany). A comparative Study

300 Seiten, € 24,95, ISBN 978-3-8306-7635-5

BAND 98

Floribert Mavungu-ma-Nlandu

L'école catholique en RDC dans la dymanique de la Convention sco
de 1977 en processus de révision. Perspectives pastorales pour un projet de développement intégral

660 Seiten, € 39,95, ISBN 978-3-8306-7679-9

BAND 99

Benedikt Hankyu Cho

Universale Concretum. Die Bestimmung des unterscheide
den Gesammelten Werken von Joseph Rat

248 Seiten, € 24,95, ISBN 978-3-8306-

EOS Editions Sankt Otti
www.eos-books.com | mail@e